GEORGE GASCOIGNE

THE AUTOGRAPHED TITLE PAGE OF
GASCOIGNE'S COPY OF PETRARCH

GEORGE GASCOIGNE

Elizabethan Courtier
Soldier, and Poet

By C. T. PROUTY

Benjamin Blom
New York

Printed in U.S.A. by
NOBLE OFFSET PRINTERS, INC.
NEW YORK 3, N. Y.

To

FREDERICK S. BOAS

Preface

THE PRESENT WORK is the result of some seven years regular and intermittent study, which I began as a graduate student at Columbia University, carried on as a research student at Cambridge University, and completed as a Research Fellow of the Folger Shakespeare Library. Parts of the first four chapters, dealing with the life of Gascoigne, were submitted in my dissertation at Cambridge. The opportunity to revise these and to write this volume came to me through the invaluable appointment as Research Fellow at the Folger Shakespeare Library.

My thanks are due Dr. F. S. Boas, who directed the initial stages of my research at Columbia, and Mr. F. L. Lucas of King's College, Cambridge, who supervised my dissertation. I am also grateful to other members of the English faculties of Columbia and Cambridge for their helpful assistance.

Dr. J. Q. Adams, Director of the Folger Library, Dr. James McManaway, his Assistant, and Dr. Giles E. Dawson, the Reference Librarian, have all read the manuscript and have been untiring in giving information and advice. To them, as well as to the other members of the Folger staff, I am pleased to render grateful acknowledgment.

To my colleagues at the University of Missouri—Dr. A. H. R. Fairchild, who has given generously of his time and advice, and Dr. R. L. Ramsay, who has read and corrected the manuscript—I am indebted.

The late Dr. R. B. McKerrow placed me, along with many another young student, in his debt for a variety of kindnesses, and it is with his permission that an article which originally appeared in *The Review of English Studies* is here reprinted as Appendix III.

The scholar's wife appears in the usual "last-but-not-least" category. In this instance, however, anything that I might say can only faintly suggest the real contribution she has made. In transcribing documents, in revision and counsel she has spent many a weary hour. The sixth appendix, dealing with "Ladies of the Court," is the result of her individual research.

It is a pleasure to offer further thanks to Dr. and Mrs. James G. McManaway who have read the page proof. All others who have assisted me will see the fruits of their labors in the succeeding pages and will know of my gratitude.

Acknowledgments are due the following publishers: Cambridge University Press for permission to quote from J. W. Cunliffe's *The Complete Works of George Gascoigne;* D. C. Heath Co. for permission to quote from J. W. Cunliffe's *Supposes and Jocasta;* Oxford University Press for permission to quote from C. S. Lewis's *The Allegory of Love* and Smith and de Selincourt's *Spenser's Poetical Works;* Macmillan Company for permission to quote from John Berdan's *Early Tudor Poetry;* Modern Library for permission to quote from John Addington Symond's *The Renaissance in Italy.*

C. T. PROUTY

Columbia, Mo.
October 11, 1941

Contents

APPENDICES

Bibliographical Note

IN QUOTING from documents I have modernized the spelling, except in a few instances where the true meaning seemed to require the original form. In all instances, however, I have preserved the original spelling of proper names. No attempt has been made to punctuate.

In quoting from printed books of the period I have modernized only to the extent of substituting "s" for long "s" and using "i," "j," "u," "v," and "w" according to current usage. A few of the more elaborate abbreviations have been silently lengthened.

In referring to Gascoigne's writings, I give volume and page references to J. W. Cunliffe's *The Complete Works of George Gascoigne* (2 vols., Cambridge, 1907–10), known hereafter by the short title *"Works."* All those passages which first appeared in *A Hundreth Sundries Flowres* are quoted from my forthcoming edition of the *Flowres*. In references to such passages I give the number of the poem in my edition, as well as a reference to Cunliffe's edition.

The following abbreviations are employed:

Bib. Soc. Trans.	*Bibliographical Society Transactions*
Cal. S. P. Dom.	*Calendar of State Papers, Domestic, 1547–1580*
Cal. S. P. Dom. Add.	*Calendar of State Papers, Domestic, Addenda, 1566–1579*
Cal. S. P. For.	*Calendar of State Papers, Foreign, 1572–1574*
CHEL	*Cambridge History of English Literature*
Chanc.	Chancery
D & O	Decree and Order Books of the Chancery
DNB	*Dictionary of National Biography*
Harl. Soc. Pub.	Harleian Society Publications
Hist. MSS Comm. R.	*Historical Manuscripts Commission Reports*
IPM	Inquisition Post Mortem
KB	King's Bench, Court of
MLR	*Modern Language Review*
MLN	*Modern Language Notes*

OED	*Oxford English Dictionary*
Pat. Roll	Patent Roll
PCC	Prerogative Court of Canterbury
Proc.	Proceedings
PMLA	*Publications of the Modern Language Association*
PRO	Public Record Office
RES	*Review of English Studies*
STC	*Short Title Catalogue*
St. Ch.	Star Chamber, Court of
S. in Ph.	*Studies in Philology*
VCH	*Victoria County History*

GEORGE GASCOIGNE

Prologue

For Gaskoygnes death, leave of to mone, or morne
You are deceived, alive the man is stil:
Alive? O yea, and laugheth death to scorne,
In that, that he, his fleshly lyfe did kil.

For by such death, two lyves he gaines for one,
His Soule in heaven dooth live in endles joye
His woorthy works, such fame in earth have sowne,
As sack nor wrack, his name can there destroy.

But you will say, by death he only gaines.
And how his life, would many stand in stead:
O dain not Freend (to counterchaunge his paynes)
If now in heaven, he have his earnest meade.
For once in earth, his toyle was passing great:
And we devourd the sweet of all his sweat.

WHETSTONE

THE MIDDLE YEARS of the sixteenth century are likely to be passed over or dismissed with generalizations. The student of the history of poetry reads Wyatt and Surrey, particularly as their verses appear in *Songes and Sonettes,* and then, with a passing nod to the other miscellanies, proceeds to Spenser. Similarly the beginnings of secular drama receive attention, especially since Professor A. W. Reed's discoveries concerning the Rastell group, but again the tendency is to pass lightly over mid-century drama, where *Gorboduc, Roister Doister,* and *Gammer Gurton* are stereotyped as the first pale ghosts of tragedy and comedy. Lyly is still singled out as the first Elizabethan writer of comedy, and Kyd and Marlowe as our first tragic dramatists. Lyly also reigns supreme as the founder of Elizabethan prose. There are, of course, very real reasons for this seeming disregard of the work of such men as Gascoigne, Turbervile, Googe, Howell, Church-yard, and Whetstone. The beginning of a great literary movement is interesting because of its innovations; the climax, because of its intrinsic genius; but the intervening period of consolidation and careful experimentation is necessarily pedestrian, although not lacking some indications of the future. In comparison with the innovators, Wyatt and Surrey, or the great figures, Lyly, Marlowe, Spenser, and Shakespeare, Gascoigne and his contemporaries are likely to be dull. The great men are obviously great, but the little men yield reward only after long and patient study. The work of the little men—the establishment of ordered prose, principles of dramatic structure, the pentameter line and the iambic foot—can be stated in a few words, and it is far easier to accept the *fait accompli* than to attempt an explanation of why and how the work of consolidation was accomplished.

To attempt such an explanation of the life and writings of George Gascoigne, the chief poet of the young Elizabeth's court, is the purpose of this study. If we can understand what Gascoigne wrote and why he wrote as he did, we shall learn something tangible about the literature which Lyly, Marlowe, Shakespeare, Greene, and Nashe knew in their youth. In 1579 E.K., in the glosse of the November Eclogue, spoke in admiration of Ma. George Gaskin a wittie gentleman, and the very chefe of our late rymers, who and if some partes of learning wanted not (albee it is well knowen he altogyther wanted not learning) no doubt would have attayned to the excellencye of those famous Poets. For gifts of wit and naturall promptnesse appeare in hym abundantly.[1]

Later, though contemporary poetry was of such excellence as to reveal the faults of Gascoigne's verse, his importance was still recognized. In 1586 Webbe[2] thought it well to quote the words of E.K., while in 1589 Nashe observed:

Who ever my private opinion condemneth as faultie, Master *Gascoigne* is not to bee abridged of his deserved esteeme, who first beate the path to that perfection which our best Poets have aspired too since his departure; whereto he did ascend by comparing the Italian with the English, as *Tullie* did *Graeca cum Latinis.*[3]

As late as 1615 Gascoigne's able pioneering was noted by Tofte.

But this nice Age, wherein wee now live, hath brought more neate and teirse Wits, into the world; yet must not old George Gascoigne, and Turbervill, with

---

[1] *The Poetical Works of Edmund Spenser,* p. 463.
[2] Webbe, *A Discourse of English Poetrie,* p. 33.
[3] "To the Gentlemen Students of both Universities," in Robert Greene's *Menaphon,* p. 12.

such others, be altogether rejected, since they first brake the Ice for our quainter Poets, that now write, that they might the more safer swimme in the maine Ocean of sweet Poesie. . . .[4]

These aspects of Gascoigne's writings have been observed by later critics, but, as far as I know, there has been no specific attempt to examine his work closely with an aim to establishing the criteria which are there exemplified. To know, as well as we can, why Gascoigne wrote as he did and why he chose the subjects which he did is to approximate from afar the critical judgment of his age and that of his great successors.

Likewise a knowledge of Gascoigne's life aids in our comprehension of his work and, almost more important, it reveals at least one social pattern of Elizabethan England. The value of this latter concept is well realized in Professor Berdan's opening lines of his *Early Tudor Poetry*:

But positively for the modern American to adopt the point of view of the six-teenth century Englishman, to see that life unmodified either by the glamour of romanticism or by the working of his own personal equation, and fully to appreciate the unconscious and unexpressed motives for their actions, is im-possible. Nevertheless the degree of our success in achieving this impossibility measures the value of our literary judgments.[5]

The particular pattern which Gascoigne's life illustrates is that of the vicissitudes of the fortunes of both individuals and families in the tran-sitional world of the sixteenth century. Professor Moore Smith's admi-rable study of the Withypoll family exemplifies most clearly this pattern of flux. Yeomen from Gloucestershire, the Withypolls established them-selves as merchant tailors of London in the fifteenth century. By 1550 the family had acquired the "seat" of Christ Church Place in Ipswich, late religious property, and the sons were well on the road to success with careers in the university and the Inns of Court. Fifty years later the family was extinct: the sons either failed in their attempts to achieve greatness or died young. So too, the Gascoignes, established in Bedford-shire in the fifteenth century by a younger son of the Yorkshire family,

<hr>

[4] "To the Courteous Reader" in Tofte's translation of Benedetto Varchi's *The Blazon of Jealousie* (1615), p. 64. This is not an introductory letter to the translation, which is con-cluded on p. 62. Instead, it apologizes for the old-fashioned meter and style of the poem, "The Fruits of Jealousie," which is appended. I have used the Folger Shakespeare Library copy.

[5] Page 1.

held large estates in the county but were extinct in the male line by the early years of the seventeenth century.

More interesting than the pattern of the rise and fall of a family is that of the careers of young men of good lineage. Gascoigne, Turbervile, and Whetstone came of well-established families and all three tried to make their fortunes by attaching themselves to the world of the court. Each, however, encountered bad fortune: Whetstone, like Gascoigne, claimed to have been cheated by his father, and Turbervile, also like Gascoigne, was in difficulties with the Privy Council. As were all Elizabethans, these early poets were frequently in the law courts. Googe's marital difficulties, singularly like those of Gascoigne, were decided by Cecil as Gascoigne's were by Sir Nicholas Bacon. When the future was most ominous, Gascoigne, Churchyard, Whetstone, and Barnaby Riche sought their fortunes in the Dutch wars. The world was changing, and the old methods of advancement were disappearing. New families were looming large in the Elizabethan sky, and young men did their best to chart the right course to fame and fortune. Of these young men Gascoigne was typical: he tried careers in the court, the law, soldiering, and finally literature; but in none achieved complete success. It is the story of these attempts which occupies the first four chapters. The remainder of the volume reverts to the first consideration, the writings of George Gascoigne examined as to sources, principles of composition, and technique.

I. The Youth

First of my life, which some (amis) did knowe,
I leve mine armes, my acts shall blase the same
Yet on a thorne, a Grape wil never growe,
No more a Churle, dooth breed a childe of fame.
But (for my birth) my birth right was not great
My father did, his forward sonne defeat.

WHETSTONE

ON EASTER MONDAY in the year 1557, the woodwards of the Queen's Majesty's Honour of Ampthill in the county of Bedford discovered that the great stag which had much haunted Willhamstead Wood had at last lain out of Bickering Park, the western part of the Honour.[1] This news was brought to Sir William Dormer, Master of the Game of the Honour, who, knowing the stag to be a very forward deer for that time of year, was desirous to kill him for Queen Mary. Therefore, Sir William sent for one Edmond Conquest, as well as certain other gentlemen dwelling near-by, to be partakers of the pleasure in hunting the stag, as also to help kill the same stag. After being stirred, the stag fled from Bickering Park unto another wood, that of Sir John Gascoigne, called Cardington Wood, and from thence drew homeward to Bickering Park where Sir William made the kill and sent the carcass up to his dread Sovereign Lady.

Although the hunt had thus ended, Sir John Gascoigne was much moved by news of the trespass on Cardington Wood and in great rage and fury gathered together his son, George Gascoigne, gent., and his yeomen, Moore, Morgan, and ffawstener, as well as divers other riotous and evilly disposed persons—not only his retainers but also other light and

---

[1] The ensuing account is a condensed paraphrase of PRO St. Ch. 4, VI/11, a petition made to the Queen by Edmond Conquest, who sought a writ of subpoena to bring Sir John and George Gascoigne into the Star Chamber. This petition is undated, but the year must be 1557, since Conquest gives the day of the assault as April 19, describes the day as near Easter, and addresses the bill to Queen Mary. Reference to Fry, *Almanacks for Students of English History*, shows 1557 the only tenable year.

idle persons meet and ready to such purpose. The company of twenty thus assembled were armed with weapons invasive and defensive, to wit, staves, bills, swords, bucklers, pitchforks, and partisans, and were led by Sir John Gascoigne into Cardington Wood, where they encountered Edmond Conquest riding homeward. Conquest, seeing his supposed friend Sir John Gascoigne and thinking no harm, rode forward all alone having no man or weapon with him. On drawing near, Conquest, as befitted a gentleman, dismounted, put off his cap and saluted his friend, who with gentle countenance resaluted. Suddenly and unwarily, however, Sir John Gascoigne struck with a long staff at Conquest's arms, so that the latter lost the use of both his arms and hands and was no longer able to hold his bridle. Sir John, not therewithal contented, eftsoons struck at him again so furiously and unmanfully that his own company bade him cease for shame. And so at the last he ceased and, leaving Conquest in great peril of his life, passed on his way through the wood. Whereupon, Conquest, being thus beaten, was at the last, though with much ado, conveyed home to his house—not without divers times swooning by the way. For seven days after, he was fain to keep his bed and was brought thereby to such extremity that he was more like to die than live.

This account of the mishaps of one day in the life of Edmond Conquest presents us with the first of many references in the legal documents of the reigns of Queen Mary and Queen Elizabeth to George Gascoigne, son and heir of Sir John Gascoigne of Cardington, Bedfordshire. As we shall see, such events seem to have been usual in the lives of father and son.

What is unusual, however, is to find the good Yorkshire name of Gascoigne, with its memories of the famous Lord Chief Justice, familiar to the residents of Bedfordshire. With Thomas Fuller[2] we may be curious as to how the family "straggled" thus far to the south. But whereas Fuller is satisfied with the explanation that Sir William Gascoigne, "Controler of the House" to Cardinal Wolsey,[3] being a younger son of the Gascoignes of Gawthorpe of Yorkshire married the inheritrix of Cardington manor, we wonder what meaning he attaches to his own evidence: namely, a John Gascoigne listed a few pages before as a knight of the shire for Bedford and one of the Commissioners who, in 12 Henry VI, returned the

[2] Fuller, *The History of the Worthies of England*, I, 129.
[3] *Ibid.* Also noted in Schelling, *The Life and Writings of George Gascoigne*, p. 3.

names of the gentry of Bedfordshire.[4] The truth of the matter seems to be that this John was second son to James Gascoigne who first established the Gascoigne family in Bedfordshire. James married Jane, daughter and sole heir of Baldwin Pygot, Lord of Dodyngton and Cardington. From this marriage, James gained three sons and probably considerable property; but these advantages were soon lost, since two of the sons were killed in the Battle of Barnet, and the manor of Cardington, the erstwhile property of the Pygots, came into the hands of the family of Winter. The surviving son, George, for whom the poet was undoubtedly named, was notable only as the father of Sir William, the real founder of the family fortunes, who by marrying Elizabeth Winter brought the manor of Cardington back to the Gascoigne family.[5]

Sir William's efforts at advancement were not limited to marriage, since he, even as William Cecil who early attached himself to the household of the Earl of Hertford, saw the value of an eminent patron and became a member of the household of the most powerful man in England, Cardinal Wolsey. Finally Sir William rose to be "Controler of the House." He was an unusual type of man to occupy such an office in the service of the magnificent prelate, but his acquisitive nature created a strong bond between master and servant. Fuller describes him thus:

A rough Gentleman; preferring rather to *profit* then *please* his *Master.* And although the *pride* of that *Prelate* was far above his *covetousnesse;* yet his *wisedome,* well knowing *Thrift* to be the *fuell* of *Magnificence,* would usually digest advice from this his *Servant,* when it plainly tended to his own *emolument.*[6]

When Wolsey fell from favor, Sir William, like many another friend of a great man, avoided the ruin which came upon his patron. Once again there is a parallel with Cecil, who wisely retired to Wimbledon when Warwick brought Somerset to the Tower. Sir William appears to have retired to Cardington, where he obviously had enjoyed some position, having been twice sheriff in the early years of Henry's reign.[7]

---

[4] Fuller, *op. cit.,* I, 121.

[5] *Visitation of Yorkshire, 1563–4,* Harl. Soc. Pub., XVI, 139, contains the above genealogical information. Professor Schelling (*op. cit.,* p. 3) notes the descent from James Gascoigne but does not discuss the establishment of the family in Bedfordshire.

[6] Fuller, *op. cit.,* I, 129.

[7] *Ibid.*

Though one patron had completed the circuit of Fortune's wheel, there was no reason why another might not be in the ascendant. Such a man was John Neville, Lord Latimer, whose family, like Gascoigne's, had connections in the North.[8] Sir William became steward to Lord Latimer, increased the boundaries of Cardington manor, and having seen at least one grandson born to carry on the family name and fortunes, died, leaving his heir, Sir John Gascoigne, well supplied with the goods of this world.[9]

This Sir John, father of George Gascoigne, had, some time before his father's death, returned to the family county of Yorkshire to find a bride. Probably while visiting his cousins at Gawthorpe he had met Margaret, daughter of Sir Robert Scargill of the near-by manor of Thorpehall.[10] Margaret and her sister Mary, wife of Marmaduke Tunstall of Thurland, were the coheirs to whom descended the considerable property noted in the Inquisition Post Mortem taken on Sir Robert. Thus the union of Sir John and Margaret Scargill was a prosperous one which augured well, at least financially, for the three children who were born to them. George, the eldest, was born sometime between 1535[11] and 1540, while soon after came a second son, John, and a daughter, Elizabeth.[12]

"Of Sir John Gascoigne," says Professor Schelling,[13] "little is known save that he inherited the patrimonial estates of Cardington and married Margaret, daughter of Sir Robert Scargell." Fortunately, the petition of Edmond Conquest and other surviving records present certain facts concerning this knight's public, as well as private, life.

Sir John was a Member of Parliament for Bedford in 1542, 1553, and 1557.[14] He also served as a Justice of the Peace,[15] but it is from his private activities that we learn most about this country squire. At Easter, 1556, Cardinal Pole, the last Catholic Archbishop of Canterbury, made his metropolitan visitation of the diocese of Lincoln—of which Bedford is part. One of the many matters reported to him at that time was the case

---

[8] Dugdale, *The Baronage of England*, I, 313.

[9] PRO St. Ch. 5, L 33/28, a dispute about boundaries between Sir John and Lord Latimer, reveals these facts.

[10] PRO Chanc. IPM (Ser. 12) CLXXXV, 60, on Sir Robert Scargill (d. 1530) mentions Margaret, the wife of John Gascoigne. Professor Schelling (*op. cit.*, p. 4) notes the marriage from the pedigree (*supra*, n. 5) but gives no date.

[11] *Vide infra*, Appendix I, for a discussion of the date of birth.

[12] *Vide supra*, n. 5.   [13] *Op. cit.*, p. 4.

[14] Willis, *Notitia Parliamentaria*, III (pt. 2), 25, 54.   [15] PRO St. Ch. 5, G 2/7.

of Sir John Gascoigne, who had been taken in adultery with one Anne Drewry. Sir John appeared before the authorities and apparently was let off lightly with an injunction not to have further relations with Anne Drewry but to return to his wife. Sir John promised but, adds the record, "promisso non stetit." Anne Drewry did not appear and so was excommunicated.[16]

The identity of Anne Drewry and the story of her subsequent relations with Sir John are indicated by the latter's will, made in April, 1568.[17] In his testament Sir John says, "And where also I have granted one annuity or yearly rent of Twenty pounds unto Anne Drewry sometime my servant for the term of her life my meaning will and intent is That my said son George within one year after my decease shall procure the same to be paid or compounded within such sort that the same may be discharged." In other words the son and heir was made responsible for the annuity of his father's "sometime servant" and mistress.

This affair with a servant girl and the previously noted attack on Edmond Conquest well reveal the private character of Sir John Gascoigne. His public activities as a Justice of the Peace are indicated somewhat by a Star Chamber proceeding and by a letter of the Bishop of Lincoln. In 1562 Sir John petitioned Queen Elizabeth for a writ of subpoena against Thomas Ardern *et. al.,* whom he accused of stealing wood.[18] This document recounts the supposed robbery and then, in an evident attempt to blacken Ardern's character, tells of the wounding of one Thomas Walker at a riotous party and the subsequent death of this man in Ardern's home. The latter is also accused of secretly burying the body without a view being taken by the coroner or any declaration being made to Walker's wife. This attack enraged Ardern who, dismissing the robbery charge in a few words, replied that not only had Walker's wife been with her husband but that she and others present had been called before Sir John Gascoigne who, as Justice of the Peace, investigated the matter. Thus, according to Ardern, it could be seen that Sir John was making use of knowledge

---

[16] Strype, *Ecclesiastical Memorials,* III (pt. 2), 391.

[17] PCC 12 Babington. The will has been noted before, but not the significance of this annuity. Modern spelling has been used in this quotation and will be used throughout for all unpublished documents. No attempt has been made to punctuate. The original spelling of names has been preserved.

[18] PRO St. Ch. 5, G 2/7.

gained in a public capacity to prosecute one against whom he had long borne a grudge.

It was not long after this dispute that the Privy Council became interested in the religious beliefs of the Justices of the Peace, who could, by reason of their position, be most influential in determining the general acceptance of the new religion. In this connection Sir John Gascoigne, J. P., was considered by the authorities at Westminster. On October 17, 1564, the Privy Council addressed inquiring letters to all the bishops of England, asking them to classify those who were already Justices of the Peace according as they were favorable, indifferent, or hostile to the proceedings of the government in matters of religion.[19] Further, the bishops were asked to name persons who, in their opinion, were fit to be put into office. To this end they were asked to consult those of the leading men of their dioceses who were favorable to the government and with their help to make suggestions for the remedying of disorders, the fuller repression of popery, the maintenance of justice, the promotion of God's gospel, and the punishment of those who afflicted the godly and maintained the perverse and ungodly. Roughly estimated, the total of justices marked favorable is 431; marked indifferent, neuter, or not favorable, 264; hinderers or adversaries, 157. The dioceses reported to be most hostile to the government were those of the North and the West: Carlisle, Durham, York, Worcester, Hereford, and Exeter. Staffordshire was troubled by a knot of hinderers led by the Vernons, and in Buckinghamshire Sir Robert Drury, Sir Robert Peckham, and Sir William Dormer were the leaders of a large band of men "not fit to be trusted."[20] The Bishop of Lincoln reported that in Bedfordshire John Gascoigne, knight, John Cawlbeck, esq., and John ffuller, esq., were noted as "hinderers,"[21] while Lewis Dive, Thomas Pygott, and Thomas Dive were commended as being "earnest in religion."[22]

Such, then, are the facts which survive concerning Sir John Gascoigne, father of the poet. He was a public official, a Catholic, and a man of

---

[19] "A Collection of Original Letters From The Bishops To The Privy Council, 1564," ed. by Mary Bateson, *Camden Miscellany,* IX, 1895, Camden Society Publications, LIII, Preface, iii.

[20] *Ibid.,* p. iv.   [21] *Ibid.,* p. 28.

[22] *Ibid.,* pp. 28, 29. As will appear later, George Gascoigne was well acquainted with Sir William Dormer, Lewis Dive, and their families.

strong emotions. Of his wife, Dame Margaret Gascoigne, less is known, but the surviving records reveal her litigious nature, which is interesting, if one places any credence in theories of heredity.

As has been noted, Margaret and her sister, Mary Tunstall, were the coheirs of Sir Robert Scargill. The quarrelsome nature of the two sisters was not aroused by the dispersal of their father's estate, but on the death of Lady Scargill the two were soon in dispute over a gold casting bottle.[23] Petitions were filed in Chancery, witnesses were examined, and the case wound its weary way, with Sir John Gascoigne and Sir Marmaduke Tunstall ably seconding their wives.[24] Evidently Dame Margaret emerged triumphant, since the first bequest in her will was a "gold casting bottle for sweet waters" to the Lady Catlin.[25]

The other records concerning Dame Margaret relate to difficulties between her and her son George. These will appear in due course, but for the present we must be content with the "casting bottle" episode and with her relationship to some rather important people. Cuthbert Tunstall, Bishop of London and later of Durham, was a first cousin to Marmaduke Tunstall.[26] More closely related to the poet and his subsequent writing was Sir Martin Frobisher, the explorer and adventurer, whose paternal great-grandfather had married a sister of Sir William Scargill, Dame Margaret Gascoigne's grandfather.[27] In his introductory letter to Sir Humphrey Gilbert's *A Discourse of a Discoverie for a New Passage to Cataia,* George Gascoigne says: " . . . *because I understoode that* M. Fourboisir *(a kinsman of mine) did pretend to travaile in the same* Discoverie."[28]

From both his father and his mother, therefore, George Gascoigne received the proud heritage of a substantial ancestry, along with the advantages of reasonable prosperity. Accordingly, it is to be expected that

[23] PRO Chanc. Proc. (Ser. II) C3, 71/73.

[24] PRO Chanc. D & O C 33/27, fols. 140r, 362r, 441v.

[25] PCC 4 Carew. The will has been noted before, but not this bequest. Ward, "George Gascoigne and His Circle," *RES,* II (1926), 34.

[26] *Visitation of Yorkshire,* Harl. Soc. Pub., XVI, 327–28.

[27] Rev. J. Hunter, *South Yorkshire, The History and Topography of the Deanery of Doncaster* (London, 1828), I, 32. Both Hazlitt (*The Complete Poems of George Gascoigne,* I, xvi) and Schelling (*op. cit.,* p. 4) use Gascoigne's statement to show the relationship but give no reference to substantiate the assertion therein contained.

[28] *Works,* II, 564.

the son and heir was given a fitting education at Cambridge and later at Gray's Inn. We have no definite information regarding Gascoigne's education before he went up to Cambridge and, in fact, only his own words to show that he did attend the university. It will be well, then, to examine the poet's few references to his academic experience.

> (*And* Cantabridge, *shal have the dignitie,*
> *Whereof I was, unworthy member once*) [29]

> ... such lattyn as I forgatt att Cantabridge,... [30]

> If *Nevynsone* my maister were not plaste,
> Since by his helpe I learning first embraste. [31]

> ... suche English as I stale in westmerland ... [32]

From these quotations it is apparent that Gascoigne had some schooling in Westmoreland—somehow or other "stolen"—that he attended Cambridge and that his master was one Nevynson. Both the cryptic reference to Westmoreland and the time of his stay at Cambridge, as well as subsequent events in his life, are clarified by an examination of the surviving information about Stephen Nevynson.

Stephen Nevynson, later prebend of Canterbury, was a native of Carlisle, second son of Richard Nevynson of Newby, Westmoreland, and a first cousin of Christopher Nevynson, who mentions him in his will. A pensioner of Christ's College in 1544, he became Bachelor of Arts in 1544/5, Master of Arts in 1548, and Doctor of Laws in 1553; during the years 1547–61 he was a fellow and tutor of Trinity College. In the reign of Mary, Nevynson, like many of his coreligionists, found solace in secret personal devotion to the Protestant cause, but with the accession of Elizabeth he became more articulate, gained preferment, and was a man so favorable to the new religion as to write to Lord Burghley advocating a policy of "not showing mercy to those who are disaffected towards Queen Elizabeth." Such is the brief account [33] of the master whom the son of a Catholic squire held in high esteem.

Other information concerning Nevynson aids considerably in an

---

[29] *Ibid.*, II, 168.   [30] *Ibid.*, II, 477.   [31] *Ibid.*, I, 180.
[32] *Ibid.*, II, 477. These were all noted by Schelling (*op. cit.*, p. 5).
[33] C. H. Cooper and T. Cooper, *Athenae Cantabrigienses*, I, 426. *DNB* "Stephen Nevynson."

understanding of the man and clarifies, somewhat, his relations with his pupil. In the time of Mary, Stephen Nevynson was still interested in property in Westmoreland, for an Early Chancery Proceeding[34] lists him as coplaintiff with Thomas Blekinsop of Holbecke against Robert Dalston, Thomas Kendall, and Leonard Dent in an action concerning lands in King's Mowbray, Westmoreland. This action, I think, shows that the Cambridge tutor had not abandoned either his interest or his property in his native county. Like Archbishop Grindal, who long remembered his native Cumberland, Stephen Nevynson continued his association with Westmoreland. With this connection between Nevynson and Westmoreland in mind, we may, perhaps, see, in Gascoigne's reference to the English he "stole" in Westmoreland, an early relation between the poet and his Cambridge master. There is, however, another possible explanation for Gascoigne's curious statement.

That there was close contact between the family of Sir John Gascoigne and the Gascoignes of Gawthorp, as well as the Scargills, is shown by the records. We have noted that Sir John returned to Yorkshire for his bride, and the will of Dame Margaret shows clearly her feeling for her old home and her Scargill relatives.[35] This lady not only made provision for the transportation of her body to the parish church of Whitecerke, but directed her executor to pay the expenses of those who accompanied the cortège from Bedford to Yorkshire. John Conyers, grandson of Dame Margaret's maternal uncle, was sole executor as well as the recipient of a considerable legacy. In addition, there were bequests to several Scargills and Conyerses, and to relatives of the Conyers family. The bulk of Dame Margaret's estate was given to these northern relatives. If Dame Margaret were so closely bound to her family as the will indicates, it is logical to infer that she must frequently have journeyed north and that her son George did likewise. A glance at the map shows how near to the borders of Westmoreland were the manors of Scargill, Thorpe, and Gawthorpe; so the clue to that enigmatic reference to English stolen in Westmoreland may well lie in a visit by young George Gascoigne to

[34] PRO Early Chanc. Proc. C1/1404, 50–56.
[35] *Vide supra*, n. 25. Here, as before, the terms of the will are for the first time noted and discussed.

his relatives. There was, most probably, a tutor for Gascoigne's young cousins, and, if the young man joined them in their lessons, he would indeed be "stealing" his education.

Another strange series of coincidences shows a further link between Stephen Nevynson and George Gascoigne; this is the connection of both with the county of Kent and, more particularly, the town of Nonnington, near Dover. In the early years of the reign of Queen Mary, Stephen Nevynson brought action in the Chancery[36] in behalf of his ward, Thomas Nevynson, an infant of eight years. The defendants, the President and Scholars of Magdalen College, Oxford, and Thomas Waren, mayor of Dover, are accused of trying to cheat the child out of his inheritance. Some six years before, Waren and Christopher Nevynson (Stephen's first cousin) decided to divide between them certain lands which they held by lease from Magdalen College. Soon after this agreement Christopher assigned his share to his son Thomas; but, although the rents were paid, Waren and an avaricious new President, having secured possession of the lease, tried to exact double rents; failing in that, they tried to get possession of the land. Whether or no such seeming chicanery succeeded is, by reason of the absence of certain Chancery records, unknown.

This Christopher Nevynson, described in the above document as being of Addisham, is briefly noted in the *Athenae Cantabrigienses*[37] as having been renowned as a lawyer. In other records we find that he held the lease of the Vicarage of Nonnington,[38] as well as that of Addisham. This latter bit of information appears from the fact that the vicar of Addisham married Nevynson's widow and sought to inherit, not only the wife, but her husband's property as well.[39]

The importance of these facts becomes evident when we realize that some years later one Edward Boyes of Nonnington, in the county of Kent, married Elizabeth, the wealthy widow of William Bretton, only to have this lady transfer her affection and property to George Gascoigne. If Christopher Nevynson had land in Nonnington, and if his cousin

---

[36] PRO Early Chanc. Proc. C1/1457, 13.   [37] Cooper and Cooper, I, 106.
[38] Hasted, *A History of the County of Kent*, III, 711.
[39] PRO Early Chanc. Proc. C1/1386, 26, 27.

Stephen was intimate enough with him to become guardian of the son Thomas, it is almost certain that Stephen Nevynson knew Edward Boyes, a son of the family who were manor holders in Nonnington and Fredville. Did Stephen Nevynson continue his friendship with his cousin's widow? Did he, after his appointment as prebend of Canterbury, ride over to Addisham and stop at Nonnington? Was it through Nevynson that Gascoigne first met Elizabeth Bretton, for love of whom he became involved in many a legal dispute? These are questions which the records do not seem to answer, but certainly the coincidences are indeed suggestive.[40]

Turning again to the consideration of Gascoigne's education, we see that the career of Nevynson furnishes us with only broad, limiting dates for the poet's residence at Cambridge, which must have been between 1547–61, when Nevynson was fellow and tutor of Trinity. As a son of a knight Gascoigne would have been a fellow commoner, and therefore it is not surprising that we do not find his name in any of the surviving records of Trinity College. Although neither Nevynson's life nor the records give definite information, a forward date may be set by Gascoigne's admission to Gray's Inn during 1555.[41] It is thus reasonable to assume that the poet was at Cambridge between 1547 and 1555.

If this assumption is correct, it is likely that it was at Cambridge that the poet first met his good friend Bartholomew Withypoll. This young man, son of a second generation of merchant tailors, was sent to Gonville Hall in Easter, 1554, by his father, Edmund Withypoll, who was occupied in the business of founding a family.[42] Bartholomew did not accompany his brothers, Edward and Paul, to Gray's Inn, but engaged in diplomatic affairs, for in 1562 he was secretary and messenger to Sir Thomas Challoner in Spain.[43] In 1572 Gascoigne wrote a poem of advice to Withypoll, shortly before the latter set off on a journey to Genoa.[44] Here they appear to be close friends, but what their relations had been in the intervening years we do not know. Bartholomew may have been in and around London while his brothers were at Gray's Inn, and the brothers as well

---

[40] References for the material on Edward Boyes, Elizabeth, and Gascoigne appear below in connection with the poet's marriage. Cf. also Appendix III.

[41] Foster, *Register of Admissions to Gray's Inn*, p. 25.

[42] Smith, *The Family of Withypoll*, pp. 20, 21, 55.

[43] *Ibid.*, pp. 55–58.   [44] *Works*, I, 344. No. 67.

as "Batte" may have been the poet's friends. Whatever the circumstances and details, it is interesting to note the possibility of this early contact at Cambridge.

However high the original hopes of both Sir John Gascoigne and Edmund Withypoll regarding the advantages of a legal education to their sons, there is no evidence that George Gascoigne, or Edward, or Paul Withypoll made professional use of their training. In his early days at Gray's Inn,[45] the poet tells us that he read his law books.[46] At least in the beginning of his career in London, Gascoigne was seriously interested in his studies, but soon this interest waned, while in the ascendant were things more near to the heart of a young man. We know, for example, from the petition of Edmond Conquest that, in the spring of 1557, the young student was home for the holidays, enjoying hawking and hunting in the Queen's Majesty's Honour of Ampthill.

Before he completely abandoned a legal career, however, the poet, perhaps through the good offices of his father, entered the last Parliament of Philip and Mary as Burgess for Bedford Borough.[47] This Parliament met on January 20, 1557/8, adjourned in March, and resumed its session in November, when the Members heard the news that ended a Catholic England.[48] On the morning of November 17, 1558, while George and his father were assembled in the Commons,[49] news was brought to the Lords of the death of Queen Mary. The Commons were summoned into the Lords, where Archbishop Heath, Chancellor of England, pronounced these words:

The cause of your calling hither at this time, is to signifie unto you, that all the lords here present are certeinlie certified, that God this present morning hath called to his mercie our late sovereigne ladie queene Marie. Which hap as it is most heavie and greevous unto us, so have we no lesse cause another waie to rejoise with praise to almightie God; for that he hath left unto us a

---

[45] For a discussion of the poet's admission to Gray's Inn and other George Gascoignes, *vide infra*, Appendix II.

[46] *Works*, I, 348. No. 70.

[47] *Parliamentary Papers* (London, 1878), XVII, 396. *Vide infra*, Appendix II, for a more detailed discussion of George Gascoigne in Parliament.

[48] Willis, *op. cit.*, III (pt. 2), 54.

[49] It is almost certain that they were present, since *The Journals of the House of Commons* are exact in the accounting of absences from sessions.

true, lawfull and right inheritrice to the crowne of this realme, which is the ladie Elisabeth, second daughter to our late sovereigne lord of noble memorie king Henrie the eight, and sister to our said late queene, of whose most lawfull right and title in the succession of the crowne (thanks be to God) we need not to doubt. Wherefore the lords of this house have determined with your assents and consents, to passe from hence into the palace, and there to proclame the said ladie Elisabeth queene of this realme, without further tract of time. Whereto the whole house answered with evident appearance of joy, God save queene Elisabeth, long may queene Elisabeth reigne over us.[50]

Not only did George Gascoigne hear the first proclamation of Queen Elizabeth, but he, the young law student, also took part in her coronation. By reason of their ownership of lands whose title carried the perquisite of being almoners in coronation proceedings, John Neville, Lord Latimer, Sir Edward Bray, and Sir John Gascoigne were entitled to serve in this capacity in the coronation of Queen Elizabeth. Fortunately, at least for the survival of this item of information, Sir John Gascoigne was sick and was unable to leave Cardington. He therefore had his son George made his deputy. Also unable to appear was Lord Latimer, who, according to Sir John Gascoigne,[51] was at the time "prisoner in the fleet." One Henry Darcy was admitted as his deputy, so the only "surviving" member of the original trio was Sir Edward Bray. The fee receivable for the office of almoner was a tun of wine and the silver alms dish. A sum of money was, however, allowed in lieu of the dish, which could not be divided. In spite of this means of division, there was no sharing of the fee, for Sir Edward Bray took both money and wine. Some time later, in 1564, Sir John brought a petition in Chancery for his share of the fee and it is from this document that our information comes. Sir Edward answered Sir John's charge by saying that the fee had belonged to him and Lord Latimer, since "time out of mind and the said Sir John Gascoigne in respect of his lands hath been but an Aider unto the said Lord and the said defendant." Once again the solution of the problem is lacking, but we do know, as a result of this dispute, that George Gascoigne had an official part in a solemn court function.

It was probably about this time that the learned Littleton proved "a

---

[50] Holinshed, *The Whole Volume of Chronicles*, III, 1170.

[51] PRO Chanc. Proc. (Ser. II) C3, 76/82. This proceeding was noted by Miss Genevieve Ambrose in "George Gascoigne," *RES*, II (1926), 165. Miss Ambrose did not quote from the document nor give any of the details.

dawe,"[52] and the poet found the law full "darke."[53] From the law Gas-coigne tells us that "he shotte to catch a courtly grace."[54] There is no evidence to show any exact time, but since in the introductory comments to his five theme poems he says that "He had (in middest of his youth) determined to abandone all vaine delights and to retourne unto Greyes Inne,"[55] and since one of the friends referred to in these remarks did not enter Gray's Inn until 1563,[56] his return must have been subsequent to that year. In view of the fact that Gascoigne married Elizabeth Bretton in 1561,[57] it is likely that he enjoyed his gay days at court before this date. It seems, therefore, that his attempts at achieving a courtly grace began at about the time of the accession of Elizabeth.

In the lines written on the theme, *Sat cito, si sat bene*,[58] the poet de-scribes his first introduction to court life. He was overwhelmed by the vision of "stately pompe." Some of his fellows were at court and their stories of life and pleasure incited in him the desire to be a part of such a world of life and beauty. Finally he came to court and sought to cut a figure.

> Then peevishe pride pufft up my swelling harte,
> To further foorth so hotte an enterpryse:
> And comely cost beganne to playe his parte,
> In praysing patternes of mine owne devise. . . .[59]

In order to maintain this expenditure, the poet says,

> Of every ferme I then lette flye a lease,
> To feede the pursse that payde for peevishnesse,
> Till rente and all were falne in suche disease,
> As scarse coulde serve to maynteyne cleanlynesse:
> They bought, the bodie, fyne, ferme, lease and lande,
> All were too little for the merchauntes hande.[60]

This seemingly straightforward account of financial ruin presents somewhat of a problem, however, because we should expect to find some records of these debts in the form of recognizances and indentures.

---

[52] *Works*, I, 348. No. 70.   [53] *Ibid.*
[54] *Ibid.*   [55] *Ibid.*, I, 62. No. 57.   [56] Foster, *op. cit.*, p. 31. John Vaughan, 1563.
[57] *Vide infra*, Appendix III.
[58] *Works*, I, 66. No. 60. I cannot share Miss Ambrose's feeling (*RES*, II [1926], 165–166) that this poem describes his attendance at the coronation. A visit to any court function would inspire like feelings.
[59] *Works*, I, 67. No. 60.   [60] *Ibid.*

Examination of the Close Rolls shows, however, that it is not until 1563 and 1564 that Gascoigne's name appears with any frequency. Nevertheless, these records reveal one interesting item of information which may explain the financing of the poet's early expenditures. On July 10, 1563, Sir John appeared in Chancery and acknowledged that he owed his son George £1,000 if the property due to descend to the latter and his heirs were otherwise disposed of.[61] This type of acknowledgement and the translation of inheritable property into cash was not an unusual thing if the heir got the cash, but George Gascoigne did not; instead, he agreed to his father's disposal of the property to Thomas Colby of London, under terms which eliminated any claim he might have to the £1,000.[62] Mrs. Oldfield is puzzled by the poet's seeming acquiescence in this matter.[63] Surely a man who had spent some years at Gray's Inn studying the law would not be taken in by so transparent a scheme. The only valid explanation which I can see is that Gascoigne owed his father considerable sums of money and that he took this means to repay the debt by subtracting it from his future inheritance. It may be objected that there is no record of any such debt of the son to his father. To such an objection one may reply that in legal proceedings there are frequent references to recognizances and indentures which do not appear in any of the rolls where such documents were entered. The fact is that documents of this nature were entered on the Rolls as a form of protection and that a fee had to be paid for such entry. What need was there for Sir John to "protect" a debt owed him by his son? The father had control of the land and could, even if the son did not agree, balance accounts in his will.

[61] PRO Close Roll 650, 5 Eliz. pt. 21, no. 98. Noted by Mrs. Genevieve Ambrose Oldfield, "New Light on the Life of George Gascoigne," RES, XIII (1937), 134.
[62] Oldfield, op. cit., p. 134.   [63] Ibid.

II. The Worldling

I once bemoned the decayed and blasted estate of M. Gascoigne: *who wanted not some commendable parts of conceit and endevor: but unhappy* M. Gascoigne, *how Lordly happy, in comparison of most-unhappy* M. Greene?

HARVEY

IN HIS ADOLESCENT INFATUATION with the gay, fashionable life of the court, George Gascoigne was typical of an age when Elizabeth continued that process of the centralization of power in and around the court which was one of the chief political devices of the Tudors. A comparison of the lives of George and his brother John with that of their father reveals the growth of this interest in London and in the court. Sir John was content to live in Cardington, superintending his estates, but both his sons sought advancement through attendance at the Inns of Court. A similar pattern may be traced in the Withypoll family, as well as in the lives of George Turbervile, Barnabe Googe, and George Whetstone. The will-o'-the-wisp which urged these young men into the world of fashion was the hope of gaining favor and with it, success. Sir Nicholas Bacon and Lord Burghley were shining examples of this royal road to fortune, while the Dudley family showed how soon the sins of the father could be disregarded if the sons achieved the favor of the sovereign. But for every story of success there were ten of failure, and George Gascoigne's life during the period 1558–72 is a harsh exemplum of the ruin which Fortune could distribute more easily, perhaps, than success.

The chief events in the poet's life during these years may be stated briefly. He continued his life at court and married a rich widow. No longer able to afford the life of fashion, he retired for two or three years to the manor of Willington in Bedfordshire, but soon returned to London and Gray's Inn in an attempt to rehabilitate his fortunes. After 1567 he again retired to the country, this time to Cardington, with brief periods of residence at Walthamstow and possible sojourns in London. His legal and financial difficulties increased in spite of this rustication. He became embroiled in a lawsuit with his brother, another with Thomas Colby, and finally in a dispute with the Earl of Bedford, which reduced him to ignominious imprisonment in Bedford gaol.

Although such an account may be rehearsed quite simply, the manifold lawsuits, Gascoigne's troubles with his wife's second husband, his so-called disinheritance—all these are complicated. It seems best, therefore to establish a chronology, and the first step is the approximation of the date when the poet was "cast off by the court." Two autobiographical poems, "The greene Knights farewell to Fansie"[1] and "Gascoignes wodmanship,"[2] contain important evidence. The first of these is quite detailed in its story:

> The glosse of gorgeous courtes, by thee did please mine eye,
> A stately sight me thought it was, to see the brave go by:
> To see there feathers flaunte, to marke their straunge devise,
> To lie along in Ladies lappes, to lispe and make it nice:
> To fawne and flatter both, I liked sometimes well,
> But since I see how vayne it is, *Fansie* (quoth he) *farewell.*

> When court had cast me of, I toyled at the plowe
> My fansie stoode in straunge conceipts, to thrive I wote not how:
> By mils, by making malte, by sheepe and eke by swyne,
> By ducke and drake, by pigge and goose, by calves & keeping kine:
> By feeding bullockes fat, when pryce at markets fell,
> But since my swaines eat up my gaines, *Fansie* (quoth he) *farewell.*

> In hunting of the deare, my fansie tooke delight,
> All forests knew, my folly still, the mooneshine was my light:
> In frosts I felt no cold, a sunneburnt hew was best,
> I sweate and was in temper still, my watching seemed rest:
> What daungers deepe I past, it follie were to tell,
> And since I sigh to thinke thereon, *Fansie* (quoth he) *farewell.*

> A fansie fedde me ones, to wryte in verse and rime,
> To wray my griefe, to crave reward, to cover still my crime:
> To frame a long discourse, on sturring of a strawe,
> To rumble rime in raffe and ruffe, yet all not worth an hawe:
> To heare it sayde there goeth, the *Man that writes so well,*
> But since I see, what Poetes bee, *Fansie* (quoth he) *farewell.*

---

[1] *Works,* I, 380–81.
[2] *Ibid.,* I, 348–52. No. 70.

At Musickes sacred sounde, my fansies eft begonne,
In concordes, discordes, notes and cliffes, in tunes of unisonne:
In *Hyerarchies* and straynes, in restes, in rule and space,
In monacordes and moving moodes, in *Burdens* under base:
In descants and in chants, I streyned many a yel,
But since Musicians be so madde, *Fansie* (quoth he) *farewell*.

To plant straunge countrie fruites, to sow such seedes likewise,
To digge & delve for new foũd rootes, where old might wel suffise:
To proyne the water bowes, to picke the mossie trees,
(Oh how it pleasd my fancie ones) to kneele upon my knees,
To griffe a pippine stocke, when sappe begins to swell:
But since the gaynes scarce quite the cost, *Fansie* (quoth he) *farewell*.

Fansie (quoth he) *farewell,* which made me follow drommes,
Where powdred bullets serves for sauce, to every dish that cõmes:
Where treason lurkes in trust, where *Hope* all hartes beguiles,
Where mischief lieth still in wayte, when fortune friendly smiles:
Where one dayes prison proves, that all such heavens are hell,
And such I feele the frutes thereof, *Fansie* (quoth he) *farewell*.

The first stanza shows us the familiar figure of the poet as courtier, but in the second, the erstwhile gallant becomes the man behind the plow. Then in successive stanzas he becomes hunter, poet, musician, horticulturist, and soldier. The time limits of these varied activities are quite clear. I have shown that his entry into the court circle occurred at about the time of Elizabeth's accession[3] and I shall show that he departed for the Dutch wars in 1572.[4] Although the limits are thus established, the internal chronology remains uncertain. We know, for example, that he returned to Gray's Inn after being cast off by the court, but the "farewell" contains no mention of this. Matters are not simplified by the "wodmanship" poem, which traces Gascoigne's unsuccessful career as university student, law student, courtier, and soldier. Here again, the return to Gray's Inn is omitted, as are any references to the rustic interlude of the "farewell." Other evidence does, however, enable us to place the court period as before the return to Gray's Inn and to date this return as subsequent to 1563.[5]

As has been noted in chapter i, Gascoigne associated his court period with financial difficulties. Here the Close Rolls are of considerable value,

---

[3] *Vide supra,* chap. i.   [4] *Vide infra,* chap. iii.   [5] Cf. *supra,* n. 3; *infra,* n. 9.

for they show not only his financial transactions but also his place of
of residence. During the year 1561 the name of George Gascoigne appears only once in the Close Rolls,[6] but for the next year there are eight
entries in which the poet is concerned. The year 1563 lists five entries;
1564, two; 1565, none; and 1566, two. In 1561 the poet is described as of
Cardington, but in 1562 his regular residence appears to have been Willington, with occasional residence at Gray's Inn. The following year
records Willington with one reference to Gray's Inn. From this time on,
however, all references to Willington cease and Walthamstow appears
for the first time in 1564. The two years 1566 and 1567 refer only to
Gray's Inn.[7]

The meaning of these entries and places of residence, when compared
with the poems noted, seems to be that Gascoigne continued his court
life through the year 1562 and part of 1563. After that he devoted himself to agricultural pursuits until he returned to Gray's Inn to resume
the study of the law. I base this conclusion on the following facts. During 1562 and 1563 George Gascoigne, either alone or jointly with his
father, paid considerable sums of money to various London merchants.
£600 was paid to one Thomas Wood of London, gent.; 200 marks was
paid to John Peers, citizen and fishmonger, of London. Another fishmonger and citizen of London, John Marshall, received £200. Then
there followed a series of bonds given to John Rawlyns of The Tower
of London. There is nothing in these various bonds to indicate that
George or his father was purchasing goods, lands, or services; and the
occupations of the various second parties suggest that they were owed
money. In other words, these bonds seem to me to be payments of debts.

Such a theory of prodigal expenditure for the years 1561–63 is strengthened by other facts and persons mentioned in these Close Roll entries.
In November, 1562, there was entered a bond of £200 to be paid by
George Gascoigne of Willington, to Arthur Hall of Grantham, provided the latter, within a specified time, has been in the city of Toledo,

---

[6] *Vide infra,* Appendix IV, for a brief listing of all the Close Roll entries referring to
Gascoigne, with date, place of residence, and particulars.

[7] The description of residence cannot be taken with absolute certainty. Gascoigne may
have been in continuous residence at Willington, but on coming up to London and staying
for a week at Gray's Inn, he might well describe himself as of the latter place. Nevertheless,
the residence stated is indicative.

in Spain, and provided the traveler gives proof of this journey. Such a bond is the official recording of a bet, i.e., Gascoigne bets that Hall will not get to Toledo and back by a certain time. The friendship indicated by this bet is confirmed by an entry of January 28, 1562/3, in which Gascoigne guarantees a debt of Hall's in the sum of £100. This Arthur Hall,[8] though a member of Gray's Inn, was no serious student of the law. He is chiefly known to us as the translator of Homer, but in 1562 he was known as a tavern brawler, skilled in the use of the dagger. A wealthy orphan, his wardship had been given to Sir William Cecil in whose home in London he lived. Through Cecil, Hall had entry to the court, and we can thus see two connections with Gascoigne: Gray's Inn and the court. The poet's friendship with such a brave young gallant is further evidence of a gay spendthrift existence and confirms the hypothesis that sometime in the autumn of 1563 Gascoigne left the court and retired to the manor of Willington, which he had leased from one John Gostwick as a suitable country residence for himself and his wife, Elizabeth Bacon Bretton Boyes. Final proof of the date and duration of residence at Willington is found in a suit brought by Gostwick. According to this, George and Elizabeth resided at Willington from 1563 until 1564/5.[9]

In the midst of his life as a courtier, in fact on November 23, 1561,[10] George Gascoigne married Elizabeth, the widow of William Bretton and apparently the wife of Edward Boyes. The poet's marriage has posed many problems. Was Elizabeth really married to Boyes? Was she a near kinswoman to Sir Nicholas Bacon? Was she divorced from Boyes? These and other questions have been answered by an examination of certain legal documents and the wills of several members of the Bacon family.

Elizabeth Bacon, daughter of John Bacon of Hesset, was a distant cousin of Sir Nicholas Bacon, Lord Keeper of the Great Seal of England; but her uncle, Francis Bacon, seems to have been more solicitous of her

[8] H. G. Wright, *The Life and Works of Arthur Hall of Grantham*. Wright makes no mention of these bonds nor does he indicate any relation between Hall and Gascoigne other than the notice of "the pretie and pythie conceites of M. George Gascoigne" in Hall's introduction to his translation, *Ten Books of Homers Iliades* (1581).

[9] *Vide infra*, n. 72.

[10] For this date and all other references to the marriage and its attendant problems, see Appendix III.

welfare than her more famous relative. She soon established herself by a marriage, in 1545 at the parish church of Hesset, to William Bretton, a well-to-do citizen of London. By him she had several children, one of whom was Nicholas Bretton, the poet. On January 12, 1558/9, William Bretton died, leaving behind him considerable property.

Sometime between January, 1558/9, and April 7, 1559, Elizabeth found a second husband in "one Edward Boyes of Nonnington in Kent." This gentleman came of a good family and subsequently held positions of some note in his native county. Ostensibly the marriage was a desirable one, but later events point to rather questionable behavior on the part of Boyes. It is probable that he married Elizabeth in order to control not only her property, but that of her children as well, since some years later we find the Bretton children suing Edward Boyes for the recovery of their possessions which had "casually comen into" his hands. It is the original bill of this case which finally settled the problem of whether or no Elizabeth married Boyes. The children, speaking of their mother's second marriage, say: " . . . That one Edward Boyes of Nonnington in the county of Kent by and under colour of a pretended marriage solemnized between the said Edward and the said Elizabeth." The details of this ceremony are not amplified, but it seems certain that there was no doubt of its validity in the mind of Elizabeth Bacon's father, who, in his will of April 1559, mentioned Elizabeth as his "daughter Boyes," and also referred to "Mr. Boyes my son-in-law."

Of the life and activities of Elizabeth between her marriage to Boyes and that to George Gascoigne, nothing is at present known, save one legal document which may or may not refer to her. This is a petition to the Queen for a writ of subpoena to bring Edward Boyes, his wife Elizabeth, and "divers other as well women as men" into the Star Chamber.[11] Christopher Rythe, the plaintiff, seeks redress for the unlawful seizure of his property, the parsonage of Ealing, in the county of Middlesex. The grounds for a Star Chamber proceeding are the usual ones of forcible entry with the usual weapons invasive and defensive. Rythe claimed that having bought the lease of the parsonage from Thomas Bawghe, grandson of the late chancellor of St. Paul's, he was denied access by Edward

---

[11] PRO St. Ch. 5, R41/39 contains the petition and answer, while St. Ch. 5, R12/23 contains the interrogation and answers of witnesses.

Boyes, Elizabeth his wife, and others. The various bills, replications, and interrogatories present a vivid picture of the embattled defenders thrusting pikes through the fence palings and indulging in amusing repartee with Rythe and the constable, but we learn nothing about Boyes's title to the parsonage nor do we gain any further information about Boyes.

It seems probable, however, that these principals are the same as the relict of William Bretton, and her second husband. In the first place, the date is consistent with the known facts: Boyes and Elizabeth were married between January and April, 1559; the "Battle of Ealing" was fought in the second week of Lent, 1559, and Ash Wednesday was February 1, 1559.[12] Secondly, there is the negative evidence of the various pedigrees of the Boyes family, none of which lists any but the one Edward who had a wife at this time.[13] Thirdly, the fact that the Bawghes were descended from a good stock and that Christopher Rythe was acquainted with at least two members of the Inns of Court suggests that this was not entirely a local affair.[14]

If Elizabeth Bacon was the lady involved in the affair at Ealing, she was then defending her husband's rights with considerable vehemence. But within the next two years she evidently came to suspect the intentions of her new husband, for she seems to have considered her marriage to Boyes not legal. This must have been the case, unless she calmly contemplated bigamy, for on November 23, 1561, she married George Gascoigne at Christchurch Newgate. How Elizabeth met Gascoigne cannot be definitely ascertained. As I have pointed out, Stephen Nevynson knew the poet and probably knew Elizabeth. On the other hand, the family of Bartholomew Withypoll owned property in Walthamstow,[15] and it was to a cottage in Walthamstow, owned by Elizabeth,[16] that Gascoigne retired on his return from Holland. It is possible that, either as a student at Cambridge or later at Gray's Inn, George may have visited "Batte" or his brothers at Walthamstow. Perhaps Elizabeth Bacon may have had, through her influential cousin, Sir Nicholas, some position at court.

---

[12] Fry, *Almanacks for Students of English History,* Table 5.

[13] *Vide infra,* on Edward Boyes, in Appendix III.

[14] Dr. Mark Eccles (*Christopher Marlowe in London,* p. 107) has information showing that a Christopher Rythe was a Middlesex magistrate. It is probably the same man.

[15] Smith, *The Family of Withypoll,* p. 13.

[16] The property is listed in the will of William Bretton, PCC 51 Welles. Noted by Schelling, *The Life and Writings of George Gascoigne,* p. 50.

There is, however, no mention of her name in any of the surviving documents which concern ladies at court.

Following their marriage, George and Elizabeth seem to have resided for a short time in the Redcross Street home of William Bretton, since a Close Roll recognizance prescribes payment of certain sums of money at the tenement, "wherein the said George Gascoigne now inhabiteth and wherein one William Bretton lately inhabited and dwelled set and being in Redcross Street in the parish of Saint Giles without Cripplegate of London."[17]

But, as we now learn for the first time through the records, provision had been made of a home in Bedfordshire for the young couple. Elizabeth's uncle, Francis Bacon of White Friars in Fleet Street, was a man of considerable wealth, if one may judge by the bequests of his will,[18] and Elizabeth's father being dead, this uncle took upon himself the duty of providing a jointure for his niece.[19] To this end, Francis Bacon entered into an indenture with Sir John Gascoigne on May 14, 1562, six months after the marriage. The terms of this agreement were that Sir John,

for divers good and reasonable causes and considerations . . . and for a jointure to be assured to and for Elizabeth then and now wife of George Gascoigne [should allow Bacon to make a recovery of Sir John's manor of Eastcottes], and of divers lands tenements rents recoveries and divers and sundry other things in Cardington And also of all that his [Sir John's] part or portion of the Barony of Bedford with all and singular the rent realties and service thereunto belonging in the said county of Bedford and of divers and sundry other lands tenements rents reversions services and hereditaments in Hawnes Elmstowe and Bydenham in the said county of Bedford.

Bacon having thus gained title to these lands was, by terms of the agreement, to allow them "to the only use of the said Sir John Gascoigne for term of his life and after his decease to the use of the said George Gascoigne and Elizabeth his wife and of the heirs of the body of the said George lawfully begotten." The following day, May 15, 1562, Sir John

[17] PRO Close Roll 625 (4 Eliz. pt. 22) no. 29. *Vide infra,* Appendix IV, for acknowledgement of Close Roll entries noted by previous researchers.

[18] PCC 10 Sheffeld.

[19] This and the following details are from a hitherto unknown case in Chancery which Thomas Colby, to whom George and his father sold the lands bought by Francis Bacon, brought to recover certain deeds from the executors of Francis Bacon. PRO Chanc. Proc. (Ser. II) C3, 41/22. The case will be discussed below. It should be noted that its date and terms confirm the date of the marriage as 1561.

and George made an indenture to Francis Bacon guaranteeing their performance of this agreement.

However, Sir John was still alive after the making of these indentures, and accordingly the manor and the lands therein mentioned were not yet the property of George and Elizabeth. Probably because of this fact Gascoigne sought a suitable country home for his bride and himself, and rented, on May 20, 1562, from one John Gostwick, the latter's manor of Willington in the county of Bedford. It was to this country home that Gascoigne retired after being "cast off" by the court in 1563. The lease, enrolled on the Close Rolls,[20] is to all intents a very ordinary arrangement, but all was far from peaceful in the relations between Gascoigne and John Gostwick, as I shall show below. For the present, it will be well to follow events chronologically, because in this way Gascoigne's troubles may be more easily understood.

Sometime in the spring of 1562, Edward Boyes, Elizabeth's second husband, and George Gascoigne had become involved in legal difficulties regarding their respective marriages to Elizabeth. The matter was, by the summer, under consideration in the ecclesiastical Court of the Arches, but hot tempers were not satisfied with the law and on the night of September 30, 1562, there was a great fray in Redcross Street between the two "husbands" and their retainers.[21] The next day Sir Nicholas Bacon issued a Chancery order committing the problem of who was Elizabeth's legal husband to three new judges. Other items in this order provided for the impounding of the household effects at the home in Redcross Street—although Elizabeth was allowed to live there—and for the delivery of goods belonging to Gascoigne that Boyes had in his possession and vice versa. Finally, both men were forbidden to have access or repair to Elizabeth "in the mean season." Gascoigne and Boyes signed a £500 bond to observe this latter order, but once again there was an argument. What did the term "in the mean season" signify? Did it mean until the Feast of All Saints, by which time Bacon had ordered Gascoigne to be ready to settle the matter, or did it mean until the case was settled? The poet held to the former interpretation and no sooner repaired to his wife than Boyes sued him for £500 on the bond. Thereupon Gascoigne peti-

[20] PRO Close Roll 617 (4 Eliz. pt. 14) no. 33.
[21] Noted by Schelling (*op. cit.*, p. 9) from *Machyn's Diary*.

tioned Sir Nicholas for relief from this unjust persecution, alleging that the reason the case was not settled was because Boyes and his attorney kept delaying the proceedings. In May 1563, a Chancery injunction prevented Boyes from continuing his action.

In the meantime there were other disputes at law which arose from Elizabeth's marriage to Boyes. In his will, William Bretton left his children £500, due to him from Thomas and James Bacon, brothers to Sir Nicholas. Boyes, having possession of the obligation signed by Thomas and James Bacon, brought suit against the latter to collect the £500. In addition, Boyes had other documents which belonged to Elizabeth as executrix of her first husband's estate. To recover these, as well as the obligation of the brothers Bacon, George and Elizabeth brought a petition, on October 7, 1562, to Sir Nicholas, to make Boyes return these papers.[22] How Sir Nicholas disposed of these attacks on his brothers is not known; the records appear to be missing. In the spring of 1573 James Bacon died, and his will shows an obligation to Elizabeth Gascoigne for property bought by Bacon from Richard Bretton, the eldest son of the deceased William.[23] No mention is made of Boyes, so it is likely that Sir Nicholas had decided that matter with speed. However, the troubles of the Bretton children and Boyes were by no means over, as we shall see.

Elizabeth Bretton brought to her third husband not only her own trials and tribulations but also those of her first husband, William Bretton. In the spring of 1562, Sir Ambrose Jermyn, in his capacity as executor of the last will and testament of Robert Ashefeilde of Suffolk,[24] sued George Gascoigne. The story is rather complicated, but its essentials can be given briefly without doing violence to the many details. It seems that Robert and Henry Ashefeilde bought certain lands in Cambridge and Bedford from King Henry VIII. At the same time William Bretton also bought lands from the King and, to make sure of his title, decided to secure letters patent confirming the purchase. The Ashefeildes, in order to save the cost of getting their own letters patent, had Bretton include their

---

[22] PRO Chanc. Proc. (Ser. II) C3, 71/71. Noted by Ward ("George Gascoigne and His Circle," *RES,* II [1926], 41). See also Appendix III.

[23] Ward, *op. cit.,* p. 39.

[24] PRO Chanc. Proc. (Ser. II) C3, 104/47. The bill and answer are undated, but a Chancery Order of April 25, 1562 (C 33/25 fol. 301ᵛ), refers to this matter and thus dates the proceeding approximately. It is interesting to note that Thomas Colby was Jermyn's attorney.

lands with his, but this economy proved expensive. The lands were never returned, so Jermyn, as executor of Robert, to whom had descended the property of his brother Henry, invoked the law to secure for the children of Robert Ashefeilde this property which had now come into the possession of George Gascoigne and his wife Elizabeth. The case dragged on until June 21, 1564, when one clause of a judgment awarded, provisionally, 100 marks to the Ashefeildes.[25]

Either the expenditures for these various legal difficulties or a dissatisfaction with the living arrangements at Willington, where Gostwick and his wife were also in residence, may have been the cause of Gascoigne's resumption of his studies at Gray's Inn in 1564 or 1565.[26] His return was celebrated by poems written for five of his friends,[27] and the literary interest shown in these continued with exceptional vigor during the next two years: the *Supposes* and the *Jocasta* were both presented in 1566.[28]

We are, of course, uncertain as to how seriously Gascoigne considered his studies, but we do know that, in addition to his interest in the drama, he found time to enjoy a number of friends. There are the five for whom he wrote on his return: Francis and Anthony Kinwelmarshe, John Vaughan, Alexander Neville, and Richard Courtop.[29] Francis Kinwelmarshe, admitted to Gray's Inn in 1557,[30] was Gascoigne's collaborator in the translation of *Jocasta*,[31] and a contributor to *The Paradyse of Daynty Devises*,[32] and may well have been the Francis Kinwelmarshe who was elected to Parliament from Bossiney, Cornwall, in 1572.[33] The family was probably originally of London[34] and it may have been that

---

[25] PRO Chanc. D & O C33/29, fol. 317ʳ. However, the award was still being debated in July, 1565. (Chanc. D & O C33/31, fol. 304ʳ.) After this there are no further entries, and the terms of the judgment almost certainly point to the fact that Gascoigne lost.

[26] Gascoigne was made an ancient of Gray's Inn in 1565 (British Museum, Harleian MS 1912, fol. 238ᵛ).

[27] The five poems are entitled "Gascoignes memorie," (*Works*, I, 62–70. Nos. 57–61).

[28] These dates are from the title-page of each play. (*Works*, I, 187, 244.)

[29] The names are prefaced to each poem, *q.v.*

[30] Foster, *Register of Admissions to Gray's Inn*, p. 27.

[31] *Works*, I, 260, 307.

[32] *The Paradise of Dainty Devises*, ed. by Rollins. Biographical notice, Introduction, p. liv. Poems Nos. 9, 11, 13, 18, 19, 21, 40, 41, and 75 are signed "F.K." Rollins also attributes No. 98 to Kinwelmarshe.

[33] *DNB* "Francis Kinwelmarshe."

[34] Dr. Rollins (*op. cit.*) gives Mrs. Stopes's discovery of an entry in the parish register of Allhallows, London, which lists the christening on Oct. 18, 1538, of Francis, the son of Rich-

the sons, as they achieved success, took up residence in the country. Anthony Kinwelmarshe, admitted to Gray's Inn in 1561,[35] may then be the
Anthony Kinwelmarshe of Wing, Buckinghamshire, who was friendly
with the Dormer family.[36] Nothing, aside from his admission in 1562–3,[37]
is known about John Vaughan. The frequency of this name prevents
identification. Concerning Alexander Neville there seems to be more
information. In 1560 he translated Seneca's *Oedipus* and later he was
secretary to Archbishop Parker.[38] As to the last of the five friends, Richard
Courtop, who entered in 1559,[39] little is known. There was a Richard
Courtop of Cranbrook, Kent,[40] but we cannot be certain if he was the
law student or if he is to be identified with the defendant in a Chancery
action of 1562.[41]

Other friends at Gray's Inn would include the brothers Withypoll, as
well as Arthur Hall, who was admitted in 1556.[42] Among the senior
members of the Inn was Christopher Yelverton, the author of the epilogue to *Jocasta,* of whom Gascoigne wrote the following:

> But hold my tale to *Rugge* and all the rest
> Of good Grayes Inne, where honest *Yelverton,*
> And I *Per se* sometimes yfeere did rest,
> When amitie first in our brests begonne,
> Which shall endure as long as any Sunne
> May shine on earth, or water swimme in Seas,
> Let not my verse your lawlike minds displease. . . .[43]

---

ard Kyndelmershe. A document which I have found confirms this fact of London origin. A
Chancery suit (Early Chanc. Proc. C1/1445, 45) was brought by Richard Kinwelmershe of
London, mercer, against John Sparke of London, merchant tailor.

[35] Foster, *op. cit.,* p. 29.   [36] *DNB* "Francis Kinwelmarshe."   [37] Foster, *op. cit.,* p. 31.

[38] There is no record of Alexander Neville's admission to Gray's Inn; Gascoigne's reference
is, however, presumptive evidence of his being a member. There seems to be confusion regarding the identity of this young poet who, in the preface to his translation of Seneca
(1560), gives his year of birth as 1544. *DNB* describes him as brother to Thomas Neville,
Dean of Canterbury, and son of Richard Neville of South Leverton, Notts., by Anne, daughter of Sir Walter Montell. I have found several Chancery Proceedings instituted by Alexander
Neville of South Leverton, Notts., against his mother Anne, the widow of Sir Anthony Neville (Early Chanc. Proc. C1/1455, 21–25; C1/1455, 26–30). These date from 1553 and
could hardly have been instituted by a boy born in 1544. There is a need for a study of this
secretary of Archbishop Parker (Strype's *Life . . . of . . . Parker,* II, 433) and author of *De
Furoribus Norfolciensium Ketto Duce* (1575), and *Academiae Cantabrigiensis Lacrymae*
(1587).

[39] Foster, *op. cit.,* p. 28.   [40] *Visitation of Kent,* Harl. Soc. Pub., XLII, 200.

[41] PRO Chanc. D & O C33/25, fol. 330ʳ.   [42] Foster, *op. cit.,* p. 26.   [43] *Works,* I, 181.

Yelverton in 1552[44] entered Gray's Inn, where his father had been a Reader of the Inn in 1535 and 1542.[45] Especial care seems to have been taken of the strict observance of the Revels,[46] and Yelverton was much interested in the performance of plays at such times. His rise to the position of Justice of the King's Bench occurred long after the death of Gascoigne. William Rugge, mentioned with Yelverton, was an older member of the Society who had become Dean of the Chapel.[47] Another senior member was Serjeant William Lovelace, described by Gascoigne as "Serjeant *Lovelace,* many ways my friend."[48] The worthy Serjeant, a Canterbury man,[49] did, as we shall see, come to Gascoigne's aid when the poet was in serious trouble. He evidently favored young poets, since Barnabe Googe expressed his gratitude by dedicating his poems *"To the ryght worshipfull M.* William Lovelace *Esquier, Reader of Grayes Inne."*[50] As a lawyer Lovelace held high offices; he was Archbishop Parker's counsel-in-law, as well as steward of the liberties of the Cathedral of Canterbury.[51] His death in 1576, a year before the poet's, was presumably accidental, since on May 3, 1577, Henry Bynneman licensed a ballad entitled, "The briefe course of the accidentes of the deathe of Mr. Serjeant Lovelace."[52] Although the name of his friend Lovelace occurs on a number of documents in Gascoigne's various legal actions, there appears on others the name of Thomas Colby, also a Reader of Gray's Inn. Presumably Gascoigne was at one time friendly with this senior member, but by 1568 the two were enemies.

The return to the fellowship of Gray's Inn and life in London was but a brief interlude in the inexorable succession of disasters which reduced the once gay young man to the status of a soldier of fortune in the Dutch wars. From the time of his marriage, Gascoigne was almost continually in the courts; even during his sojourn at Gray's Inn there was litigation. This constant trouble may have been one cause of his final abandonment of the law. What other reasons there may have been are unknown, but by 1567–68, Gascoigne was farming in Cardington,[53] and we may be certain that he had once again retired to the country.

[44] Foster, *op. cit.,* p. 23.   [45] Dugdale, *Originales Juridicales,* pp. 292–93.

[46] *Ibid.,* p. 285.   [47] Fletcher, *The Pension Book of Gray's Inn, 1569–1669,* p. 5.

[48] *Works,* I, 181.   [49] PRO St. Ch. 5, L47/14.

[50] Googe, *Eglogs, Epytaphes, and Sonettes,* p. 24.

[51] Strype, *The Life and Acts of Matthew Parker,* II, 168.

[52] Arber, *Transcript of the Registers of the Company of Stationers of London,* II, 312.

[53] *Vide infra,* Appendix V.

From 1565 on, Gascoigne's troubles were of three kinds: those involving his wife, her children, and Boyes; others concerning his inheritance from his father; and a third group best described as the results of his own quarrelsome nature. The question of Elizabeth's marriages was settled by November 1565, as we know from a suit brought by the Bretton children.[54] Their mother had been divorced from Boyes, but, since this divorce was subsequent to her marriage to Gascoigne in 1561, the decree had given her permission to marry again. Where and when this ceremony was performed is at present unknown. Although this matter was ended, George and Elizabeth found that they were by no means free of other litigation. William Bretton had feared for his children if his wife married again, so he inserted a clause in his will which transferred, in the event of Elizabeth's remarriage, receipt of the income from property left to his children from his widow to John Bacon, her father, and one Lawrence Eresby.[55] Shortly after the death of William Bretton, John Bacon died, leaving as executors of his estate his son, George Bacon, his brother, George Bacon, and a friend, Thomas Andrewes.[56] These executors seem to have succeeded John Bacon in the task of watching over the inheritance of the Bretton children, for, on November 7, 1564, George and Elizabeth Gascoigne gave a bond of £1,000 to the two George Bacons and Thomas Andrewes. The mother and stepfather were bound to manage carefully the property of the Bretton children which they had, to give the children their lawful bequests, and to maintain them with the revenue received.[57] If George and Elizabeth failed to observe these terms, they would forfeit the £1,000. Surely a strange state of affairs if Elizabeth's own brother and her uncle had to require from her such a large bond for the performance of what was a matter of motherly affection! This bond indicates that either George or Elizabeth was suspect, and that the children needed protection.[58] From the course of later events it becomes evident that such protection was necessary, since many years later the children sued George Gascoigne for their inheritances.

For the moment, however, matters progressed rather peacefully, but

[54] PRO Chanc. Proc. (Ser. II) C3, 27/51. [55] Ward, *op. cit.*, p. 36. [56] PCC 16 Chaynay.
[57] PRO Close Roll 693 (7 Eliz. pt. 21) no. 43.
[58] Other evidence, showing the questionable dealings of the pair, is revealed by the fact that in 1568 George Gascoigne and Elizabeth, his wife, were summoned into the Guildhall of the City for a Lord Mayor's inquiry into the question of the property of the children of William Bretton. (*Complete Poems of George Gascoigne,* ed. by Hazlitt, I, xviii, xix.)

there was still the common foe, Edward Boyes. In November 1566, the Bretton children brought a petition in Chancery to force Edward Boyes to return to them certain property left them by their father.[59] Boyes not only had control of land and tenements, as well as goods and chattels, but also had collected the rents. Unfortunately the technicalities of the law prevented justice; Boyes, in his reply to the petition, pointed out that the children were not of legal age to bring an action and furthermore they were not of the age designated in their father's will as the time for them to receive their inheritances. Sir Nicholas Bacon, evidently concurring in this view, on June 9, 1567, issued a Chancery degree suggesting that George and Elizabeth should join with the children in bringing action against Boyes.[60] This they did in the same month, with Thomas Colby as their attorney.[61] Boyes countered at once with his usual reliance upon technicalities by saying that the matter pertained to the ecclesiastical courts and that a Chancery decree of October 1, 1562,[62] released him from any claims regarding this property. The plaintiffs' reply to this was an affirmation of their rights, but what finally happened we do not know. There is, so far as I have been able to discover, no further mention of this case in Chancery decrees, so it may be that the matter was heard by Commissioners whose proceedings and decrees appear to be missing.

Meanwhile, Sir John Gascoigne had been busy fighting with his neighbors. A lengthy and acrimonious dispute between Sir John and Lord Latimer appears frequently in Star Chamber records.[63] Some of Latimer's woodwards went by night to Sir John's wood of Cardington, which bounded the property of Lord Latimer, and cut down trees which they then tossed over the hedge into their master's wood. Sir John called the constable and took back the cut timber, claiming that all was done peaceably, but there were accusations of riot, and the entire company appeared before the local justices, charged with a breach of peace. Then Sir John took the matter to the Star Chamber, where a great array of witnesses was marshaled and everyone called everyone else a riotous and lying fellow. This action, begun in 1565, lasted about a year. By that time Sir John was in dispute with another of his neighbors about boundaries. The new

---

[59] PRO Chanc. Proc. (Ser. II) C3, 27/51.   [60] PRO Chanc. D & O C33/35, fol. 172ʳ.
[61] PRO Chanc. Proc. (Ser. II) C3, 202/7.   [62] *Vide infra,* Appendix III.
[63] PRO St. Ch. 5, L33/28; N2/24.

opponent was Reginald Grey, who after a great deal of legal battling secured for himself the family title of Earl of Kent, only to die shortly after the victory. The suit between Sir John and Grey is known to us only through the Chancery decrees, but among these is a reference, on November 28, 1567, to Sir John's being ill.[64]

Apparently Sir John's illness was a serious one because he had begun preparations for the disposal of certain of his properties. On November 11, 1567, Sir John and George received a patent allowing them to grant to Thomas Colby and Elizabeth, his wife, the manor of Eastcottes, alias Cotton, which Sir John and George held from the Crown.[65] The next day an indenture conferring this grant was enrolled on the Close Rolls.[66] Subsequently Sir John gave two bonds to Colby, guaranteeing the performance of the articles of indenture.[67]

These preparations were indeed those of a man whose days were nearing their close; Sir John Gascoigne died on April 4, 1568.[68] His will, made two days before, was proved June 1, 1568. The terms of this deathbed testament, together with Whetstone's observation that the poet was disinherited, have raised the question of Sir John's real intentions toward his son and heir. Elsewhere I have examined in detail the provisions of the will, as well as the evidence of certain hitherto unexamined documents, and have been able to show that George Gascoigne received from his father's estate property with a yearly value of £135 and from his mother other lands worth £60 per annum. The possession of such a competence can hardly be called evidence of disinheritance.

The thought of disinheriting his son was, however, in Sir John's mind, as we learn from the legal proceedings resulting from certain bequests in this knight's will. The first of these concerned the manor of East-

---

[64] PRO Chanc. D & O C33/35, fols. 327ʳ, 349ᵛ.

[65] PRO Pat. Roll 1051, 10 Eliz., pt. XI, m. 16 (31). This bears the date Nov. 11, 10 Eliz., which is an error, for by that time Sir John had been dead seven months. It should be 9 Eliz., i.e., 1567. This entry was noted by Mrs. Oldfield (RES, XIII [1937], 133), but the matter of the date was not discussed.

[66] PRO Close Roll 769 (10 Eliz. pt. 13) m. 46ᵈ. Although the Roll is 10 Eliz., this entry is dated Nov. 12, 9 Eliz., and confirms my conclusion in n. 65.

[67] PRO Close Roll 769 (10 Eliz. pt. 13) m. 48ᵈ; this membrane records two bonds: one on Dec. 15, 10 Eliz. and the other on March 10, 10 Eliz.

[68] Appendix V, "The 'Disinheritance' of George Gascoigne," contains a detailed examination, of which the ensuing account is an abstract. All references are to be found in this appendix.

cottes, which Sir John, shortly before his death, had sold to Thomas Colby. Now it will be remembered that this was the same manor which Francis Bacon had bought from Sir John Gascoigne as a dowry for his niece, Elizabeth. According to the terms of the original indenture, Sir John was to continue possession until his death, when the property was to revert to Elizabeth. Evidently Sir John was timorous about his plan to sell this property, for he not only had his son George join with him in the patent but also added to his will stern admonitions that George was to allow Colby quiet and peaceable possession of the property. Somehow or other Colby induced the poet to sign a bond guaranteeing possession, but ere long the redoubtable George very nearly tricked Colby out of Eastcottes.

Another source of irritation was the ownership of the manor of Fenlake Barnes, the parsonage of Cardington, which Sir John left to his son John. In a devious way it becomes apparent that Sir John had, in 1562, sold this manor to his son George for £200. After the death of his father, George took possession of the parsonage and proceeded to collect the tithe lambs due him as owner of the property. The lambs were, however, too young to be taken from the ewes; so Gascoigne, after branding them with a Roman "H," left the lambs in the common pasture. Hereupon Dame Margaret and John raided the common pasture and took the tithe lambs, which they put among Dame Margaret's own flock. Strangely enough, this whole flock happened one day to break through into George's pasture. The poet and his shepherd, fortunately on hand, divided the tithe lambs, drove back Dame Margaret's flock, and blocked up the hole in the hedge. The upshot of this was another raid by Dame Margaret, John, and their retainers, armed with the usual weapons invasive and defensive. Thus the matter came into the Star Chamber, where for the first time we learn of George's claim to Fenlake Barnes, of Sir John's fear of trouble over this property, and of a melodramatic deathbed scene, in which Sir John wished to disinherit his son George, but was dissuaded by the maternal tears and pleadings of Dame Margaret. The proceedings are a masterly portrayal of this whole episode. Dame Margaret's imprecations at George's shepherd, a disparaging reference to hawking staves no bigger than a man's thumb, a temporizing answer saying that daggers were carried behind the backs of the raiding party in order to avoid frightening the shepherd—all these give vivid life to the great Cardington sheep-stealing.

This action continued for a weary time in the courts. George evidently won in the Star Chamber, for in the Chancery Decree Books there appear references to a suit brought by John against George concerning the ownership of Fenlake Barnes.[69] If the variety of the Chancery decrees is any indication, the problem seems to have been a complicated one. John, however, eventually won title to the parsonage, for his daughter, Anne, many years later mentions the parsonage of Fenlake Barnes as a bequest.[70]

The eventual ownership of Fenlake Barnes is, however, of relatively little importance in comparison with the information in the proceedings concerning the problem of Gascoigne's disinheritance, his relations with his father, and his rather unpleasant troubles with his mother and brother. The replication of John Gascoigne shows that George was not disinherited, but that his father thought of such procedure. The reasons which might cause Sir John to disinherit his son are also suggested. It was claimed by the poet that his father had given him the lease of Fenlake Barnes. We know also that Sir John agreed to sell the manor of Eastcottes to Francis Bacon and that he later sold the same property to Thomas Colby. Whether or no the Fenlake Barnes and Eastcottes properties were legally conveyed to George Gascoigne and Francis Bacon cannot be proved, but, since both matters got into the courts, it seems to me that there was something questionable about Sir John's actions in both instances. Therefore, when Sir John reputedly accused his son of "evil doings," one is led to wonder whether Sir John's own "evil doings" might have been the origin of the misunderstanding between father and son. Certainly Sir John's deathbed censures of his son refer to business matters; there is nothing in the document referring to matters of personal conduct. On the other hand, as we have seen, George and Elizabeth were suspected by both the Bacons and the Lord Mayor in the matter of the Bretton children's estate. Fathers and sons have fought over money, and the proverb, "to hate like brothers," is all too common for us to wonder greatly over this unfortunate family relationship. A complicating factor may also be seen in the fact that Sir John was a strong Catholic,

---

[69] PRO Chanc. D & O C33/40 fols. 319ᵛ, 410ᵛ, 419ʳ.
[70] PCC 59 Huddlestone.

whereas his son made slighting references to the faith of his father. Then, too, George's marriage was not one to find favor with his family. Both father and mother came of old families, while the Bacons of Hesset were yeoman stock. Moral scruples could scarcely have been a matter of conflict between father and son, if we remember Anne Drewry, "sometime my servant." Sir John could hardly task his son with a wild life at court, but the son could naturally be very angry at the gift of an annuity to a mistress, particularly a servant girl. There seems to have been blame on both sides, but time did not heal the breach; rather George ceased to have any relations with either his mother or brother.[71]

While George was fighting with his brother, another lawsuit was brought against him.[72] This time the plaintiff was John Gostwick, from whom the poet had rented the manor of Willington as a suitable home for his new bride. The indenture, which seemed such an ordinary business transaction, contained, however, elements of trouble, for Gostwick suddenly claimed to have been tricked. A word about John Gostwick will better prepare our understanding of the agreement about Willington manor. Sir John Gostwick of Willington, was, like Sir William Gascoigne, a member of the household of Cardinal Wolsey. In 1529 he bought Willington manor from Thomas, Duke of Norfolk. Sir John, having used his court influence to increase the boundaries of his estates, left considerable property to his son William. This William died without issue, and the estate reverted to William, the brother of Sir John. This latter William died in 1549, leaving as his heir his son, the John Gostwick of our story. Apparently the acquisitive nature of the family was not inherited by this John, who made any number of unfortunate leases and whose actions can best be described as those of a feeble-minded person. In 1562 Gostwick leased Goldington Manor to Francis Russell, Earl of Bedford, whose mother was the widow of William, the son of Sir John Gostwick. The indenture by which Bedford leased Goldington somehow or other got into the hands of Richard and George Ackworth, largely, one gathers, through the foolishness of John Gostwick. In the

---

[71] It is not strange, in view of what is learned from these trials, that Dame Margaret did not mention her son George in her will (PCC 4 Carew), which was probated March 10, 1575, a few months after the poet's return from Holland. This matter puzzled Mrs. Oldfield (*op. cit.*, pp. 134–35).

[72] PRO Chanc. Proc. (Ser. II) C3, 71/85.

dispute that resulted, Gostwick was described as "being a man of great simplicity and having little or no understanding." Out of similar troubles the unfortunate Gostwick was helped by his father-in-law, Sir William Peter, who was, however, unable to get back other properties which his son-in-law had leased to one Alexander Scroggs.[73]

The good folk of Bedfordshire, as we learn from various records, were not slow to take advantage of this simple soul. One of the more interesting of these records is the case of Frances Bosgrave.[74] This child's father was at first much concerned over Gostwick's simplicity and of his own volition went to Sir William Peter telling the latter that Gostwick "was a very simple witted man and wanted discretion to order or use himself." Bosgrave feared for the poor fellow whom he had heard say that he (Gostwick) "was very ready and willing to give . . . to sell and convey away his said possessions and goods to any person or persons which would ask or take the same." With Christian charity, Bosgrave advised Sir William Peter to get a bond in a large sum from Gostwick to prevent the sale or lease of any property. This was done, but when Bosgrave saw that Peter was not enforcing the bond, he decided to have a share in the spoils. To this end he persuaded Gostwick that, being simple-witted, he was also impotent. Such inability to produce offspring should be compensated for by good deeds to his fellowmen. One good work suggested was the granting of an annuity to Bosgrave's four-year-old daughter, Frances. This was duly accomplished and poor Gostwick brought a petition to Sir Nicholas Bacon to be relieved of the resulting debt.

At about the time when Gostwick was devoting his life to good works, he leased the manor of Willington to George Gascoigne. In 1568[75] Gostwick brought action against Gascoigne, claiming the lease had been effected by fraud. Gostwick's story was that Gascoigne had come to him with the news that Sir William Peter was planning to bring legal action and would get possession of all his property. Gostwick, in great terror,

---

[73] VCH, Bedfordshire, III, 203, 263.

[74] PRO Chanc. Proc. (Ser. II) C3, 70/39. Also Chanc. D & O C33/40, fol. 356r; C33/41, fol. 25r.

[75] The original bill and answer are undated, but a Chancery order (C33/37, fol. 298r) notes the delivery of a subpoena to George Gascoigne and bears the date Nov. 25, 1568. Presumably the action began late in 1567 or early in 1568.

transferred all his property to this friend in need, at the friend's suggestion. Time, however, proved that Sir William brought no action; therefore Gostwick asked Gascoigne for the return of his property, but without success.

Gascoigne's answer to this bill tells a far different story:

[This document is badly torn and worn.]
. . . and also he [Gostwick] and Elizabeth his wife upon sundry their misdemeanours being in very great displeasure with the right honourable Sir William Peter knight—[torn] in consideration he meant to pay his debts in time convenient As also by reformation of their disordered Lives to recover the favour and benevolence of the said Sir William—[torn] to let the same with other his lands and tenements to his most commodity and advantage And that in consideration thereof as well the said complainant [Gostwick] as the said Elizabeth did . . . let—[torn]—m[anor] house of Willington in the county of Bedford furnished with all such kinds of furniture plate household stuff and Implements as then remained in and about the said h[ouse]—And that he this defendant would take to sojourn or Board the said complainant and Elizabeth his wife with such convenient number of [servants]—as between the said parties might be reasonably concluded and agreed Whereupon this defendant reckoning to pleasure the said complainant being a gentleman somewhat [allied?]—[torn] [c]ommodious a house being within the county aforesaid And very near the mansion and abiding of this defendant his father And other his kinfolk and Allies within the said county And—[torn] therein as might deserve no blame or rebuke in the Judgement of Sir William Peter did travel with the said Complainant unto the said Sir William as well for the—[torn] that the same Sir William Peter might be made privy unto the determination of the complainant in the granting and devising of the said house with the rest of his manor lands and—[torn] Whereupon the said Sir William Peter very willing that this defendant should have the said manor house and lands in lease at the hands of the said Complainant upon reasonable Rent—[torn]— . . . .

Hereupon Gascoigne recites the indenture found on the Close Rolls by which Gostwick leased the property. He adds that he was unable to furnish such a large house with such fine furniture as was then in it, so to keep the same he paid "a great yearly rent" and took in to live with him Gostwick and his wife, four servants, two maids, and six horses, all of which was "a great charge and expense." Complications arose when Elizabeth Gostwick "conveyed out of the house plate household stuff and furniture" which she took to her disreputable friends for sale. The disappearance of these goods and chattels put the poet in a difficult position, for an inventory of the contents of the house was attached to the indenture which he had signed. To avoid both damage and slander which might arise out of such thefts while he was in occupancy, George told Gostwick and asked what he proposed to do. Simple Gostwick found the charges true and was much ashamed, "for the defendant bare great love to the plaintiff." Therefore, in reparation for the great injury done to Gascoigne and because Gostwick saw his wife "continue her disordered life," he gave all his property to Gascoigne, with the proviso that the poet would support both husband and wife. "So," says Gascoigne, "they [the Gostwicks] lived with the said defendant for the space of one whole year." For two years Gascoigne continued to occupy Willington and Gostwick said nothing at all, and when "about two or three years past"[76] Gascoigne removed from Willington, he took with him some of the contents of the house, and enjoyed possession of them without let or hindrance until evilly disposed persons urged Gostwick on to this suit. The charges of intimidating Gostwick are completely denied.

That Gascoigne was the victim of unjust persecution is most unlikely; the other information which we possess about Gostwick's affairs indicates that his simple nature was exploited by his neighbors, and the evidence certainly points to rather questionable tactics on the part of Gascoigne. In fact, all financial transactions in which Gascoigne was involved seem to have been questionable.

Whatever may have been the cause, the fact is that from the time of his marriage George Gascoigne became involved in more and more lawsuits, which brought him to financial ruin. Typical of such law disputes is one brought by Sir Richard Verney.[77] This has to do with the property that Gascoigne possessed as a result of his dealings with John Gostwick. Unfortunately the bill and answer are undated, and there are no references in the decree books which can help in ascertaining the time. However, it must have been subsequent to the leasing of Willington and the deed of gift. Briefly the matter is this: Anne, the relict of William

---

[76] These references confirm my hypothesis about Gascoigne's residence. Elizabeth Gostwick's thefts occurred soon after Gascoigne leased Willington. Then John Gostwick lived with the poet for a whole year, i.e., until 1564. "Two or three years past," i.e., 1565/6, Gascoigne removed from Willington. This would be about the time of his return to Gray's Inn.

[77] PRO Chanc. Proc. (Ser. II) C3, 185/39.

Gostwick, the father of John, died before receiving her share of the estate of her husband. In the time between the death of her first husband and her own demise, she married Sir Thomas Verney, the father of the plaintiff. The property which she should have had and which should have descended to Sir Richard came into the possession of Gascoigne, presumably by the deed of gift from John Gostwick, although Verney does not mention this. Gascoigne replied that Anne's inheritance had already been settled and denied any responsibility.

There is, so far as I have searched, no record of the outcome of this dispute, but this and other cases accumulated rapidly. The sheep-stealing dispute and the Gostwick case kept the poet in the courts through the years 1567, 1568, 1569, and 1570, as is shown by frequent references[78] in the Chancery Decree Books. On November 6, 1568, Gascoigne, described as of Walthamstow, gave a bond of 200 marks to Richard Ratcliffe.[79] Evidently he was in need of money, since if this was not paid by December first, £100 was to be paid on the sixth at the dwelling house of Barnard Garter, notary, in Christchurch Way in Newgate.[80] Neither the bond nor the installment was paid, for a Chancery order of April 24, 1569, shows that Ratcliffe brought action against Gascoigne.[81] In like manner, a bond[82] given to William Pelham of Brokelsby, Lincolnshire, for £300 was not paid, and on May 31, 1568, a Chancery order refers to an action brought by Pelham.[83] Other Close Roll entries show the poet giving bonds amounting to £2,600 and 1,500 marks in the years 1566–70.[84] Some of these may have been for value received, but there is no evidence of any lands acquired from any of the persons mentioned. If value was received, it was for goods and purchases, but more probable is the explanation that these were debts. The lawsuits were of course costing money, but there must have been other reasons for this expenditure. Why was the poet so anxious to sell his inheritance to Sir George

---

[78] PRO Chanc. D & O, Gascoigne v. Gascoigne, C33/37, fol. 402ʳ; C33/40, fols. 319ᵛ, 410ᵛ, 419ʳ. Gostwick v. Gascoigne, C33/37, fols. 298ʳ, 402ʳ; C33/41, fol. 193ʳ.

[79] PRO Close Roll 767 (10 Eliz. pt. 11) m. 33ᵈ.

[80] It may be that this is the author of *The Tragicall And True Historie which happened between two English lovers.* 1563, Tottel, 1565.

[81] PRO Chanc. D & O C33/40, fol. 5ᵛ.

[82] PRO Close Roll 756 (9 Eliz. pt. 30) m. 16ᵈ. This may not be the poet for the description is "of London."

[83] PRO Chanc. D & O C33/37, fol. 79ʳ. [84] *Vide infra*, Appendix IV.

Speke for a comparatively small sum?[85] Why had he in 1566 tried to sell Eastcottes to John Wynche?[86] I can only suggest that he soon tired of his resolve to study law and left Gray's Inn to return to the life of a young gallant. There is no evidence to prove this, but he must have been spending his money in some way and the gay life in London seems the obvious answer.

By 1570 Gascoigne was in great difficulty. His brother was suing for Fenlake Barnes, and the Chancery ordered the property to be sequestered until ownership was decided.[87] The Gostwick case was still in the courts,[88] and finally the poet became involved in a dispute with the Earl of Bedford. This is known to us only through the Chancery Decree Books, where it is said that Gascoigne had summoned Bedford on a writ of "audita querella."[89] This writ was used on the common law side of Chancery to reopen, on the basis of new evidence, a suit in which the new plaintiff had been defeated. Therefore we may deduce that, sometime before, Bedford had brought action against Gascoigne and had been successful. Probably the original dispute concerned land, for that is the usual dispute heard in the common law side of Chancery.[90] The documents of this class are exceedingly fragmentary, one rolled bundle of about fifty documents being all that remains of the proceedings for the reigns of Elizabeth, James I, and Charles I. My examination of these documents revealed that a good many were concerned with land held from the Crown by letters patent. In 1562 Sir John received letters patent allowing him to alienate, that is to sell, to Francis, Earl of Bedford, and Sir George Conyers, his lease held of the Crown of the manor of Cardington, Bedfordshire.[91] The use of the manor was reserved to Sir John and his heirs. Perhaps some disagreement over the manor of Cardington was the cause of trouble between Gascoigne and the Earl of Bedford.

By the spring of 1570 George Gascoigne was in a lamentable condition. He was still involved in a number of lawsuits, all of which were decided against him. The temporary good fortune, shown by the recent

[85] PRO Close Roll 772 (10 Eliz. pt. 16) m. 36d.
[86] PRO Close Roll 729 (9 Eliz. pt. 3) no. 10.
[87] *Vide supra*, n. 78.   [88] *Ibid.*
[89] PRO Chanc. D & O C33/40, fols. 334r, 359r, 413r; C33/41, fol. 2v.
[90] PRO Class Number: C89.
[91] PRO Patent Roll 985, 4 Eliz., pt. 10, m. 3(56). Noted by Mrs. Oldfield (*op. cit.*, p. 132).

grant to him of two patents, seemed of little value. On February 17, 1569, Gascoigne had been granted the wardship and marriage of Richard Bretton, together with a retroactive annuity of £15 from Bretton's estate, beginning with the day of William Bretton's death.[92] On the first of June, in the same year, a patent had been granted to the poet to hold all the lands and hereditaments which Sir John had held of the Crown in chief.[93] No lands are specified in this patent, and, since we know that Dame Margaret disposed of Cardington manor in her will,[94] that John Gascoigne gained possession of Fenlake Barnes,[95] and that Thomas Colby had Eastcottes,[96] it is clear that this patent applied only to the manor and one-quarter of the Barony of Bedford, which was left by Sir John. Thus this seeming advantage was of little value to Gascoigne, while the annuity was a comparatively small sum for one involved in such large transactions as are shown by the Close Rolls.

The final evidences of financial ruin are in the Chancery decrees, where, among the entries of Friday, April 21, 1570, we find the following order:[97]

John Gascoigne pl } John Raynold hath made oath that the def lieth in
George Gascoigne deft } Bedford gaol upon an execution whereupon he can not appear, Therefore a dedimus potestatem is awarded to Lewis Dive and Robert Newdigate esquires to take the answer of the defendant. . . .

Among the orders for Monday, May 29, 1570, occurs another entry:[98]

George Gascoigne pl } Memorandum that this day Mr Sergeant
ffraunces Earl of Bedford deft } Lovelace and Mr Colby are by order of this court assigned to be of counsel with the said George Gascoigne touching a matter depending in this court brought by him against the deft upon an "audita querella."

Fortune's wheel had completed its circuit: the brave young gallant lay in Bedford gaol upon an execution of an order of debt; he was assigned

---

[92] PRO Patent Roll 1060, 11 Eliz., pt. 8, m. 10. Noted by Mrs. Oldfield (*op. cit.*, p. 137).
[93] PRO Patent Roll 1056, 11 Eliz., pt. 4, m. 26. Noted by Mrs. Oldfield (*op. cit.*, p. 138), who did not examine the problem of just what this patent really included.
[94] PCC 4 Carew.
[95] *Vide supra*, n. 69. This property was disposed of by John's daughter, Anne, in her will.
[96] Gascoigne sued Colby in 1576 to recover the manor. (Chanc. D & O C33/51, fol. 320^r.)
[97] PRO Chanc. D & O C33/40, fol. 319^v. Another decree (C33/40, fol. 410^v) records an attachment against George Gascoigne, awarded to the sheriff of Bedford.
[98] PRO Chanc. D & O C33/40, fol. 413^r.

counsel by the court—a form of legal aid. The men whose names appear in these Chancery entries were both friends and enemies of the poet: Lovelace and Colby we have met before; whereas Lewis Dive was to receive, some years later, the dedication of the repentant sinner's moral tract, *A delicate Diet, for daintiemouthde Droonkardes.*[99]

The most curious feature of these Chancery orders is the fact that Colby was assigned as counsel to the poet, for it was in this same year that Colby brought action against Dame Margaret Gascoigne, William Drury, doctor at the civil law, and one Jacob,[100] as well as against Gascoigne and his servant, John Rogers,[101] for the recovery of the deeds and papers relating to the manor of Eastcottes. Obviously unfriendly to the poet, Colby was a strange choice for a lawyer. Presumably his influence was counterbalanced by "worthy Serjeant Lovelace."

How George Gascoigne fared in Bedford gaol and when he was released are, unfortunately, unknown, but we do know that the autumn of 1570 found his various cases still in the courts. Colby succeeded in getting a court order forcing Dame Margaret to produce the deeds and papers which related to Eastcottes[102] and which were in her possession. Whether Colby succeeded with William Drury, the executor of Francis Bacon's will, who admitted to the possession of the indenture by which Francis Bacon sought to give a jointure to his niece, Elizabeth, is also unknown. A certain amount of crooked work was afoot, for George Gascoigne, in an attempt to trick Colby out of Eastcottes, had given deeds for part of the property to his servant, John Rogers.[103] It would be tedious to follow the ramifications of these land disputes, but appar-

---

[99] *Works,* II, 453. Dive was a person of some eminence in Bedfordshire, as appears from the frequency with which his name occurs in legal records appointing him to take the depositions of witnesses, to take answers and the like (PRO St. Ch. 5, L33/28; Chanc. D & O C33/33, fol. 2ʳ; C33/35, fol. 349ᵛ; C33/37, fol. 402ʳ; C33/40, fol. 319ᵛ). He was a cousin german to Grey of Wilton, with whom he served at Guisnes (Holinshed, *The Whole Volume of Chronicles,* III, 1138). Here, according to Holinshed, both Dive and Grey escaped through a breach in the walls. Later, at Calais, they were both captured and held for ransom (Chanc. Proc. [Ser. II] C3, 56/99). Grey had to sell the family seat of Wilton to gain freedom and at the same time paid 400 crowns for Dive. The latter was accused of not paying the remainder to the Lady Creseques, their captor, and her agent, Philip Didato, brought an action in the English courts for the recovery of this ransom. More to our purpose is the fact that Lewis Dive's son, John, married Douglas, the daughter of Sir Anthony Denny and for this lady Gascoigne wrote a poem of advice (*Works,* I, 341. No. 66).

[100] PRO Chanc. Proc. (Ser. II) C3, 41/22.   [101] PRO Chanc. Proc. (Ser. II) C3, 47/43.
[102] PRO Chanc. D & O C33/41, fol. 171ʳ.   [103] *Vide supra,* n. 101.

ently Colby was successful, for in 1576, when Gascoigne's fortunes were
in the ascendant, the poet brought action against Colby for the recovery
of the lands.[104]

After the spring of 1571 Gascoigne's name disappears from all the
legal records. Where he lived and what he was doing we do not know;
we can only conclude that, having fallen on evil days, he was living
in retirement.

[104] PRO Chanc. D & O C33/51, fol. 320^r.

III. The Soldier

Wel leave I hear, of thriftles wil to write,
Wit found my rents, agreed not with my charge:
The sweet of war, sung by the carpet knight,
In poste haste then shipt me in Ventures Barge.
These lusty limes, Saunce use (quod I) will rust:
That pitie were, for I to them must trust.

WHETSTONE

BY THE SPRING of 1572 a sudden crisis occurred in Holland, and Gascoigne made ready, as Harvey says, "to try other conclusions in the Lowe Countries." The rebellion of the Dutch offered him a way out of a seeming impasse; indeed, what other opportunity was there? Having failed as a lawyer and a courtier, Gascoigne was in a desperate plight. His only chance of recouping his fortunes was through a sudden ascendant of Fortune's wheel—a wheel that revolved more rapidly in war than in peace. Like Mount Hermer, whose son recites the masque for the Montague marriage, Gascoigne "gan nowe prepare himself to save his pawne, or else to leese his pheares."[1] On All Fools' Day, 1572, the Dutch Sea-Beggars under La Marke challenged Spanish supremacy in the Low Countries. The city of Brill was no sooner captured than other towns, among them Flushing, declared for the Stadtholder, William of Orange.[2] In England enthusiasm for the war ran high, for what attractions were offered! A chance of fame and fortune, an opportunity to fight the hated Spaniards, and an occasion to strike a blow at the Romish cause! Men like Sir Humphrey Gilbert saw that Holland was England's first line of defense against Spain and Rome;[3] others, like Rowland Yorke, sought personal gain.[4] By the end of May the first band of volunteers ready to

---

[1] "Pheares" is a variant spelling of "fers," the queen in chess.
[2] Camden, *The History of The most Renowned and Victorious Princess Elizabeth*, p. 184.
[3] *Vide, passim,* Gilbert's letters to Burghley, *Cal. S. P. For.,* Docs. Nos. 491, 530, 546, 550, 556, 557.
[4] *Vide infra,* n. 80, for a brief account of Yorke.

leave England was given a sort of unofficial blessing by the appearance
of the Queen for their muster at Greenwich. The origin of this band of
men is described by one of their number, Sir Roger Williams,[5] whose
account of the war closely parallels Gascoigne's verse narrative, "Dulce
Bellum Inexpertis."[6] Williams thus describes his companions:

Amongst the *Londoners* were divers Captaines and souldiers, who had served
some in *Scotland,* some in *Ireland,* others in *France.* And having nothing to
doe, with the countenance of some great men who favoured the cause, and the
small helpes of the deputies of *Flushing,* Captaine *Thomas Morgan* levied a
faire company of three hundred strong. . . .[7]

Gascoigne must have been one of these volunteers, since upon their
arrival they at once saw action, which the poet describes.[8] He could not
have come over later with Sir Humphrey Gilbert, as this latter company
were too late for the skirmishes before Flushing, and Gilbert, immediately he arrived, set out on an expedition which is mentioned by Gascoigne after his original reference to "a *Flushyng* fraye."[9] Probably
Gascoigne owed his inclusion in Morgan's group to the good offices of
one of the "great men who favoured the cause," but who this was we
do not know.

The volunteers arrived at Flushing on June 6[10] and were received by
the Governor, M. de Saras, as Morgan informed Burghley in a letter
which also told of the rout of the Portuguese fleet under the Duke of
Medina and the capture of a prisoner who "confessed" that they had
two priests aboard who "conjured" for good weather—the implication
is evident to any good Protestant.[11] Within a few days, the English were

[5] Williams, *Actions of the Lowe Countries.*

[6] *Works,* I, 139–83.   [7] Williams, *op. cit.,* p. 56.

[8] For a detailed proof of this and for the first recognition of the importance of Williams
in connection with Gascoigne, see my article, "Gascoigne in the Low Countries," *RES,* XII
(1936). The ensuing discussion is an amplification of this original study by means of various
letters found in *Cal. S. P. For.*

[9] *Vide infra,* n. 15.

[10] *Cal. S. P. For.,* No. 419. Captain Thos. Morgan to Burghley. This date of arrival and
Gascoigne's references to immediately subsequent events are sufficient to show that a hitherto
unknown reference to a George Gascoigne in the *Journals of the House of Commons* (noted
in vol. I, 101) is not applicable to the poet. The entry is for June 9, 1572, and follows details concerning a dispute between Reginald Grey, Earl of Kent, and Lord Compton. It reads:
"George Gascoigne and Thoms. Cobbe being produced." Gascoigne and Cobbe are obviously
produced as witnesses in the Grey-Compton case.

[11] *Cal. S. P. For.,* No. 419. Morgan to Burghley.

involved in fighting. The Spanish attempted to strengthen the fortifications of the near-by town of Middleburgh and were perceived by the
garrison of Flushing, who sallied forth, attacked, and so routed the
Spaniards that the latter had to discover their identity to their own rear
guard to avoid being shot. This encounter was so successful that the
English captains sought and gained permission for an afternoon attack.
According to the professional soldier, Williams, this encounter was a
good skirmish of two hours, "in which time our men came twice to
the push of the pike." Further proof of its excellence was found in the
fact that the English lost 100 men, killed and wounded; the Spanish,
400.[12] These are the only battles in or near Flushing of which I can find
mention in Williams's account or in the dispatches of Morgan and Gilbert. Therefore the following stanza by Gascoigne was evidently written
about the brave deeds of his first military encounter.

> For I have seene full many a *Flushyng* fraye,
> And fleest[13] in *Flaunders* eke among the rest,
> The bragge[14] of *Bruges,* where was I that daye?
> Before the walles good sir as brave as best,
> And though I marcht all armde withouten rest,
> From *Aerdenburgh* and back againe that night,
> Yet madde were he that would have made me knight.[15]

The next encounter which Williams mentions, after the skirmishes in
the neighbourhood of Flushing, is the expedition to Bruges, which was
led by Sir Humphrey Gilbert, who had some difficulty with the Governor, M. de Saras. The Flushingers were not at all pleased with this
Governor, sent them by the Prince of Orange, and at one time asked
Morgan to take his place, but the latter refused.[16] When Gilbert arrived
before Flushing on July 10, 1572, he received a chilly reception, for M. de
Saras was well disposed toward the French volunteers among the garrison. Sir Humphrey came ashore and in diplomatic fashion told the
Governor that he and his company had come to relieve the Dutch of
their misery, to restore their ancient liberties, and concluded with a pro-

---

[12] This account is found in Williams, *op. cit.,* pp. 57–60.
[13] Plundered.
[14] *OED* gives "the challenge at a game like poker." Here, the challenging of Bruges by
Sir Humphrey, who tried to bluff the Spaniards into surrender.
[15] *Works,* I, 160, st. 95. [16] Williams, *op. cit.,* p. 63.

testation of his own zeal for the Protestant cause. When these honeyed words did not persuade de Saras to provide billets for 1,200 Englishmen, Gilbert, with a gesture of bluff, pretended to make ready to leave. This unfriendly reception was not approved by the townspeople, who saw in the English a welcome addition and insurance against Spanish attack;[17] so they threatened to pull down the walls to let the English in. After a tense night, during which the English, in full armor, stood before the gates to guard themselves against a surprise attack from the French, a compromise was reached. By the fourteenth all was well, and Sir Humphrey and de Saras were banqueting each other.[18]

On Thursday, the seventeenth, began the expedition to Bruges,[19] a counterattack designed to relieve the town of Mons, where Count Lodowick was besieged. With a force of 2,400, 1,400 of whom were English, Gilbert took ship from Flushing to New-Haven on the mainland, and marched from there to Ardenburgh, where a base was established. The next night de Saras and Gilbert sent 800 men to get as near the town of Sluys as possible. Williams was one of this band, but whether Gascoigne accompanied them is unknown. At any rate, their lack of military experience prevented them from taking the town, and they passed the night outside Sluys. In the morning the enemy, seeing their numbers, sent out an attacking force. The noise of the battle roused Gilbert and Saras, who marched forward. The resulting increase in the number of attackers led the Spanish Governor to temporize, which he did so well that the triumphant English arrived to take possession, only to be forced to retreat to Ardenburgh. Although the Governor of Sluys had advised Alva of the presence of the English, Gilbert tried an attack on Bruges, which ended with Sir Humphrey "swearing divers oaths" at the refusal of the Spanish to surrender. Once again the valiant band retired to Ardenburgh. Two days later news came of a supply train marching from Ghent to Bruges, and Lieutenant Rowland Yorke, one Tristan, a Frenchman, and Ambrose Duke, a Walloon, were placed in charge of a party that was to make an ambush. Williams, too, was a member of this expedition, which succeeded by a clever trick, much to the gratification of that worthy

---

[17] *Ibid.*, p. 69.

[18] Gilbert's arrival and troubles are, with one exception, noted in *Cal. S. P. For.*, No. 491, Gilbert to Burghley.

[19] *Cal. S. P. For.*, No. 491. No. 478 (anonymous) also tells of this expedition.

soldier. Ambrose Duke, "an expert soldier who had seene service on horsebacke," gathered a motley group of farm horses, which were arrayed to resemble cavalry. As the supply train entered the small glade where the volunteers lay in wait, a volley was fired and the "cavalry" rushed forth so that the Spaniards thought a great force was attacking them.[20] Twenty-three pieces of artillery, as well as munitions, were taken, and it was this fact that Gilbert stressed in his report to Burghley; little was said about Sluys or Bruges.[21] However, Burghley got the whole story from one of his many agents.[22]

Gascoigne's lines upon this redoubtable expedition well reflect the general disorder with which it was governed. Sir Humphrey, desirous of playing the conquering hero, stood baffled before the walls of Bruges, while the poet remembered only the march from Ardenburgh to Bruges and back again, "all withouten rest."

The outcome of the final efforts of de Saras and Gilbert was tragic. Foiled twice, they decided to tackle a third objective, the city of Tergoes on the island of Beveland. The enemy, seeing approaching ships, laid an ambush so that when the English landed and marched inland a short distance they were surrounded. Those who suffered most were in the van with Captain Morgan, since Sir Humphrey and de Saras retired at the first shot. A camp was made for the night at Barland, from whence an attack was launched upon Tergoes. Again bad generalship resulted in a great slaughter; so it was with no regret that the troops embarked for their return to the near-by island of Walcheren, with its chief city, Flushing. A fine stratagem was marred when a foolish officer of certain troops that were hidden ashore after the main contingent embarked, fired a shot at the Spaniards who were coming to retake possession of Barland. After this mishap, the shore party were taken on board.[23]

Returned to Walcheren, Gilbert's company did not billet in Flushing, because, by an arrangement made with de Saras, only 200 Englishmen were allowed in the town; all others could enter only when provided with passports.[24] However, the near-by town of Southland provided comfortable if somewhat exposed quarters. The Spanish of Middleburgh, thinking to take advantage of the precarious fortifications of Southland,

---

[20] The story of the Bruges expedition comes entirely from Williams, *op. cit.*, pp. 69–73.
[21] *Cal. S. P. For.*, No. 491.   [22] *Ibid.*, Nos. 504, 511.
[23] Williams, *op. cit.*, pp. 74–78   [24] *Cal. S. P. For.*, No. 492.

sent a raiding party whose aim was to get between the English and Flushing. Although the enemy were within sight when news was brought to Southland, the volunteers rallied and, after a fierce hand-to-hand engagement, repulsed the attack. As Williams remarks, "There can bee no brave encounter without men slaine on both sides. True it is, the fewer the better conduct; but the more dyes, the more honour to the fight." [25] About 250 English were slain to prove the honor of the fight, among them Captain Bourcher, whose noble deeds Gascoigne celebrated in "An Epitaph upon Captaine *Bourcher* late slaine in the warres in Zelande." [26] This poem, phrased in the quaint conceit of the words of the tombstone, "Marmaduke Marblestone," tells us that Bourcher lay in bed wounded upon the day of the Spanish attack; nevertheless, he called for arms and cried, "I wyll to fielde and God before." This brave resolve cost the weakened man his life.

Gilbert evidently shared Williams's views of the "braveness" of this skirmish since he wrote to Burghley that on August 9, the English served valiantly and killed divers Spaniards, making them run three miles "like peasants." At the same time, Sir Humphrey was still worried about the French. More were on their way, so this noble man of action sought the Queen's permission to foment trouble between the townspeople of Flushing and the French. He "will take the town's part and will die for it and all his people with him except they cut all the French in pieces and the governor also." Such action is urged also because Gilbert claims the French have a similar plot against the English. [27] Williams, the soldier, never mentions frictions with either French or Walloons, but rather praises both for their brave actions. I have thought it well, however, to include Gilbert's troubles with de Saras and the French to show the general spirit of jealousy and dissension against which Gascoigne exclaims in "Dulce Bellum" and other poems and under which Gascoigne himself suffered.

The hopes of the English were raised by their successful repulse of the Spanish, so another attack on the city of Tergoes was planned. [28] About

---

[25] Williams, *op. cit.,* p. 80. Pages 78–80 tell the story of the return to the island of Walcheren.

[26] *Works,* I, 73. No. 68. Williams, *op. cit.,* p. 80.   [27] *Cal. S. P. For.,* No. 530.

[28] This and the following account are from Williams, *op. cit.,* pp. 80–86. The dates are from *Cal. S. P. For.,* No. 546 (Gilbert to Burghley); No. 547 (Thos. Wal to Burghley).

the twenty-fifth of August, the company landed once again at Barland, and, having learned a lesson from the last attempt, pretended a double landing so that the enemy could not make an ambush. Little else about the art of war was, however, known to Gilbert or de Saras. Their men were insufficient to surround the town; their artillery too small to breach the walls. Quarrels between Gilbert and de Saras made a massacre of an attempt to scale the walls. The Prince of Orange sent reinforcements, who were of less skill and experience than the volunteers. Finally poor generalship ended the siege. Alva, learning of the plight of Tergoes, dispatched a body of men under Mondragon to its aid. This latter general, having arrived at the mainland of Bergen-ap-Zoom, found La Marke in control of the sea, but no one on the Dutch side seemed aware that at low tide the water between the island and the mainland was only four feet deep. Mondragon marched his men across and camped overnight within a short distance of the town, without any news of his arrival reaching the English. The next day the defenders, being in touch with the relief party, sallied forth to a skirmish. But let Williams continue: "While wee were in hot skirmish with the garrison, *Mondragon* passed his men through the towne *pel mel* with ours."

At this point further siege was useless, and the soldiers were discouraged. Gilbert had been writing equivocal letters to Burghley, attempting to excuse the length of the siege by pointing out that Elizabeth could have possession of all the islands.[29] Evidently Captain Morgan had become disgusted with Gilbert's blundering, for Junius de Jonge wrote, on September 25, to Sir Henry Killigrew, telling of a quarrel.[30] On the twenty-seventh Gilbert wrote to Burghley saying he was sure the latter would not condemn him without a hearing. He added that he hoped to take the city soon.[31] Nothing was achieved, however, until Mondragon broke the siege on October 21.[32] This disaster was too much; Gilbert and his men had had enough and wanted to go home. Vain were the pleas of Sir William Morgan, lately come from the French wars[33] and sent by Orange to induce them to stay. Too many defeats and too few victories had

[29] *Cal. S. P. For.*, Nos. 546, 550, 556, 557.
[30] *Ibid.*, No. 572.
[31] *Ibid.*, No. 576.
[32] Motley, *The Rise of the Dutch Republic*, II, 415.
[33] *DNB* "Sir William Morgan."

broken their morale and home they went. The company probably shared Gascoigne's views.

> I was againe in trench before *Tergoes,*
> (I dare not say in siege for bothe mine eares)
> For looke as oft as ever Hell brake lose,
> I meane as often as the Spainish peares,
> Made salie foorth (I speake this to my pheares)
> It was no more but which Cock for a groate,[34]
> Such troupes we were to keepe[35] them up in coate.[36]

This adventure into the wars of the Low Countries brought death and wounds to some; fame and fortune to none. Whatever hopes Gascoigne may have had of recouping his fortunes disappeared completely as Mondragon entered besieged Tergoes. The return to England, empty-handed, must have been a cruel blow to Gascoigne, who was no better off than he had been in the spring of 1572. There still remained one possible avenue of escape from his impoverished condition. He had the ability to write poetry which had been well received in court and legal circles and he had friends in high places. Judging by the poems which he wrote during the winter of 1572–73, we see that Gascoigne decided to put the two together and find a patron.[37]

Arthur, Lord Grey of Wilton had succeeded his illustrious father but had yet to gain enduring fame as the friend of Edmund Spenser.[38] The noble lord was evidently, at this early date, interested in poets and poetry: we find that he favored Gascoigne enough for the latter to write a poem to him, asking for patronage.[39] Grey, probably at his estates in Bedfordshire, had invited the returned soldier to hunt the winter deer. Gascoigne's shot missed the intended quarry, whereat his host reproached him for being a poor marksman. The poet replied in verse, elaborating the theme of shooting awry. Everything that he had attempted had gone

---

[34] Equivalent to the modern "You pays your money and you takes your choice."

[35] "Such poor troops we were to keep them in the city."

[36] *Works,* I, 160, st. 97.

[37] *Works,* I, 344 (No. 67); 73 (No. 68); 75 (No. 69); 348 (No. 70); 354 (No. 74). The dates of some of these are self-evident; the others are noted below in the discussion of Gascoigne's writings.

[38] *DNB* "Arthur Grey."

[39] *Works,* I, 348. No. 70. See introductory remarks by Gascoigne.

wrong, and most recently the attempt at soldiering had so disgusted him that he had renounced the wars. Such being the case, "unlesse your lordship deigne, to traine him yet into some better trade, it will be long before he hit the veine, whereby he may a richer man be made."[40] That this appeal was favorably received by Grey is shown by the poem written on the poet's return to Holland on March 19, 1572/3, which is addressed in a far different vein to the same lord.[41] Gone is the rather resigned tone; gone, too, the lament for past misfortune. The patron is addressed as a friend, not as a great personage from whom one begs a favor. It is evident that affairs are in a better condition, and there is hope for the future.

But why did Gascoigne return to Holland and the wars of which he had recently spoken so bitterly? To answer this, it is necessary to learn what other events took place after his return to England in October, 1572. Gascoigne had ventured his pen in the service of another noble lord, Anthony Browne, Viscount Montague.[42] The occasion was the double wedding of Anthony Browne, Montague's son and heir, to Mary, daughter of Sir William Dormer by his second wife, Dorothy Catesby, and of Robert Dormer, brother of Mary, to Elizabeth, daughter of Lord Montague by his second wife, Magdalen Radcliffe.[43] This alliance and the families involved had curious ramifications. Both Dormer and Browne were Catholics, but the former seems to have been leaning to the Protestant cause; at least he and his wife were in dispute over the marriage, as we know from a letter written by Sir Francis Englefield, an English Catholic refugee at Louvain, to Jane, Duchess of Feria.[44] This famous lady was Dormer's daughter by his first marriage, to Mary Sidney.[45] Englefield and the Duchess favored the marriage because it would strengthen the position of the Dormer family in the Catholic world; but it is evident that young Robert Dormer had Protestant sympathies, for his mother purposely avoided the discussion of religion or politics with him. How ardent the Brownes were in the Catholic cause is hard to

[40] *Ibid.*, I, 350.   [41] *Ibid.*, I, 354. No. 74.

[42] *Ibid.*, I, 75. No. 69. See introductory remarks.

[43] Pedigree of Anthony Browne, Viscount Montague: British Museum, Add. MS 5689, fol. 154. Pedigree of Dormer: *Visitation of Buckinghamshire*, Harl. Soc. Pub., LVI, 41.

[44] *Cal. S. P. Dom. Add.*, p. 284, No. 45.

[45] *Vide* Dormer pedigree, and H. Clifford, *The Life of Jane Dormer, Duchess of Feria,* ed. by Rev. J. Stevenson, S.J. 1887.

say, for Lord Montague's father had shared in the plunder of the religious establishments,[46] while Lord Montague himself had been a member of Mary's Privy Council.[47] The whole affair is filled with the plots and counterplots of the time; intrigue by the exiles complicated matters.

Just how much Gascoigne knew of all this and how much, if at all, he was involved in it cannot, at present, be known. It is, however, interesting to note that Mary Browne, sister to Anthony who married Mary Dormer, was the mother of Shakespeare's Earl of Southampton.[48] Perhaps she and Henry Wriothesly were present at the wedding. The temptation to follow these ramifications is strong, but of one thing we may be sure: Gascoigne had known, either at court or in London, members of the Browne family, for it was they who entreated the poet to devise some lines which would give them an excuse to wear Venetian costumes. To this end Gascoigne devised a masque which centered upon the connection between the Montagues of Italy and those of England. As Professor Schelling has pointed out, the reference to the Capulets reveals contemporary interest in the Romeo-Juliet story told by Arthur Broke and Painter.[49] Far from being a love story, however, this wedding celebration is an excursion into the siege of Famagusta and the battle of Lepanto.[50]

The evident success of these poetic ventures written for Grey and Montague may have been the cause of Gascoigne's decision to publish his poems. If Grey was favorable to his work and if Montague, as we shall see below, rewarded him, it would be wise to publish; by thus making his work more widely known, he might secure further patronage, even from the Queen herself.[51] Therefore Gascoigne began to arrange his poems and to write new ones, but precautions had to be taken. A gentle-

---

[46] *VCH, Sussex*, I, 515.

[47] James Dallaway, *A History of the Western Division of the County of Sussex* (London 1815), I, 291.

[48] Sir Sidney Lee, *A Life of William Shakespeare* (London 1916), p. 658.

[49] Schelling, *The Life and Writings of George Gascoigne*, p. 48.

[50] For the importance of these events in dating the masque, *vide infra*, chap. vi, pp. 173–174.

[51] This aim in publication is supported by Gascoigne's own words in "The Epistle to the Reverend Divines" which prefaced the revised *Posies* (*Works*, I, 5). Gascoigne's acknowledgment of his authorship of *A Hundreth Sundrie Flowres* is so obvious in this letter, that I have deferred a refutation of Mr. Ward's erroneous theory of "multiple authorship" to my edition of *A Hundreth Sundrie Flowres*.

man, even though he had the example of Googe, Howell, and Turbervile,[52] could not allow the world to think that he published his poems in order to make money. Therefore Gascoigne devised a series of introductory letters which would exonerate him from any blame in the matter. As the time for printing drew near, sudden disaster, appearing from an unexpected quarter, necessitated great speed in the printing of the book. Unfortunately, the volume was unfinished when the poet had to leave for Holland. Indeed he had not finished writing certain passages necessary to its completion and had to send them back from Holland.[53]

No attempt has hitherto been made to explain this sudden departure while the book was going through the press, because previous investigators have seemingly been unaware of the details concerning the poet's experiences in Holland. Hazlitt is completely lost in his references to the poet's adventures in Holland, asserting that Gascoigne returned to England in 1573 to find *A Hundreth Sundrie Flowres* already published;[54] Professor Schelling and Mr. B. M. Ward both say that he went to Holland in March, 1571/2, and did not return to England until the autumn of 1574;[55] while Dr. Cunliffe maintains that Gascoigne went first to Holland in March, 1572/3.[56] The above account of the wars of 1572 shows that Gascoigne was in Holland at that time, and elsewhere I offer proof that Gascoigne returned to England with Sir Humphrey Gilbert soon after October 21, 1572.[57] The matter has been complicated by the poet in his account of his martial experiences found in "Dulce Bellum Inexpertis," where, after the reference to the siege of Tergoes, he says:

> Since that siege raysde I romed have about,
> In Zeeland, Holland, Waterland, and all,
> By sea, by land, by ayre, and all throughout,
> As leaping lottes, and chance did seeme to call,

[52] Googe, Howell, and Turbervile do not mention the reward received from the printer nor do they excuse themselves for such payments. They are protected by their dedications. A great point in Gascoigne's introductory letters to *The Posies* is a denial of receiving any money.

[53] *Vide infra,* chap. vii.

[54] *The Complete Poems of George Gascoigne,* ed. by Hazlitt, I, Introduction, xix–xxv.

[55] Schelling, *op. cit.,* pp. 54, 60. *A Hundreth Sundrie Flowres,* ed. by Ward, Introduction, pp. xvii ff.

[56] Cunliffe, "George Gascoigne," *CHEL,* III, 203.

[57] C. T. Prouty, "Gascoigne in the Low Countries," *RES,* XII (1936).

Now here, now there, as fortune trilde the ball,
Where good *Guyllam* of *Nassau* badde me be,
There needed I none other guyde but he.[58]

The next reference to affairs of war is to the siege of Ramykins, which took place in the summer of 1573.[59] The poet deliberately omits reference to his return to England for two possible reasons: first, by appearing to have been absent from England in the winter of 1572–73 he had a good defense against the objections raised against his book by the authorities; second, certain events of that season were best ignored and forgotten.

One mysterious poem of this winter is that entitled *"Gascoignes councell given to master* Bartholmew Withipoll, *a litle before his latter journey to Geane.* 1572."[60] This is the young man who was at Cambridge at about the same time as the poet and whose brothers were at Gray's Inn. Evidently he and Gascoigne had continued their friendship and were involved in certain plans for the future. This fact appears in the closing lines, with their reference to Sir William Morgan and James a Parrye. The poet promises to pray daily for "Batte" and for "Pencoyde." in *The Posies,* a marginal annotation identifies "Pencoyde"[61] as Sir William Morgan of Pencoyde. From the tenor of the poem it seems that Morgan was to accompany Withypoll, while Gascoigne, if James a Parrye made good what he had said, was to meet Withypoll and Morgan at the Spa.[62] What these four were planning is a mystery, but it evidently fell through, for in the spring of 1572/3 Morgan went to Ireland.[63] Who James a Parrye was is uncertain. There is a James a Parrye of Herefordshire, who appears in the records in conflict with a friend of Gascoigne's, James Scudamore.[64] Parrye was trying to get the wardship of one of his young relations away from Scudamore, to whom it had apparently been given by Burghley as one of the unofficial perquisites of a courtier. Parrye appears likewise in various questionable affairs, such as an attempt to trick the magistrates of Hereford.[65] Whether or no he is the same

---

[58] *Works,* I, 160, st. 99.
[59] *Ibid.,* I, 161, st. 102. Motley, *op. cit.,* III, 379.
[60] *Works,* I, 344. No. 67.
[61] *Ibid.,* I, 347. This marginal note is not in the *Flowres.*
[62] The watering place in the Low Countries.
[63] *DNB* "Sir William Morgan."
[64] PRO St. Ch. 5, A55/33, S32/40.
[65] PRO St. Ch. 5, A8/10, A47/28, A29/5, A53/9.

individual as the one referred to by Gascoigne cannot be proved, for the name is not unusual; but it may be that he was, since the Parrye in the records seems to have had some position in the world.

Perhaps some plotting was afoot and the threat of discovery forced the poet to leave England. More certain reasons for Gascoigne's return to the wars are to be found in the oft-quoted anonymous letter sent to the Privy Council and endorsed "Against Georg Gascoyne y^t he ought not to be Burgess."[66] This document bears neither month nor year date, but previous investigators have been content to accept the year of 1572 and the month of May (?), which the editor of the *Calendar* appended to the document without a shred of authority, as far as I have been able to discover.[67] A recapitulation of the terms of this letter may serve to furnish a date and may explain certain curious features of the document.

Certaine objections why George Gascoigne oughte not to be admitted to be a Burgesse of the Parliament

First he is indebeted to a greate nomber of personnes for the which cause he hath absented him selfe from the citie and hath lurked at villages neere unto the same citie by a longe time, and nowe beinge returned for a burgesse of Midehurste in the countie of Sussex, doethe showe his face openlie in the despite of all his creditors

Item he is a defamed person and noted as well for Manslaughter as for other greate crymes

Item he is a common Rymer and a deviser of slaunderous Pasquelles againste divers personnes of greate callinge

Item he is a notorious Ruffianne and especiallie noted to be bothe a spie; an Atheist and godlesse personne

For the which causes he is not meete to be of the counsaile of the highe courte of Parliament

One fact noted in this letter is that Gascoigne actually was returned as a Burgess for Midhurst. The letter does not say that he intends to stand for election but that he has been elected. Schelling[68] is content to accept the verdict of the editors of the *Athenae Cantabrigienses*[69] to the effect

---

[66] PRO State Papers Domestic, LXXXVI, no. 59. Noted by Schelling (*op. cit.*, pp. 11, 12).

[67] *Cal. S. P. Dom. Vide, passim, Complete Poems of George Gascoigne*, ed. by Hazlitt, Introduction, pp. xx, xxi; Schelling, *op. cit.*, p. 11; Cunliffe, "George Gascoigne," *CHEL*, III, 203.

[68] *Op. cit.*, p. 12.   [69] Cooper and Cooper, *Athenae Cantabrigienses*, I, 374.

that Gascoigne did not sit in Parliament. What evidence is there for such a view? None that I have been able to discover. However, if Gascoigne were elected to Parliament, we should expect to find a record in either the writs of return of members or an enrollment of his name in one of the rolls kept by the clerks of the House. Search of these records reveals no mention of his name as a Burgess for Midhurst at any time in Elizabeth's reign.[70] The answer to this seeming impasse was suggested to me by Professor J. E. Neale. Frequently a member died after his election and what is now called a by-election was set in motion. The names of new members elected under such circumstances very seldom appear in the records. The lists were made up at the time of a general election and writs, returned some months after, were probably not kept with the regular writs; thus they could very easily be lost.

If this hypothesis be accepted, how does it relate to the facts known about the poet? First, it is well to note that the division for which he was returned was Midhurst in Sussex. Among the manuscripts of the Sussex collection is one which relates to the election of burgesses from Midhurst:

Midhurst has sent Burgesses to Parl^t from 4 Ed.2 to this time [late eighteenth century]. The Burgesses were chiefly divided between the late Lord Montacute and the late Sir Jn. Peachy B^t....[71]

We know that Gascoigne wrote a masque in celebration of a Montague wedding, that the poet knew the family of the noble lord, and that the seat of the family was Cowdray House, at Midhurst in Sussex.[72] From these known facts it seems logical to deduce that Lord Montague was responsible for the poet's return as burgess and that such a favor was a reward for the writing of the masque.

Since the date of the masque is the autumn of 1572,[73] we might conclude that the election to Parliament occurred in the same winter. There had been a general election in April, 1572, for the Parliament which was in session from May 8, 1572, to June 3, 1572, and which was not convened

---

[70] "Return of the Name of Every Member of the lower house of the parliaments of England Scotland and Ireland. 1213–1874," *Parliamentary Papers*. There are also MS lists of additional writs in the PRO.

[71] British Museum, Add. MS 5690, fol. 24.

[72] *VCH, Sussex*, I, 515. [73] *Vide infra*, chap. vi, pp. 173–74.

again until February 8, 1574/5.[74] The fact that Parliament was not in session at the time of Gascoigne's election makes the hypothesis even more credible. Thus far I have not been able to ascertain the date of death of either of the two Midhurst burgesses elected in 1572, but this does not disprove the hypothesis. It may be that the poet was a member of an earlier Parliament, but I feel that the masque, Lord Montague, and Midhurst are related to the question of the poet in Parliament.

Although parliamentary immunity would protect him from his creditors,[75] who obviously wrote the letter to the Privy Council, Gascoigne probably feared a possible investigation into the other charges mentioned. That of manslaughter possibly refers to a duel, although I have been unable to find any record of one. More serious perhaps is the charge of atheism, which some years later was also directed against Christopher Marlowe. It will be remembered that Marlowe was accused of Catholic sympathies, so it was not strange for "atheism" to include Catholic leanings. As I have noted, the Montagues and the Dormers were Catholics; so, too, was James Scudamore, and Catholic friends might well prove embarrassing to a man charged with "atheism." The accusation of "slanderous Pasquelles" is borne out by Harvey in an obituary, which, although noted by Cunliffe,[76] has never been quoted:

> Me thinkes thou sckornist seigniores,
> And gibist at thrise mightye peeres....[77]

Obviously there is some reason in the charge, and I show below certain similarities between events in "The Adventures of Master F. J." and those in the life of the Earl of Leicester.[78] There are, moreover, contemporary innuendoes in many of the poems, the significance of which seems lost. Finally, the charge of "Ruffianne" is confirmed by other evidence. As I have shown above, one of the poet's friends was the notorious Arthur Hall, who can easily be described as a "Ruffianne." Rowland Yorke, whom the poet mentions,[79] was a brave man in the Dutch wars, but his

---

[74] Willis, *op. cit.*, III, pt. 2, 88.
[75] "And as for Merchants, though I finde the most
Hard harted men and compting cunningly...."
[*Works*, I, 182, st. 206.]
[76] Cunliffe, "George Gascoigne," *CHEL*, III, 201.
[77] *Letter-Book of Gabriel Harvey, A.D. 1573–80*, ed. by Scott, p. 69.
[78] *Vide infra*, chap. vii, p. 193. [79] *Works*, I, 359. No. 74.

London reputation was bad. Of him Camden says:

This *York* was a *Londoner,* a man of a loose and dissolute Behaviour, and desperately audacious, famous in his time amongst the common Hacksters and Swaggerers, as being the first that, to the great Admiration of many at his Boldness, first brought into *England* that bold and dangerous way of Foining with the Rapier in Duelling.[80]

Rowland Yorke's father, Sir John, had been a famous and respectable man, holding office as the sheriff of London in 1549 and as Master of the Mint in 1551.[81] Further, Sir John's sister was the mother of Martin Frobisher, whom we have noted as a kinsman of the poet.[82] Thus there is a twofold connection between Gascoigne and this notorious swaggerer, who, in January 1586/7, sold to the Prince of Parma the town of Zutphen.[83] Acquaintance and possibly friendship with two such persons as Arthur Hall and Rowland Yorke are enough to make us realize how much truth there was in the use of the appellation, "Ruffianne." Hazlitt's theory that the charge was "doubtless exaggerated and over-coloured"[84] must now be consigned to limbo.

The matter of spying is more difficult of proof. True it is that one Herle accompanied Gascoigne and Yorke on their return to Holland on March 19, 1572/3.[85] William Herle was in Burghley's employ and had written letters to his master from Holland in 1572.[86] By May 1578, Rowland Yorke was acting as a messenger of Sir Francis Walsingham.[87] Gascoigne also seems to have been employed by the Secretary, but not until 1576, when he reported on the taking of Antwerp. Walsingham's *Journal* records that on Wednesday, November 21, 1576, Gascoigne returned from the Low Countries. According to another record, he was paid upon a warrant signed by the Secretary.[88] Whether or no Gascoigne began his service under Walsingham in 1572 or 1573 is unknown. The fact that he lists as companions Herle and Yorke, one of whom we know

---

[80] Camden, *op. cit.*, p. 397.   [81] *DNB* "Sir John Yorke."

[82] *Visitation of Yorkshire 1563–4*, Harl. Soc. Pub., XVI, 357.

[83] *Allen's Defense of Stanley* (Chetham Society, 1851), pp. xxvi, xlv.

[84] *The Complete Poems*, ed. by Hazlitt, I, Introduction, xxi.

[85] This is known by a printed marginal notation to "Gascoignes voyage into *Hollande*," which notation appears only in *The Posies* (*Works*, I, 359).

[86] *Cal. S. P. For.*, *passim*, Herle to Burghley.

[87] C. T. Martin, ed., "Journal of Sir Francis Walsingham," *Camden Miscellany*, VI, 36.

[88] Cunningham, *Extracts from the Accounts of the Revels at Court, in the Reigns of Queen Elizabeth and King James I*, p. xxxi.

was then employed by the government, together with the allegation of the document, leads me to think that Gascoigne may have had some understanding with Walsingham.

Such an understanding would have been helpful, but it would not quash the investigation of the charges brought against him. The career of Robert Poole, one of the assistants at Marlowe's murder, is sufficient proof of the lot of spies.[89] What action—if any—the Council took against the poet is not known, since the proceedings for those years are fragmentary. At any rate the decision with regard to Parliament was a matter for the House, not the Privy Council. This we know from the record of a certain John Smythe, who in June, 1572, had been accused of the same thing, i.e., becoming a burgess to avoid the payment of his debts. That the House was jealous of its privilege is shown by the fact that on this occasion the immunity of John Smythe from his creditors was upheld.[90] If the matter against Gascoigne had proceeded very far, it is likely that notice of it would have survived in the *Journals*.

We can only conclude that the poet decided, somewhat hurriedly, to leave England until the affair blew over. Therefore with *A Hundreth Sundrie Flowres* nearly off the press, Gascoigne, in the company of Yorke and Herle, departed from Quinborough (Queenborough) on March 19, 1572/3.[91] The trials and tribulations of this voyage are well narrated in the poem addressed to Lord Grey, a copy of which Gascoigne sent to his printer for inclusion in the unfinished *Flowres*.

Where Gascoigne was and what he was doing immediately after his return to Holland in March, 1572/3, we do not know: the poet makes no reference to military engagements before August; the *Calendar of State Papers* lacks any news until June; the *Rélations Politiques*[92] is also silent for the period from March until June; and Sir Roger Williams tells us that the main body of English did not return to Holland until a few days before May 25.[93] At the same time Williams does note that Morgan's own band under Rowland Yorke had returned some months before.

[89] Boas, *Marlowe and His Circle* (Oxford 1928), chap. ii.
[90] *Journals of the House of Commons,* I, 55.
[91] *Vide* n. 57, for reference to proof of this date.
[92] Kervyn de Lettenhove and van Severen, *Rélations Politiques Des Pays-Bas et de l'Angleterre sous le régne de Phillippe II.* Hereafter referred to as *Rélations Politiques.*
[93] Williams, *op. cit.,* p. 93. Williams gives no date, but the details which he does give can be dated by reference to Motley *(op. cit.).*

Therefore we can only conclude that after his shipwrecked landing at Brill, Gascoigne was either at that town or else engaged in the manifold attempts to relieve Haarlem.

By the twenty-fifth of May the English had returned to Holland in some numbers, but dissension at once broke out. The rank and file had been promised their wages on landing. These were not paid, and the men refused to join their commanders in the Baron of Battenburgh's naval venture to relieve Haarlem. Some seem to have yielded at the last and embarked with Yorke's and Captain Morgan's company.[94] Since Williams refers, as we have seen above, to the return of Yorke's and Morgan's company, and since we know that Gascoigne returned with Yorke, it is reasonable to assume that the poet was one of Morgan's officers and a member of Battenburgh's expedition. The details of this venture vary according to the source. Williams says that the ships were insufficiently manned,[95] while an anonymous dispatch from Antwerp[96] says that the Dutch had 125 sail, in comparison with the 60 sail of the Spanish fleet. Whatever may have been the relative strength of the enemy, Williams emphasizes their warlike appearance: "They advanced towards us triumphing with Drummes, Trumpets and glistering armours, with great courage; so as the sight quailed the courage of our white-livered Generall and cowardly Admirall."[97] These latter gentlemen turned their ships in flight and escaped to a harbor called the Cage. The others, thus left unsupported, were driven in rout by the Spaniards. Some were lucky enough, by reason of their shallow draft, to escape over the sand-bars; but others, including "two Hoyes, where *Yorke* and Captaine *Morgans* companie was, were boarded and burned," their occupants escaping by leaping into the water, and recovering the shore. Once again ineffectual leadership brought disaster to the Dutch cause, so it is little wonder that Gascoigne's references to war were such as caused Gabriel Harvey to note in the margin of "Dulce Bellum Inexpertis": "A sory resolution for owre Netherland Soldiours. A good pragmatique Discourse; but unseasonable, & most unfitt for a Captain, or professed Martiallist."[98]

Such a judgment was natural on the part of a scholar who experienced

[94] Williams, *op. cit.*, pp. 93–94.　[95] *Ibid.*, pp. 93–94.
[96] *Rélations Politiques*, VI, 752. Document No. 2592.
[97] Williams, *op. cit.*, p. 93. The following details are from this source.
[98] Smith, ed., *Gabriel Harvey's Marginalia*, p. 165.

vicariously the glories of war in books and theoretical discourse. In an abstract fashion Gascoigne himself, in the 1560's, would, very probably, have taken a heroic view; but his judgment of war proceeded from personal experience, wherein he found little that was heroic and much that was base. We have noted Sir Humphrey Gilbert's bad management, a characteristic which showed itself in Battenburgh and Admiral Norris Brand. Treachery, more than inefficiency, played its part, and while treachery is always, in the heroic tale, the work of the villain, the leaders in these wars were ready for bribery. In June 1573, Antonio de Guaras wrote to the Duke of Alva that an Englishman had offered to deliver Flushing to the Spanish and suggested that a deal might be made with Colonel Chester for the assassination of the Prince of Orange,[99] yet Chester was the man for whom this same Prince wrote a praising letter to Lord Burghley.[100] One anonymous letter, written from Delft on July 11, 1573, to someone in England, tells of suspected treachery and mentions Captain Morgan as informing the Prince of the actions of a person who seems to be a clergyman.[101] The manuscript is in very bad condition, but it indicates that Captains "Piers" and "Gascon" have had something to do with the suspected man. Information is also given that Piers made off with 2,000 guilders, his soldiers' pay.

In the same letter are other references to the English volunteers. The writer reports that in conversation the Prince of Orange said:

... he knewe not what to judge of such a regiment, for Capten Chester also woulde not serve under y° regiment of Morgan. "Yet," said he, "Mr. Herle[102] toulde me otherwyse, and Mr. Chester beinge with him, I, askinge hym by Mr. Herle whether he woulde, ye or noe, and he by words in english said: Yea as Mr. Herle toulde me, and by his owne wordes and semblance I perceaved," said he, "his meaning was suche, and nowe he is chaunged." ...

Chester was probably jealous of Morgan, and the fact that the men were unpaid seemingly made feeling stronger.

Whatever the reason, the English retired from action and were billeted in Delft and The Hague—the latter a town of rare charm according to both Williams and Gascoigne.[103] The writer of the letter in which

[99] Rélations Politiques, VI, 778. No. 2600.
[100] Ibid., VII, 27. No. 2661.   [101] Ibid., VI, 791. No. 2609.
[102] The appearance of Gascoigne's companion, Herle, is most interesting.
[103] Williams, op. cit., p. 109. Works, I, 166.

Piers, Gascon, and Chester are mentioned notes this retirement from the siege of Haarlem in these words:

There went not owte 600 Engleshmen to this exploite [a sally to bring relief to Haarlem], for Capten Yorke and his compaignie . . . by ordinance remayne in the Hage, and divers others of other bandes, as also Mr. Morgan, Gascon and Pers and theire men, in the Hage, and other stragglers, which alwaies absente themselves from service in townes and villaiges.

The ordinance may have been the result of the Prince's troubles with his English allies, whom he had no money to pay. Bad feelings increased on both sides until Orange finally called Morgan and Chester to make up their accounts and leave, since he had found others who would serve him more cheaply.[104]

Before this final rupture, the English were engaged in one more action. On July 14, 1573, Haarlem, starved into surrender, yielded to the butchery of Alva, who meant to make an example of a city that defied the might of Spain.[105] When, however, Alva sought to besiege Alkmer, his troops rebelled. At this juncture the Dutch transferred their greatest activity to the island of Walcheren in Zeeland, where the city of Middleburgh was in Spanish hands.[106] Some time before August 4, 1573, Colonel Morgan and his regiment came from Holland to Walcheren and were engaged in the siege of the fort of Ramykins.[107] Gascoigne's account of this encounter contains details not found in Williams's record and is an interesting example of the poet's reaction to the cowardly and treacherous conduct of the defenders:

> Well let that passe. I was in rolling trench,
> At *Ramykins,* where little shotte was spent,
> For gold and groates their matches still did quenche,
> Which kept the Forte, and forth at last they went,
> So pinde for hunger (almost tenne dayes pent)
> That men could see no wrincles in their faces,
> Their pouder packt in caves and privie places.[108]

---

[104] *Cal. S. P. For.,* No. 1221. Morgan to Burghley.

[105] Grimeston, *A General Historie of the Netherlands,* p. 392.

[106] Williams, *op. cit.,* pp. 100–6.

[107] The details of this and subsequent events at Middleburgh are, except where noted, from Williams (*op. cit.,* pp. 118–30). The date August 4 is from Grimeston (*op. cit.,* p. 396). Grimeston (*ibid.,* pp. 396, 406–10) also relates events around Middleburgh.

[108] *Works,* I, 161, st. 102.

From this account it appears that Gascoigne was aboard one of the ships (rolling trench) that threatened Ramykins from the sea. Grimeston corroborates Gascoigne's contempt for the Spanish; the former says that the defenders, seeing the preparations made against them, began to take fright and called a parley.[109] Then, without a shot being fired, they abandoned their position. However, there is no reference to bribery, which Gascoigne takes to be the chief cause of surrender.

With Ramykins in Dutch hands, the way to Middleburgh was undefended; but news of the plight of the city had been brought to Alva, who dispatched a fleet under Beauvois and a land force under Mondragon, whose relief of Tergoes has been noted above. The ensuing action is not fully described by Gascoigne; but since he gives the main points of his share in the many skirmishes, it will be well to consider his story before entering upon a detailed account of the action.

> Next that I servde by night and eke by daie,
> By Sea, by lande, at every time and tide,
> Against *Mountdragon* whiles he did assaie,
> To lande his men along the salt sea side,
> For well he wist that *Ramykins* went wide,[110]
> And therfore sought with victuall to supplie,
> Poore *Myddleburgh* which then in suddes[111] did lie.[112]

Williams, Captain Morgan,[113] and Grimeston all tell of the attempts of Beauvois to land Mondragon's troops so that they could relieve Middleburgh. The coast near the city was well guarded and several naval skirmishes took place. The defenders of Middleburgh sallied forth and set up some artillery to cover a landing, but to no avail. Thereupon Beauvois decided to circle the island to find a safe landing. According to Williams, the Dutch and English followed the fleet, but Morgan told Burghley that the Spanish fooled his men by landing at a perilous place called "the Hage" (on the island, not The Hague of Holland). Grimeston, in more detail, shows the Spanish strategy. They sailed almost out of sight and suddenly returned, passed through a narrow strait and ar-

---

[109] Grimeston, *op. cit.*, p. 396.   [110] Ramykins had surrendered.
[111] "Middleburgh was flooded by a high tide."
[112] *Works*, I, 161, st. 103.
[113] *Cal. S. P. For.*, No. 1130. Morgan to Burghley, Aug. 16. For Williams and Grimeston, *vide supra*, n. 107.

rived at a place called "the Powder, or the Haek, a league from Campuere, there to unlade their victuals and so to have it carried by carts to Middlebourg." This action took place on August 13.

Although Mondragon was thus able to get to Middleburgh, Beauvois was not yet out of harm's way, nor was the garrison of Middleburgh, who, being relieved by Mondragon, marched to the "Haek" to embark. A land attack upon the Spaniards at "Haek" ended in a draw, although Morgan's company fought bravely. It was to this skirmish that Gascoigne referred in these lines:

> And there I sawe full many a bold attempt,
> By seelie soules best executed aye,
> And bravest bragges[114] (the foemens force to tempt)
> Accomplished but coldely many a daye,
> The Souldiour charge, the leader lope away,
> The willing drumme a lustie marche to sounde,
> Whiles ranke retyrers gave their enimies ground.[115]

After this vain attempt the Dutch commanders decided to risk a naval engagement; so a large part of the army were embarked. Yorke, "with a great number of young *English* gentlemen and souldiers, the most Collonell *Morgans* Company," was aboard the vice admiral's ship.[116] Both sides were ready to fight: soon the ships grappled one another and boarding parties set to work. The Dutch fought so well that the enemy put before the wind in an attempt to escape, and many of their ships got away, although Williams proudly tells of the two-and-thirty that were captured, burnt, or run aground. Morgan recites the same story of victory in a letter to Burghley and dates the action as August 26.[117]

Morgan does not, however, inform the Lord Treasurer of the debate that broke out between him and one of his captains, George Gascoigne. The latter tells in some detail of this naval battle and the unfortunate luck that was his.

> The shippes retyre with riches full yfraught,
> The Souldiours marche (meane while) into the towne,
> The tide skarce good, the winde starke staring naught,
> The haste so hoate that (eare they sinke the sowne)[118]

[114] "Challenges."   [115] *Works*, I, 161, st. 104.
[116] Williams, *op. cit.*, p. 124.   [117] *Rélations Politiques*, VI, 809–10. No. 2624.
[118] "ere they cast the sounding lead."

They came on ground, and strike all sayles adowne:
While we (ay me) by backward saylers ledde,
Take up the worst when all the best are fledde.

Such triumphs chance where such Lieutenants rule,
Where will commaundes when skill is out of towne,
Where boldest bloudes are forced to recule,
By Simme the boteswayne when he list to frowne,
Where Captaynes crouch, and fishers weare the Crowne.[119]
Such happes which happen in such haplesse warres,
Make me to tearme them broyles and beastly jarres.

And in these broyles (a beastly broyle to wryte,)
My *Colonell,* and I fell at debate,
So that I left both charge and office quite,
A Captaynes [120] charge and eke a Martials state,
Whereby I proved (perhaps though all to late)
How soone they fall whiche leane to rotten bowes,
Such faith find they, that trust to some mens vowes.[121]

These accusations which the poet levies against the sailors, and the lack of initiative on the part of the commanders who allow themselves to be ruled by fishermen that "weare the Crowne," find confirmation in Grimeston's account of the naval battle. This historian, writing many years after the encounter, has no need, as did Morgan and Williams, to make a triumph for the English and Dutch, and he tells us that the larger ships of the Dutch fleet were unable, by reason of the tide, to pursue the flying Spaniards.[122] Only a few of the lighter vessels could do this. Thus we see that Gascoigne was not without justice in condemning the sailors who mismanaged things. Of course the reason for his anger is obvious: the ship he was on did not get a chance to share in the spoil of the Spanish vessels. By the time Gascoigne and his fellows arrived, there was little, if anything, left.

[119] "when fishermen have charge."

[120] Gascoigne is called captain in the letters and in the notes of Barnaby Riche, which are quoted in *A True Discourse Historicall of the Succeeding Governors in the Netherlands And The Civill Warres there begun in the yeere 1565.,* Translated and Collected by T[homas] C[hurchyard] Esquire and Ric. Ro., p. 19: ". . . the citie of Harlem . . . had . . . received the Garrison of the said Prince of Orange . . . bringing thither his armie, consisting of Wallons and Frenchmen, under their Captaines: also Englishmen and their Captaines, by name, . . . Captaine Cotton, Captaine Christopher Hunter, Captaine Candish, Captaine George Gascoyne and others, which were all voluntaries. . . ." This passage corroborates my theory that Gascoigne took part in the attempts to relieve Haarlem in the spring of 1573.

[121] *Works,* I, 162, sts. 107-9. [122] Grimeston, *op. cit.,* p. 398.

The "broyle" was not soon forgotten; when, after the flight of the Spanish Admiral, Beauvois, the English were sent to billet on the island of Strayne,[123] matters came to a head. Gascoigne decided to quit his regiment "where no good rules remayne." Discipline was "vayne" and "selfe will" stood "for martiall lawe." It seems, on the basis of what we have seen of the management of affairs and the frequent corruption, that the charges were true. All who fought were not heroes, and thus the poet came to have a view of warfare which, as Harvey said, was not in tune with his times.

Having decided to quit his regiment, Gascoigne went to the Prince of Orange, who was, in September, 1573, at the pleasant town of Delft.[124] The poet told the Prince that because of the contention in his company he wanted leave until Christmas.[125] But before he could depart with the passport given him by the Prince, Gascoigne received orders to remain. The cause was that Gascoigne's "Colonell was nowe come to the Courte" and, according to the poet, the Prince wished to effect a reconciliation. On October 6 Morgan was summoned from Strayne and told to make up his accounts.[126] Surely the two events are the same. Although Gascoigne does not name his "Colonell," we have seen from the poet's own words that he was in many actions in which, according to Williams and to Morgan's own letters, Morgan took part. It is well to remember that Yorke is identified many times by Williams as Morgan's lieutenant and that Yorke was Gascoigne's companion. If, then, Morgan was the colonel in question, was it likely that the Prince who planned to discharge Morgan was interested in patching up a quarrel? It seems particularly unlikely when we learn that on October 13 Colonel Chester was also told to make up his accounts and was discharged.[127] Chester refused the passport offered him until a passport covering all his captains and "all the captaynes that were gone from the Collnel Morgan, which have byne

---

[123] Williams (op. cit., p. 125) and Morgan (Cal. S. P. For., No. 1221) both tell of the English retirement to Strayne. Gascoigne mentions Strayne (Works, I, 163, st. 111) and then relates his departure to Delft (ibid., sts. 112–14).

[124] Cal. S. P. For., No. 1173. Orange to Killigrew, Sept. 20, 1573.

[125] This and the ensuing details are from "Dulce Bellum" (Works, I, 163, 164, sts. 114–18).

[126] Cal. S. P. For., No. 1221. Morgan to Burghley. Delft, Nov. 12, 1573. That Morgan was Gascoigne's colonel is shown by Grimeston (op. cit., p. 407), who says that at this time Orange, because of some spleen toward Morgan, made Chester colonel of the English forces.

[127] Rélations Politiques, VI, 824–27. No. 2634.

synce, as it were, under Mr Chester." But the writer of the letter which contains this information doubts if any will leave and lose six months' pay.[128] Thus the real reason of Gascoigne's failure to depart for England was a financial one. If all the English stood together, they had a better chance of collecting their wages, but George Gascoigne would be the last to admit that his actions were motivated by money. Morgan was still in Holland on November 12, 1573, and at that time wrote to Burghley telling of his troubles in getting any money from the Prince.[129]

Whatever may have been Chester's and Morgan's opinions about the Prince of Orange, Gascoigne was fervent in his admiration of the patriot. Chester evidently became reconciled, because on January 4, 1573/4, Orange sent him back to England with a letter to Lord Burghley which contains a multitude of complimentary references to the bearer.[130] But while Gascoigne was in Delft, the Spanish army under Julian Romero took The Hague and threatened both Delft and Leyden. In the correspondence we find Morgan telling Burghley of the ease with which the Spanish captured The Hague on October 30.[131] Although he might have escaped by boat, Gascoigne stayed on in Delft, scorning to leave the Prince, like a rat deserting a sinking ship.[132] At this time occurred one of the unhappy events which seemed continually to dog Gascoigne's every move.[133]

During a sojourn at The Hague, probably that of the preceding July, Gascoigne had given his picture to "a worthie dame" with whom he had had an affair. Some time after The Hague was taken by the Spanish, this lady wrote a love letter to the poet and sent it to Delft by her maid, who was, of course, stopped at the tower gate. Upon her reply that she brought a letter to Captain Gascoigne, the Dutch at once became suspicious, thinking the letter might be part of a plot to betray the town. The lover was not so infatuated with this token of affection but that he realized the implication of a letter from an enemy town. Straightway he showed it to the Prince, who believed him and gave permission for him to answer. This did not calm suspicion, and the poet bitterly remarks that he was allowed outside the town only if there was a skirmish. All

[128] *Ibid.*   [129] *Vide supra*, n. 126.
[130] *Rélations Politiques*, VII, 27. No. 2661.   [131] *Cal. S. P. For.*, No. 1221.
[132] *Works*, I, 165, st. 121.   [133] *Ibid.*, pp. 165 ff.

in all, Gascoigne and his men, who seem to have accompanied him in his original departure from his regiment, passed a most unpleasant time at Delft.

By December, Requesens, who had replaced Alva in the command of the Spanish operations, began the preparation of a fleet to relieve Mondragon, then in dire straits at Middleburgh.[134] Prince William assembled a navy to oppose such a force, and Gascoigne tells us that he was put in charge of a hoy.

> There once agayne I served upon seas,
> And for to tell the cause and how it fell,
> It did one day the Prince (my chieftayne) please,
> To aske me thus: *Gascoigne* (quoth he) you dwell
> Amongst us still: and thereby seemeth well,
> That to our side you beare a faithfull harte,
> For else long since we should have seene you starte.[135]

In the next stanza the poet reveals that his men had already departed, and since we know that Chester left about the first of the year,[136] and, since elsewhere we find that Chester returned in March,[137] it seems that Gascoigne was for a time a lone adventurer in the Low Countries. At any rate he was pleased with the appointment and was evidently in the fleet that harassed the Spanish coming from Antwerp to a rendezvous at Bergen-op-Zoom.[138] But before this fleet under Sancho D'Avila could reach Bergen, news came overland of the utter rout of the fleet of Julian Romero. Then, as Gascoigne says, D'Avila returned to Antwerp. Thus on January 29 Mondragon was abandoned, but this worthy leader held out until February 18, when an honourable surrender was concluded.[139]

The success of his forces inspired generosity in the Prince, for Gascoigne tells us that, some time after, he received 300 guilders in addition to his pay, a most welcome reward. In retrospect, however, the poet sees that "hope is [the] harbenger of all mishappe," because shortly after the receipt of this money, there began a sequence of events which ended in disaster and imprisonment.[140] In March the English volunteers, newly

---

[134] Motley, *op. cit.,* II, 524. Grimeston, *op. cit.,* p. 417.   [135] *Works,* I, 167, st. 134.

[136] *Rélations Politiques,* VII, 27. No. 2661.   [137] *Ibid.,* VII, 79–80. No. 2697.

[138] Williams (*op. cit.,* pp. 128–33) presents a full account of the naval engagement. Cf. Williams's and Gascoigne's accounts for the latter's part in the battle.

[139] Grimeston, *op. cit.,* pp. 417, 423.

[140] The account of this and succeeding events is in "Dulce Bellum" (*Works,* I, 141–74).

raised by Chester, left England,[141] and Gascoigne records their arrival. The Spanish were in constant communication with Elizabeth concerning the English who were fighting in Holland.[142] The Queen protested that those who left had no support from her, but it is amusing to note that efforts to stop Chester's return were not initiated until the colonel was safely out of England. Thereupon Chester's father was summoned before the Privy Council, where he protested that he had never been able to control his son.[143] This trouble about English intervention is important, for it was partially responsible for Gascoigne's later imprisonment.

According to the poet, requested by Orange to take command of a company of volunteers, he determined "to loose the saddle or the horse to winne" and agreed. The spring had passed when, in May, Gascoigne and his men were engaged in fortifying Valkenburgh, an outpost to the defences of Leyden.[144] The subsequent adventures of this company are reported in different ways by various authors. Gascoigne's story is lengthy and makes out a good case for his conduct. Briefly, he says that the fortifications of Valkenburgh were less than half complete when the Spanish advance began. The English, only 500 strong, were confronted with 3,000 of the enemy. Had the fort been completed, 2,000 men would have been needed to hold it; so when news came that a far stronger fort at Alphen had been taken, there was nothing to do but retreat to Leyden. Gascoigne is particular to point out that he and his men were in a very dangerous position at Valkenburgh; they had no food or military supplies and the colonel had warned the Prince of the danger. Little help could be expected from Leyden, and the hard treatment accorded them by that city was soon to be known. A temporary plan to make a stand at Maesland Sluys (Maassluis) was abandoned when the Spanish attacked Valkenburgh. In a rout the English fled three miles to Leyden, hoping to find refuge; but the gates of the city were closed against them and their pleas were vain. Why they were refused admittance Gascoigne does not say, but presumably the Dutch suspected some sort of trap to enable the Spaniards to take the city. The wretched company thus caught between the

---

[141] *Rélations Politiques,* VII, 80. No. 2698.

[142] *Ibid.,* VII, 65, No. 2689; 80, No. 2698; 117, No. 2722.

[143] *Ibid.,* VII, 79–80. No. 2697.

[144] The date is from Grimeston (*op. cit.,* pp. 434–35). Gascoigne's version is from "Dulce Bellum" (*Works,* I, 141–74).

city's walls and the approaching enemy had to make the best possible
bargain with the Spaniards. Gascoigne and Captain Sheffield, in a parley
with De Licques and Mario, made an arrangement whereby they were
all to be shipped back to England. All was carried out according to the
terms of surrender, except that Gascoigne and the captains were held
prisoner for four months; the soldiers were returned some time in June.[145]

Grimeston's account of this affair[146] is far more complete than Gascoigne's and gives rise to the theory that the English had made a bargain
with the Spaniards. According to this historian, the English left Valkenburgh without encountering a single Spaniard. They retired near to
Leyden, where they took up positions and finally engaged in a hot skirmish. The Dutch, seeing this from the walls of the city and noting that
not a single man fell on either side, feared the worst. Then Chester, entering Leyden, told the defenders that if he were forced he would retire
to The Hague. The Dutch planned a stratagem whereby upon a certain
signal the English were to retire and let the city's artillery have an opening for an attack upon the Spaniards. No sooner were the English returned to their trenches than they treacherously marched to the enemy
and surrendered. Grimeston adds that the English were well rewarded
for such conduct by the Spanish, who stripped them of their possessions
and forced the majority to labor as pioneers while the others were imprisoned at Haarlem. A few, he says, managed to escape to England.

Motley,[147] who seems to be using a Spanish source, dates the action as
of May 26 and, although he does not comment on the abandonment of
Valkenburgh, he says that the Dutch, not without reason, suspected the
English and for that reason would not let them into Leyden.

A letter from Requesens,[148] the Spanish commander-in-chief, casts
some light on the happenings and supplies a good reason for the return
of the English as well as for the imprisonment of their leaders. This account maintains that Valkenburgh was so well fortified that cannon were
necessary to attack it. The Spanish attacked bravely, putting the English
to flight. Several were killed and the remainder surrendered to the Baron

---

[145] This date is deduced from a letter of Requesens to Jean de Boischot (Boissu, the Dutch
admiral) dated June 4, 1574, which tells of the Spanish plan to return the English to their
own country (*Rélations Politiques*, VII, 164–65. No. 2745).

[146] Grimeston, *op. cit.*, pp. 434–35.   [147] Motley, *op. cit.*, II, 552.

[148] *Rélations Politiques*, VII, 164–65. No. 2745.

de Licques. Four hundred of these were led to Haarlem, and although they deserved death for their part in fighting against the King of Spain, the latter, being such a good friend and cousin to the Queen of England, was willing to spare their lives, if the Queen would recall the English who were in Holland and would punish them. Further he would return them to England. All the while, however, Requesens is anxious that the Queen allow a fleet coming from Spain to revictual in England. This seems to be the main point: the officers are held as hostages for the revictualing of the fleet, and the return of the men is to prevent further aid from England to William of Orange.

The truth of the loss of Valkenburgh probably lies in an average of these various reports. Certainly the Dutch had cause to be suspicious of the English, who many times were suspected of treachery, but we are forced to choose between Gascoigne and Requesens as to the strength of the fort. At any rate Gascoigne denies any charge of bad treatment after his capture or of bad faith on the part of the Spaniards. He says that the men were sent home and Requesens's letter seems to support this.

Some four months later[149] the imprisoned captains were released and thus they returned to England in the early weeks of October, 1574. Gascoigne says nothing of the revictualing of the Spanish fleet and guesses that the captains were held either for ransom or so that the Spaniards could discover how important their persons were considered by the English authorities.

The erstwhile warriors were glad of their freedom, and Gascoigne's joy at his release may perhaps account for his definite abandonment of the career of soldier of fortune.

> How so it were, at last we were dispatcht,
> And home we came as children come from schoole,
> As gladde, as fishe which were but lately catcht,
> And straight againe were cast into the poole:
> For by my fay I coumpt him but a foole,
> Which would not rather poorely live at large,
> Than rest in pryson fedde with costly charge.[150]

The troubles of war were at an end, but soon the returned captain found others to take their place.

---

[149] *Works*, I, 175, st. 170.   [150] *Ibid.*, st. 171.

IV. The Repentant Sinner

What is this world? a net to snare the soule,
A mas of sinne, a desart of deceit:
A moments joy, an age of wretched dole,
A lure from grace, for flesh a toothsome baight.
Unto the minde, a cankerworm of care:
Unsure, unjust, in rendring man his share.

WHETSTONE

THE JOY with which the prisoner of war returned home was soon counteracted by the news which awaited him. His book, *A Hundreth Sundrie Flowres,* had raised a storm of objection. A change in his philosophy of life, long foreshadowed, followed this final blow and the poet, court gallant, and soldier played his final scene as a repentant sinner.

Why this change came about and whether or no it was sincere are problems which merit careful consideration. The evidences of Gascoigne's moral philosophy after his last return from the wars are found in the introductory verses to the expurgated, rearranged, and enlarged edition of *A Hundreth Sundrie Flowres* which appeared under the new title of *The Posies,* as well as in the introductory remarks which prefaced *The Complaynt of Phylomene, The Droomme of Doomes day, A delicate Diet, for daintiemouthde Droonkardes,* and the very nature of these various works.

The first of the letters which preface *The Posies* is headed: "To the reverende Divines, unto whom these Posies shall happen to be presented, George Gascoigne Esquire (professing armes in the defence of Gods truth) wisheth quiet in conscience, and all consolation in Christ Jesus."[1] On reading this formidable salutation, one wonders what reverend divines are meant. The text of the letter suggests a possible answer:

It is verie neare two yeares past, since (I beeing in Hollande in service with the vertuous Prince of Orenge) the most parte of these Posies were imprinted, and

---

[1] *Works,* I, 3–8.

now at my returne, I find that some of them have not onely bene offensive for sundrie wanton speeches and lascivious phrases, but further I heare that the same have beene doubtfully construed, and (therefore) scandalous.[2]

He continues:

It were not reason (righte reverende) that I shoulde bee ignoraunt howe generally wee are all *magis proni ad malum quàm ad bonum*. Even so is it requisite that I acknowledge a generall reformation of maners more necessarie to bee taught, than anye Whetstone of Vanities is meete (in these dayes) to bee suffered. And therefore as youre gravitie hathe thought requysite that all ydle Bookes or wanton Pamphlettes shoulde bee forbidden, so might it seeme that I were woorthie of great reprehension, if I shoulde bee the Aucthour of evill wilfully, or a provoker of vyces wittingly.[3]

From these lines certain facts emerge. First, the poet lists what were evidently the charges brought against the *Flowres;* secondly, the divines to whom he addresses the letter apparently had the power to forbid "ydle Bookes or wanton Pamphlettes." The divines who thus had the power of censorship were the Queen's Majesty's Commissioners, also described as the Court of High Commission.[4] If Gascoigne is writing an apology to the Queen's Commissioners, it seems evident that the book defended had been banned. Unfortunately, all records of the proceedings of the Commissioners for the years in question are missing, but Dr. Greg[5] has found an entry in *The Decrees and Ordinances of the Stationers' Company, 1576–1602*, which shows that even the revised version, *The Posies*, was seized by the Commissioners in 1576.

The objections to the volume had evidently not been satisfied by the revisions which the poet made. The changes are of a rather strange nature, the most noticeable of which is the transformation of "The Adventures of Master F. J." into an Italian story attributed to a fictitious author, Bartello. In addition, the names of persons and places are changed, while the scenes of amorous encounters, as well as one poem elaborating cuckoldry, are omitted. The only other changes are the omission of a few seemingly innocuous poems and attempts to disconnect Gascoigne's name from several of the love poems.

[2] *Ibid.*, I, 3. [3] *Ibid.*, I, 4.
[4] Phoebe Sheavyn, *The Literary Profession in the Elizabethan Age* (Manchester, 1909), pp. 39 ff. *Vide* R. G. Usher, *The Rise and Fall of the High Commission*, for an understanding of our lack of knowledge of this Court during its early years.
[5] Greg and Boswell, *Records of the Court of the Stationers' Company*, pp. lvii, 87.

Nevertheless, Gascoigne was in trouble over his *Flowres* and became further involved, as we have seen, with the supposedly revised text. His answers to the charges of obscenity and scandalmongering are interesting. First, he maintains that many authors who have reformed their lives after a riotous youth have not disdained the poems of their youth.[6] A few lines further on, he cites the example of the famous Calvinist divine, Theodore Beza, who in youth wrote poems which were scarcely of a religious nature.[7] Secondly, he appeals to patriotism, saying that he has been an English poet, not one employing foreign terms or those that smell of the inkhorn.[8] How well this echoes Ascham on the pernicious influence of Italy! The third item of his defense is the affirmation of his desire, as a poet, to obtain a patron; he has, he says, exercised his pen to the end that someone might realize his worth and employ him "in some exercise which might tende both to [his] preferment, and to the profite of [his] Countrey."[9] Finally, he advances a twofold excuse for the objectionable poems: it would have been a waste to discard poems which contained much of value simply because of certain undesirable passages, and even those might have value "as a myrrour for unbrydled youth, to avoyde those perilles which [he] had passed." Above all, he hoped that those poems which would "content the learned and Godlye Reader" would also "purchase" him "lyking with the honourable aged."[10]

The second letter, "To al yong Gentlemen, and generally to the youth of England," emphasizes the idea that these memories of a misspent youth "may serve as ensample to the youthfull Gentlemen of England, that they runne not upon the rocks which have brought [Gascoigne] to shipwracke."[11] This idea is also noted in the last letter, "To the Readers generally," but the bulk of that epistle dilates upon the combination of good and evil to be found in all things as well as in these poems, with the final excuse that the majority of the lines were written for other men.[12]

Certainly, if we take these letters at their face value, Gascoigne had abandoned vain delights and was at the time of writing desirous of two things: patronage and popular realization of the moral worth of the works of his youth. This interest in didacticism was present in the poet's

---

[6] *Works*, I, 4.   [7] *Ibid.*, I, 6.   [8] *Ibid.*, I, 5.

[9] *Ibid.*, I, 5.   [10] *Ibid.*, I, 5.   [11] *Ibid.*, I, 9, 14.   [12] *Ibid.*, I, 16.

own works as early as the year 1565 and is to be found in the writings
of his contemporaries. Is it serious or feigned? Was the forswearing of
green youth's delights merely a pose designed to bring favors and rewards? At the time of his return to Gray's Inn, in the year 1565, Gascoigne
first wrote poems which reveal the repentant sinner. Particularly in that
on the theme, *Sat cito, si sat bene,*[13] which was given by Alexander
Neville, we find a rather bitter reflection on the financial ruin which the
"glistring Courte" brought to the would-be courtier. It is easy to say, "The
Fox and the Grapes; if Gascoigne had been a successful courtier he would
not have been bitter." The point, however, seems to be that the way of
lavish expenditure which Gascoigne had followed was not the way to
attain preferment. Therefore the poet was angry with himself for his
precipitate pursuit of advancement by a false course. A natural corollary
of this perception of personal error was an attack on the customs of the
time. The old methods of advancement were disappearing, and, in the
resultant chaos, where tradesmen and merchants achieved fame and fortune, the former virtues of family and the maintenance of a household
were no longer held in esteem. Loyalty to subordinates and dependents
is shown to be a thing of the past in "A gloze upon this text, *Dominus
iis opus habet,*"[14] which, though not one of the sequence of themes, is
closely allied with them. The method here employed well illustrates the
feudal point of view of the hierarchy of society. Beginning with kings
and princes, Gascoigne descends the social scale, showing that each class
disregards its obligations. The princes do not grant anew the office of a
deceased holder; instead, the reversion of the revenues of an office accrues
to the Crown. In similar manner "Dukes Earles and Barons bold, have
learnt like lesson nowe." They desert their country estates, leaving their
servants and retainers to shift for themselves. All is taken by the lords.
Finally, after castigating the clergy, Gascoigne shows the plowman pinch-
ing out his pence and patching his russet cloak. The opening lines of the
poem notice the connection between the poet's own career and these
views of the present age. He has found by bitter experience that each man
is for himself.

Clearly, Gascoigne's reasons for viewing his world with a jaundiced
eye cannot be fairly ascribed to failure in his attempts to be a courtier.

[13] *Ibid.,* I, 66. No. 60.   [14] *Ibid.,* I, 70. No. 62.

The matter is not so simple: it is rather an instance of personal experience begetting a wider view of the world in which the individual lives. By his own experience he had discovered that greed, not a lavish purse, was the order of the day, and the results of that realization were not personal attacks on particular people, nor indeed the poetically fashionable attacks upon the hectic life of the court, with unfavorable comparisons to the quiet life. The last was the subject matter of Petrarch and Wyatt; Gascoigne's theme was that of Langland.

It will be remembered that Gascoigne, in "The Epistle to the Reverend Divines," asserted that he was an English poet employing English epithets, not those of the inkhorn. Therefore it is not strange that he should follow the typically English subjects of Piers Plowman. More important, perhaps, than a traditional view is the fact that many of Gascoigne's contemporaries were prefacing their publications with affirmations of the morally didactic value of literary compositions. Painter, in the introductory letter to Ambrose Dudley, Earl of Warwick, prefixed to *The Palace of Pleasure,* uses words almost identical with Gascoigne's:

... and although by the first face and view, some of these stories may seeme to intreat of unlawfull love, and the foule practises of the same, yet being throughly reade and well considered, both old and yonge may learne how to avoyde the ruine, overthrow, inconvenience and displeasure, that lascivious desire and wanton will doth bring to their suters and pursuers. All which maye render good examples, the best to be followed, and the worst to be avoyded: for which intent and purpose be all things good and bad recited in histories, chronicles, and monumentes, by the first authors and elucubrators of the same.[15]

Surely *The Mirrour for Magistrates* represented not only the vagaries of Fortune's wheel but, as well, the ruin caused by evil actions, which should be avoided if one desired the rewards of a good life. Adlington found that the very light and merry matter of *The Golden Asse* tended to a good and virtuous moral, and remarked that "therfore the Poets feined not their fables in vain, considering that children in time of their first studies, are very much allured thereby to proceed to more grave and deepe studies and disciplines, whereas otherwise their mindes would quickly loath the wise and prudent workes of learned men, wherein in

---

[15] Painter, *The Palace of Pleasure*, I, iii.

such unripe years they take no sparke of delectation at all."[16] Pettie[17] echoes the same refrain of the moral didacticism of literature, while Spenser,[18] learning that youths had been "too vehemently" carried away with his *Hymnes,* resolved "to amend, and by way of retractation to reforme them, making in stead of those two Hymnes of earthly or naturall love and beautie, two others of heavenly and celestiall."

Such concepts were by no means the particular property of the Elizabethan world, but were well rooted in the medieval past.[19] The exempla of the church and Chaucer's retraction both consider that a story or tale teaches old and young to avoid the pitfalls of the world. In fact Gascoigne compares himself to Chaucer in one of the introductory letters prefaced to "The Adventures of Master F. J." in *A Hundreth Sundrie Flowres:*

And the more pitie, that amongst so many toward wittes no one hath bene hitherto encouraged to followe the trace of that worthy and famous Knight *Sir Geffrey Chaucer,* and after many pretie devises spent in youth, for the obtayning a worthles victorie, might consume and consummate his age in discribing the right pathway to perfect felicitie, with the due preservation of the same.[20]

This defense of poetry against the attacks of philosophers and moralists has a long and varied history. Sidney's reply to Gosson's attack is, of course, the best-known Elizabethan work on the subject. My purpose is not to discuss Gascoigne's part in the development of this critical argument, since the larger aspects of the problem are well dealt with in J. E. Spingarn's *Literary Criticism of the Renaissance* and Gregory Smith's *Elizabethan Critical Essays.* I have tried only to show that before Sidney's time, English authors were defending themselves against attack on moral grounds. Whether their defense was truthful and honest or a mere subterfuge I am in no position to say. However, I do feel that it is unwise to assume that all men are Machiavellis when they discuss their personal view of spiritual and ethical matters.

In judging Gascoigne's change from court gallant to a writer of moral

[16] Wm. Adlington, *The Golden Asse of Lucius Apuleius,* "Abbey Classics," p. 2. (Dedicatory Letter to Thomas, Earl of Sussex.)

[17] Pettie, *A Petite Pallace of Pettie His Pleasure,* Vol. I, "The Introductory Letters," *passim.*

[18] *The Poetical Works of Edmund Spenser,* p. 586.

[19] *Vide passim* Farnham, *The Medieval Heritage of Elizabethan Tragedy;* Wright, *Middle-Class Culture in Elizabethan England.*

[20] *A Hundreth Sundrie Flowres* [1573], p. 203.

and godly works we should not at once accuse him of hypocrisy. In estimating the intellectual and spiritual beliefs which brought about the transformation, we are indebted to Dr. Willard Farnham's excellent analysis of that seeming contradiction in the Renaissance temperament which he so well calls "Gothic Espousal and Contempt of the World."[21] I can do no better than to survey Dr. Farnham's illustrations, particularly those which have a connection with Gascoigne, and thus show that in our poet were the forces which led him to become a repentant sinner rejecting the world.

As we shall see, Gascoigne translated Innocent III's *De Contemptu Mundi*[22] and imitated Petrarch's *De Remediis Utriusque Fortunae*,[23] both of which works Dr. Farnham discusses as illustrations of that growing spirit of contempt of the world which accompanied man's increasing interest in all of life's activities. Innocent, who traced the misery of man's life from the corruption of birth to the corruption of death, raised the papacy to the peak of its temporal power. Similarly, the Petrarch who gloried in his love for Madonna Laura and his fame as the laureate undertook, in the *De Remediis,* to prove that the joys of life are but a snare and a delusion. This conflict is well illustrated by Dr. Farnham in Boccaccio,[24] Lydgate, and Chaucer,[25] to all of whom the conquering reality was the contempt of the world or, as C. S. Lewis so well phrases it:

In the last stanzas of the book of Troilus, in the harsher recantation that closes the life and work of Chaucer as a whole, in the noble close of Malory, it is the same. We hear the bell clang; and the children, suddenly hushed and grave, and a little frightened, troop back to their master.[26]

Men could indulge for a while their fondness for and preoccupation with the things of this world; but always in the background was the ultimate reality of the vanity of all things human, which were pitfalls for the unwary in their quest for final salvation.

Gradually men came to understand and to sympathize with the unequal struggle of things mortal against the certainty of death, and from this understanding Dr. Farnham shows the growth of Elizabethan

---

[21] Farnham, *op. cit.,* chap. ii. The ensuing discussion, limited as it must be, does not do justice to Dr. Farnham's fine work.
[22] *Vide infra,* chap. viii, pp. 269–70.   [23] *Vide infra,* chap. viii, pp. 264–65.
[24] Farnham, *op. cit.,* chap. iii.   [25] See *Ibid.,* chap. iv, for Lydgate and Chaucer.
[26] Lewis, *The Allegory of Love,* p. 43.

tragedy. Such comprehension does not, however, invalidate the domi-
nance of the theme of contempt of the world, whose literary appearances
in England are noted by Dr. Farnham.[27] In 1547 William Baldwin's *A
Treatise of Morall Philosophie* gave voice to contempt for the world. The
same year saw Robert Whyttynton's translation of Seneca's *De Remediis
Fortuitorum,* Petrarch's inspiration. In 1556 George Covile translated
Boethius' *De Consolatione Philosophiae,* and in his dedication to Queen
Mary uttered the pious hope that men would learn by it to contemplate
the reality of Heaven. In the year 1576 Gascoigne and Henry Kirton
both translated Innocent's *De Contemptu Mundi,* the former as part of
his *Droomme of Doomes day* and the latter, under the title, *The Mirror
of mans Lyfe.* To Kirton's version is appended Stephen Gosson's first
published verse, his *Speculum Humanum,* and a stanza from this reveals
only too clearly the opinion of one of Gascoigne's contemporaries. The
following is Gosson's description of man.

> A lame and lothsome lymping legged wight,
> That dayly doth Gods froune and furie feele:
> A crooked cripple, voyde of all delight,
> That haleth after him an haulting heele,
> And from *Hierusalem* on stilts doth reele:
> A wretch of wrath, a sop in sorow sowst,
> A bruised barke with billowes all bedowst.
>   A filthie cloth, a stinking clod of clay,
> A sacke of sinne, that shall be swallowde aye,
>   Of thousand hels, except the Lord doe lende
> His helping hand, and lowring browes unbende.[28]

When we find Gascoigne announcing his reformation and his desire
for serious work, can we be too sure that he was feigning and was not
seeking repentance for his wayward youth? To his friend Lewis Dive
he dedicates his tract against drunkenness, saying:

And too make amendes for the lost time which I misbestowed in wryting so
wantonlie: I have of latter dayes used al my travaile in matters both serious
and Morall.[29]

Gascoigne had delighted in the joys of the flesh, but had found only

[27] *Op. cit.,* pp. 55–60.
[28] Gosson, *The Schoole of Abuse and A Short Apologie of the Schoole of Abuse* (1579),
p. 76.
[29] *Works,* II, 453.

trouble arising from such pleasures. Being a man of his times, he turned to the ultimate reality of Heaven and scorned the world he had known, but even though he repented, trouble was still his friend.

The unhappy reception accorded *A Hundreth Sundrie Flowres* was only an indication of what was to follow the poet's return to England in the autumn of 1574. The following verses from Whetstone's *Remembraunce* indicate this.

> When my plain woords, by fooles misconstred were
> by whose fond tales reward hild his hands back
> To quite my woorth, a cause to settle care:
> within my brest, who wel deserv'd, did lack.
> for who can brook, to see a painted crowe:
> Singing a loft, when Turtles mourn belowe.
>
> What man can yeld, to starve among his books,
> and see pied Doultes, uppon a booty feed?
> What honest minde, can live by fav'ring looks,
> and see the lewd, to rech a freendly deed?
> What hart can bide, in bloody warres to toile:
> when carpet swads, devour ye Soldiers spoile? [30]

Hard days indeed, but Gascoigne's known activities during 1575 show that he faced the future with considerable courage and hope. He revised *A Hundreth Sundrie Flowres* and published it in the spring of that year under the new title, *The Posies of George Gascoigne*.[31] The actual date of publication is uncertain, but it was subsequent to the last day of January, 1574/5, when one of the prefatory letters was written. The first two of these letters are from "my poore house at Waltamstow in the Forest,"[32] and we may infer that Gascoigne had again retired to the house once owned by William Bretton. Whether or no Elizabeth was there with him is impossible of proof. In fact all references to her, in any of the records which I have examined, end in 1568. Some investigators feel that "Dan Bartholmew of Bathe" is autobiographical and reveals a quarrel and separation between George and Elizabeth.[33] This again is

[30] Whetstone, *A Remembraunce of the wel imployed life, and godly end, of George Gaskoigne Esquire*, ed. by Arber, p. 21.

[31] For a discussion of the date of publication, *vide* Dr. Greg's review of Ward's partial reprint (*The Library*, VIII, [1927] 272).

[32] *Works*, I, 8, 14.

[33] Schelling, *The Life and Writings of George Gascoigne*, p. 52. *A Hundreth Sundrie Flowres*, ed. by Ward, Introduction, pp. xx–xxii.

a matter impossible of proof, but I will show below what deductions may be drawn from internal evidence.[34] As a matter of fact, it seems very unlikely that the lady of "Dan Bartholmew" was Elizabeth. It is, however, disconcerting not to know more of the poet's wife.

By April 26 Gascoigne finished *The Glasse of Government,*[35] the unique English example of the Dutch prodigal-son play,[36] which type of dramatic composition he had most probably encountered while in the Low Countries. This is prefaced by a short letter to Sir Owen Hopton, whom the poet claims as kinsman by alliance[37] and to whom he was indebted for "sundrie great curtesies." Whether these were the result of a possible incarceration in the Tower, of which Hopton was Lieutenant, we do not know. More probably they were courtesies of assistance during troublesome times. There is no introductory letter explaining the poet's reform or the good intent of the play. The actions of the wayward youths who neglect their studies and come to ruin bear only too close a parallel to Gascoigne's own career to need any editorial comment.

Some time before July, 1575,[38] Gascoigne evidently received a commission from the Earl of Leicester to undertake the composition of at least part of the festivities which were to be presented during the Queen's progress at Kenilworth. It seemed that the long-desired patronage and preferment were at hand. It was even possible that the Queen might favor Gascoigne's verses and that that way lay the chance to recoup low-fallen fortunes. Two accounts of the Kenilworth visit survive: the letter of Robert Laneham unto his good friend, Master Humfrey Martin, mercer, and Gascoigne's own account, both of which are printed in Nichols's *Progresses of Queen Elizabeth.*[39] Gascoigne evidently collected manuscripts of the various entertainments, but he does not appear to have been completely certain of the authorship. *The Princely Pleasures at the Courte*

[34] *Vide infra,* chap. vii, pp. 219–20.

[35] The Dedication is thus dated. (*Works,* II, 3.)

[36] *Vide* Herford, *Studies in the Literary Relations of England and Germany in the Sixteenth Century,* pp. 149–63.

[37] The only relationship which I can discover is that Sir Owen Hopton's great-great-great-great-great-grandfather married a Mary Scargill (*Visitation of Somersetshire,* Harl. Soc. Pub., XI, 56–57). This would be a blood relationship, not a relationship by marriage; thus I can only conclude that one of Elizabeth Bacon's relatives was, in some way unknown, connected with the Hoptons.

[38] Elizabeth came to Kenilworth on July 9, 1575. (*Works,* II, 91.)

[39] Nichols, *The Progresses and Public Processions of Queen Elizabeth,* I, 426–523.

at Kenelworth was first printed, without the editor's name, but with the ascription of each part to its author, in a quarto edition, in 1576.[40] Unfortunately the unique copy was destroyed by fire in 1879.[41] The first collected edition of Gascoigne's works, that of 1587, contained *The Princely Pleasures* but lacked the letter of "The Printer to the Reader."[42]

The pleasures of the Queen's stay at Kenilworth were indeed elaborate. Fireworks, masques, and pageants were accompanied by a plenitude of verse and prose which flattered the guest.[43] Hunnis, Master of the Chapel; Badger, Beadle of Oxford; Ferrers, sometime Lord of Misrule in the Court; Mulcaster, Master of the Merchant Taylors School; Goldingham, and Gascoigne all shared in the literary composition.[44] Gascoigne did the lion's share of the writing; but was unfortunately prevented by the weather from displaying his *magnum opus,* a masque concerned with Diana's nymph, Zabeta.[45] However, he did on the third day of the Queen's stay appear as a "Savage man"[46] or, as Laneham[47] describes him, an "Hombre Salvagio, with an oken plant pluct up by the roots in hiz hande, himself forgrone [overgrown] all in moss and ivy; who for parsonage, gesture, and utterauns beside, coountenaunst the matter too very good liking; and had speech to effect." The savage man reveals that he desires to know the cause of such celebration, and a conversation with Echo conveys the necessary information, well honeyed with complimentary references to Elizabeth and Leicester.[48] Thus informed the savage man falls on his knees before the Queen and offers his submission in lines that have a double meaning, as for example these:

> Since I, which live at large,
>   a wilde and savadge man:
> And have ronne out a wilfull race,
>   since first my lyfe began:
> Doe here submit my selfe,
>   beseeching you to serve:
> And that you take in worth my will,
>   which can but well deserve.[49]

[40] *Works,* II, v.   [41] *Ibid.*   [42] *Ibid.,* II, 569–70.
[43] Nichols, *op. cit.,* I, 430–50.   [44] *Works,* II, 92–95, 102, 105, 106.
[45] *Ibid.,* II, 120.   [46] *Ibid.,* II, 96.   [47] Nichols, *op. cit.,* I, 436.
[48] Gascoigne's verse on this occasion is found in *Works,* II, 96–102.
[49] *Ibid.,* II, 100.

How fitting these are to a savage man—and how suitable for a poet of decayed fortune who wishes to be well employed! It is little wonder that, when Leicester desired Gascoigne to provide a farewell, the latter should devise a brief "shewe" wherein he appeared as another forest dweller, Sylvanus.[50] The wild man and Gascoigne were to be identified in the Queen's mind, if poetic repetition could effect such a connection.

On both occasions Elizabeth showed certain marks of favor to the "Hombre Salvagio." For the first I quote Laneham's anecdote:

Az thiz Savage, for the more submission, brake hiz tree asunder, kest the top from him, it had allmost light upon her Highness hors head; whereat he startld, and the gentleman mooch dismayd. See the benignittee of the Prins; as the footmen lookt well to the hors, and hee of generositee soon calmd of himself . . . "no hurt, no hurt!" quoth her Highness.[51]

Gascoigne must have been glad indeed to hear those words which released him from blame. Later the Queen exhibited a kindly interest in Sylvanus. As she set out for a hunt, Sylvanus appeared and ran by her side, reciting the lines of his "shewe." But let Gascoigne tell what occurred:

Here her majestie stayed her horse to favour *Sylvanus*, fearing least he should be driven out of breath by following her horse so fast. But *Sylvanus* humbly besought her Highnesse to goe on, declaring that if hys rude speech did not offend her, he coulde continue this tale to be twenty miles long. And therewithall protested that hee had rather be her majesties footeman on earth, then a God on horseback in heaven, proceeding as followeth.[52]

Such a mark of royal favor and such a nicely turned compliment as Gascoigne here both received and employed indicate the opportunity for and desire of royal patronage. It is no wonder then, that on the next occasion which the poet had of gaining the royal attention he was glad to be able to present, even at secondhand, the character of a forest dweller to recall to the Queen the poet of Kenilworth. Such an opportunity was offered by the Queen's September progress to Woodstock, where an elaborate entertainment was presented.[53] At this time was pronounced "The Tale of Hemetes the Heremyte."[54] This early pastoral tale in prose

[50] *Ibid.*, II, 120–31. [51] Nichols, *op. cit.*, I, 437–38. [52] *Works*, II, 123.
[53] Cunliffe, "The Queenes Majesties Entertainment at Woodstocke," *PMLA*, XXVI (1911), 92–137. This is a reprint of the unique quarto in the British Museum. *Vide infra*, chap. vii, p. 223.
[54] *Works*, II, 473–510.

evidently had a favorable reception, because Gascoigne presented an elaborate and costly manuscript of "The Tale" as a New Year's gift to the Queen.[55] In this manuscript "The Tale" is rendered by Gascoigne in English, Latin, Italian, and French and is adorned with a preface and several emblematic illustrations. A discovery by Mr. B. M. Ward indicates that the drawings were done by Gascoigne[56]—another example of his versatility—but for present purposes the preface is most interesting. In this, Gascoigne recites his unsavory past, his repentance and suffering, and his great desire for royal favor. To this end he makes a "glosse" upon the adage "that thonder 'often tymes bruseth the bones, wthowt blemyshing of ye flesh/ or (as some have held opynyon) y^t hathe byn sene to breke the sword, without hurt don to the scaberd.' "[57] Gascoigne's interpretation follows:

And this allegorycall exposicōn of *Thoonder,* have I pretely pyked owt of myne owne youthfull pranks/ fyndyng by deare experyens, that God (seeing the crokednes of my wayes) hath brused my bones though not blemyshed my fleshe/ and broken my swerd not touching the skaberd/ he hath overwhelmed my pryvy thoughts wth contynuall regreats, though owtwardly I march amongst the ranks of delightfull darlyngs/ he hath brused my bones wth the scourge of repentãnce, though my body beare the shew of a wanton and waveryng worldling/ and he hath broken the blade of my headye will, though the skaberd of my wishinge remayn hole & att lybertye/.[58]

He continues to discuss this interpretation, and, after apologizing for the rudeness of his translations of "Hemetes" in the passage concerning his knowledge of Italian, Latin, French, and English, he makes his request for patronage.

Behold here (learned pryncesse) nott *Gascoigne* the ydle poett, wryting tryfles of the greene knighte, but *Gascoigne* the *Satyricall* wryter, medytating eche

---

[55] As shown by the dedication. The MS is British Museum, Royal MS 18 A xlviii. Noted by Cunliffe (*Works,* II, 581).

[56] Mr. Ward ("George Gascoigne and His Circle," *RES,* II, 39–40) notes a letter from G. Le Gascoigne to Sir Nicholas Bacon, dated Jan. 1, 1577. This letter, now in the possession of the Marquess of Townshend, has an emblematic drawing of a man on horseback and a man about to mount a barebacked colt. It is a true emblem with the inclusion of a "posy"— "Aliquando tamen proficit qoo [quo] sero sapit." The accompanying letter to Bacon tells that Gascoigne planned to present emblems to "all my Lords and good friends at Court." The significance of the drawing is the poet's oft-employed conceit of his "unbridled" youth and the final guiding hand of reason. The fact that Gascoigne drew this emblem shows that the sketch in the MS of "Hemetes," as well as the emblematic drawings therein, were also done by him.

[57] *Works,* II, 474.   [58] *Ibid.,* II, 475.

Muse that may expresse his reformacōn/ fforgett (most excellent lady) the poesies w^(ch) I have scattered in the world, and I vowe to wryte volumes of proffitable poems, wherw^(th) yor ma^(tie) may be pleased/ Only employ me (good Quene) and I trust to be proved as dillygent as *Clearchus,* as resolute as *Mutius,* and as faythfull as *Curtius*/.[59]

The ensuing year found Gascoigne successful both in his efforts as a "*Satyricall* wryter" and in his desire for royal service. Sometime after April 15, 1576, when he wrote "The Epistle Dedicatorie" to Arthur, Lord Grey of Wilton, he published the first original nondramatic poem in blank verse in the English language, *The Steele Glas.*[60] The letter to Lord Grey, whose favor to the poet has been noted above, continues the outpouring of remorse over a wasted youth and the disastrous repercussions of *A Hundreth Sundrie Flowres:* "I am derided, suspected, accused, and condemned: yea more than that, I am rygorously rejected when I proffer amendes for my harme."[61] There are references to adversaries whose indentities are as much lost as the scandals to which some of the poems evidently refer. Whetstone's *Remembraunce*[62] contains passages which tell of the poet's suffering and of his enemies; but unfortunately I have been unable to discover any means of elucidating the cause of the troubles or of naming the people involved. We can only point out that Gascoigne had real or imaginary enemies who attempted to thwart his advancement.

Such foes did not, however, limit his literary productivity. Published with *The Steele Glas* was *The Complaynt of Phylomene,* also dedicated to Lord Grey by a letter dated April 16, 1576, and, like the epistle to the former, written at Walthamstow.[63] *The Complaynt* was not a new poem, but, as we learn from the letter to Grey, had been begun in 1562 or 1563. While he was refurbishing this old poem and writing *The Steele Glas,* Gascoigne was evidently engaged in the translation of Pope Innocent III's *De Contemptu Mundi,* which composed the first part of that lengthy tract, *The Droomme of Doomes day.*[64] The other two parts of this moralistic call to piety and virtue are from a yet-unknown source, and the translation must have entailed a great deal of time and effort. Since *The Droomme* was published some time after May, 1576,[65] it would seem that

---

[59] *Ibid.*, II, 477.   [60] *Ibid.*, II, 135–74.
[61] *Ibid.*, II, 135.   [62] Whetstone, *op. cit.*, pp. 20–21.   [63] *Works,* II, 177.
[64] Professor Schelling (*op. cit.*, p. 96) first noted this source.
[65] *Works,* II, 214. Thus the date of the "Epistle Dedicatorie."

Gascoigne had followed his New Year's resolution with labors exemplifying his reformed way of life. *The Droomme* is dedicated to the Earl of Bedford, Gascoigne's erstwhile opponent in the law courts, with whom he had apparently become reconciled. The "Epistle Dedicatorie" again laments the past, but, more than any previous utterance, is concerned with the poet's sincere interest in the problems of "Devinitie" and "morall Philosophie."[66] Bedford was certainly a man of great spiritual qualities if he read *The Droomme* in its entirety!

Aside from such labors of repentance, Gascoigne engaged in other literary matters designed to assist in his rehabilitation. On April 12, 1576, he wrote a "Prefatory Epistle" to Sir Humphrey Gilbert's *A Discourse of a Discoverie for a New Passage to Cataia.*[67] This "Epistle" purports to give the reasons for publication. Gascoigne, having gone to visit his former general, at the latter's home in "Limehowse," was shown the tract which Gilbert had originally written to persuade Raleigh to allow him to risk the voyage. Having asked permission to take the pamphlet home with him for further perusal and having read it at his leisure, he became so convinced of its merits that he undertook to have it printed. As I have shown elsewhere, he employed the same device of introductory letters to avoid the responsibility of publishing *A Hundreth Sundrie Flowres,* and there are contemporary examples of a similar nature.[68] The fiction was one which would undoubtedly enhance Gascoigne's relations with Gilbert, and thus with a considerable number of Gilbert's friends. In the same year he wrote prefatory commendatory verses for Turbervile's *The Noble Arte of Venerie,*[69] for Thomas Bedingfield's translation, *Cardanus Comforte,*[70] and for Hollyband's *The Frenche Littelton.*[71]

By August Gascoigne's labors among the works of the Church Fathers[72] produced yet another moral treatise, *A delicate Diet, for dain-*

[66] *Ibid.,* II, 212.   [67] *Ibid.,* II, 562–66.

[68] *Vide* introductory letters to *A petite Pallace of Pettie his Pleasure,* where an identical case is related.

[69] *Works,* II, 559.   [70] *Ibid.,* II, 561.

[71] *Works,* II, 558. Hitherto it has been thought that this commendatory verse was Gascoigne's first published work. The use of the posy "Tam Marti Quam Mercurio," which never appears elsewhere before 1575, points to a later date. A discovery by A. W. Pollard ("Claudius Hollyband," *Bib. Soc. Transactions,* XIII [1916], 253–72) shows that the date 1566 on the title-page of the first edition of *Littleton* is an error for 1576.

[72] Professor Schelling (*op. cit.,* p. 97) indicated the source as St. Augustine's *De Ebritate.* There is no such work by Augustine. For a complete study of the source, *vide infra,* chap. viii, p. 274.

tiemouthde Droonkardes, which he dedicated to Lewis Dive of "Broome-ham," Bedfordshire.[73] The recipient of this honor was, as I have noted above, closely connected with many of the legal disputes of the Gascoigne family, and it was for his daughter-in-law, Douglas Dive, that Gascoigne wrote a poem.[74] In the introductory letter appears information which reinforces the evidence of the dedications of other works to the Earl of Bedford and Lord Grey. Gascoigne refers to the former as "my Lord and Maister" and to the latter as "your good Lord and myne." A close friend at this time was John Dive, son of Lewis and husband to Douglas, whom the poet twice calls "brother."[75]

On August 22, 1576, shortly after the publication of *A delicate Diet,* Gascoigne received what he had so long desired—royal employment. His strenuous literary efforts or his friends, Bedford, Grey, and Gilbert had proved to the world that "the ydle poett" was no more; that a reformed character had supplanted the riotous youth. Two letters written by Gascoigne to Burghley and references to the poet by Sir Amyas Paulet and Walsingham, as well as Dr. Cunliffe's conclusive attribution of *The Spoyle of Antwerpe* to Gascoigne,[76] show that the poet was sent by the government to observe affairs in the Low Countries. On September 15, 1576, Gascoigne wrote to Burghley from Paris[77] concerning affairs in the French court and the effect of the news from Holland. He ended by saying that he would soon be an eyewitness of the "stirs" in Flanders. However, on October 7, 1576, he was still in Paris, because of possible French intervention in the Low Countries and because of the contradic-tory aims of the King, the Queen Mother Catherine de Medici, and the Duc de Guise.[78] Five days later, according to Sir Amyas Paulet, he left Paris for Antwerp.[79]

Soon after his arrival, Gascoigne witnessed that appalling devastation of the city so vividly described in his pamphlet, *The Spoyle of Antwerpe.* His first dated references in this news-letter are to the Spanish bombard-ments of the city on the nineteenth and twentieth of October,[80] and by that time, he had been in residence at the house of the English Merchant

---

[73] *Works,* II, 453, 454.   [74] *Ibid.,* I, 341. No. 66.   [75] *Ibid.,* II, 453, 454.
[76] *Ibid.,* II, vi.   [77] PRO S.P. 70, CXXXIV, No. 796, fol. 169.
[78] PRO S.P. 70, CXL, No. 829, fol. 23.
[79] *Cal. S. P. For.,* No. 955. This and the two preceding are quoted by Arber (*An English Garner,* VIII, 142–43).
[80] Gascoigne gives these dates (*Works,* II, 591). The entire account covers pp. 587–99.

Adventurers for several days. As later events showed and as the Adventurers themselves willingly admitted, the presence of the soldier-poet in their establishment undoubtedly did much to save them from the savage attack of the Spanish.

One difficulty in attempting any consideration of the sack of Antwerp comes from the fact that the Spanish mutinies, which broke out after the fall of Haarlem in 1573, had occurred again.[81] Therefore, it is difficult to know to what degree the men were under the command of Requesens, Philip's commander-in-chief, or even of their own company leaders. Discontented soldiers were the main cause of the rape of the city, which had hitherto taken no active part in the war. Sancho D'Avila had for some time been in command of the Spanish garrison at the Castle of Antwerp,[82] and was there stationed to protect the city, not to pillage it. However, the great wealth of the city was its undoing. D'Avila, becoming chief of the mutiny, saw at his feet Antwerp, with as much gold and wealth as Cortez and Pizzaro found in Mexico and Peru.

Of the ensuing events Gascoigne gives an objective account, which agrees in all respects with that found in Motley. He tells of the taking of the near-by town of Maestrecht, which Motley dates as October 20, 1576.[83] Then the mutineers in the vicinity, hearing of a force sent from Brussels, began to assemble at the Castle. On November 2 the relief force arrived and began the preparation of defenses, but by the next morning some 5,000 mutineers were assembled at the Castle.[84] Don Alonso and Francesco de Valdes came from Maestrecht with 1,000 horse and 500 footmen. Julian Romero and his men came from Lierre, while various companies of mutineers left Aelst (Alost) late on the night of the third and, after their arrival the next morning, waited only for a drink before assailing the city.[85] Of this assault Gascoigne gives two accounts: a composite one gathered from all the sources available, and the story of his own personal experiences. The latter conveys almost too vividly the dreadful scene of carnage and destruction.[86] Gascoigne was at dinner

---

[81] Motley, *The Rise of the Dutch Republic*, III, 82–91.
[82] *Ibid.*, III, 97.
[83] *Ibid.*, III, 96. Gascoigne's account, *Works*, II, 591.
[84] Motley, *op. cit.*, III, 99–100. Gascoigne, *Works*, II, 592.
[85] Motley, *op. cit.*, III, 104, 105. Gascoigne, *Works*, II, 592, 593.
[86] Gascoigne, *Works*, II, 594–95.

in the English House when the attack first began and, after a short tour of exploration, he returned to request the governor to close and lock the gates. Even though this was done, there was great trouble with the Spaniards, who seemed unwilling to accept King Philip's placard of protection. Finally the mutineers gained entrance and, after taking considerable spoil, killed four Englishmen. Gascoigne makes no boast of his efforts to mitigate the danger, but says, "I used mine uttermost skyll and ayde for the safegarde of theyr lyves, aswell as mine owne."[87] The truth of this statement was proved by a letter which Thomas Heton, Governor of the English merchants at Antwerp, wrote to the Privy Council on November 10, 1576, and which was brought to England by Gascoigne.

The discourse of the tragedies we omytt, and referre the same to be reported to your Lordes by Mr George Gascon, whose humanitie in this tyme of trouble we for our partes have experimented.[88]

On Wednesday, November 21, 1576, Walsingham records in his Journal: "Mr Gascoigne came out of the Low Countries with lettres."[89] A record in the accounts of the Treasurer of the Queen's Chamber confirms this:

Paid uppon a warrant signed by Mr Secretaire Walsingham dated at Hampton Court xxi November 1576 to George Gascoigne gent for bringing of L[etter]'es in post for her Ma[jes]ties affaires frome Andwarpe to Hampton Courte. xx^{li}[90]

Thus had Gascoigne carried out his royal commission as an agent of Burghley and Walsingham. That he was an agent and not, as Miss Ambrose[91] would have us believe, an ambassador, is shown by two facts. First, the letters written to Burghley and the items in Walsingham's "Journal" are obvious evidence of his position. Secondly, "A Catalogue of English Ambassadors in Foreign Countries,"[92] which Miss Ambrose

[87] Gascoigne, *Works*, II, 598.
[88] *Cal. S. P. For.*, No. 1010. Noted by Schelling (*op. cit.*, p. 85).
[89] C. T. Martin, ed., "The Journal of Sir Francis Walsingham," *Camden Miscellany*, VI, 29. Noted by Schelling (*op. cit.*, p. 82).
[90] Cunningham, *Extracts from the Accounts of the Revels at Court, in the Reigns of Queen Elizabeth and King James I*. The introduction (p. xxxi) contains among other records those of the Treasurer of the Chamber, where this reference is found. Schelling (*op. cit.*, p. 83) quotes this and gives a very fragmentary reference. It is worth noting that in January, 1576/7, Thomas Churchyard received a similar payment for a similar piece of work, bringing letters from Dr. Wilson in the Low Countries. Probably Gascoigne knew Churchyard at this time.
[91] G. Ambrose, "George Gascoigne," *RES*, II, (1926) 168.
[92] British Museum, MS Birch 4104.

gives as authority, bases its inclusion of Gascoigne as "Ambassador to the Netherlands" upon the evidence of the two letters which the poet wrote to Burghley. These letters contain no evidence whatsoever to substantiate such an assertion. In other words, the "Catalogue" has no independent value.

The letters do, however, contain one fact which has seemingly hitherto been overlooked. In that written on October 7, 1576, Gascoigne says:

I have a matter depending in the Court of Wards before your honor [Burghley was Master of the Court of Wards] concerning an account for Brettons lands. I humbly beseech your honors favor therein for stay of process until my return for I mean to spend this winter (or as long as shalbe thought meet) in service of my country....

Once again the affairs of the Bretton children were causing Gascoigne some concern. The matter is explained by a recognizance which he had given in June, 1575.[93] This was a bond to the Queen of £500 as guarantee that he would pay the arrears standing against him for the lands of William Bretton. Evidently an action had been brought, or else a court order had been issued, to make him settle the accounts of the children's property. In consequence of such an action or order Gascoigne was forced to give a bond. Since the arrears amounted to £426, and the bond to £500, it is evident that he was between the upper and the nether mill-stones. The money had probably been spent, and from what information is available it seems unlikely that the poet could lay his hands on any such sum. He therefore must have succeeded in postponing the execution of the bond. Indeed, it is possible that he postponed it until his death. Some of the bonds in the Wards' Book are struck through as canceled; others have remarks entered against them; but this bond is neither struck through nor annotated. One wonders if Gascoigne cheated his foster children even in death.

One other legal record of the year 1576 is the entry in the Chancery Decree and Order Books which is tantalizing by reason of its lack of information.

3 July 1576

George Gascoigne pl ⎱ The said deft made oathe that he
Thomas Colbeye deft ⎰ cannot make answer for want of
certain Evidences and writings which are in the country.[94]

---

[93] PRO Court of Wards, Wards 9/266, fol. 76.   [94] PRO Chanc. D & O C 33/51, fol. 320^r.

This seems to indicate that Gascoigne was suing Colby for lands, probably the much fought-over manor of Eastcottes. Unfortunately, the bill and answer are not to be found nor are any further Chancery orders.

The employment as government agent was one piece of good fortune which came to the poet in the hard years after his return from Holland. Other events may have been unhappy; but the letters to Burghley, as well as *The Spoyle of Antwerpe,* show him well pleased with his task, which was originally destined to last the winter of 1576-77.[95] The sudden culmination of the Spanish mutinies in the pillage of Antwerp made it necessary that the news be taken to England. Therefore, as we have seen, Gascoigne returned on November 21 with letters from the Merchant Adventurers. His own report to the Privy Council was probably identical with his pamphlet which Richard Jones printed in November, 1576.[96]

Obviously the way to further success lay in royal patronage. "Hemetes" had proved an acceptable New Year's gift, so another such present was prepared for January 1, 1576/7. This was *The Grief of Joye,* a series of elegies on the general theme of the vanity of man's life, in imitation of Petrarch's *De Remediis Utriusque Fortunae.*[97] The term "song" is employed instead of "elegy," and only three were completed. In the dedication to Elizabeth, Gascoigne says that the lines were written during the vacant hours of his past summer's royal service.[98] When the fourth song ends in the middle of a line with the note,

Left unperfect for feare of Horsmen,[99]

one wonders if, in the midst of the spoil of Antwerp, Gascoigne was calmly composing rhyme-royal stanzas as a New Year's present for the Queen.

The dedication does not lament the poet's wasted youth, nor is it an exposition of a theme with a personal application; it is, rather, the reflection of a man surveying his past life. The style is biblical:

> The lyfe of Mann (my most *gracious and soveraigne lady*) is besett withe sundrie enemyes, and subjected to manye perilles. Neither have wee in this worlde any joye that maie be accoumpted sure and stable, nor yet any suche stabilitie, as maie yelde us sufficient cause of perfect Joye and contentation. But amongst all other occurrents, I have noted, that even in greatest prosperities,

---

[95] The letter of Oct. 7 makes this statement.

[96] Arber, *An English Garner,* VIII, 141.

[97] Gascoigne's own statement. (*Works,* II, 514.) [98] *Ibid.,* II, 514. [99] *Ibid.,* II, 557.

Man is oftentymes burdened with greate cares, and bearethe continually on his shoulders an untollerable weight of wooes./ Soe that owre age seemethe (unto mee) a flyeng chase, continuallie hunted withe Callamities./ And even as the harte, hare, or Foxe, do oftentymes light in the nett or snare (unseene) whyles they flye to eschew the open mowthed hownde, in like manner do we most comonly fall into the botomles pitt of abuse, whiles wee seeke things that seeme most necessarie for sustentation of owre bodies/ [100]

This is the language of the Bishop's Bible, so largely used by the scholars who prepared the King James version. It is a more real utterance of the early years of Queen Elizabeth's reign than any Italianate sonnet; we often forget the tremendous production of serious religious tracts of the time. As many a recent scholar has been at some pains to point out, the medieval tradition did not disappear with the suppression of religious establishments. As the monasteries and abbeys endured as the residences of the new rich, so the ideas of salvation and the snare of the world lived on in the minds of men. The doctrine of transubstantiation could cause brother to turn on brother, but nothing altered the spiritual bases which underlaid man's thought. Heaven and hell were tremendous realities to Faustus, in spite of Marlowe's reputation as an atheist. When Gascoigne wrote these lines to his Queen, he was not a Puritan or a Catholic, he was a man of his time.

Even as the temptation is strong to see in the closing lines of *Faustus* a comment on Marlowe's early death and in *The Tempest,* Shakespeare's renunciation of the active life, so, too, in this dedication of his last work it is tempting to see Gascoigne's final reflections on his own life and experiences. "The Epistle Dedicatorie" of *The Droomme of Doomes day,* addressed to the Earl of Bedford, closes with the sentence, "From my lodging where I finished this travayle in weake plight for health as your good L: well knoweth this second daye of *Maye.* 1576."[101] Perhaps the illness was recurrent; certainly the dedication of *The Grief of Joye* is calm and in a way resigned; if the Queen is pleased with the four songs of vanity, then Gascoigne will endeavor to print them. Otherwise

. . . withowt confirmation of your favorable acceptauns (your Matie well knoweth) I will never presume to publishe any thing hereafter/ and that being well considered (compared also withe the unspeakeable comfort whiche I have conceived in your Maties undeserved favor) maie sufficientlie witnes

---

[100] *Ibid.,* II, 513. [101] *Ibid.,* II, 214.

withowt further triall, that doubtfull greeves, and grevous doubtes, do often accompany oure greatest Joyes./[102]

Where Gascoigne was during the spring and summer of 1577 is unknown, but by the autumn he was in Lincolnshire, probably at the manor of Burghe, which was the property of the Bretton children.[103] According to Whetstone's *Remembraunce,* the poet died at "Stalmford," which could mean either the Bretton estate or Whetstone's home, both of which were near Stamford. For some time before his death, according to Whetstone, Gascoigne was sick; finally, feeling death upon him, he called for his wife and son.

> My loving wife, whose face I fain would see,
> my love I give, with all the welth I have:
> But sence my goods (God knoweth) but slender bee
> most gratious Queene, for Christ his sake I crave
> (not for any service that I have doon)
> you will vouchsafe, to aid her and my Sonne.
>
> Come, come deer Sonne, my blessing take in parte,
> and therewithall I give thee this in charge:
> First serve thou God, then use bothe wit and arte,
> thy Fathers det, of service to discharge.
> which (forste by death) her Majestie he owes:
> beyond desarts, who still rewardes bestowes.[104]

Thus having bade farewell, George Gascoigne died peacefully on October 7, 1577.[105] Still living were his wife Elizabeth and their son William, both

---

[102] *Ibid.,* II, 514.

[103] PRO Patent Roll 1060, 11 Eliz., pt. 8, m. 10. Noted by Ward ("George Gascoigne and His Circle," *RES,* II, 37), who does not give the reference.

[104] Whetstone, *op. cit.,* p. 26.

[105] There have been attempts to surround with mystery the date and place of Gascoigne's death. Mr. B. M. Ward (*RES,* II, 169) clings to Anthony a Wood's statement that Gascoigne died in Essex and attempts to substantiate this by noting the granting of letters of administration in Oct., 1578, on the estate of George Gascoigne "nuper de Walthamstow." The fact that Gascoigne lived at Walthamstow is no proof that he died there. What reason is there to doubt Whetstone's account? Certainly Anthony a Wood, writing a hundred years later, may not have known of this pamphlet. As a matter of fact, Gabriel Harvey did not know the circumstances of Marlowe's death. Why then should we be seriously concerned with the venerable Anthony, whose many errors in no way detract from the magnitude of his labors? The fact that letters of administration were not granted until some eleven months after death is no reason to question Whetstone's account. Wills were often not probated until some months after death and Inquisitions Post Mortem were frequently held as late as a year after death. This is true of that taken on Sir John Gascoigne.

Mr. William Kittle (*George Gascoigne April 1562–January 1, 1578 OR EDWARD DE VERE,* Washington 1930) believes that "George Gascoigne" was but a pseudonym for the Earl of Oxford. Whetstone, it seems, made up the obituary at Oxford's request!

of whom died within ten years' time. Letters of administration were taken on Elizabeth Gascoigne's estate by Richard Bretton in 1585.[106] The son, who is known to us only by the pedigree and by Whetstone's reference, was old enough to sail with Sir Francis Drake on the voyage to Cartagena and Nombre de Dios on September 14, 1585. The first stop was at San Domingo, where unfortunately the lad was killed.[107]

From this scanty evidence it is possible only to suggest the date of the son's birth. It is unlikely that he was born before October, 1562, when the dispute was raging with Boyes, for certainly if he had been alive, there would have been mention of him in some of the many documents. Probably he was born by 1565, since it is improbable that he was much under twenty when he set out with Drake. It is ironic that the son should have followed his father's example of seeking fortune in wars and should have been killed on his first adventure. The father lived through many a perilous exploit; the son had not his father's luck—at least in the wars.

George Gascoigne completed the circuit of ambition, struggle, and disillusionment; his son knew only the first of these, and, dying young, he left no one to carry on the Gascoigne name in Bedfordshire. The changing world of Tudor England had seen another family rise but to fall.

[106] Ward, "George Gascoigne and His Circle," *op. cit.*, p. 37.
[107] *Visitation of Bedfordshire*, Harl. Soc. Pub., XIX, 116. The date of the expedition is from the *Cambridge Modern History* (Cambridge 1903), III, 301.

V. The Court Poet

Chawcer *by writing purchast fame,*
And Gower *got a worthie name:*
Sweete Surrey, *suckt* Pernassus *springs,*
And Wiat *wrote of wondrous things:*
Olde Rochfort *clambe the stately Throne,*
Which Muses *holde, in* Hellicone.
Then thither let, good Gascoigne *go,*
For sure his verse, deserveth so.

BYNNEMAN

UPPON SATURDAIE, which was the fourteenth daie of Januarie, in the yeare of our Lord God 1558, about two of the clocke at after noone, the most noble and christian princesse, our most dread sovereigne ladie Elisabeth, by the grace of God queene of England, France and Ireland, defender of the faith, &c: marched from the tower, to passe thorough the citie of London toward Westminster, richlie furnished, and most honourablie accompanied, as well with gentlemen, barons, and other the nobilitie of this realme, as also with a notable traine of goodlie and beautifull ladies, richlie appointed.[1]

To such charming ladies of the court as these George Gascoigne wrote poems of love, and in so doing he was following a tradition older than that of Dante or Petrarch. Medieval and then Renaissance poetry found a part of their inspiration in the social world that regarded proficiency in the art of love as one of the essential attributes of a gentleman. Mr. Lewis[2] has recently given us a masterly account of the growth, both social and literary, of the idea of romantic love; but so far as I know there has been no attempt to analyze the precise nature of that concept of love which the courts of Edward, Mary, and the young Elizabeth considered the

[1] Holinshed, *The Whole Volume of Chronicles,* III, 1172.

[2] *Vide passim,* Lewis, *The Allegory of Love,* chaps. i, ii, vii. See also Vernon Lee [Violet Paget], *Euphorion,* Vol. II, "Mediaeval Love;" Crane, *Italian Social Customs of the Sixteenth Century,* chaps. iii, iv, xi. This list could be extended, but I have found these three books the most valuable for the present study.

basis of social relations.[3] As Mr. Lewis makes clear, the ideas of love were fostered in both the feudal society of Provence and the urban world of *quattrocento* Italy. Very naturally each social order modified or emphasized certain characteristics according to its own system of values. Therefore, although we may truthfully say that the love poetry of Renaissance England had its inspiration in Dante, Petrarch, and their followers, we must, if we are to understand the contents of *A Hundreth Sundrie Flowres,* ascertain not only the exact nature of early Elizabethan ideas of love but also the activities and standards of the court poets who expressed their environment.

Thus we may ask certain questions whose answers will reveal those stereotypes of thought and behavior which George Gascoigne accepted as axiomatic. What, for example, was his definition of love? Was it the Neoplatonism of Dante or the more mundane passion of Ariosto? Had the rules for the conduct of true lovers changed since the days of Andreas Capellanus? Did Gascoigne and his fellows restrict their verses to amorous subjects and, if they did not, what limits did they observe in those writings which may be called court poetry? Likewise we should be curious as to Gascoigne's idea of what really constituted good poetry. What was the form of his language, and in what metrical patterns did he compose? These questions may be easily grouped in three classifications—*Concepts of Love, Court Poetry,* and *The Poet's Desiderata*—so that we may more readily understand the bases on which to evaluate Gascoigne, one of the earliest Elizabethan courtier poets.

CONCEPTS OF LOVE

Gascoigne's *A Hundreth Sundrie Flowres* contains many short poems of love, but more consistent evidence from which to deduce his idea of love may be drawn from the two narratives, "The Adventures of Master F. J." and "Dan Bartholmew of Bathe,"[4] which deal with the poet's affairs or, if some may doubt this, at least with persons in love. The story

---

[3] Crane's magnificent work *(op. cit.)* begins its discussion of England with Tilney's *Flower of Friendship* (1568), but Crane is, by the size of his work, prevented from an examination of the nature of the varying concepts of love, and is primarily interested in social customs per se.

[4] For a discussion of the manner of composition, the literary value, and the autobiographical nature of these two stories, *vide infra,* chap. vii.

of "F. J." has never been reprinted in its original form; however, the revised version as found in *The Posies*[5] contains the majority of the original details. It must be remembered that in the first edition F. J. is not an Italian, but a young Englishman traveling to the North, where he is to be entertained by some of his relatives. Arrived at his destination, F. J. promptly becomes enamored of a married woman, Elinor, who first learns of the "fervent fire" kindled in the lover's breast when she receives from him a letter "(besprent with salt teares, and blowen over with skalding sighes)." The lady, who, like an expert in the game of chess, knows the correct response to such an opening move, replies that "she coulde not perceyve any part of his meaning . . . yet gave him thankes." To this our hero counters with a lyric celebrating Love's victory over King David, Solomon, Hercules, and Sampson. If such great men were unable to resist the assaults of Love, how can F. J.? The affair continues in the same vein: letters are exchanged and the lover composes poems to advance his suit; indeed, the whole very closely resembles a game of chess with each move balanced by the opponent, who seems only to desire that the queen be not too easily taken; she has no desire to win the game. After the lovers have, for some little time, enjoyed the fruition of their desires, the fortunes of F. J. enter their declination: he becomes jealous of Elinor's secretary and as a result takes to his bed, where he lies consumed by suspicion and disgust with himself for having become infected with that suspicion. At length he reveals the cause of his sickness, but his most devout protestations of belief in her constancy are of no avail against her anger, which is increased by her knowledge that the charge is true. In a last vain attempt to regain her favor, F. J. tasks his mistress with having an affair with her secretary, to which accusation she replies, "And if I did what then?" Finally recognizing defeat, the lover ends his adventure with his best poem, which begins with her retort and ends with a wish that she sometime suffer a like rejection.

The divisions of this story are about equal: the seduction of Elinor comprises the first half and the decline of F. J.'s fortunes, the second. Such equality is not found in "Dan Bartholmew,"[6] where the main concern

---

[5] *Works,* I, 383–453. References may be checked here, but I quote from the first version as found in *A Hundreth Sundrie Flowres.*

[6] *Works,* I, 96–137.

is with the unfaithfulness of the lady, Ferenda Natura. The story of Dan Bartholmew's successful love and his song of triumph occupy less than one-quarter of the total; whereas the remainder is concerned with Ferenda's faithlessness, Bartholmew's reaction to her conduct, and the temporary reconciliation of the lovers. Unlike F. J., Dan Bartholmew cannot accept the rejection of his love by the simple expedient of writing a poem; instead, he discourses dolorously and suffers so acutely his lady's "dark disdain" that he is brought near to death. Our lover of Bath seems more seriously infected with his passion than F. J., and in fact, love seems to mean far more to him.

But do these two stories contain a synthesis of love that would have been accepted by the ladies and gentlemen of Queen Elizabeth's court? Certainly F. J. and Dan Bartholmew would not agree on the significance of love, and indeed their respective attitudes are ultimately in conflict. We are fortunate, however, in possessing a contemporary treatise on the doctrines and theories of love, which will aid the resolution of these two problems. This is Etienne Pasquier's *Le Monophyle,* which, in 1572, Geoffrey Fenton translated under the title of *Monophylo.*[7] In the first place we shall see that several mutually exclusive definitions of love were prevalent, and secondly that the fact of Fenton's English translation emphasizes the validity of those ideas in England as well as in France.

In 1554 Etienne Pasquier, a young courtier, published his first work, *Le Monophyle,*[8] a discussion of love based as to its form on the Platonic dialogues and as to its content upon the ideas which he found current in the fashionable world of the French court. In 1572 appeared Fenton's carefully literal English translation, entitled *Monophylo.* The *mise en scène* is quickly discerned when we learn that shortly after the French King raised the siege of Metz, a group of gentlemen soldiers, feeling a great need for relaxation from the rigors of war, decided that each should, in turn, entertain the entire group at his home, and since but few were married, each host should provide such "honest and best spoken gentle-

---

[7] Fenton, *Monophylo, . . . A philosophicall discourse . . . of love.* The *STC* does not list this as a translation of Etienne Pasquier's *Le Monophyle,* Paris 1554, but F. I. Carpenter, *A Reference Guide to Edmund Spenser* (Chicago 1923), p. 139, notes the French original. I have used the Folger Shakespeare Library copy. A full study of the problem would require a lengthy examination of the history of the ideas of love and an exhaustive survey of the writings of Gascoigne's predecessors and contemporaries—tasks far beyond the scope of the present work.

[8] *Oeuvres Choisies d'Etienne Pasquier,* ed. by Feugère, I, x.

women as the place and tyme could any wayes afforde, so should there be an equall sort of companie."[9]

Among the group thus gathered together there were three men and one woman who were particularly interested in the doctrines of love. The first of these was Monophylo, "so extreemely passioned with love, as all his thoughts and devotions tended directly to his Mystresse, upon whom he committed ydolatrie, as making hir the onely Idoll of his secrete contemplations."[10] The second was the good courtier, Glaphyro, "not so deeply distressed as he, preferring a civill and curteous behaviour to the Ladies . . . then to professe singuler love."[11] Phylopolo, "the last and youngest of them all delighting in a liberty of affection, without any peculiar choyse or regard, . . . tryfled with them [the ladies] with . . . a livelye libertie of speache and affection . . . with his skoffes and pleasaunt toyes."[12] The latter two, tiring of the dull amusements and conversation of the rest of the party, propose to a certain Madame Charyclea that she undertake with them a discussion of the manifold problems of love.

To this end they retire to a sylvan arbor, where they find Monophylo lamenting his pangs of love. Glaphyro "yeelded compassion in respect of the martiredome he endured, [but] *Phylopolo* made a skoffe at his passion, as esteeming love no other thing than a substaunce of follye."[13] The lovelorn Monophylo is baited on the question of faithfulness to one mistress who is absent. Phylopolo advises taking advantage of all opportunities for conquest, a remark that provokes the following reply from the faithful lover:

I protest here to abhorre his opinion, notwithstanding it be grounded uppon good and auncient lawes, drawne out of the Registers of *Venus* Temple at Rome, whose tenor bare expresse permission to execute our actuall will on all as occasion offered.[14]

The argument continues until Monophylo in desperation invokes the example of the faithfulness in marriage required by the Church as a final rebuke to the advocate of promiscuity.

At this point the symposium evolves into a discussion of marriage and love, the central problem of which is thus enunciated by Monophylo:

[I am] sorie from the bottom of my hart (which here I pronounce in the sight

[9] Fenton, *op. cit.*, fols. 1ʳ, 1ᵛ.   [10] *Ibid.*, fol. 1ᵛ.   [11] *Ibid.*, fols. 1ᵛ–2ʳ.
[12] *Ibid.*, fol. 2ʳ.   [13] *Ibid.*, fol. 4ᵛ.   [14] *Ibid.*, fol. 8ᵛ.

and testimonie of God) that we must be driven to erect a double kinde of love, as one to consist in mariage and the other without.[15]

But this is not a solution which is accepted merely because it is propounded—a fact which Monophylo well recognizes, and he continues with the reasons for such a double standard. The fault lies in the corruption of the institution of marriage. Men marry to secure dowries and are abetted in such practices by rascally lawyers. To understand the evil of such conduct one has only to consider the example of Licurgus, for

... that grave lawgiver and Philosopher shutting all dowries out of his common wealth, woulde not that mariages should proceede upon any other pretence than by an only and hartie love: So that it is not to be marveyled, if such as enter that holy state at this day defiling their affections, with covenauntes and condicions of money, finde this difference in love to the great blemishe and often prejudice of their husbandes, who not being truelye and equally cuppled, see their wives for the most part delight in an other, to whome it seemes the heavens had predestinate them from the beginning. . . .[16]

From this frank admission and defense of adultery arise a variety of minor digressions, but the theme of the remaining hundred pages of the first book is this basic contradiction between the avowed rules of the society and the conduct of that society. The significance of this conflict has, I think, been fully realized by Mr. C. S. Lewis in his *Allegory of Love,* where he shows the continual attempts of medieval and Renaissance poets and philosophers to find some resolution of the problem.[17] Through Lewis's remarkably clear analysis one sees that the *volte face* of Andreas Capellanus, "the last stanzas of the book of Troilus . . . the harsher recantation that closes the life and work of Chaucer as a whole . . . the noble close of Malory . . ."[18] are not mere convention, but are the inevitable statements of men who were unable to solve the problem except

[15] *Ibid.,* fol. 10ʳ. This is the reality, but for proof that Monophylo would prefer true love to culminate in matrimony, *vide infra.* It is this very inconsistency between the ideal and the reality that was responsible for the unsettled, in fact, chaotic, morality of the Renaissance. For an excellent presentation of this general topic of morality, cf. Vernon Lee (*op. cit.,* I, "The Italy of the Elizabethan Dramatists").

[16] Fenton, *op. cit.,* fol. 10ᵛ.

[17] The attempted reconciliations of the theory of love and the doctrine of marriage by the school of Chartres are discussed by Lewis (*op. cit.,* pp. 87–111); the contribution of Chaucer to this problem is stated on p. 197; Gower's, on pp. 218–21; while the whole study of the *Faerie Queene* (chap. vii) is concerned with the view that Spenser's chief aim was to reconcile the opposing views.

[18] Lewis, *op. cit.,* p. 43.

by denying the validity of what they had written. Important for our purposes is the realization that the problem of the twelfth century was still the problem of the sixteenth, and that the solutions of the various members of our sylvan symposium are reflections of the opinions of greater men and poets.

Monophylo attempts a further defense in two arguments. Forced to admit the divine origin of marriage, he nevertheless appeals to nature: "doe you not see in common wealthes well ordered . . . that many things are suffered for necessitie sake, which other wayes, being esteemed evill, should be also abolished."[19] Finally he is forced to the crux of the problem—his own definition of the nature of love. Here there is no agreement with his fellows and here is his best defense. If love be accepted in his definition, then one must also accept his double standard, unless one wishes to reform the entire system of *mariage de convenance*. For him

love takes his being, neyther of a heavenly influence, nor conformitie of conditions, nor lastlye of a custome or mutuall conversation, what other thing shall I tearme him to be, than a mocion sturring I know not how, which is farre more easie to be felt in our hartes, then uttered by speech . . . therefore [the philosophers] did figure unto us an *Androgina,* by whome they ment a man composed of the Masculine and Femenine sexe, and he standing in his state of perfection, swelled in such mortall pryde agaynst the Gods, that by that meanes he was afterwardes devided into two. But it is most manifest that this unitie of the two halfes, is not ment by a conjunction of the bodyes, but by the communion of the myndes . . . Love is then a power lying betweene the two worse extremities, not setting his originall upon this common lust, and yet, though longe hee doe reject it, at last he doth admit it: the same being the cause (as I beleeve) why all our church lawes in the consomation of a true mariage (wherin ought to consist the marke and ende of true friendship) require not but the consent of the parties: as though this true love of mariage ought not to passe but under a conformitie of mindes, and not by any lust or suggestion of the fleshe.[20]

With this definition of love we are, in some respects, very near to the ideas of the *Vita Nuova,*[21] although it should be realized that Monophylo

---

[19] Fenton, *op. cit.,* fol. 18ᵛ.

[20] *Ibid.,* fols. 34ʳ–36ʳ. I have changed the order of the original and this is indicated by three dots. The figure of Androgina and the attendant explanation of love are found in Plato's *Symposium,* 189 E.

[21] J. B. Fletcher's *The Literature of the Italian Renaissance* (pp. 43–53) may be compared with Vernon Lee's "Mediaeval Love" (*op. cit.,* Vol. II) for a brief understanding of Neo-

does not deny the physical but reluctantly admits it. Likewise, nothing is said of the Neoplatonic concepts of love for woman leading to an understanding of the divine love that is the Godhead. Nevertheless, Monophylo's definition does rest upon the mystic one-that-is-two, and in this essential he presents something that is alien to the laws of adultery within the system of courtly love, as codified by Andreas Capellanus. But most important is the fact that Monophylo could not have arrived at his definition unless Dante had written the *Vita Nuova,* and Petrarch, his songs in praise of Madonna Laura. Men had to be led to the belief that love was something other than the sophistications of Ovid and the formalizations of Guillaume de Lorris before they could attempt that concept of spiritual affinity stated by Monophylo.

As Monophylo finishes his definition, Madame Charyclea gives it her hearty endorsement, and this is too much for the author, Pasquier, who has all the while been hidden in the bushes near by to overhear the discussion. Such bowdlerizing of his ideas cannot be tolerated; so, after briefly explaining his appearance, he launches into his own definition of love:

... it is no lesse commendable to seeke out the true propertie of love, wherein nature, even from the begynning of our age, hath hid within us a secret instruction: then by a dissembled arte, to be guyded and taught by an Orator or Phisition [22] who in tymes past have bene dryven out of common wealthes, the one for corrupting the bodyes, the other for infecting the mindes and manners of men: where love being imprinted in us, by so excellent a mistresse and workewoman, hath had alwayes an Empire over us: by him the worlde had his being, and in him it hath multiplyed: and by him even trees and other insensible things seeme to take their encrease one of an other: so that right necessarie and noble is the desire of my *Charyclea,* to seeke out his condition and nature ... And heare, I put my selfe of the beadroll of the happiest crewe in the worlde, seing it is the pleasure of the mightie God of love, to chose me for

---

platonic love. More exhaustive is Robb's *Neoplatonism of the Italian Renaissance* (chap. vi); while W. G. Dodd's *Courtly Love in Chaucer and Gower* (pp. 1–20, 21–37; Andreas's rules, pp. 5–8) is an excellent supplement to Lewis *(op. cit.)* for an understanding of Andreas and the Ovidian elements.

[22] This seems to be a reference to Ovid. Cf. *Ars Amatoria,* I, 1–8, 357; *De Remediis Amoris (Remediarium Amoris),* ll. 9–10:

> "Quin etiam docui, quo posses arte parari,
> "Et quod nunc ratio est, impetus ante fuit."

one of his,[23] to the ende to instruct and acquaint me with his armes, which hereafter wyll be more intollerable to me, than if he had called me to his trayne, when eyther by age or other needefull occasions, I should be lesse apt to attende him: And herein (good Ladies) you may beleeve me, (as one to whom untrue reportes are hatefull) that such is the straunge and haggarde nature of love, that if we defie him in our tender yeres, he will punishe our olde age with such sharpe passions and plagues of his power, that (in the common gase and skoffe of the world) he will bring us at last to marche under his banner.[24]

Thus, with banners flying and followed by his vassals, Amor, the feudal baron carrying a volume of Ovid in his hand, invades the arbor where only a little before the shades of Dante and Beatrice had been present and Monophylo had discoursed of Neoplatonic love. The intellectual basis of the latter depends upon the individual's state of mind: Monophylo grieves over the absence of his mistress and meditates upon the significance of his love. Pasquier, on the other hand, is advocating a system wherein individual perception of love is of no account. Every gentleman must know of love, and a systematized code of behavior is an easy way to fulfill the requirements. Courtly love inextricably mingled Pagan, Christian, and feudal customs in its concept of Amor,[25] and relied heavily on Ovid, and it is precisely these trappings of mythology and rhetoric which Pasquier here advocates: his Amor comes straight from the Middle Ages, but with garments new-furbished by the poets of the Renaissance.

Phylopolo, however, cares little for such an elaborate masquerade. Since he is a straightforward sensualist who sees no need to gild the lily, we are not surprised with his definition:

The efficient or originall cause by the which we love a Ladye, is in deede the selfe same instinct which you say breedes in us as it were by the permission of heaven: but the ende and purpose why we love is, to possesse whollye, pleasauntlye, and absolutely, and so every one of us doth love, as one daye to possesse at our pleasure. . . .[26]

---

[23] This idea, though feudal, must have some connection with Ovid's doctrine that the lover is a soldier in love's forces. Cf. *Ars Amatoria*, I, ll. 35–36, 131–32; also *Remediorium Amoris*, ll. 3–4:

> "Parce tuum vatem sceleris damnare, Cupido,
> "Tradita qui toties te duce signa tuli."

The idea is, of course, a common one. Cf. "Cupido Conquered" in Googe's *Eglogs, Epytaphes, and Sonettes* (1563), pp. 107–27.

[24] Fenton, *op. cit.*, fols. 52ʳ–52ᵛ.

[25] Lewis, *op. cit.*, chap. i.   [26] Fenton, *op. cit.*, fol. 39ᵛ.

Finally, Glaphyro, the diplomatic courtier, defines love with but minor dissent from the others:

> ... certaine olde Philosophers ... holde that love dependes not but uppon a certaine desire of beautie ... you have to note that beautie lyeth not altogither in the bodie, but hath also hir residence in the partes of the minde: the one is called beautie simplie, and the other good behaviour, not onely in good maners and outward fashions of conversation, but also hath a speciall perticipation wyth vertue, even as the beautie of the bodie restes not altogither in the lineamentes and feature of the face, but also in a good composition and universall proporcion of all the other parts of the bodie ... my opinion is that the verie first daye wherein we are betrayed by love we feele a certaine sparke of this beautye which is in our Ladies ... as there is diversitie of beauties, so also everie one enclining according to his perticuler fancie, some delightes in the properties of the minde, other takes pleasure in the personage. . . .[27]

It is hardly an accident that the courtier, Glaphyro, echoes, almost directly, the words of Pietro Bembo as found in the fourth book of *Il Cortegiano*.[28] Perhaps more important than Glaphyro's reliance upon the teachings of Castiglione as to the qualities of the perfect courtier is his presentation of the idea of love as an abnormal state of existence—as a disease to be cured. In so doing he presents the other aspect of Ovid's writings: Pasquier's Amor is guided by the *De Amore* or *Ars Amatoria,* while Glaphyro would surely prefer to read *De Remediis Amoris.* As Lewis[29] has observed, the courtly lovers of the Middle Ages and the Renaissance took Ovid quite seriously, never realizing the implicit flippancy of a classical handbook of love, with its companion piece describing the means of curing the disease.

Although it would be possible to elaborate these various concepts of love and marriage, enough has been said to show that there was in the middle years of the sixteenth century no unanimity as to the nature of or the definition of love. To these four different points of view could be added others from other sources,[30] but the value of Pasquier's symposium

---

[27] *Ibid.*, fols. 55ʳ–56ʳ.

[28] Castiglione, *The Book of the Courtier, Done into English by Sir Thomas Hoby, 1561,* "Everyman's Library," pp. 303–5.

[29] Lewis, *op. cit.,* pp. 6–8.

[30] For example, the prosaic empiricism of married love is found in Edmund Tilney's *A briefe and pleasant discourse of duties in Marriage, called the Flower of Friendship.* I have consulted the seemingly unique Folger Shakespeare Library copy, printed by Abell Ieffs in 1587, which imprint is not noted in the *S.T.C.* The first edition is 1568 and thus applies to the period in question.

lies in the fact that it belongs to the very time during which Gascoigne wrote and may fairly be considered as a statement of the general attitudes toward the subject, with which we would expect him to be familiar. That all of these views find expression in Gascoigne's verse seems a confirmation of the significance of Pasquier's book.

"Dan Bartholmew of Bathe" is perhaps the best example in which Gascoigne reflects Monophylo's concept of love and, in particular, the "Dolorous discourses"[31] reveals the lover who has given his allegiance to his lady and who remains faithful to her. Of the origins of this love we know little, except that Dan Bartholmew fell in love and after initial success was forced to absent himself. Returning, he found that another had taken his place; whereupon sorrow and care became his companions. His love was such that he could not, with Phylopolo, merely seek other conquests; nor could he, with Pasquier, take refuge in the system of love, although it cannot be denied that there is much in the various poems of this sequence that could be used to support such a contention. The essential quality of "Dan Bartholmew" is that love is here shown to be a force which profoundly affects the lover. Dan Bartholmew's "Triumphes" or his "last will" are *tours de force,* while any comparison of these with the "Dolorous discourses" must reveal the intense sincerity of the latter. It may be a profanation of divinity to compare this and the *Vita Nuova,* but the same powerful force is in both. Dante's love for Beatrice leads to the composition of *La Divina Commedia;* Bartholmew's love for Ferenda has no conclusion, but one fact is inescapable.

> For well thou knowest, I must thy partner be
> In bale, in blisse, in solace, and in smarte.[32]

It may, of course, be said that this is better described as a sincere love affair, not one which exhibits a diffused reflection of the Neoplatonic love of Dante for his Beatrice. Surely the love of Tristram for Isolde was equally sincere, as was that of Launcelot for Guinevere, and these affairs have no relation to Neoplatonic love. But the matter is not quite so simple. The stories of Tristram and Launcelot were given literary expression in an age which still respected the ideals of courtly love, but those ideals soon became systematized.[33] When Andreas drew up his code of

---

[31] *Works,* I, 106 ff.   [32] *Works,* I, 115. "D.B." No. 3.

[33] It is well to remember that Chaucer's *Troilus,* which presents an illicit love affair, is the great love story of the Middle Ages. *Aucassin and Nicolette* is, of course, an exception.

law, and love was best expressed in an allegory, formalism destroyed individuality: the courtier was no longer a lover; he became a reflection of the lover.[34] In like manner, the ideal love of Dante became popularized through the poems Petrarch wrote to Madonna Laura; yet, while supposedly imbued with deep spiritual love, Petrarch found time and opportunity to beget bastards. In one respect, however, courtly love and Neoplatonic love had one common ideal, and that was in the sincerity and reality of the emotion of love.[35] The followers of Dante and Petrarch at least gave articulation to the spiritual aspects of love, even though their practice fell from this standard, and it is because we find a person like Monophylo sincerely advocating a somewhat modified Neoplatonic love that I see a certain kinship between his view of love and that revealed in Dan Bartholmew's "Dolorous discourses." Furthermore, both Monophylo and Dan Bartholmew are dealing with love that is open and honest, not the adulterous love of Tristram for King Mark's wife or of Launcelot for King Arthur's.[36]

Aside from this one poem, the various parts of "Dan Bartholmew" follow traditional themes. The description of Ferenda given by the Re-

[34] This seems but another manifestation of the sociological truism that systemization and institutionalization of any individual idea inevitably result in stagnation and decay.

[35] It may be objected that there is a vast difference between mere faithfulness and spiritual ennoblement. But who can read Dante's lines on Paolo and Francesca and not feel that the poet found a spiritual value in their love?

> "E quella a me: 'Nessun maggior dolore
> che ricordarsi del tempo felice
> nella miseria; e ciò sa 'l tuo dottore.
> " 'Ma s'a conoscer la prima radice
> del nostro amor tu hai cotanto affetto,
> dirò come colui che piange e dice.
> " 'Noi leggiavamo un giorno per diletto
> di Lancialotto come amor lo strinse:
> soli eravamo e sanza alcun sospetto.
> " 'Per più fiate li occhi ci sospinse
> quella lettura, e scolorocci il viso;
> ma solo un punto fu quel che ci vinse.
> " 'Quando leggemmo il disiato riso
> esser baciato da cotanto amante,
> questi, che mai da me non fia diviso,
> " 'la bocca mi baciò tutto tremante.
> Galeotto fu il libro e chi lo scrisse:
> quel giorno più non vi leggemmo avante.' "
> [*Inferno*, V, ll. 121–38.]

[36] Although Monophylo is forced to admit of a double standard, his ideal is matrimony (*vide supra*). I can find nothing in "Dan Bartholmew" to indicate that the affair is adulterous; rather the closing lines of the "Dolorous discourses" indicate matrimony.

porter carefully imitates Petrarch's description of Laura[37] and Ariosto's of Alcina.[38] The song of triumph[39] is another rehandling of an old theme, which Gascoigne had used before in "The Adventures of Master F. J.":[40] his love is more fair and true than Helen, Cressid, or Venus. The "libell of request exhibited to Care"[41] tells of his youthful rebellion against Love, who now in his age is afflicting him with the pangs of retribution, and at once we think of the words of Pasquier, quoted above, which tell of Love's vengeance on those who rebel against him in youth. Pasquier would indeed have approved these productions of one of Love's men, and in "The Adventures of Master F. J." and the other poems of *A Hundreth Sundrie Flowres* there are further examples of this same attitude.

In the poem, "To make a lover knowne, by playne Anatomie,"[42] we find a complete catalogue of the physical aspects of a lover: the hair is "unkempt"; the eyes, "hollowe" and "dazled"; the cheeks, "wan & wrinckled"; the arms are worn out with beating on his breast; within his chest sorrow, the smith, beats upon the anvil, his heart, while the lungs serve as the bellows and "sighs ascend for smoke." Although Gascoigne later tells us that this was not composed as a serious poem, he many times slips into the same vein when writing quite seriously, as is seen in "I smile sometimes although my griefe be great," where occurs this stanza:

> Some say they find nor peace, nor power to fight,
> Which seemeth strange: but stranger is my state:
> I dwell in dole, yet sojorne with delight,
> Reposed in rest, yet weried with debate.
> For flatte repulse, might well apease my will
> But fancie fights, to trie my fortune still.[43]

Another, and perhaps better, illustration of the same type of thing can be found in the fourth poem of "F. J.," of which two stanzas will suffice.

> *In prime of lustie yeares, when Cupid caught me in*
> *And nature taught the way to love, how I might best begin:*
> *To please my wandring eye, in beauties tickle trade,*
> *To gaze on eche that passed by, a carelesse sporte I made.*

---

[37] Cf. Petrarch, Canzone XV ("In quella parte dov' Amor mi sprona").

[38] Cf. Ariosto, *Orlando Furioso*, VII, ll. 11–15; also Ariosto's Twenty-Second Sonnet ("Madonna, sete bella").

[39] *Works*, I, 100. "D.B." No. 2. [40] *Ibid.*, I, 414. "F. J." No. 8.

[41] *Ibid.*, I, 118. "D.B." No. 6. [42] *Ibid.*, I, 37. No. 48. [43] *Ibid.*, I, 40. No. 52.

With sweete entising bayte, I fisht for many a dame,
And warmed me by many a fire, yet felt I not the flame:
But when at last I spied, the face that pleased me most,
The coales were quicke, the woode was drie, & I began to toste.[44]

The more sensual aspects of love exist chiefly in "The Adventures of Master F. J.," since the theme of that story is the straightforward seduction of another man's wife. Such behavior is a direct parallel to the various adulteries of courtly love, found in the romances and typified by Launcelot and King Arthur himself, and reappearing in later stories, such as *Amadis of Gaul.* In none of these, however, is there such a callous gloating as in the seventh poem of "F. J."

That selfe same day, and of that day that hower,
When she doth raigne, that mockt Vulcane the Smith:
And thought it meete to harbor in hir bower,
Some gallant gest for hir to dally with.
That blessed hower, that blist and happie daye,
I thought it meete, with hastie steppes to go:
Unto the lodge, wherein my Lady laye,
To laugh for joye, or ells to weepe for wo.
And lo, my Lady of hir wonted grace,
First lent hir lippes to me (as for a kisse:)
And after that hir body to embrace,
Wherein dame nature wrought nothing amisse.
What followed next, gesse you that knowe the trade,
For in this sort, my Frydayes feast I made.[45]

Something of the same spirit may be suggested by Wyatt's "They flee from me, that sometime did me seke,"[46] but it is in Ariosto that a parallel is found when Alcina seduces Ruggiero,[47] and when Sacrapant contemplates Angelica as follows:

But to himselfe thus *Sacrapant* doth say,
B' it that my lord of *Anglant* were so mad,
To take no pleasure of so faire a pray,
When he both time and place, and power had,
Yet am I not obliged any way,
To imitate a president so bad,
Ile rather take my pleasure while I may,
Than waile my want of wit another day.[48]

[44] *Ibid.,* I, 398. "F. J." No. 4.   [45] *Ibid.,* I, 413. "F. J." No. 7.
[46] *Songes and Sonettes* (1557), ed. by Arber, p. 40.   [47] Ariosto, *Orlando Furioso,* VII, 29.
[48] Sir John Harington, *Orlando Furioso in English Heroicall Verse* (1st ed., 1591), I, 57.

In their casual flippancy Gascoigne and Ariosto have much in common, and indeed both are characteristic of the *cinquecento*—in Italy, a time of decay and satire and in England, of sedulous imitation of Italian standards. As Gabriel Harvey noted, Gascoigne had his full share of levity, but in this characteristic, which appears to owe much to Ariosto, his contemporaries do not seem to share. Googe, Turbervile, and Howell are very serious in their verse where we find nothing quite comparable to "Gascoigns Anatomie,"[49] "Gascoignes araignement,"[50] "Gascoignes libell of Divorce,"[51] "Gascoignes Recantation,"[52] "Of all the byrds that I do know,"[53] or *"Gascoignes councell given to master* Bartholmew Withipoll."[54] Harington is perhaps the next Englishman to exhibit a similar jesting spirit, which is well exemplified in the final stanza couplets of his translation of *Orlando*—a translation, incidentally, expressing the original better than any other English version. One wonders how much the *Metamorphosis of Ajax* owed to the penance of translation imposed on Harington by the Queen.

In a more courtierlike vein that would have pleased Glaphyro is the second poem of "The Adventures of Master F. J.," of which the final sonnet stanza is typical:

> For when
> I first beheld that heavenly hewe of thyne,
> Thy stately stature, and thy comly grace,
> I must confesse these dazled eyes of myne
> Did wincke for feare, when I first viewd thy face:
> But bold desire, did open them agayne,
> And bad mee looke till I had lookt to long,
> I pitied them that did procure my payne,
> And lov'd the lookes that wrought me all the wrong:
> And as the Byrd once caught (but woorks her woe)
> That stryves to leave the lymed twigges behind:
> Even so the more I strave to parte thee fro,
> The greater grief did growe within my minde:
> Remediles then must I yeeld to thee,
> And crave no more, thy servaunt but to bee.[55]

If, however, separate poems may be found which illustrate the various concepts of love as enunciated by the members of the symposium in

---

[49] *Works,* I, 37. No. 48.   [50] *Ibid.,* I, 38. No. 49.   [51] *Ibid.,* I, 42. No. 53.
[52] *Ibid.,* I, 51. No. 56.   [53] *Ibid.,* I, 455. No. 21.   [54] *Ibid.,* I, 344. No. 67.
[55] *Ibid.,* I, 389. "F. J." No. 2.

Fenton's *Monophylo,* it must not be concluded that Gascoigne was following now one and now another idea of love. Rather, different lines
from the same poem may illustrate a number of different concepts.
Pasquier simply created type characters who would advocate the varying
ideas that were an essential part of the intellectual baggage of any who
pretended to the court circles of society. Love was the most important
social activity of the upper class, but courtly love had become a debased
excuse for adultery which infected even Dante's first imitator, Petrarch.
Sir Thomas Wyatt could sing of Neoplatonic love and yet admit that
though he was innocent of the charge of seducing nuns, he had had
several affairs. In Italy, Bembo could be portrayed as condemning fleshly
lust, while his own excursions into such adventures were widely known;
and, finally, Aretino could compose *I Sonnetti Lusoriosi* and yet paraphrase
the Psalms. As Vernon Lee remarks of the problem of evil in Renaissance
Italy,[56] there was a wide discrepancy between avowed ideals and conduct.
From this situation resulted an infinite variety of contraries, and the
essential conflict between love and marriage was hidden in a morass
wherein the conceits and language of the imitators of Dante spread like a
stagnant film to cover sensual promiscuity. Amor, the feudal baron, the
Cupid of Ovid who could be described as a Christian saint, and the
Venus who betrayed Vulcan were as useful to a corrupt moral system as
were perfumes to a society that lacked the means of sanitation. So in
Gascoigne we find a variety of concepts of love and a language in which
to express conventional ideas drawn from the medieval and the Italian
Renaissance background.

COURT POETRY

A cursory examination of *Songes and Sonettes* and the manuscripts
which preserve the verses of early Tudor courtiers reveals the fashion of
love poetry, but there is nothing in either printed book or manuscripts to
tell us how seriously these poets regarded their ladies and their love affairs.
From what we know of the Italian followers of the Neoplatonic cult, it
does not seeem that reveling in the ethereal and mystical aspects of love's
potent force excluded the mundane expediency of favoring friends, complimenting patrons, and philosophizing in a sententious vein. Petrarch
found time to write complimentary verses to Rienzi, Colonna, and Mala-

[56] Vernon Lee, *op. cit.,* Vol. I, "The Italy of the Elizabethan Dramatists."

testa,[57] as well as to pose as a philosopher in his satires. Neither Wyatt nor Surrey limited their verse production to their love affairs, but could with equal facility say farewell to the river Tagus or castigate the city of London. So we may well wonder what limits the later court poets set for themselves. Was all experience their domain or were they chiefly interested in love, compliment, personal reflection, and fashionable satire?

George Turbervile, one of Gascoigne's friends, in a palinode to his last published volume of verse,[58] described the manifold activities of a court poet in words that are most revealing:

> Two things in cheefe did move me thus to write,
> And made me deeme it none offence at all:
> First Ovids works bedeckt with deepe delight,
> Whom we of Poets second best doe call.
> I found him full of amours every where:
> Each leafe of love the title eke did beare.
>
> Then next I lived in place among the moe,
> Where fond affection bore the cheefest sway,
> And where the blinded archer with his bow
> Did glaunce at sundry gallants every day:
> And being there, although my minde were free,
> Yet must I seeme love wounded eke to be.
>
> I sawe how some did seeke their owne mishap,
> And hunted dayly to devoure the hookes
> That beuty bayted, and were caught in trap,
> Like wilfull wights that fed on women's lookes:
> Who being once entangled in the line,
> Did yelde themselves, and were content to pine.
>
> Some other minding least to follow love,
> By haunting where dame Venus darlings dwelt,
> By force were forst Cupidos coales to proove,
> Whose burning brands did make their minds to melt,
> So as they were compeld by meere mischaunce,
> As others did, to follow on the daunce.

---

[57] Cf. the sonnet "L'aspettata vertù che 'n voi fioriva," which ends:
    "Pandolfo mio, quest' opere son frali
      "al lungo andar; ma 'l nostro studio è quello
      "che fa per fama gli uomini immortali."
This is but one of the complimentary themes, but it is interesting because of its frequent appearance.
[58] Turbervile, *Tragical Tales and Other Poems*, pp. 403–5.

Some eke there were that groapt but after gaine,
That faynd to frie and burne with blooming heate
Of raging love and counterfetted paine,
When they (God wot) had slender cause to treate:
But all was done to make their Ladies deeme
How greatly they their beuties did esteeme.

And then (O gods) to vew their greeful cheeres,
And listen to their fonde lamenting cries,
To see their cheekes deepe dented in with teares,
That day and night powred out from painful eyes,
Would make a heart of marble melt for woe,
That sawe their plights, and did their sorowes know.

And all for lacke of ruthe and due remorse,
Their cruel Ladies bore so hard a hand,
And they (poore men) constraynd to love perforce,
And fruitlesse cleane to sowe the barrain sand:
That unto me, who privie was of all,
It was a death, and grieved me to the gall.

Then for my friends (as divers loved me well)
Endite I must some light devise of love,
And in the same my friends affection tell,
Whom nothing mought from beauties bar remoove:
My pen must plead the sillie Suters case,
I had my hire, so he mought purchase grace.

Some otherwhile, when beautie bred disdaine,
And feature forst a pride in hawtie brest,
So as my friend was causelesse put to paine,
And for good will might purchace slender rest:
Then must my quill to quarels flatly fall,
Yet keepe the meane twixt sweete and sower brall.

Somtimes I must commend their beauties much
That never came where any beautie lay,
Againe somwhiles my mates would have me tutch
The quicke, bicause they had received the nay:
And thus my pen, as change of matter grew,
Was forst to grief, or els for grace to sue.

Thus did I deale for others pleasure long,
(As who could well refuse to do the like?)
And for my self somtimes would write among

As he that lives with men of war must strike.
I would devise a Sonet to a dame,
And all to make my sullen humor game.

This statement of a poet's activities is most helpful in judging Gascoigne's productions. First, it establishes a confirmation of the Ovidian influence which was evident in the preceeding discussion of the concepts of love. Ovid, however, occupies second place among the poets, according to Turbervile, and it seems a fair presumption that first place was assigned to Petrarch.[59] Second, we are told of the court circle's preoccupation with the poetic expression of the themes of love.[60] Third, we learn that Turbervile, and thus presumably his contemporaries, wrote a variety of poems for friends.[61] Finally, it seems that poets were unable to resist writing complimentary verses in their own behalf.

That Gascoigne wrote in and for the court circle is shown by his poems: one is written for Sir John Scudamore, gentleman usher to Queen Elizabeth and father of the famous Sir James Scudamore;[62] another is addressed to "a Gentlewoman in Court";[63] several contain appeals to ladies of the court;[64] still others are addressed to such persons as Zouche, Lady Grey of Wilton;[65] Bridges, Lady Sands;[66] a Countess;[67] while a large

[59] The question of sources found in Gascoigne has been dealt with above, and we may note here the following evidence from the title-page of Gascoigne's *A Hundreth Sundrie Flowres:* "Gathered partely (by translation) in the fyne outlandish Gardins of Euripides, Ovid, Petrarke, Ariosto, and others: and partly by invention, out of our owne fruitfull Orchardes in Englande."

[60] The subject matter of *Songes and Sonettes* and the various British Museum MSS of early Tudor poems (many of these are printed in Hebel and Hudson's *Poetry of the English Renaissance,* New York, 1929) are evidence for this truism, but the actual words of a contemporary seem worthy of attention.

[61] Both Wyatt (*The Poems of Sir Thomas Wiatt,* ed. by Foxwell, p. 174 [No. 9]; pp. 217–18 [No. 12]) and Surrey (*The Poems of Henry Howard, Earl of Surrey,* ed. by Padelford, p. 71 [No. 21]; p. 79 [No. 27]) have poems written as by a lady, and these may probably be considered as written for a friend. Otherwise there seems to be little evidence of the custom among the poets of the reign of Henry VIII.

[62] *"L'Escu d'amour,* the shield of perfect love," *Works,* I, 340. No. 47. In the notes of my edition I shall offer proof that this poem concerns Scudamore and not the Earl of Oxford as some believe.

[63] "When daunger kepes the dore, of lady beauties bowre," *Works,* I, 88. No. 14.

[64] "Give me my Lute in bed now as I lye," *Works,* I, 338. No. 37. "This tenth of March when Aries receyv'd," *Works,* I, 333. No. 24.

[65] "These rustie walles whome cankred yeares deface," *Works,* I, 53. No. 51.

[66] "In Court who so demaundes what dame doth most excell," *Works,* I, 52. No. 50.

[67] "Desire of Fame would force my feeble skill," *Works,* I, 336. No. 32.

group contain incidental references to famous persons.[68] At a later time Gascoigne himself confirmed the fact that he wrote love poems for other men: "And out of all doubt, if ever I wrote lyne for myself in causes of love, I have written tenne for other men in layes of lust."[69] Several poems obviously belong to this class of composition: for example, there is the poem written for Scudamore; another is headed "A letter devised for a young lover";[70] while a third is written as by a woman, "An absent Dame thus complayneth."[71]

In addition to these poems of his and others' loves, there are three distinct classes of verses not mentioned in Turbervile's palinode. There are many poems which do not celebrate love, but which are written merely to compliment or befriend a particular person. To these are closely linked what may be described as occasional verses. And finally there are the satiric and moralistic poems.

The first group is well represented by the poem in "prayse of a Countesse."[72] Conventional conceits are prosaically forced into rhymes: Pallas is so jealous of the Countess's gifts as to combat the poet's efforts to praise her; Mars deserts Venus for the beauteous Countess; and Phoebus stands in dread of her beams, as does Cynthia. But nowhere is there any mention of love. The poet is "sometimes hir servaunt, now hir friend," who has "presumed in friendly wise to spend, this ragged verse in honor of hir name." This method of elaborating a conceit, employed more effectively in such a poem as *Gascoignes prayse of* Bridges, *nowe Ladie* Sandes,"[73] is carefully enunciated in his "Certayne notes of Instruction," the first critical English treatise on poetry:

If I should undertake to wryte in prayse of a gentlewoman, I would neither praise hir christal eye, nor hir cherrie lippe, &c. For these things are *trita* & *obvia*. But I would either finde some supernaturall cause whereby my penne might walke in the superlative degree, or els I would undertake to aunswere for any imperfection that shee hath, and thereupon rayse the prayse of hir commendacion.[74]

---

[68] "Dulce Bellum Inexpertis," 'Peroratio,' *Works*, I, 179–82. *The Grief of Joye*, "The Seconde Songe," *ibid.*, II, 526–32. The Dedicatory Letters to *The Glasse of Government*, *ibid.*, II, 3. *The Steele Glas*, *ibid.*, II, 135–37. *The Complaynt of Phylomene*, *ibid.*, II, 177. *The Droomme of Doomes day*, *ibid.*, II, 211–14.

[69] *Works*, I, 16.   [70] *Ibid.*, I, 462. No. 40.   [71] *Ibid.*, I, 335. No. 27.

[72] *Vide supra*, n. 67.   [73] *Vide supra*, n. 66.   [74] *Works*, I, 465–66.

Bridges's imperfection was "the blemishe on hir browe" which, we learn, was caused by the anger of Cupid who, unable to resist the lady's beauty, fell in love with her. The god, in revenge for this trick played upon him by Dame Nature, "sodeynly with myghtie mace, gan rap hir on the pate," and so Bridges bore a scar even from her cradle. Likewise the imperfection of a dark complexion is lessened when one realizes that Cleopatra, a true lover faithful until death, had a similar coloring.[75]

Not a direct compliment, but, instead, a poem written to better the position at court of an anonymous lady is that beginning "This tenth of March when Aries receyv'd."[76] Employing the conventional astrological introduction, found, for example, in Chaucer's "House of Fame"[77] and in Barnabe Googe's "Cupido Conquered,"[78] Gascoigne tells the story of a lady to whom the freshness of spring brings only a recognition of her lack of love. The concluding stanza urges the ladies of the court to be kind to this unfortunate. The ladies are also implored to "lend you me some relief" by the anonymous gentlewoman,[79] who tells of her unsought-for marriage, which soon blossomed into love, only to fade into despair when her husband was imprisoned.

The method of these poems is reminiscent of the *exemplum*: a narrative is related and an appeal for a desired course of conduct is based upon the logic of the story. Marriage brought love and happiness; but dire circumstances changed all this to sorrow, wherefore the ladies should take pity and lend relief. Similar in manner but of different matter is "Gascoignes wodmanship."[80] The poet was enjoying the hunting of the winter deer in the company of Lord Grey of Wilton; although many opportunities were offered, Gascoigne was unable to hit a single creature. Being chided by his host, Gascoigne wrote a poem in which he traced his poor marksmanship throughout his life: he had shot awry at an academic career, a legal career, and finally he had missed the mark completely when he tried to become a soldier. Therefore he besought Lord Grey "to traine him yet into some better trade." This appeal is the real reason for the poem, yet Gascoigne followed the method advocated in his "Certayne notes of Instruction" of grounding it "upon some fine invention,"[81] here the

[75] *Works*, I, 454. No. 9. [76] *Vide supra*, n. 64.
[77] *The Complete Works of Geoffrey Chaucer*, ed. by Robinson, p. 332.
[78] Googe, *op. cit.*, p. 107. [79] *Vide supra*, n. 64.
[80] *Works*, I, 348–52. No. 70. [81] *Ibid.*, I, 465.

invention being the conceit of shooting awry. Another "invention" is the basis of "Gascoignes voyage into *Hollande*,"[82] which was written

> To shew my Lord what healplesse happe ensewth,
> When heddy youth will gad without a guide. . . .

The story is that of shipwreck due to insufficient skill, and the analogy is plain: "heddy youth" is a ship without a proper pilot.

In subject matter as well, Gascoigne explored a vein neglected by his predecessors but used by both Turbervile and Churchyard, namely, a poetic rendition of events in the life of the author. Churchyard tells of his experiences in the Scotch wars;[83] Turbervile, of his voyage to Russia;[84] but Gascoigne personalizes the verse essay or history. As we shall see below, in connection with "Dulce Bellum Inexpertis" and *The Spoyle of Antwerpe,* he emphasizes the importance of the individual reaction to events. This same point of view is found in his love narratives. In these, however, he avails himself of the models of his predecessors. The love story with interpolated poems is as old as Boccaccio's *Filostrato.* Gascoigne, though using this conventional framework in "The Adventures of Master F. J.," tells his own story and thus follows the autobiographical tradition of Turbervile and Churchyard. To this, however, he adds his own contribution—the importance of individual psychological reaction. Likewise "Dan Bartholmew of Bathe" is a personal narrative, but its formal ancestry is somewhat complicated. Since it is, unlike "The Adventures of Master F. J.," entirely in verse, it may be considered a descendant, in its form, of such a medieval poem as Chaucer's *Troilus;* but whereas *Troilus* is one poem, "Dan Bartholmew" is composed of a series of poems with verse links and, as such, is far closer to the scheme of Petrarch's *Rime,* where we have a series of short poems dealing with various manifestations of the love of Petrarch for Laura. But this analogy can only be suggested, not forced to any definite conclusion. What we may conclude is that Gascoigne was aware of his literary heritage and, within a framework derived from the past, used new materials, modified by his individuality.

[82] *Ibid.,* I, 354–63. No. 74.
[83] Thomas Churchyard, *The First Parte of Churchyardes Chippes, containing twelve severall labours,* Thomas Marshe, 1575. Reprinted by J. P. Collier, n.d. "The siege of Leeth" (pp. 8–31); "The siege of Edenborough Castle" (pp. 200–212).
[84] Turbervile, *Tragical Tales,* pp. 370–91.

More truly occasional verse is *"Gascoignes councell given to master Bartholmew Withipoll,"*[85] when the latter's voyage to Genoa offers the poet a double opportunity to tease his friend upon former trips to that land of infamy and to catalogue, in mock-serious vein, the dangers of wicked Italy. It is particularly in poems of this nature that Gascoigne displays his best efforts. He can handle narration in an almost conversational tone, and the light easy flowing result is in distinct contrast with either Churchyard's or Turbervile's rather sententious versifying. The jesting spirit of *"Gascoignes councell"* appears in other pieces which may not truly be described as occasional; but in these, his light touch is productive of verse which is reminiscent of Chaucer's best irony, a type of verse unfortunately too rare in English poetry of the Renaissance and after. The lines "in prayse of a Gentlewoman, whose name was Phillip"[86] are an excellent case in point. One thinks of Catullus and Skelton; but Gascoigne's delightful *double entendre* is a far cry from the pretended sensibility of the first and the anvil-pounding humor of the latter. It is such a poem as would have delighted the members of the Scriblerus Club, and we can only regret that it has been omitted from the anthologies. Another poem of the same type that has escaped notice because it was excluded from *The Posies* is "Eyther a needelesse or a bootelesse comparison betwene two letters,"[87] where, in rather simple and unadorned style, the poet shows very good and amusing reasons why the lady should prefer G.[ascoigne] to B.[oyes].[88]

This simple style is characteristic of the really best poems of Gascoigne, wherein his muse is that of the great tradition of English poetry. "Gascoignes Lullabie,"[89] "Gascoignes gardnings,"[90] and the lines written "In that other ende of his sayde close walke"[91] are such as to make us wish he had never seen the *Songes and Sonettes* or heard of Petrarch. A stanza like this:

> You that have spente the silente nighte
> In sleepe and quiet reste,
> And joye to see the cheereful lighte
> That ryseth in the East:

---

[85] *Works,* I, 344–47. No. 67. [86] *Ibid.,* I, 455. No. 21. [87] *Ibid.,* I, 502. No. 38.
[88] For a discussion of Gascoigne's troubles with Boyes, *vide supra,* chap. ii.
[89] *Works,* I, 44. No. 55. [90] *Ibid.,* I, 352. No. 71. [91] *Ibid.,* I, 353. No. 72.

> Nowe cleere your voyce, nowe cheare your heart,
> Come helpe me nowe to sing:
> Eche willyng wight come beare a parte,
> To prayse the heavenly King.[92]

seems incredibly remote from

> *And yet they be but sorrowes smoke,*
> *my brest the fordge where fury playes,*
> *My panting hart, it strikes the stroke,*
> *my fancie blowes the flame alwayes,*
> *The coles are kindled by desire*
> *and* Cupide *warmes him by the fire.*[93]

But seemingly we cannot have the one without the other and we may be glad that Gascoigne's satiric poems are in a style more simple than elaborate. The themes given Gascoigne by John Vaughan and Richard Courtop as a condition for admission to their fellowship, when the poet "(in middest of his youth) determined to abandone all vaine delights and to retourne unto Greyes Inne," are interesting examples.[94] The first, on the theme *Magnum vectigal parcimonia,* is a tract for the times, portraying the financial ruin attendant upon those who seek to achieve courtly position and wealth by a lavish expenditure. At first glance, this seems to be in the great tradition of satire upon courtly or fashionable life which extends from Horace and Ovid to Wyatt, with many examples by the way, as in Petrarch and Alain Chartier. A comparison with Wyatt's "Myne own John Poins" at once reveals a great difference: instead of Wyatt's philosophical point of view and classical allusions, Gascoigne deals with concrete figures:

> The common speech is, spend and God will send,
> But what sends he? a bottell and a bagge,
> A staffe, a wallet and a wofull ende. . . .[95]

The life of a wandering beggar awaits the courtly spendthrift, in comparison with whom "Hick, Hobbe and Dicke with cloutes uppon their knee" are rich indeed. They have money safely hidden away, and Davie Debet never enters their parlor. Where Wyatt is concerned in "Myne own John Poins" with the loss of personal integrity, Gascoigne here reveals

---

[92] *Ibid.,* I, 55. No. 63.
[93] *Ibid.,* I, 116. "D.B." No. 4.
[94] *Ibid.,* I, 62–70. Nos. 57–61.
[95] *Ibid.,* I, 64. No. 59.

the tangible financial ruin of those who pursue Lady Meed. It is to the spirit of *Piers Plowman* that we must look for the source of Gascoigne's earthy realism. Gone are the conceits, the inventions, and in their place is the real language of real men.

This same truly English heritage is found in the dilation of Richard Courtop's theme *Durum aeneum & miserabile aevum*[96] and in "Gascoignes gloze uppon this text, *Dominus iis opus habet.*"[97] Give Gave, the plowman, Dame Alyson his wife, their son Sim, and Mawde the maid, come straight from the "fair field full of folk" whom Piers saw from the Malvern Hills. The graphic procession of "the woman wantonesse" and her "ticing traine" is a very real reflection of the Lady Meed.

> Pride in hir pocket playes bo peepe, and bawdrie in hir braine.
> Hir handmaides be deceipte, daunger, and dalliance,
> Riot and Revell follow hir, they be of hir alliance:
> Nexte these commes in Simme Swash, to see what sturre they keepe.
> Climme of ye Clough then takes his heeles, tis time for him to creep.
> To packe the pageaunt up, commes Sorowe with a song. . . .[98]

In the other "theme" compositions, Gascoigne is close to his school days, with a store of proverbs, homilies, conceits, and fine "inventions." They are pedestrian pieces, although Alexander Neville's theme, *Sat cito, si sat bene,* is close to the poet's own experience and thus is dealt with in a more straightforward manner.

As Turbervile shows, all the literary productions of the court poet were closely related to the ideas and customs of the social world. There was a fashionable tradition for poems of love and compliment, while occasional, narrative, and satiric verse were not cast in so strict a mold. The literature of ideas, the *Arcadia* and its ideals of fashionable conduct, *The Faerie Queene* fashioning the moral virtues—these were still in the future. Before they could be written, the period of apprenticeship had to continue: the language still needed enrichment through translation and imitation; ideas of form and theory could come only through the work of the lesser men, and Gascoigne had to continue his exploration of literary ideas, conceits, and forms. The court poets of the next generation are reputed better poets, but for the majority the field of endeavor was nearly the same as for Gascoigne, and for many it was far more limited.

[96] *Ibid.,* I, 69. No. 61.   [97] *Ibid.,* I, 70. No. 62.   [98] *Ibid.,* I, 69–70. No. 61.

THE POET'S DESIDERATA

Puttenham's comments on Wyatt and Surrey, in his *Arte of English Poesie,* furnish a valuable basis from which to estimate the ideals of poetic composition which guided Gascoigne and his fellows. The recent editors of *The Arte* have shown that we must now think of that work as having been begun in the late sixties.[99] Thus Puttenham is really a contemporary of Gascoigne, Googe, and Turbervile, and his remarks on poetry would presumably have had the sanction of these men, who undoubtedly judged their work as a continuation of and an improvement upon that of their predecessors. If this last be true, why have the critics given us the picture of the burgeoning of poetry in Wyatt and Surrey, followed by a seeming dormancy until there unfold the flowers of Sidney and Spenser? Puttenham, I think, gives a clue to the answer:

In the latter end of the same kings raigne sprong up a new company of courtly makers, of whom Sir *Thomas Wyat* th'elder & *Henry* Earle of Surrey were the two chieftaines, who having travailed into Italie, and there tasted the sweete and stately measures and stile of the Italian Poesie as novices newly crept out of the schooles of *Dante Arioste* and *Petrarch,* they greatly pollished our rude and homely maner of vulgar Poesie, from that it had bene before, and for that cause may justly be sayd the first reformers of our English meetre and stile.[100]

Evidently, then, Puttenham thought that the chief work of these men lay in such polishing and reforming of meter and style, and it is in respect to these two qualities in the work of Wyatt and Surrey that we must judge Gascoigne. Since we have Gascoigne's own remarks on the making of poetry, it will be well to list briefly his various ideas.[101]

1–13. Technique and language:

    1–2. Ground the poem upon some fine invention, taking heed to follow this invention to the end;

    3–4. Follow throughout the metrical pattern with which you begin, placing every word so that its natural stress appears. (Here occurs the statement that in English poetry only the iambic foot is used, although formerly others were employed);

    5. Avoid polysyllabic words;

---

[99] *The Arte of English Poesie* (1589), ed. by Willcock and Walker, pp. xliv–liii.
[100] *Ibid.,* p. 60.
[101] "Certayne notes of Instruction concerning the making of verse or ryme in English," *Works,* I, 465–73.

6–7. Avoid rhyme without reason. How to find a rhyme;

8–11. Employ the figures and tropes of prose, avoiding strange words and using the English phrase to frame the style to perspicuity;

12. "This poeticall licence is a shrewde fellow, and covereth many faults";

13. The use of the caesura.

14. On various meters:

(1) "Rythme royall is a verse of tenne sillables, and seven such verses make a staffe, whereof the first and thirde lines do aunswer (acrosse) in like terminations and rime, the second, fourth, and fifth, do likewise answere eche other in terminations, and the two last do combine and shut up the Sentence";

(2) Ballad:

(a) . . . "a man may write ballade in a staffe of sixe lines, every line conteyning eighte or sixe sillables, whereof the firste and third, second and fourth do rime acrosse, and the fifth and sixth do rime togither in conclusion";

(b) "You may write also your ballad of tenne sillables rimyng as before is declared, but these two were wont to be most cōmonly used in ballade, which propre name was (I thinke) derived of this worde in Italian *Ballare,* whiche signifieth to daunce";

(c) . . . "those kinds of rimes serve beste for daunces or light matters";

(3) "Rondlette . . . doth alwayes end with one self same foote or repeticion";

(4) Sonnets: . . . "some thinke that all Poemes (being short) may be called Sonets, as in deede it is a diminutive worde derived of *Sonare,* but yet I can beste allowe to call those Sonets whiche are of foureteene lynes, every line conteyning tenne syllables. The firste twelve do ryme in staves of foure lines by crosse meetre, and the last twoo ryming togither do conclude the whole";

(5) "Dyzaynes, & Syxaines . . . are of ten lines, and of sixe lines, cōmonly used by the French";

(6) Verlay: . . . "a long discourse in verses of tenne sillables, whereof the foure first did ryme acrosse, and the fifth did aunswere to the firste and thirde, breaking off there, and so going on to another termination";

(7) Internally rhyming quatrains: "There are also certaine Poemes devised of tenne syllables, whereof the first aunswereth in termination with the fourth, and the second and thirde answere eche other";

(8) Poulter's measure: . . . "the long verse of twelve and fourtene sillables . . . it doth consist of Poulters measure which giveth xii. for one dozē and xiiii. for another."

15. Length: . . . "avoyde prolixitie and tediousnesse."

16. The proper subjects of the various meters:

(1) . . . "riding rime [Chaucer's decasyllabic couplets] serveth most aptly to wryte a merie tale";
(2) "Rythme royall is fittest for a grave discourse";
(3) "Ballades are beste for matters of love";
(4) "Rondlettes moste apt for the beating or handlyng of an adage or common proverbe";
(5) "Sonets serve as well in matters of love as of discourse";
(6) "Dizaymes and Sixames for shorte Fantazies";
(7) "Verlayes for an effectual proposition";
(8) "Poulters measure . . . best for Psalmes and Himpnes."

These various rules, admonitions, and comments fall into three classifications: (1) technique, (2) metrical patterns, (3) language. "Technique" includes such items as employment of the iambic foot, coincidence of tonic and word accent, variable use of the caesura, continuation of a line pattern throughout a poem, careful attention to rhyme, and, finally, the preservation of a normal word order, using understandable, not archaic or foreign words. To us all this may seem gratuitous, but most of these precepts are to be found in Professor Courthope's summary of Surrey's contribution to English prosody.[102] Since it is a fact that Surrey's poems reflect these same characteristics and are for that reason something new in English verse, we must not lightly dismiss Gascoigne's articulation of the rules and his reasons for propounding them.

The problem of the iambic foot may perhaps seem strange, but with only a brief backward glance we can well understand the necessity for such a rule. Gascoigne, lamenting that English "Rithmes" have only this one foot, recognizes that it had not always been thus and quotes a line containing two anapests. But his failure to understand why this latter measure is no longer acceptable is explained by his remarks on Chaucer:

Also our father *Chaucer* hath used the same libertie in feete and measures that the Latinists do use: and who so ever do peruse and well consider his workes,

---

[102] Courthope, *A History of English Poetry,* II, 92–100.

he shall finde that although his lines are not alwayes of one selfe same number of Syllables, yet beyng redde by one that hath understanding, the longest verse and that which hath most Syllables in it, will fall (to the eare) correspondent unto that whiche hath fewest sillables in it: and like wise that whiche hath in it fewest syllables, shalbe founde yet to consist of woordes that have suche naturall sounde, as may seeme equall in length to a verse which hath many moe sillables of lighter accentes.[103]

This failure to understand the iambic pattern of Chaucer's verse began long before, with Lydgate. Later, Hawes and Barclay were of an age that no longer comprehended the metrical significance of inflectional endings or the normal accent of the Romance languages.[104] Not only pronunciation had changed, but vocabulary as well. This change resulted in Hawes's production of such lines as this:

> A mynute vi houres, and vi houres a yere,[105]

or this

> By Musykes toure walked most goodly.[106]

The first of these may perhaps be read with some meaning, if one follows Gascoigne's theory about the scansion of the Latinists,[107] but the second is nothing else than prose. The older poets were not alone in their failure to understand the Chaucerian iambic pattern. Wyatt has many lines that cannot be scanned either by the system of Pynson's *Chaucer* advocated by Miss Foxwell[108] or by relying on Dr. Tillyard's theory that Wyatt's irregularity is a conscious one.[109] Not only does Wyatt seem rough to us, but he most certainly did to Gascoigne and his contemporaries. The very fact that lines appear in different forms in both the Harington MS and in Tottel indicates this.[110] The changes noted by Courthope make the

---

[103] "Certayne notes," *Works*, I, pp. 467–68.

[104] Professor Saintsbury's excellent interchapter (*A History of English Prosody*, I, 370–77) details this change at more length. On the breakdown of the metrical pattern after Chaucer, Berdan (*Early Tudor Poetry*, pp. 50–55) is most helpful.

[105] Stephen Hawes, "The Pastime of Pleasure" in Neilson and Webster's *Chief British Poets of the Fourteenth and Fifteenth Centuries* (Boston, 1916), p. 250.

[106] *Ibid.*

[107] Cf. Berdan (*op. cit.,* pp. 121–25) for a fuller consideration of this problem.

[108] Foxwell, *A Study of Sir Thomas Wyatt's Poems,* chap. vi.

[109] Tillyard, *The Poetry of Sir Thomas Wyatt,* p. 21.

[110] Courthope (*op. cit.,* II, 146) discusses this and gives examples. I realize that I am presenting what now has come to be regarded as an old-fashioned attitude toward Wyatt, but the concept of Wyatt as a greater poet than Surrey, and the immediate ancestor of Donne, does not seem to me fully proved.

Tottel versions regular in scansion, and that these changes were purpose-
fully made seems quite true. After Surrey's day, Wyatt's reputation suffered greatly, as is shown by Sidney's omission of his name from the list
of English poets.[111] Furthermore, since Surrey's verse is regular to a
modern ear and Wyatt's is not, the conclusion is strengthened: if we can
easily scan Surrey and Gascoigne, then our pronunciation is not greatly
different from theirs, but it is far different from Wyatt's. Thus with Surrey's regularity as his model, it is not strange that Gascoigne clung with
steadfast faith to the iamb and reflected this desire for regularity in his
emphasis on the preservation of the same pattern throughout a poem.

The coincidence of tonic and natural emphasis is definitely related to
this recognition of the iambic pattern and to the Elizabethan poets' inability to scan the work of their predecessors. The shift from the Romance
accent to that of modern English is particularly noticeable in Middle
English words of French origin, such as nature, vertue, season, and
reason. Accenting the final syllable results in greater regularity in the
following lines from Wyatt:

> Thy vertue to let; though that frowerdnes[112]
>
> Nature that gave the bee so seet a grace[113]

Such accentuation would, however, have seemed unnatural to Gascoigne,
and he obviously found Surrey's skillful coördination of the verse and
word accent more understandable and more in harmony with a regular
system of versification. But here again the literal following of a rule made
Gascoigne's regularity too obvious and harsh.

The strictures regarding natural word order, as well as the avoidance
of archaic and strange words, are also related to this same problem. An
unnatural word order could result from a changing language, or could
be the effort of an inferior poet to achieve a correct accentual pattern. In
condemning this latter, Gascoigne is attacking artificiality in manner,
exactly as he attacks artificiality of language resulting from the use of
archaic and strange words. This faint foreboding of Wordsworth's mani-
festo is emphasized in rule no. 8: "You may use the same Figures or

---

[111] Sir Philip Sidney, *An Apologie for Poetrie* (1595, ed. by Arber, 1868), p. 62. Webbe
(*A Discourse of English Poetrie*, p. 33) also omits Wyatt from his list of English poets.
[112] Foxwell, ed., *The Poems of Sir Thomas Wiat*, Sonnet 13, p. 13.
[113] *Ibid.*, Epigram 13, p. 27.

Tropes in verse which are used in prose, and in my judgement they serve more aptly, and have greater grace in verse than they have in prose."[114]

More directly related to Surrey's achievements are Gascoigne's theory and practice of rhyming. He warns against rhyme that spoils the "invention" and rhyme without reason. Though he does not say so, he follows Surrey in avoiding weak-syllable and double rhymes, generally using, instead, an accented rhyme of a monosyllabic or dissyllabic word. Particularly facile is his rhyming in what he calls the "Verlaye" with the pattern *ababa cdcdc* and so forth, where there are sequences of unrhymed lines ending *acd*.[115] The effort is not too far removed from blank verse. If he had allowed himself a variable caesura and a run-on line, this form, which is, so far as I can discern, unique, would have had interesting possibilities.

The necessity for rule was a principle which had to be firmly established before poets could venture to break away in variation. Thus Gascoigne establishes the position of the caesura after the fourth syllable in a pentameter line, after the eighth in a fourteener, and the middle of eight and twelve-syllable lines. For some unknown reason, he allows any position in rhyme royal, and we can only wonder why he did not perceive the resulting fluidity.

All these remarks about the construction of the individual line are an articulation of the usage which had been established by Surrey and which Gascoigne solidified in practice. He was equally interested in metrical forms and here again he developed tradition by usage. The most significant fact about Gascoigne's poetry is, in my judgment, that the bulk of it was written in three typically English meters: rhyme royal, poulter's measure, and blank verse. There are approximately 3,000 lines of rhyme royal, 2,500 of poulter's, and 3,000 of blank verse. In the number of poems written in each, poulter's leads with 27 appearances; rhyme royal appears 9 times; and blank verse is found only in *Jocasta* and *The Steele Glas*. It is in the long poems and the play that the latter two amass their large totals and therein lies their importance. Chaucer had used rhyme royal in *Troilus*, Sackville had employed it in his *Induction*, but prior to Gas-

---

[114] "Certayne notes," *Works*, I, 469.
[115] An example of the verlay is "Gascoignes voyage into *Hollande*." (*Works*, I, 354. No. 74.)

coigne the long poem in this meter had been used exactly as Gascoigne describes it: "for a grave discourse." In "Dan Bartholmew," "Dulce Bellum," and *The Grief of Joye* it descends to earth and walks with mere mortals. The amorous narrative, the personal essay, and a description of the ladies of the court are intensely individual expressions, wherein the personality of the poet is of importance. To the long poem Gascoigne gave the spirit of the Renaissance—the emphasis on the individual reaction and emotion—which remained so long thereafter buried beneath the weight of the pastoral, the euphuistic, and the religious traditions. The drama became the mode of expression, and it is not until much later that we find the emergence of that type of long poem for which Gascoigne opened the way.[116]

Poulter's measure and its near relative, the fourteener, had their day, but blank verse soon established its unquestioned position as the English dramatic meter, and here Gascoigne's use of the form had a definite influence. *The Steele Glas,* the first original English poem in blank verse, extends the use of this meter to satire and, although *Gorboduc* antedates *Jocasta,* Gascoigne's dramatic translation gave further currency to the form. The drama, *The Misfortunes of Arthur,* appearing in 1587, offered verse little different from that of *Jocasta,* with its strict iambic pattern, fixed caesura, and end-stopped lines. In the same year that the gentlemen of Gray's Inn were content to follow the model of twenty years before, Christopher Marlowe's "mighty line" marked the final coming of age of dramatic blank verse. In its nondramatic form, however, this measure remained subordinate to the couplet and stanzaic patterns.

A Hundreth Sundrie Flowres and its expanded and purified second edition contained neither *The Steele Glas* nor *The Grief of Joye;* it was primarily a volume of popular love poetry, written in traditional metrical forms on traditional themes. Gascoigne's lament on the prevalence of poulter's measure is abundantly justified in his own works, where, as we have noted, it appeared in twenty-seven separate poems. The subject matter of these ranges from the power of love to the imminence of death, with a consequent need of faith. Between these extremes are the long

[116] Rhyme royal was, of course, used by Daniel in his *Complaint of Rosamund* and by Shakespeare in *Lucrece,* but these seem to me to be definitely in the "bookish" tradition of *Troilus.* I am concerned more with the tenor of Gascoigne's long poems than with the actual pattern. The familiar and the personal, emphasized by Gascoigne, are infrequent elsewhere.

narrative masque written for the Montague-Dormer weddings, conventional love poems, and the amusing mock-heroic "last will and Testament" of "Dan Bartholmew." Satire and compliment are also written in this form, where the length of individual poems varies from the 10 lines of the first poem of "F. J." to the 381 of the masque. The singsong rhythm and the couplet rhyme made this an easy and therefore a most popular metrical form of the middle years of the century. The lack of discipline which it encouraged was largely responsible for the inferiority of the poetry of this period. The original blame must, of course, lie with Surrey, who, by using it in both his love poems and his Biblical paraphrases, gave it an initial impetus that long continued. Wyatt originated poulter's, but used it in only a few poems.

The other meters mentioned by Gascoigne all find illustration in Wyatt, so it will be well to retrace our path to survey the prosody of Puttenham's two "reformers" of English verse and the continuity of their work in Gascoigne. Miss Foxwell's analysis[117] of the poems in the Egerton MS reveals that Wyatt employed approximately thirty-one different metrical patterns, and an examination of the Devonshire MS adds some ten more, if we include such variants as a rhyme royal of four-syllable lines and other departures from the fixed octo- or decasyllabic line. Great as is our debt to Dr. Tillyard[118] for pointing out that several of the patterns belong to the songs which were developed under Dunstable in the court of Henry VI, we must not lose sight of the fact that Wyatt was an experimenter in verse forms. He used the sonnet and *ottava rima* with almost equal frequency, approximately twenty-five of each. The quatrain in varying line lengths comes next with twenty-three appearances, while *terza rima* with twelve, and the *rondeau* with eight appearances follow in order. Although Surrey's poems[119] are fewer in number, they exhibit an equally significant frequency analysis: poulter's measure occurs in eighteen poems, the sonnet, in fifteen, while *terza rima, ottava rima,* quatrains of varying line length, and stanzas of four, six, eight, ten, and seventeen lines appear occasionally. The predominating line is the decasyllabic, with some of six and eight syllables, as well as the twelve and

---

[117] Foxwell, *A Study of Sir Thomas Wyatt's Poems,* Appendix D.
[118] Tillyard, *op. cit.,* p. 15.
[119] *The Poems of Henry Howard, Earl of Surrey,* ed. by Padelford, Vol. I.

fourteen of poulter's. The total number of blank-verse lines, though large, comes from the translation of the *Aeneid*. As we have seen, Gascoigne employs poulter's more frequently than any other measure, although it is curious to note that his second favorite on the basis of incidence is the sonnet, which always follows the English model established by Surrey. Gascoigne's definition of three quatrains and a couplet of decasyllabic verse is indeed helpful when we find Googe[120] labeling all short poems as sonnets and Turbervile failing to include a single correct example in his *Epytaphes, Epigrams, Songs and Sonets*.[121] The sonnet form appears separately sixteen times and twice as a stanza form, once with a four-syllable link, and again with the last line of one stanza being repeated as the first line of the next. Other stanza forms are rhyme royal in nine poems; the six-line ballad of six, eight, or ten syllables used in seventeen poems; eight lines composed of two quatrains used twice; a six-syllable quatrain appearing once, and, finally, a seemingly unique invention used in two poems, the eleven-line stanza (55555555325), rhyming *abbaac-ccdee* or *ababbccdeed*. In long non-stanzaic poems the quatrain, with twelve examples, follows poulter's measure, while the verlay, as defined by Gascoigne, is used five times, and six syllable couplets, once.[122]

From this evidence it seems possible to reach certain conclusions. Wyatt was essentially a translator and experimenter; in translation he reproduced as far as possible the metrical schemes of his originals, as, for example, his *ottava rima* translations of Serafino's *Strambotti*. Not only did he use the traditional English song patterns, but he also experimented on the basis of these meters and those of his translations; so that we find, for instance, the rhyme-royal pattern appearing in six, eight, and ten-syllable lines. Such experimentation fulfills a very necessary function; but there must be an ensuing period of consolidation and standardization, if the correct means of expression are to be found. The very fact that Surrey employed only between one-third and one-half of Wyatt's metrical patterns is, I think, real evidence of the former's contribution. In

---

[120] Googe, *op. cit.* The half title on p. 75 is "Sonettes"; thereafter follow thirty-six poems, of which only four are true sonnets.

[121] I have used the Folger Shakespeare Library copy of the 1570 edition.

[122] Gascoigne has no true example of the "rondlette," but otherwise he uses all the forms which he discusses. His total number of metrical patterns is fifteen, if the varying line lengths are counted separately.

comparison with Wyatt, Surrey was an original poet, in that he translated less, imitated instead, and confined his endeavors to those media which he found congenial. It is significant that Surrey established the English sonnet form. The standardization which Surrey effected in the technique of the individual line emphasizes his similar contribution in the metrical patterns. We have noted, however, that the long poem was not found in either Wyatt or Surrey, and the use of this type of composition by Gascoigne and Turbervile is accompanied by a considerable interest in the metrical forms suitable for such productions.

The source of this interest may perhaps be explained by Professor Berdan's definition of the two phases of Petrarchan imitation:

There are two sharply differentiated phases in Petrarchan imitation, (a) the quattrocento imitation of separate poems, and (b) the cinquecento imitation of the *Rime* as a whole. As confusion reigns without this distinction I have tried to mark it by calling the first *Petrarchism* and by keeping the Italian term *Petrarchismo* for the second.[123]

Both Wyatt and Surrey belong to the tradition of *Petrarchism*, but Gascoigne felt the influence of *Petrarchismo* and the attendant necessity for grouping his poems around one person. Both "The Adventures of Master F. J." and "Dan Bartholmew of Bathe" are examples of this. There is evidence that the poems of the first were written some time before the prose narrative, and that "The Reporter" of the second was created only as a means of linking a series of separate poems, which may or may not have been composed originally in connection with the romance of Ferenda and Dan Bartholmew.

Petrarch's *Rime* may be considered as a unit, in that all the poems center on the poet's love for Madonna Laura; they are a series of infinite variations upon a single theme. The ecstasy of a moment, the rapture of a glance, the sorrow of absence—all these evanescent emotions are frozen into changelessness at the perfection of their being. But such crystallization of intangibles George Gascoigne did not understand. For him the unity of ideas, the variations of a theme, meant only one thing, and that was telling a story. While Petrarch indirectly told the story of his love for Laura, Gascoigne recited the events that transpired in the love affair of Dan Bartholmew and Ferenda. All we really learn of the emotional

---

[123] Berdan, *op. cit.*, p. 460.

reactions of the hero is that when he was happy he was very, very happy
and when he was sad, he was very, very sad. So, too, in individual poems,
Gascoigne achieves a beginning and an end by narrating events. The
poem beginning "This tenth of March," which has been discussed above,
is an excellent case in point.[124] The poet decides to go for a boat ride in
the springtime; he hears a lamenting voice; he rows to the spot whence
comes the sound; he hears a lady sing woefully because she is unhappy
in the spring when all the world is gay; she sees him and stops; after one
more stanza the poet also stops. The same narrative method is used in
praising "Bridges, *nowe Ladie* Sandes."[125]

It is this interest in narration that explains Gascoigne's attention to the
metrics of long poems based on personal experience, which are infrequent
in the *Songes and Sonettes*. With both Turbervile and Gascoigne the
long poem is popular, and naturally we find the latter experimenting
with suitable stanza forms. Rhyme royal is used for "The Reporter" in
"Dan Bartholmew"; more popular is the "ballade," the six-line stanza of
a quatrain and couplet used in both a tetrameter and pentameter line.
Two independently rhyming quatrains compose another stanza, while
the quatrain itself appears in varying line lengths. Gascoigne's unique
development of the eleven-line stanza, with varying line lengths, we have
noted above.

One poem written in this stanza form celebrates F. J.'s seduction of
Dame Elinor. Gascoigne, as the anonymous narrator, makes this comment on the poem: "This Ballade, or howsoever I shall terme it, percase
you will not like, and yet in my judgement it hath great good store of
deepe invention."[126] The invention, upon which it will be remembered
Gascoigne insisted every poem should be grounded, is indeed "deepe."
Phoebus, jealous of the lady's beauty and seeking by all possible means to
"staine hir name," finally conceived the dastardly plot of casting his
"parching beames" into her eyes. Thus potential suitors received a severe
case of sunburn, since the eyes of the lady were the source of beauty's

---

[124] *Works*, I, 333. No. 24. The influence of medieval allegory is obvious, but I shall confine
consideration of such elements in Gascoigne to the section which will deal with Gascoigne,
the moralist. The medieval element in the love poems is slight and is also a part of the Italian
tradition; so I do not feel it belongs in the present discussion. Equally irrelevant are the narratives of *The Mirror for Magistrates*, which are medieval and objective. With Gascoigne the
emphasis in narration is on the individuality of the author. Events are important as they affect
the hero. This is truer of "F.J." than of "Dan Bartholmew."

[125] *Works*, I, 52. No. 50.   [126] *A Hundreth Sundrie Flowres*, p. 238.

beams which entered the lover's eyes and, penetrating to the heart, kindled the coals of love's fire. Phoebus's stratagem all but succeeded, and only the poet's understanding of its subtleties prevented the complete ruin of the lady's reputation. Waiting until Phoebus had retired for the night, Gascoigne then gazed upon his lady and found "no parching heat at all." Dame Cynthia, contrary to her brother's behavior, showed the lady in all her beauty, and, overpowered by the sight, shrank aside to give way to the darkness which was proper for the ensuing seduction.

This type of elaborate conceit is indicative of the second achievement which Puttenham praised in the work of Wyatt and Surrey—the polishing of style, which is what Gascoigne means by "invention." The conceited style finds an easy source in Petrarch,[127] and by this I do not mean to disregard the early labors of the Provençal poets nor of Petrarch's immediate predecessors, Guinicelli, Cavalcanti, and Pistoia, nor of the flood tide of Petrarch's imitators. Their work has been discussed many times;[128] but for our purposes it is enough to realize that Petrarch best expressed to his countrymen and succeeding generations of foreigners the essence of love's nature, potentialities, and language, and it is for that reason that he has become a symbol of the poetry of Neoplatonic love. He does not achieve the complete spirituality of Dante's concepts; many times the physical beauty of Laura and his longing for her cry out with a human not a divine voice, and yet the very *raison d'être* of the *Rime* is the spiritual concept of love. In Petrarch the conscious artist wrestled with the philosopher and both at times won, but neither could achieve a complete victory. With his successors, artistry of metaphysical subtlety was complete victor, and the thoroughgoing exploitation of the conceited style was under way. This was the style that quite intoxicated the French and English "barbarians," who came over the Alps and down into a fabulous land of Roman ruins, classical learning, opulent civilization, and poetry. Once again men were infatuated with the picturesque, not the essential. Petrarch's "Passa la nave mia" so appealed to Wyatt that he rendered it in English.

> My galley charged with forgetfulnesse,
> Through sharpe seas, in winter nightes doth passe,
> Twene rocke, and rocke: and eke my fo (alas)
> That is my lord, stereth with cruelnesse:

[127] Dr. Tillyard's admonition in this respect (*op. cit.,* p. 23) is most just.
[128] *Cf.* my references, *supra,* pp. 101, 107, 108.

And every houre, a thought in readinesse,
As though that death were light, in such a case.
An endlesse wynd doth teare the sayle apace
Of forced sighes, and trusty fearfulnesse.
A rayne of teares, a clowde of darke disdayne
Have done the weried coardes great hinderance,
Wrethed with errour, and wyth ignorance.
The starres be hidde, that leade me to this payne.
Drownde is reason that should be my comfort:
And I remayne, dispearyng of the port.[129]

This type of writing, which had a strong appeal for Wyatt, Surrey, Vaux, Grimald, and the other courtly makers of the first half of the century, was for Googe, Turbervile, Gascoigne, and their fellows the very essence of poetry. Wyatt could abandon the inventions and conceits to write:

Forget not yet the tried intent
Of such a truth as I have meant;
My great travail so gladly spent
Forget not yet![130]

Surrey, though dealing largely in the jargon of love, did write "so crewell prison!" and an unknown poet cried with a passion that will always last:

Western wind, when will thou blow,
The small rain down can rain?
Christ, if my love were in my arms
And I in my bed again![131]

But these were the rare poems; the unknown authors of *Songes and Sonettes* were the men who really understood poetry. If one conceit was good, ten were better! This was the guiding principle of Gascoigne and his contemporaries, and Gascoigne was chief among them. Googe translated and wrote eclogues, so his store of love poetry is small. Howell was, in his *Arbor of Amitie,* still close to schoolboy verse exercises on the themes of virtue and honesty, while Turbervile, though running Gascoigne a close second, let his classical studies reflect themselves in his verse and did not rival Gascoigne's versatility in the exploitation of conceits. Churchyard was essentially a pamphleteer, but was in accord with

[129] *Songes and Sonettes,* ed. by Arber, p. 39.
[130] Chambers, ed., *The Oxford Book of Sixteenth Century Verse,* p. 66.
[131] *Ibid.,* p. 40.

the tradition; while Whetstone is a complete reflection of his friend and master, Gascoigne.

The earliest poems included in *A Hundreth Sundrie Flowres* are those interpolated in "The Adventures of Master F. J.," as we learn from the editor's comment: "I have heard the Aucthor saye, that these were the first verses that ever he wrote uppon like occasion."[132] The poem to which this refers is that which I have quoted above concerning the inability of famous men to withstand the assaults of love. The same "invention" is expanded in another poem,[133] "When I record within my musing mind," where Holofernes and Ovid are added to David, Solomon, and Hercules of the first poem. King David's eyes are "bedimmd" with dew by the beauty of Bersabe, whose beams are obviously such that the eye is subject to great strain in passing them on to the heart. Solomon can erect no fortifications to withstand the assaults of Pharoah's daughter, who has entrapped him in "subtill snares." Even Ovid, learned in love's lore, was beguiled by Corinna. The more examples, the better poem!

The usual figures of antiquity appear in other poems, but they are stock figures. Typical is the poem in "F. J.," beginning "Beautie shut up thy shop,"[134] which is later expanded in "Dan Bartholmew's Triumph."[135] In the first, two inventions are employed, and both caused the author considerable trouble. The poet begins "ymagining that *Beautie* having a shop where she uttred hir wares of all sundry sortes, his Ladie had stollen the fynest away, leaving none behind hir, but paynting, bolstring, forcing and such like, the which in this rage he judgeth good ynough to serve the Courte."[136] This is followed by the proud boast that his lady is, as a result of her theft, more fair than Helen or Venus, and that he is willing to defend her beauty against Theseus, Paris, or Mars. The courtiers became angry with the first theme, while Dame Elinor, being unlearned, suspected him of having a secret affair with some Helen or other, in spite of his protests that his use of the diminutive "Nell" meant Elinor. The first invention appears later in the satires, while in "Dan Bartholmew's Triumph" the second is further developed. The poet challenges and then sympathizes with Theseus and Paris. They and Menelaus were all de-

---

[132] *A Hundreth Sundrie Flowres*, p. 207. [133] *Works*, I, 94. No. 46.
[134] *Works*, I, 414. "F.J." No. 8. [135] *Ibid.*, I, 100. "D.B." No. 2.
[136] *A Hundreth Sundrie Flowres*, p. 244.

ceived by a wanton girl. Likewise deceived, poor Troilus was betrayed by Cresside, who, incidentally, died a leper.[137] Though these two ladies were reputed beautiful, his lady is more chaste and more lovely than they. Cupid dare not look on her lest he be pierced by hir "blazing beames"; Venus goes in fear lest Mars, espying this bewitching mortal, desert her; and Juno has grave concern that Jove, seeing the lady, may "melt in drops of gold." To this profusion of epithets are added several rhetorical passages of parallel structure and a conclusion marked by the appearance of the lover as Petrarch's and Wyatt's ship.

The symbolic use of these figures of antiquity constantly changes to suit the particular invention. Venus may represent beauty, Vulcan's faithless wife, or the woman married to an unsuitable husband. Menelaus is the daring instigator of the Trojan War or else a rather stupid man deceived by a wanton. Mars is useful for almost any situation.

Figures involving famous persons are, however, of small moment in comparison with the limitless world of metaphor that is revealed in the following poem:

> The straightest tree that growes upon one only roote:
> If that roote fayle, will quickly fade, no props can do it boote.
> I am that fading plant, which on thy grace did growe.
> Thy grace is gone wherefore I mone, and wither all in woe.
> The tallest ship that sayles, if shee to Ancors trust:
> When ancors slip and cables breake, hir helpe lyes in the dust.
> I am the ship my selfe, myne Ancor was thy faith:
> Which now is fled, thy promise broke, and I am driven to death.
> Who clymeth oft on hie, and trusts the rotten bowe:
> If that bowe break may catch a fall such state stand I in now.
> Me thought I was aloft, and yit my seate full sure:
> Thy hart did seeme to me a rock which ever might endure.
> And see, it was but sand, whom seas of subtiltie:
> Have soked so with wanton waves, that faith was forst to flye.
> The Fluds of ficklenesse have undermyned so,
> The first foundation of my joy, that myrth is ebb'd to wo.
> Yit at lowe water markes, I lye and wayte my time:
> To mend the breach, but all in vayn, it cannot passe the prime.
> For when the primeflud comes which all this rage begon:
> Then waves of will do work so fast, my piles are over ron .
> Dutie and diligence which are my workmen there,

---

[137] This is an interesting reference to the detail found first in Henryson's *Testament of Cresseid*, which was printed in Thynne's *Chaucer* of 1532.

Are glad to take up tooles in haste and run away for feare.
For fancie hath such force, it overfloweth all:
And whispring tales do blow the blasts that make it ryse and fall.
Thus in theis tempests tost, my restles life doth stand:
Because I builded on thy words, as I was borne in hand.
Thou weart that onely stake, wherby I ment to stay:
Alas, alas, thou stoodst so weake, the hedge is borne away.
By thee I thought to live, by thee now must I dye:
I made thee my Phisicion, thou art my mallady.
For thee I longd to live, for thee now welcome death:
And welcome be that happie pang, that stops my gasping breath.
Twice happie were that axe, would cut my rootes down right:
And sacred were that swelling sea, which would consume me quight.
Blest were that bowe would break to bring downe clyming youth,
  Which craks aloft, and quakes full oft, for feare of thine untruth.[138]

The lover is successively a plant, a ship, a tree climber, and a dike; he can, in these guises, be destroyed by an axe, a swelling sea, a broken bough, and a prime flood. Both "fickleness" and "fansie" are a swelling sea. To metaphor is added antithesis: the lady is both his "Phisicion" and his disease. Elsewhere, the lover freezes in fire, swims in bliss amid his bale, and delights in that which hurts him most. All this is seasoned with a plentiful dash of alliteration, and the result is the mélange that was fashionable court poetry.

However much the reading of this type of poetry may overwhelm us, we must not forget that it once was popular. From the perspective of today we might say that there was a dearth of poetic creation between Surrey and Spenser, but to do so is to ignore the fact that Gascoigne, Turbervile, Googe, Howell, Churchyard, and a number of lesser men were standardizing the forms of English verse and were carrying one type of the conceited style to its logical and absurd conclusion. The subtleties of the conceits which Gascoigne employed were the obvious subtleties—the piling up of the various analogies which could be related to a rather simple idea—but the method which he established is the method of Elizabethan poetry. Let us consider for a moment one of Shakespeare's sonnets:

> That time of year thou mayst in me behold
> When yellow leaves, or none, or few do hang
> Upon those boughs which shake against the cold,

---

[138] *Works,* I, 90. No. 30.

Bare ruin'd choirs where late the sweet birds sang.
In me thou see'st the twilight of such day
As after sunset fadeth in the west,
Which by and by black night doth take away,
Death's second self, that seals up all in rest.
In me thou see'st the glowing of such fire
That on the ashes of his youth doth lie
As the death-bed whereon it must expire,
Consum'd with that which it was nourish'd by
 This thou perceiv'st, which makes thy love more strong,
 To love that well which thou must leave ere long.[139]

The method is that of variations on a commonplace theme. Greatness lies in the perception of the analogies and in the movement of the verse. The connotation of the figures comes not from an industrious pilfering of trite conceits; its source is the mind of the poet, which sees the essential that is picturesque. But such observation came not full sprung from Jove's brow; one need only look at the sonnet "When forty winters shall besiege thy brow" to see an example of apprentice work that resembles in kind Gascoigne's description of himself in "Dan Bartholmew."

The conceited style in poetry was carried on by Watson, who plagiarized Gascoigne, and by Whetstone. Finally Lyly achieved in *Euphues* the apogee of fashionable prose. Sidney admired classical Senecan tragedy. All these means of expression had their brief hour and they had certain results. The verse of the middle years of the century exhausted the accumulation of trite imagery, but its method continued. *Euphues* was laughed out of court, but English prose had acquired form. The tragedy of Seneca helped to create *The Spanish Tragedy*. The polishing and reforming of Wyatt and Surrey continued, and a realization of the continuity of that work may help us to appreciate the larger values of the poems of George Gascoigne.

---

[139] Sonnet LXXIII.

VI. The Dramatist

A fine Comedie: & a statelie Tragedie
HARVEY

IN HIS POETRY, Gascoigne continued the work of his predecessors and also contributed not a little to the growing tradition of English verse. In his dramatic work we find a similar inspiration, derived from the past, coupled with an individual ability that explored new aspects of the drama and at the same time laid the foundations of the new manner of expression. His translation of Lodovico Dolce's Italian version of *The Phoenissae* of Euripides certainly owed much to the dramatic tradition of the Inns of Court, that had already seen *Gorboduc* on the boards and Seneca's tragedies translated into English. Latin comedies were no novelty in England, but *The Supposes* was in the vernacular and, being based on Ariosto's imitation of Roman Comedy, it acclimatized the model. The masque for the Montague-Dormer marriage is closely related in form to the traditional entertainments, while the "shewes" devised for the Queen at Kenilworth and Woodstock are conventional aspects of Elizabethan pageantry. Gascoigne's most original dramatic work, *The Glasse of Government,* an imitation of the Dutch prodigal-son plays, was in a form little favored in England, and we may better understand its composition if we relate it to the poet's life. Since these various works pose different problems, it has seemed well in considering them to use a sectional scheme that follows an approximate chronology.

JOCASTA

As we have seen in the preceding chapter, poetry based on Italian models flourished in court circles. Such verse was both new and fashionable. Members of the court, being the leaders of the social world, were naturally interested in all aspects of *le dernier cri*. Importations from Italy, such as forks and fantastic styles in clothes, were received with enthusiasm, and exceptional hospitality was extended to Italy's poetry. As courtiers they realized that a few choice lines, feverishly penned on a transitory bit of paper, increased the likelihood of amorous intrigue. Though paid underlings provided plays, masques, and pageants, gentlemen could and did write poetry without loss of prestige. This sharp cleavage between the propriety of different types of literary creation may be partly explained by the purposes of each. Fashionable verse was not designed for publication: it was directed to a particular person and might, if not too revealing, be read by members of the court circle. On the other hand, Richard Edwards, Sebastian Westcott, John Lyly, and the members of the Revels Office earned their livings by purveying entertainment to the court. Such men, however respectable, could not enjoy a high social position at court. Gascoigne's[1] earnest protestation that he neither desired nor received monetary rewards for his publication is contributory evidence of the social inferiority of professional authors.

Fortunately for the subsequent development of Elizabethan literature, this courtly stereotype had one considerable exception, namely the Inns of Court. There gentlemen interested in literature as an avocation produced plays, translations, and original works in prose and verse and provided a nucleus of literary life. The list of "Minervaes Men" given by Heywood in the preface to his translation of Seneca's *Thyestes* has been examined and extended by Dr. C. H. Conley, whose study, *The First English Translators of the Classics,*[2] is most valuable in its presentation of the literary activity which, during the early years of Elizabeth's reign, centered in the Inns of Court. Statesmen like Cecil, Sir Nicholas Bacon, and Leicester were associated with the Inns, while literary men such as Sir Thomas North, Thomas Sackville, Lord Buckhurst, and Sir Christopher Yelverton held positions of authority. As Dr. Conley indicates, the Inns of Court were far more centers of literary and political activity than training schools for lawyers.[3] More like finishing schools, the two Temples and the various Inns fostered the activities of young men who aimed at courtly advancement and found time to interest themselves in literature.

[1] *Works*, I, 4.
[2] The translators are discussed on pp. 20–30. The contact with the influential members of the government occupies pp. 37–41.
[3] *Ibid.*, pp. 35–37, 55–56, 95–100.

Thus when Gascoigne returned to Gray's Inn, he found himself in a milieu favorable to the extension of his literary activities. The dramatic heritage of the Inns was of long standing, and the success of *Gorboduc,* both at the Inner Temple[4] and at Whitehall,[5] must have been one of the reasons for the production of *Jocasta* at Gray's Inn sometime during 1566.[6] The universities could present tragedies in Latin,[7] but translation was popular with the young lawyers, whose politics, patriotism, and inclination favored the vernacular.

It is only in comparatively recent times that Dolce's *Giocasta* has been recognized as the source of Gascoigne's and Kinwelmarshe's translation.[8] This of course robs the play of one aspect of its importance as a translation directly from the Greek; but *Jocasta* remains, even though twice removed, the first hint of Greek tragedy in the English tongue.[9] We must not think, therefore, that the translators differed from their confreres of the Inns of Court and preferred Greek to Roman tragedy. To Gascoigne and Kinwelmarshe the principal charm of *Giocasta* probably lay in its close resemblance to the ideals of Seneca, with which they were familiar. In fact, both Dolce and his English translators found in Euripides the very qualities which they admired in Seneca and which Seneca had, in turn, imitated from Euripides. There was a certain similarity in nature between Euripides and Seneca:[10] each was the product of an ancient civilization, but both dramatists lived in a period of disintegration, when men looked only backward. The great days were over, and the Greek and the Roman

---

[4] At Christmas, 1561/2. [5] Jan. 18, 1562.

[6] The date is thus given on the title-leaf of the play. (*Works,* I, 244.)

[7] Some now-lost English plays were given, but one need only examine the list in Dr. Boas's *University Drama in the Tudor Age* (pp. 386–90), to realize the emphasis on Latin.

[8] J. P. Mahaffy, *Euripides (Classical Writers),* London 1879, pp. 134–35. Noted by Dr. Cunliffe in his edition of *Supposes and Jocasta* ("The Belles-Lettres Series," Boston, 1906, p. xxix). This edition has the Italian and English on opposite pages, and all subsequent references to both Dolce's *Giocasta* and Gascoigne's *Jocasta* are to this work.

[9] Cunliffe (*Jocasta,* p. xxix) was the first to note that Dolce based his text on the Latin version of Euripides, published at Basel by R. Winter in 1541. Dr. Cunliffe (*ibid.,* p. 126) also first pointed out that Kinwelmarshe and Gascoigne used the 1549 Aldine edition of Dolce.

[10] Since this is not the place for a lengthy examination of the sources and characteristics of Seneca, the ensuing discussion inevitably deals in generalities, which are, however, based on the following: Cunliffe, *The Influence of Seneca on Elizabethan Tragedy;* Lucas, *Seneca and Elizabethan Tragedy;* Eliot's Introduction to *Seneca His Tenne Tragedies,* ed. by Newton; and the Introduction of L. E. Kastner and H. B. Charlton to their *Poetical Works of Sir William Alexander, Earl of Stirling,* Manchester, 1921.

each found release from the realization of this inevitability in pathetic horrors and resplendent rhetoric. Euripides saw a world of cruelty and injustice against which he cried out; Seneca's recital of horrors gave new zest to jaded appetites; but whatever their specific motivations, both were generally impelled by decadence. "Second childishness" is noticeable in societies as well as in individuals: the tastes of a decadent social order are frequently analogous to those of a primitive group. Thus it was that the Elizabethans found pleasure, though perhaps from a healthier point of view, in the savagery, superficiality, and rhetoric of Euripides and Seneca. Those who could enjoy bear baiting could take pleasure in the meticulous Senecan account of cannibalistic banquets. The carefully etched rhetoric of Seneca possessed a surface glitter that was as joyfully accepted by the Elizabethans as are bright beads sparkling in the sunlight by primitive peoples today.

Indications of what Gascoigne and Kinwelmarshe found desirable in their translation are shown by their additions and elaborations. First, perhaps, are the didactic elements, those passages which were considered worthy of marginal notation or of the double commas that point out sententious lines. Bailo's advice to Antigone at the end of Act I is definitely important, with its double commas and its marginal notation "A glasse for yong women."[11] In Dolce,[12] Bailo tells Antigone to return to the palace, primarily as a means of ending the scene, but lest this seem too obvious he adds eight lines on the necessity for young girls to avoid being seen in public places, since the vulgar herd is always ready to ruin a reputation. These lines Kinwelmarshe translates fairly closely, but he adds the following eight original lines.

> „You cannot be to curious of your name:
> „Fond shewe of evill (though still the minde be chast)
> „Decayes the credite oft that ladies had
> „Sometimes the place presumes a wanton mynde:
> „Repayre sometymes of some doth hurt their honor:
> „Sometimes the light and garishe proud attire
> „Persuades a yelding bent of pleasant youthes.[13]

Such an interpolation is singularly out of place at the end of the scene, where it disturbs the continuity of action and mood. Kinwelmarshe

[11] Cunliffe, *op. cit.*, pp. 175, 177, ll. 172–92.
[12] *Ibid.*, pp. 174, 176, ll. 159–71.   [13] *Ibid.*, p. 177, ll. 181–87.

evidently thought, however, that the purposes of moral instruction were more important than dramatic effectiveness—if indeed he thought of this latter. Another "glosse" is found near the end of Act V, beside Oedipus's reflectión on the change in his estate from high to low degree. The marginal annotation, "A glasse for brittel beutie and for lusty limmes,"[14] reminds us of the frequency of this idea, found in its most popular form in Petrarch's *De Remediis Utriusque Fortunae*.[15] The vagaries of Fortune are emphasized in Oedipus's last speech which bears the seemingly topical notation, "A mirrour for magistrates."[16] Other marginal "glosses" are of the same general type with such "wise saws" as "Exile an exceding griefe to an honest mynde";[17] "Few frends in miserye";[18] "Sundrye men sundry minds";[19] "Content is riche";[20] "Age must be helped by youth";[21] "A thankles office to foretell a mischiefe";[22] "Death (indeed) yeldeth more pleasure than lyfe";[23] "No greater honor than to dye for thy countrey";[24] "We harken sometimes willingly to wofull news";[25] and the laconic "Justice sleepeth."[26]

These are, of course, commonplaces, but the sententious remark was dear to the Elizabethans, who were learning from the classics that such things could be cleverly expressed, and eloquence in the production of maxims was highly esteemed both in Italy and England.[27] Indeed, one of the reasons for translating Dolce's *Giocasta* probably lay in the diversity of sentiments which it contained. *The Phoenissae* was the longest of Euripides's tragedies and is very near in its scope to the regular trilogy.[28] Haigh's comment[29] that it was one of the three plays read in the Byzantine period indicates only too well that its fame rested largely on "the beauty and variety of its sentiments." Oedipus's ruin is dwelt on at length by nearly all the characters; Eteocles's deprivation of his brother affords the opportunity for reflection on pride and arrogance; the wanderings of Polynices mirror the harsh fate of exiles; Jocasta is torn by a love for both

---

[14] *Ibid.*, p. 409, ll. 200–209.
[15] Imitated by Gascoigne in *The Grief of Joye* (*Works*, II, 511–57).
[16] Cunliffe, *op. cit.*, p. 413, ll. 240–42.   [17] *Ibid.*, p. 201, ll. 146–47.
[18] *Ibid.*, p. 203, ll. 176–77.   [19] *Ibid.*, p. 221, ll. 350–52.   [20] *Ibid.*, p. 229, ll. 447–48.
[21] *Ibid.*, p. 273, ll. 18–19.   [22] *Ibid.*, p. 293, ll. 220–22.   [23] *Ibid.*, p. 295, ll. 15–17.
[24] *Ibid.*, p. 295, ll. 7–8.   [25] *Ibid.*, p. 363, ll. 31–32.   [26] *Ibid.*, p. 409, l. 197.
[27] Cf. Lucas, *op. cit.*, pp. 54–55.
[28] Cf. Gilbert Murray, *Euripides and His Age*, "Home University Library," pp. 148–52.
[29] *The Tragic Drama of the Greeks*, Oxford, 1925, p. 311.

her sons which culminates in a threefold death; while the reception accorded soothsayers, sacrifice for one's country, and finally duty toward the dead round out a full measure of topics for sententious reflection. Here, indeed, was all the subject matter that anyone could desire, and the translators lost few opportunities to indulge themselves.

Kinwelmarshe handles his material more freely than does Gascoigne, but both follow the same general method of paraphrase and expansion. One of the best examples of Kinwelmarshe's method occurs in the second scene of Act I, where a servant, confidant of Jocasta, indulges in a monologue. I shall give both the Italian original and the English translation:

> *Servo*. Color che i seggi e le reali altezze
> Ammiran tanto veggono con l' occhio
> L' adombrato splendor ch' appar di fuori,
> Scettri, gemme, corone, aurati panni;
> Ma non veggon dappoi con l' intelletto
> Le penose fatiche, e i gravi affanni,
> Le cure, e le molestie, a mille a mille,
> Che di dentro celate e ascose stanno.
> Non san che, come il vento e le saette
> Percuoton sempre le maggiori altezze,
> Così lo stral della fortuna ingiusta
> Fere più l' uom, quanto più in alto il trova.
> Ecco: Edìpo pur dianzi era Signore
> Di noi Tebani, e di sì bel dominio
> Stringea superbo, et allentava il freno.[30]

> [Servus] „The simple man, whose mervaile is so great
> „At stately courts and princes regall seate,
> „With gasing eye but onely doth regarde
> „The golden glosse that outwardly appeares,
> „The crownes bedeckt with pearle and precious stones,
> „The riche attire imbost with beaten golde,
> „The glittering mace, the pompe of swarming traine,
> „The mightie halles heapt full of flattering frendes,
> „The chambers huge, the goodly gorgeous beddes,
> „The gilted roofes embowde with curious worke,
> „The faces sweete of fine disdayning dames,
> „The vaine suppose of wanton raigne at luste—
> „But never viewes with eye of inward thought

---

[30] Cunliffe, *op. cit.*, pp. 156, 158, ll. 1–15.

„The painefull toile, the great and grevous cares,
„The troubles still, the newe increasing feares
„That princes nourish in their jealous brestes:
„He wayeth not the charge that Jove hath laid
„On princes, how for themselves they raigne not:
„He weenes the law must stoope to princely will,
„But princes frame their noble wills to lawe:
„He knoweth not that as the boystrous winde
„Doth shake the toppes of highest-reared towres,
„So doth the force of frowarde fortune strike
„The wight that highest sits in haughtie state.
  Lo, Oedipus, that sometime raigned king
Of Thebane soyle, that wonted to suppresse
The mightest prince, and kepe him under checke.[31]

The English version of this soliloquy owes its inspiration to the Italian, where the commonplace is briefly stated. There is a great disparity between the outward show and the inner reality of the court, but where Dolce is content with "scettri, gemme, corone, aurati panni," the English poet must put Pegasus through his paces: the crown is "bedeckt with pearle and precious stone," and we are shown further details of the court, where "the glittering mace," "the mightie halles," "the chambers huge," and "gilted roofes" are a setting for "flattering frendes" and "disdayning dames." The appeal of this lies not only in the sententious but also in the rhetorical. Eight successive lines have the same beginning of article, adjective, and substantive. Details are embroidered, and the well-satisfied author, surveying his work, appends the marginal notation "The courte lively painted." That was precisely what he had set out to do and precisely what his audience would enjoy. When men gave free reign to resplendent diction which they could express within an exact metrical pattern and within a conscious style, the English language was coming of age. There was still a long road to travel before blank verse achieved fluidity, but the essential elements are here. A detail which was to become a dominant characteristic of Elizabethan imagery is also found in this speech. The Italian "Ma non veggon dappoi con l'intelletto le penose fatiche" is rendered "But never viewes with eye of inward thought the painefull toile." "L' intelletto" becomes the "eye of inward thought" and we see the beginning of that metaphorical personification which is per-

---

[31] *Ibid.*, pp. 157, 159, ll. 1–27.

haps one of the sources of "the infinite riches in a little room" that we find in such lines as "Tomorrow, and tomorrow, and tomorrow."

Examples could be multiplied, and it is, indeed, a revelation of conscious art to compare, line for line, the original and the translation. Through such a comparison one may clearly realize that the translators were among the principal establishers of English rhetorical devices, certain phases of imagery, and the use of the realistic detail. But all is not "a golden glosse that outwardly appears;" for Kinwelmarshe, particularly in his very free paraphrases of the choral finales, falls into trite bombast which quite robs these passages of their original effectiveness. For example, we may compare the following stanza of the fourth-act chorus, where he expands three lines of the Italian into a rhyme royal stanza:

> Tu sola sei cagion ch' a Primavera
> Nascano erbette e fiori,
> E vada estate de' suoi frutti carca.[32]

> When tract of time returnes the lustie Ver,
> By thee alone the buddes and blossomes spring,
> The fieldes with floures be garnisht every where,
> The blooming trees aboundant fruite do bring,
> The cherefull birds melodiously do sing.
> Thou dost appoint the crop of sommers seede
> For mans reliefe to serve the winters neede.[33]

Kinwelmarshe knew that the medieval apostrophe to spring was held in high esteem; therefore, since opportunity offered, why not drag it in?

In contrast with his collaborator, Gascoigne reveals a much clearer sense of the fitness of things and in general makes good use of the better features of the Italian, as may be seen in the following comparison of the choral finales of Act II:

> Fero, e dannoso Dio,
> Che sol di sangue godi,
> E volgi spesso sottosopra il mondo;
> Perchè, crudele e rio,
> Turbi la pace, et odi
> Lo stato altrui tranquil, lieto, e giocondo?
> Perchè, empio e furibondo,
> Col ferro urti e percuoti

---

[32] *Ibid.*, p. 348, ll. 27–29. [33] *Ibid.*, p. 349, ll. 22–28.

La Cittade innocente
Di quel giusto e possente
Dio che n' ingombra il cor de' suoi divoti
Di contento e di gioia,
E scaccia di quaggiù tormento e noia? [34]

O fierce and furious Mars, whose harmefull harte
Rejoyceth most to shed the giltlesse blood,
Whose headie wil doth all the world subvert,
And doth envie the pleasant mery moode
Of our estate, that erst in quiet stoode,
Why doest thou thus our harmelesse towne annoye,
Which mightie Bacchus governed in joye? [35]

Gascoigne has kept closely to the original, but by wise omission has produced a well-knit stanza. The change of subject from "Dio" to "harte" is
a felicitous example of the effectiveness gained by metaphorical personification. Likewise the line "Whose headie wil doth all the world subvert"
has a connotation that does not exist in "E volgi spesso sottosopra il
mondo."

This same chorus contains an expansion very significant to one familiar
with Seneca. Dolce's second stanza reads in part:

Rivolgi, Marte, altrove
Le sanguinose prove
Dell' asta tua, con cui risvegli e desti
L' empie furie d' Averno,
Per far dell' alme altrui ricco l' inferno.[36]

Gascoigne employs an entire stanza to paraphrase these five short lines:

And thou maist prove some other way full well
The bloudie prowesse of thy mightie speare,
Wherwith thou raisest from the depth of hell
The wrathfull sprites of all the furies there
Who, when [they wake], doe wander everywhere,
And never rest to range about the coastes,
Tenriche that pit with spoile of damned ghostes.[37]

The infernal regions were one of Seneca's great resources, along with
sundry ghosts. The Stygian realm was always worthy of considerable
emphasis, since its horrors could be easily exploited. Tantalus's ghost

---

[34] *Ibid.*, p. 262, ll. 1–13.   [35] *Ibid.*, p. 263, ll. 1–7.
[36] *Ibid.*, p. 264, ll. 22–26.   [37] *Ibid.*, p. 265, ll. 15–21.

dwells at length on his sufferings and on those of Sisyphus and Tytius,[38] while the shade of Thyestes describes the "Stygion porter" and other denizens of "Plutoes pyts."[39] Hercules's presence in hell affrights the resident ghosts as well as Cerberus.[40] Thus it is not to be wondered that the young lawyer of Gray's Inn should include a passing reference to this region[41] that had already become topical through the translations of *Agamemnon, Hercules Furens, Oedipus, Thyestes,* and the *Troas,* all done before 1566 by fellow members of the Inns of Court.[42]

This particular expansion may thus owe its inspiration to external sources, but the same chorus contains yet another addition which, I think, sprang from the poet's mind and which is similar to the extensions noted in Kinwelmarshe. Dolce's third stanza contains a reference to both discord and peace. The first six lines read as follows:

> Teco ne venga ancora,
> Lasciando i nostri campi,
> Cinta di Serpi la discordia fiera,
> Che fa che ad ora ad ora
> Dell' uman sangue stampi
> La terra, e 'l buono indegnamente pera.[43]

These are translated by Gascoigne:

> And when thou hast our fieldes forsaken thus,
> Let cruell discorde beare thee companie,
> Engirt with snakes and serpents venemous,
> Even she that can with red virmilion dye
> The gladsome greene that florisht pleasantly,
> And make the greedie ground a drinking cup
> To sup the bloud of murdered bodyes up.[44]

---

[38] *Seneca His Tenne Tragedies,* ed. by Newton, I, 55.

[39] *Ibid.,* II, 101, 102   [40] *Ibid.,* I, 10, 11.

[41] An addition made by Gascoigne is found in Act V, scene 2, where the Italian (Cunliffe, *op. cit.,* p. 374, l. 168) reads:
"Or, mentre ambi n' andremo ai Regni Stigi,"
and the English (p. 375, ll. 163–64):
"But since these ghostes of ours must needes go downe"
"With staggring steppes into the Stigian reigne."
Obviously it was necessary to point out that ghosts there journeyed and that their steps were "staggering."

[42] John Studley's *Agamemnon* was entered in 1565/6. Jasper Heywood's *Hercules Furens* was printed in 1561, his *Thyestes* in 1560, and the *Troas* in 1559. Alexander Neville's *Oedipus* bears the date of translation as 1560.

[43] Cunliffe, *op. cit.,* p. 264, ll. 27–32.   [44] *Ibid.,* p. 265, ll. 22–28.

Perhaps the "gladsome greene" dyed with "red virmilion" and the "greedie ground a drinking cup" are too, too much, but the figures are pictorial, vivid, and exact. The visual imagination is called into play, and the resultant effectiveness is close indeed to

> No more the thirsty entrance of this soil
> Shall daub her lips with her own children's blood.[45]

In both is the same contrast between earth, the begetter of life, and earth, the consumer of all things mortal.

The desire for rhetorical elaboration, or the desire to express more completely and more exactly the idea of the Italian may have been the motives for this addition; but why and how Gascoigne's mind produced these figures is merely one facet of the everlasting problem whose solution would reveal the very bases of poetic imagination. Miss Spurgeon's remarkable examination of Shakespeare's imagery[46] suggests the source, but one wonders if there can ever be an explanation of that lightning flash of perception when the poet's mind sees "similitude in dissimilitude."

One example of a similar type of imagery, where the original supplies more of a clue to the nature of the translation, is found in the lines:

> Or col suo fele t' avvelena tanto,
> Che l' intelletto infermo è fatto cieco
> Al proprio ben: ma tu la scaccia, o figlio.[47]

which Gascoigne renders thus:

> And now even thee hir gall so poisoned hath
> That the weake eies of thine affection
> Are blinded quite, and see not to them selfe.[48]

"Cieco," of course, gives the original impetus, but Gascoigne develops this by personifying affection and giving the personification eyes which are blind not to their own good (Al proprio ben) but to themselves. The English version thus not only contains a fuller yet more compressed meaning, but also its metaphorical nature conveys a more clear and vivid picture to the reader or listener.

In this creative paraphrasing Gascoigne is more skillful than his collab-

---

[45] *I Henry IV*, Act I, scene 1, 5–6. Cf. *Romeo and Juliet*, Act II, scene 3, ll. 9–10.
[46] F. E. Spurgeon, *Shakespeare's Imagery and What It Tells Us*, Cambridge, 1935.
[47] Cunliffe, *op. cit.*, p. 224, ll. 384–86. [48] *Ibid.*, p. 225, ll. 410–12.

orator. Kinwelmarshe devoted his energies more to the addition of rhetorical interpolations and vivid details than to the creation of imagery. On practically every page of Acts II, III, and V (those done by Gascoigne) we can find instances of such imagery, and, since they foreshadow so closely one of the main characteristics of later verse, it seems well to give a few more examples.

> Onde cosa non è stabile e ferma;
> Ma suol cangiarsi col girar dell' ore.[49]

> „There nothing is so firme and stayde to man
> „But whyrles about with wheeles of restlesse time.[50]

> E l' uno e l' altro sanguinoso diede
> Agli Argivi, e ai Teban spettacol fiero.[51]

> From both whose breasts the bloud fast bubling gave
> A sory shewe to Greekes and Thebanes both.[52]

> Ma in vece di parole fuor per gli occhi
> Gli uscir alcune lagrime. . . .[53]

> And in [the] steade of sweete contenting words
> The trickling teares raynde downe his paled chekes.[54]

> O crudel mio destin, ben fatto m' hai
> Nascer alle miserie e alle fatiche
> Di questa morte che si chiama vita, . . .[55]

> O foule accursed fate, that hast me bredde
> To beare the burthen of the miserie
> Of this colde deathe, which we accompt for life![56]

In several of these quotations the interpolation of a single adjective adds much to the meaning, as for example "trickling teares" and "colde deathe." As we have noted in connection with Kinwelmarshe, the extra word is often added to fill out the pentameter line, but that does not invalidate its effectiveness. The adjective in the line "For plenteousnesse is but a naked name"[57] changes a bare statement into a pregnant meta-phor. The Italian, "O misera Giocasta,"[58] becomes far better as "O

---

[49] *Ibid.*, p. 228, ll. 427–28.   [50] *Ibid.*, p. 229, ll. 459–60.
[51] *Ibid.*, p. 370, ll. 118–19.   [52] *Ibid.*, p. 371, ll. 113–14.
[53] *Ibid.*, p. 372, ll. 154–55.   [54] *Ibid.*, p. 373, ll. 149–50.
[55] *Ibid.*, p. 390, ll. 25–27.   [56] *Ibid.*, p. 391, ll. 25–27.
[57] *Ibid.*, p. 229, l. 448.   [58] *Ibid.*, p. 362, l. 28.

Jocasta, miserable mother."[59] The messenger has just told of the Queen's suicide over the slain bodies of her sons, and Gascoigne's version suggests the whole tragedy of incest and fraternal war when he emphasizes Jocasta, the mother.

Such dramatic effectiveness is by no means accidental, for we find several instances of a similar nature where Gascoigne is the conscious dramatist, changing his original for a very real purpose. The third scene of Act V is an excellent case in point. Antigone, alone, laments the threefold death of her mother and brothers. Her first speech is concerned with the Queen, her mother, and in the Italian her second speech begins thus:

> Madre, perduto io v' ho, perduto insieme
> Ho i miei cari fratelli.
> O Polinice mio, tu col tuo sangue...[60]

Gascoigne omits the first two lines and begins with her direct address to Polinices.[61] Since the rest of her soliloquy is concerned with her grief on losing this particular brother, it seems clear that the omission was made both to preserve the unity of the speech and to give a dramatic opening with the initial two lines. The audience or reader has no need to be reminded that Antigone has lost her mother and two brothers, since the whole affair has been repeatedly described. In the very next scene four successive short speeches by Oedipus and Antigone are omitted, as it seems to me, for a similar reason. I quote the Italian so that the reader may see the repetition which they contain.

> *Edip.* Oimé, oimé.
> *Ant.*   E che piangete voi?
> *Edip.* I miei figliuoli io piango.
> *Ant.* Più piangereste, o padre,
> Se gli vedeste innanzi
> Pallidi e sanguinosi.[62]

These add nothing either to the narrative or the mood. Antigone has already told her father of the tragedy, and he has already lamented. Further lamentation is weakly redundant.

---

[59] *Ibid.*, p. 363, l. 25. [60] *Ibid.*, p. 380, ll. 26–28.
[61] *Ibid.*, p. 381, l. 22. [62] *Ibid.*, p. 386, ll. 33–38.

A similar elimination of a useless speech is found at the beginning of Act V, scene 2, where Dolce reads as follows:

> *Nuncio.* Misero me, che dir debb' io? quai voci,
> Quai parole formar?
>   *Creonte.*   Principio tristo.
> *Nun.* Misero me, misero me più volte.
> Nuncio di crudeltà, nuncio di morte.
>   *Cre.* Appresso l' altro mal che male apporti? [63]

The English:

> [*Nuncius*] Alas, alas! what shall I doe? alas!
> What shriching voyce may serve my wofull wordes?
> O wretched I, ten thousande times a wretch,
> The messanger of dread and cruell death!
>   *Creon.* Yet more mishap? and what unhappie newes? [64]

Certainly Creon's "Principio tristo" is both weak and out of place. By combining the messenger's two speeches, Gascoigne has Creon's first inquiry the logical one, "Yet more mishap? and what unhappie newes?"

During the debate between Eteocles and Polinices in Act II occurs a speech which Dr. Cunliffe regards as a mistranslation,[65] but which seems to me another example of Gascoigne's conscious alteration of the original for dramatic reasons. It is, I think, necessary to consider the following speech as well:

> *Pol.* Il cauto Capitan sempre è migliore
> Del temerario, e tu, più che ciascuno,
> Vile, ignorante, e temerario sei.
>   *Eteo.* Polinice, la tregua t' assecura
> A formar tai parole: . . .[66]

> *Pol.* For well I wist that cankred heart of thine
> Coulde safely kepe thy heade within these walles,
> And flee the fielde when combate should be callde.
>   *Eteo.* This truce assureth thee, Polynices,
> And makes thee bolde to give such bosting wordes: . . .[67]

If Polinices is to jeer at his brother in words strong enough to provoke the other to threaten immediate death were it not for the truce, he would hardly call Eteocles merely "rash" (temerario). Stronger words were

---

[63] *Ibid.,* pp. 358, 360, ll. 1–5.
[64] *Ibid.,* pp. 359, 361, ll. 1–5.
[65] "Notes to Jocasta," *ibid.,* p. 424.
[66] *Ibid.,* pp. 236, 238, ll. 500–504.
[67] *Ibid.,* pp. 237, 239, ll. 534–38.

needed and Gascoigne supplied them. The accusation of cowardice is sufficient to provoke the retort but "temerario," never!

The preceding discussion may, I trust, have made it clear that *Jocasta* is important not only as the second example of dramatic blank verse in English and as the first pale figure of Greek tragedy on the English stage, but also as a translation that evoked the abilities of its English authors. They were not translating as a mere exercise: they were seriously concerned with the best possible production of an English version of a Greek play, to be presented before their fellow members of Gray's Inn. Both their interests and those of their audience lay in sententious maxims, epigrams, resplendent language, and the gory details of struggle, slaughter, and suicide. To satisfy these tastes, they chose a play which dealt with a variety of human tribulations and a deal of carnage. In the longest play by Euripides, Seneca's master, they found what they desired, and an Italian translation of a Latin version of that play made the problem of translation easy for them. Kinwelmarshe best expressed himself in the elaboration of his original and in the use of an imagery that became a dominant characteristic of later English verse. Gascoigne, though following his text more closely, gave to his translation distinctive touches not far removed from genius. He, too, dealt in couplet epigrams, resplendent diction, parallelism, and other rhetorical devices, but he achieved real greatness in the creation of memorable phrases based on metaphorical personification. Perhaps most important were his slight changes derived from the impulse to perfect the dramatic structure. Few though these are, they nevertheless indicate a mind that knew not only what it wanted, but also what was dramatically desirable.

STAGING

In the same year that Kinwelmarshe and Gascoigne were occupied in their translation of *Jocasta,* the latter busied himself in the translation of another Italian play—*Supposes*—this time a comedy by the "divine Ariosto," who, some years later, was the inspiration of Spenser's nine lost comedies. The year 1566[68] thus saw considerable dramatic activity at Gray's Inn, but unfortunately we have no means, at present, of knowing

---

[68] The date of the *Supposes* is known from the title-page as found in *A Hundreth Sundrie Flowres* (Cunliffe, *Supposes and Jocasta, op. cit.,* p. 3; *Works,* I, 187).

the exact date when the *Supposes* and *Jocasta* were presented nor what methods of staging were employed. The plays, however, supply certain clues, and we learn "that there were in *Thebes* foure principall gates, whereof the chief and most commonly used were the gates called *Electrae* and *Homoloydes.*"[69] Frequent stage directions, not found in the original, indicate entrances and exits made through these two gates: *"Eteocles commeth in here by the gates Electrae"*;[70] *"Creon goeth out by the gates Homoloydes."*[71] In addition, Jocasta's palace was an integral part of the setting, as is shown by the conclusion of the first "dumme shewe."[72]

Jocasta the Queene issueth out of hir Pallace before hir twelve Gentlemen, following after hir eight Gentle women, whereof foure be the *Chorus* that remayne on the Stage after hir departure.[73]

The gates of her palace likewise formed a part of the setting, as is indicated by the following:

> ... the foure Chorus also follow hir to the gates of hir pallace.[74]

As Sir Edmund Chambers has pointed out, the raised stage was in use,[75] and Miss Campbell's careful and exact analysis makes it most likely that "the scaffold" was a proper stage and not that of the mystery and miracle plays.[76] As Chambers[77] has also suggested, the gates were probably labeled by large letters. The palace may have been merely a "case" or lath framework doorway so labeled, or it may have been a separate "house" behind the gates. The scene being "as it were in Thebes,"[78] the action is unified and continuous, and there may well have been some attempt to indicate the city by means of a painted curtain. Although this is pure conjecture, we can be certain of other mechanical aspects revealed in the dumb shows, imitated from the Italian customs of *entr'acte* shows or *intermedii.* Some sort of trapdoor arrangement was necessary for the second-act grave, where were buried the two coffins and whence arose the divided flame. The same trap was used for Curtius's "Gulfe." A chariot

---

[69] Cunliffe, *op. cit.,* p. 418. All references to both plays are to this edition.

[70] *Ibid.,* p. 209.   [71] *Ibid.,* p. 305.

[72] For a full discussion of the dumb show and its origin in the Italian *intermedii, vide* Cunliffe, *Early English Classical Tragedies,* pp. xxxix–xl.

[73] Cunliffe, ed., *Supposes and Jocasta,* p. 135, ll. 22–26.

[74] *Ibid.,* p. 155.

[75] Chambers, *The Elizabethan Stage,* III, 30.

[76] Campbell, *Scenes and Machines on the Elizabethan Stage,* pp. 94–96.

[77] *Op. cit.,* III, 30.   [78] Cunliffe, *op. cit.,* p. 133.

was used in two shows, and a "greate peale of ordinaunce," required in another, evidently had no such disastrous results as a somewhat later "peale" had in the Globe.

The *Supposes* evidently employed the conventional "houses,"[79] fairly elaborately constructed, since one stage direction reads:

Dalio commeth to the wyndowe, and there maketh them answere,[80]

and another:

Dalio draweth his hed in at the wyndowe, the Scenese commeth out.[81]

Likewise "dores" and "houses" are mentioned, so that it would seem that there were at least three distinct houses belonging to Damon, Cleander, and the feigned Erostrato. Beyond this lies conjecture: there may have been other houses to indicate the city; these may have been arranged in perspective after the Italian manner; and there may have been a back curtain. Many of the young lawyers having traveled extensively, had probably seen dramatic performances in Italy; but definite evidence of the *mise en scène* is unfortunately lacking, and we are forced to judge by internal evidence.

SUPPOSES

We would be fortunate indeed, did we know how familiar Gascoigne was with the history and original presentations of *I Suppositi*. Ariosto began his dramatic writings with the comedy *La Cassaria,* which was presented for the first time on March 5, 1508, in the theater of Ippolito d'Este, as part of the Carnival festivities.[82] The details of this first performance, preserved in a letter of Bernadino Prosperi to the Marchesana Isabella, tell of the *intermedii* and the scene "in perspective of a town with houses, churches, belfries and gardens, such that one could never tire of looking at it."[83] A year later, on February 6, 1509,[84] there was presented in the same theater for the delectation of Cardinal Ippolito, a second prose comedy, *I Suppositi,* which, if we are to believe Bernadino Prosperi, was even more successful than its predecessor.[85] According to

---

[79] On the "houses," *vide* Chambers, *op. cit.,* III, 27–29.

[80] Cunliffe, *op. cit.,* p. 67.   [81] *Ibid.,* p. 70.

[82] E. G. Gardner, *The King of Court Poets,* London 1906, p. 323. Ariosto, *Le Commedie,* ed. by Michele Catalano, I, 3.

[83] Quoted by Gardner, *op. cit.,* p. 323.   [84] Ariosto, *op. cit.,* I, 81.

[85] Quoted by Gardner, *op. cit.,* p. 325. Cunliffe (*Supposes and Jocasta,* p. 10) gives the complete Italian.

this letter writer, Ariosto himself spoke the prologue, and certain of its details may prove interesting.

E vi confessa l' autore avere in questo e Plauto e Terenzio seguitato, de li quali l'un fece Cherea per Doro, e l'altro Filocrate per Tindaro, e Tindaro per Filocrate, l'uno ne lo *Eunuco,* l'altro ne li *Captivi,* supponersi: perché non solo ne li costumi, ma ne li argumenti ancora de le fabule vuole essere de li antichi e celebrati poeti, a tutta sua possanza, imitatore; e come essi Menandro e Apollodoro e li altri Greci ne le lor latine comedie seguitoro, egli cosí ne le sue vulgari i modi e processi de' latini scrittori schifar non vuole.[86]

Ariosto imitated others as well as Plautus and Terence,[87] but more important is the fact that he applied the devices of Roman comedy to a contemporary scene. *La Cassaria* dealt with a vague period, and laid its scene in Mytilene; *I Suppositi* is concerned with contemporary events in the very city where it was first acted.[88] The characters and events belong to Renaissance, not Classic, Italy. Of the typically Roman characters only Pasiphilo survives.[89] The influence of such a modernization must have been felt in England as well as in Italy. The schools and the court presented Roman comedy, and the lawyers could well appreciate the gain effected by a modern scene. *Gammer Gurton* and *Roister Doister* had achieved a similar fusion, but, as Chambers points out, these are much closer to the interludes than to Renaissance comedy.[90] The *kudos* of Ariosto's authorship must, I feel, have marked a considerable difference between the extravagancies of farce and a comparatively well-knit comedy. The humor of situation stands somewhat higher than that of farcical action.

Gascoigne did not, however, merely translate Ariosto's prose comedy; he combined the original prose and a later verse rendition, which was composed between 1528 and 1531,[91] and in so doing he demonstrated a

[86] Ariosto, *op. cit.,* I, 86. I shall base all future references to both prose and verse renderings on this modern, carefully collated text, since there are no considerable variations noted among the early editions which would alter the translation. References are all to Volume I and will be by page and line.

[87] *Cf.* Guido Marpillero in *Giornale Storico della Letteratura Italiana,* XXXI, 291–310.

[88] The scene is Ferrara, and Cleander's lost son, Dulipo, was five years old when he was taken by the Turks at Otranto in 1480.

[89] The nurse as a stock figure belongs to classical tragedy.

[90] Chambers, *The Elizabethan Stage,* III, 27.

[91] Ariosto, *Le Commedie,* I, 291. Catalano refutes the established tradition that the verse was presented at Rome in 1519 and concludes that the prose was then used, the verse not being done until 1528–31 (*Ibid.,* I, xxvi, 291).

very real dramatic ability. Ariosto's first two comedies were written in prose; but about 1528 he devised a new comic meter, the *verso sdrucciolo* of twelve syllables, ending in a dactyl and lacking rhyme. In this form he recast *I Suppositi* and wrote his three later comedies. The verse revision of the former may, perhaps, have been due to the fact that the actors had succeeded in stealing a copy of the prose as presented in 1509 and had, in the same year, had it piratically printed. A copy of this rare work is now in the Folger Shakespeare Library and examination of it reveals that while the text is quite accurate, its abbreviations and its being solidly printed without speech indentation make it most difficult to read. The first authorized prose edition was printed in 1524, and subsequent editions appeared in 1525 and 1542.[92] The first edition of the poetic version appeared in 1551, and in 1562[93] a collected edition of the comedies contained the verse. In 1552 there was printed in Paris an edition of the play with French and Italian prose on facing pages.[94] The French title was *La Comedie Des Supposez,* from which Dr. Cunliffe thinks Gascoigne derived his title. A free translation of the Italian seems equally justifiable. At any rate, it is quite clear that Gascoigne made no use of the French version in his translation, but which editions of the Italian prose and verse he used cannot be ascertained. There are, so far as I have been able to discover, no peculiarities of any single edition which might afford a clue.

Dr. Cunliffe was the first to observe that the intermingling of details from both prose and verse clearly indicated that Gascoigne had used both versions in his translation.[95] A line-by-line comparison of the English with the two Italian versions fails to indicate one or the other as a basic text which was later revised. The unusual conclusion to which one is thus forced is that Gascoigne simultaneously consulted both the prose and the verse. The manner in which this was done and the reasons for such a method of translation present two problems whose solutions give us a new understanding of Gascoigne's skill as a dramatist.

The first scene which most clearly reveals the blending of prose and

[92] Copies of the last two are in the Folger Shakespeare Library.
[93] Two copies of the 1551 edition are in the Folger Shakespeare Library, as is one copy of the 1562.
[94] Two copies are in the Folger Shakespeare Library.
[95] Cunliffe, ed., *Supposes and Jocasta,* pp. 109–11.

verse has been noted by Dr. Cunliffe,[96] but its significant details can be briefly recapitulated. Scene 2 of Act I introduces Cleander, the aged suitor, and Pasiphilo, the parasite, and much is made of the former's age and eyesight. Cleander, though having failed to recognize Polynesta, thanks God that his vision is little worse than when he was "but twentie yeres olde." The prose reads, "venticinque, o trenta anni," and the verse "di venti anni or di trenta." Here the English follows the verse. A few lines later Cleander says he is "fiftie yeres olde," which is the verse reading, while the prose is "Io sono nelli cinquanta sei anni." Pasiphilo, in an aside, remarks, "He telles ten lesse than he is," which this time follows the prose since the verse uses "dodici." Pasiphilo's final comment, "you looke like one of sixe and thirtie, or seven and thirtie at the moste" combines details from both the prose ("trenta sei, or trent' otto") and the verse ("trentasette anni"). This mixture of details seems quite arbitrary, with Gascoigne seeming to prefer round numbers ("fiftie," and "ten") but for some reason employing thirty-seven instead of thirty-eight. One is almost led to suppose that Gascoigne was using an unknown manuscript or printed text, but the recent edition of *Le Commedie*[97] by Michele Catalano, which notes all variants found in the two manuscripts, and the first two editions of the prose, as well as the first verse edition, offers no such evidence nor does my examination of the fourteen copies of the play in the possession of the Folger Shakespeare Library.

However, the latter portions of this same scene present certain details that do offer an explanation of the method, and I quote the English, the prose, and the verse.

Cle. But pyckling in deede, whereof we have a verse:
> *The trade of lawe doth fill the boystrous bagges,*
> *They swimme in silke, when other royst in ragges.*

Pa. O excellent verse; who made it? Virgil?

Cle. Virgil? tushe, it is written in one of our gloses.

Pa. Sure who soever wrote it, the morall is excellent, and worthy to be written in letters of golde. But to the purpose: I thinke you shall never recover the wealth that you loste at *Otranto*.

Cle. I thinke I have dubled it, or rather made it foure times as muche: but, in deed, I lost mine only sonne there, a childe of five yeres olde.

Pa. O great pitie!

---

[96] *Ibid.*, pp. 110–11. The ensuing quotations are from the same pages.

[97] Ariosto, *Le Commedie*, ed. by Catalano.

Cle. Yea, I had rather have lost al the goods in the world.

Pa. Alas, alas! by God, and grafts of suche a stocke are very gayson in these dayes.

Cle. I know not whether he were slayne, or the Turks toke him and kept him as a bond slave.

Pa. Alas, I could weepe for compassion, but there is no remedy but patience; you shall get many by this yong damsell with the grace of God.

Cle. Yea, if I get hir.

Pa. Get her? why doubt you of that?

Cle. Why? hir father holds me off with delayes, so that I must needes doubt.[98]

Clean. . . . *unde versus: Opes dat sanctio Iustiniana; Ex aliis paleas, ex istis collige grana.*

Pasif. O buono! Di chi è? di Virgilio?

Clean. Che Virgilio? è d'una nostra glosa excellentissima.

Pasif. Bello e moral certo, e degno di porsi in lettere d'oro. Tu déi avere acquistato oggimai più di quello che a Otranto lasciasti.

Clean. Triplicato ho le mie facultá: è vero che io vi persi uno figliolino di cinque anni, che avevo più caro che quanta roba sia al mondo.

Pasif. Ah! troppo gran perdita veramente.

Clean. Non so se morisse o pure ancora viva in captivitade.

Pasif. Io piango per compassione che n'ho; ma sta di buona voglia che con Polinesta ne acquisterai de gli altri.

Clean. Che pensi tu di queste lunghe che Damone mi dá?[99]

Clean.   . . . *Opes dat sanctio Iustiniana.*

Pasif.   O come è buono!

Clean.   *Ex aliis Paleas* . . .

Pasif.   Eccellente!

Clean.   *Ex istis collige Grana.*

Pasif.   Chi 'l fe'? Virgilio?

Clean.   Che Virgilio?
Gli è d'una nostra glosa elegantissima.

Pasif.   Non udii il miglior mai: si dovria scrivere
In lettere d'òr. Ma torniamo al proposito.
Dovete ormai aver fatto un peculio
Maggior di quel che giá lasciaste ad Otranto.

---

[98] Cunliffe, *op. cit.,* pp. 16–17, ll. 76–105.

[99] Ariosto, *op. cit.,* pp. 93–94. Catalano does not number the lines of the prose version.

   Clean. Lo credo aver multiplicato in quadruplo;
        Ma un figliolin vi perdei, che m'era unico:
        Avea cinque anni a punto . . .
   Pasif.   Ah, fu gran perdita!
   Clean. Che valea piú che quanti danar siano
        Al mondo.
   Pasif.   Me ne duol.
   Clean.   Non so se 'l misero
        Morisse, o pur li Turchi ancor lo tengano
        In servitú.
   Pasif.   Voi mi farete piangere
        De la compassion. Ma pazienzia:
        Ne acquistarete ben con questa giovane
        De gli altri.
   Clean.   Sí, s'io l'avrò.
   Pasif.   Non c'è dubbio.
   Clean. E non ci debbe esser gran dubbio, dandomi
        Il padre queste lunghe?[100]

Within these few lines Gascoigne has followed now the prose, now the verse, and has made original additions. Cleander's uninterrupted quotation and Pasiphilo's comment thereon follow the prose, but after this the sequence of speeches follows the verse. Such alternation does not seem as capricious as the details of Cleander's age. Following the prose, Gascoigne can coin an epigrammatic couplet (similar to those found in *Jocasta*) which would be spoiled by the interjection of Pasiphilo's exclamations. On the other hand, the verse offers a transition in "Ma torniamo al proposito" and emphasizes the important fact of Cleander's lost son, which is essential to the solution of the play. That the verse is better in this respect and that Gascoigne here follows the verse seem to me to indicate that the translator exercised deliberate choice. A few lines later he reverts to the prose for Cleander's instructions to Pasiphilo regarding the marriage arrangements, and here again the poet seems to follow that version which best expresses those details necessary to the working out of the plot.

   Cle. Well, gentle Pasiphilo, go thy wayes and tell Damon I require nothing but his daughter: I wil none of his goods: I shal enrich hir of mine owne: and if this dower of two thousand ducates seem not sufficient, I wil make it five

---

   [100] *Ibid.,* pp. 304–5, ll. 235–56.

hundreth more, yea a thousand, or what so ever he wil demaund rather than faile. Go to, Pasiphilo, shew thy selfe frendly in working this feate for me: spare for no cost; since I have gone thus farre, I wilbe loth to be out bidden. Go.[101]

Clean. Va, Pasifilo mio, se mai aspetto da te piacere, e truova Damone, e digli che io non gli domando altro che sua figliuola, e non voglio da lui dote: io la doterò del mio, e se duo mila ducati non sono a bastanza, io ve ne aggiugnerò cinquecento, e mille, e quel più che vuole egli medesimo. Va, e fa quella opera che io so che tu saprai fare. Non intendo in modo alcuno di perdere questa causa. Non tardare più, va adesso.[102]

> *Clean.* Or va. S'io aspetto mai da te, Pasifilo,
> Piacere alcuno, va, truova mio suocero,
> *Idest quem spero;* e digli, se non bastano
> Li duo mila ducati, io vi vo' aggiungere
> Altri mille, e quel più che saprá chiedere
> Egli a bocca. Io non voglio del suo un picciolo,
> Se non la figlia. Va, 'l truova, e fa l'opera,
> Ch'io so che saprai far. Or va, non perdere
> Tempo.[103]

In the scenes of low comedy, Gascoigne handles his material even more freely and makes the humor definitely English, as may be observed by a comparison of the following scene with its originals.

[*Carion.*] Maister, what the divel meane you to goe seeke guestes at this time of the day? the Maiors officers have dined ere this time, which are alway the last in the market.

Cleander. I come to seeke Pasiphilo, to the ende he may dine with mee.

Ca. As though six mouthes and the cat for the seventh bee not sufficient to eate an harlotrie shotterell, a pennieworth of cheese, and halfe a score spurlings: this is all the dainties you have dressed for you and your familie.

Cle. Ah, greedie gut, art thou afearde thou shalt want?

Ca. I am afearde in deede; it is not the first time I have founde it so.

Dulipo [aside]. Shall I make some sporte with this gallant? what shall I say to him?

Cle. Thou arte afearde belike that he will eate thee and the rest.

Ca. Nay, rather that he will eate your mule, both heare and hyde.

Cle. Heare and hyde? and why not flesh and all?

Ca. Bicause she hath none. If she had any flesh, I thinke you had eaten hir your selfe by this time.

---

[101] Cunliffe, *op. cit.,* p. 18, ll. 128–38.
[102] Ariosto, *op. cit.,* p. 94.   [103] *Ibid.,* p. 305, ll. 270–78.

Cle. She may thanke you then for your good attendance.
Ca. Nay, she may thanke you for your small allowance.
Du. [*aside*]. In faith now let me alone.
Cle. Holde thy peace, drunken knave, and espie me Pasiphilo.[104]

Car. Che ora importuna è questa, patron mio, di venire per questa contrada? Non è banchiero in Ferrara che non sia ito a bere ormai.

Clean. Venivo per vedere se io trovavo Pasifilo, che io lo menassi a desinar meco.

Car. Quasi che sei bocche che in casa tua si ritruovano, e sette con la gatta, non sieno a mangiare sufficienti uno luccetto d'una libra e mezo, e una pentola di ceci, e venti sparagi, che senza piú sono per pascere te e la tua famiglia apparecchiati.

Clean. Temi tu che ti debba mancare, lupaccio?

Dulip. (Non debbo io soiare un poco questo uccellaccio?)

Car. Non sarebbe la prima fiata.

Dulip. (Che gli dirò?)

Car. Pure io non dico per questo, ma perché la famiglia stará a disagio, né Pasifilo rimarrá satollo, che mangerebbe te, con la pelle et ossa de la tua mula: direi ancora la carne insieme, se la ne avessi.

Clean. Tua colpa, che cosí bene ne hai cura.

Car. Colpa pure del fieno e de la biada, che son cari.

Dulip. (Lascia, lascia fare a me.)

Clean. Taci, imbriaco, e guarda per la contrada se tu vedi costui.[105]

> *Car.* O padron, ch'ora è questa fuora d'ordine
> D'andare a cerco? Credo che si stuzichi
> Ormai li denti, non vo' dir che desini,
> Ogni banchiere, ogni ufficial di camera,
> Che sono a uscir di piazza sempre gli ultimi.
> *Clean.* Io son venuto per trovar Pasifilo,
> Acciò desini meco.
> *Car.*   Come fussemo
> Pochi sei bocche che siamo, e aggiungendovi
> La gatta, sette, a mangiar quattro piccioli
> Luccetti, che una libra e mezo pesano
> A pena tutti insieme, et una pentola
> Di ceci mal conditi, e venti sparagi,
> Che senza piú in cucina s'apparecchiano
> Per vio e tutta la famiglia pascere.
> *Clean.* Temi, lupaccio, che ti manchi?

---

[104] Cunliffe, *op. cit.,* pp. 39–40, ll. 1–33.   [105] Ariosto, *op. cit.,* pp. 110–11.

Car.   Temone
　　　　Pur troppo.
Dulip.   (Non debbo uccellare e prendermi
　　　　Piacer di questo vecchio?)
Clean.   Dee dunque essere
　　　　La prima volta.
Dulip.   (Che dirò?)
Car.   Rincrescemi
　　　　De la famiglia, e non giá del mio incommodo;
　　　　Che quel, con che temporeggiar potriano
　　　　E con pane e coltello un poco i poveri
　　　　Famigli, tutto in duo boccon Pasifilo
　　　　Trangugiar debbia, né rimaner sazio;
　　　　Che voi, e con la pelle mangiarebbesi
　　　　E con l'ossa la mula vostra, et anco la
　　　　Carne, s'avesse pur carne la misera.
Clean. Tua colpa, che sí ben n'hai cura.
Car.   Datene
　　　　Pur colpa al fieno e alla biada, che costano.
Dulip. (Lascia pur fare a me.)
Clean.   Taci, brutto asino,
　　　　E guarda se apparir vedi Pasifilo.[106]

In his translation Gascoigne has mingled material from the prose and verse, has compressed two speeches into one, and has expanded to include byplay typical of the English tradition of *Gammer Gurton* and *Roister Doister*. Such freedom seems more necessary in the comic scenes, since they are both idiomatic and topical. The list of available food could have been literally translated, but by using English terms Gascoigne preserved the spirit of the original. The byplay of the mule is well expanded in the English manner, though here, even as in later Elizabethan drama, the character becomes incongruous. For Cleander to become suddenly a "stooge" for his servant is humorous, but it is also a definite flaw in the presentation of the character. This fondness of the Elizabethan for low humor which today seems singularly dull had a more ancient lineage than their interest in the complications of classical and Italian comedy.

It is no wonder that the vigor and animation of Shakespearean comedy owes as much to this English heritage as to the framework derived from foreign models. It has long been recognized that the *Supposes* is the

[106] *Ibid.*, pp. 324–25, ll. 738–68.

source of the subplot of Bianca and her suitors in *The Taming of the Shrew,* and it has been equally well recognized that the humor of the play lies more in Petruchio's wooing than in the devices of Bianca's youthful suitor, Lucentio, to thwart the desires of his rivals, the aged Grumio and Hortensio. The disguises, the wealth of the aged suitor, the frightened traveler who pretends to be a father, the debate between the pretended and the real father—all these are borrowed by Shakespeare from Gascoigne and Ariosto, but Shakespeare's subordination and curtailment present them in a perspective quite different from that of the *Supposes.* The raw materials were borrowed only to be transmuted.

The process of dramatic choice, of selecting now the sequence of the prose, now that of the verse, of adding or compressing, continues throughout the play. But Gascoigne's method of translation does not end with choice of order or details, for the poet was also interested in the development of prose style. By a judicious use of his sources and by paraphrase and addition he did much to establish a definite style in this first real prose comedy of the English stage. In the first scene of the play, where through the conversation of Polynesta and her Nurse we learn the bases of the action, occur the following speeches:

Ba. I can not denie but at the beginning I did recommende him unto you (as in deede I may say that for my selfe I have a pitiful heart), seeing the depth of his unbridled affection, and that continually he never ceassed to fill mine eares with lamentable complaynts.

Po. Nay, rather that he filled your pursse with bribes and rewards, Nourse.

Ba. Well, you may judge of Nourse as you liste. In deede I have thought it alwaies a deede of charitie to helpe the miserable yong men, whose tender youth consumeth with the furious flames of love. But, be you sure, if I had thought you would have passed to the termes you nowe stand in, pitie nor pencion, peny nor pater noster, shoulde ever have made Nurse once to open hir mouth in the cause.

Po. No[?] of honestie, I pray you, who first brought him into my chamber? who first taught him the way to my bed but you? fie, Nourse, fie, never speake of it for shame, you will make me tell a wise tale anone.[107]

This sequence is based on both the prose and verse.

Nutr. É vero che da principio te lo raccomandai per la compassione che io ne
avevo, per le continue preci con che mi sollecitava.
Polin. Anzi per la pensione e prezzo che tu ne traevi.

---

[107] Cunliffe, *op. cit.,* p. 9, ll. 41–62.

Nutr. Tu puoi credere quel che ti pare: tuttavia renditi certa che se io avesse
pensato che poscia voi dovessi procedere cosí inanzi, né per compassione
o pensione o prece o prezzo te ne arei parlato.

Polin. Chi la prima notte lo condusse al mio letto se non tu? Chi altri che tu?
Deh taci, per tua fé, che mi faresti dire qualche pazzia.[108]

> *Balia.* Non ti voglio negar che da principio
> Io non te ne parlassi, per grandissima
> Compassion ch'io gli avevo, e per continue
> Preci che mi faceva.
>
> *Polin.*   Anzi pur, balia,
> Perché n'avate pensione e prezio.
>
> *Balia.* Creder tu puoi ciò che ti par; ma rendeti
> Certa, che s'io pensava che procedere
> Voi doveste sí inanzi, prece o prezio,
> Compassione o pension, non erano
> Sufficienti per fartene muovere
> Da me parola.
>
> *Polin.*   Chi 'l menò alla camera,
> E poi nel letto mio, se non la balia?
> Per vostra fé, non mi fate trascorrere
> A dir qualche pazzia.[109]

The first words of the Nurse, "I can not denie but" are taken from the
verse; but the succeeding, from the prose, and the reason seems implicit
in the resultant fusion of the two. Evidently Gascoigne wanted to use the
antithesis, but he preferred "raccomandi" to "parlassi." The choice is
based on a consciousness of style and a feeling for *le mot juste*. The parallelism of Polynesta's last speech, with its two interrogative clauses, seems
another example of an interest in style, while the substitution of "pater
noster" for "compassione" in the Nurse's second speech certainly reveals
the English love of alliteration. The interpolation of the word "Nourse"
may be accidental, but it is effective in emphasizing the relationship and
in pointing out that the pander is not merely a servant.

The rendering of "continue preci" by "lamentable complaynts" recalls
the jargon of love poetry, where "disdain" must always be "darke" and
where "sighs" must always be "shriching." The original additions seem to
have a like source. The Nurse must have a "pitiful heart"; "compassion" is

---

[108] Ariosto, *op. cit.*, pp. 88–89.   [109] *Ibid.*, p. 298, ll. 83–96.

too weak for matters of love. And of course she must perceive "the depth of his unbridled affection." The long addition in the Nurse's second speech may reflect the activities of Gascoigne and his fellows, who knew of the effective persuadings of servants in the *novelle* of Boccaccio and Cinthio, and who had, themselves, probably bribed a servant more than once. The addition of such details is probably due to the desire both to introduce familiar details and to sharpen the reality of the scene.

Similar additions of the language of love are found in Dulipo's soliloquy at the end of the third scene of Act I. The figure of the moth and the flame, old even with Petrarch, appears as an antithesis and has no basis in the original:

But, alas, I find that only love is unsaciable: for, as the flie playeth with the flame till at last she is cause of hir owne decay, so the lover that thinketh with kissing and colling to content his unbrideled apetite, is commonly seene the only cause of his owne consumption.[110]

Later in this speech we encounter "the pleasant tast of my sugred joyes," as well as a "soppe of sorow" which are again the translator's own additions. Indeed, the entire speech is largely a paraphrase couched in a prose style based on parallelism, antithesis, and closely knit clauses and phrases.

One addition that seems closely related to Gascoigne's own experience is Damon's lament in Act III, scene 3, where a passage of some thirteen lines on the duty of parents toward their children is an entirely original interpolation.

For of al the dueties that are requisite in humane lyfe, onely obedience is by the parents to be required of the childe: where on the other side the parents are bound first to beget them, then to bring them foorth, after to nourish them, to preserve them from bodily perils in the cradle, from daunger of soule by godly education, to matche them in consorte enclined to vertue, too banish them all ydle and wanton companie, to allow them sufficiente for their sustentation, to cut off excesse the open gate of sinne, seldome or never to smile on them unlesse it be to their encouragement in vertue, and finally, to provide them mariages in time convenient, lest (neglected of us) they learne to sette either to much or to litle by themselves.[111]

By the year 1566, when he translated the *Supposes,* George Gascoigne was in the midst of his legal difficulties; in debt, on the one hand, and

[110] Cunliffe, *op. cit.,* p. 22, ll. 81–86.
[111] *Ibid.,* p. 54, ll. 68–84.

on the other, sued more than once by various people connected with his wife's first and second husbands. The death of his father in 1568 was to bring into the law courts evidence that the relations between Sir John Gascoigne and his son George had not been harmonious. Certainly it seems that in this reflection on the duties of parents, the longest original addition to his translation, Gascoigne was indirectly reproaching his own father for neglecting to guide his life aright and for failing to provide a suitable marriage. The interpolation is not undramatic: personal feelings do not spoil, rather they enhance, the effectiveness of the addition, the style of which is resplendent in its parallelism.

Enough has now been said to sustain certain conclusions about Gascoigne's method of translation. He evidently knew that Ariosto had written two versions of *I Suppositi,* and he seemingly had access to copies of both the prose and the verse. Our knowledge of the importation of foreign books into England is incomplete, but Gascoigne's own copy of Petrarch is evidence of his possession of at least one Italian book. Certainly among the well-traveled young gentlemen of the Inns of Court one could probably have found copies of the works of the great Ariosto. Having knowledge and possible possession of the two versions, Gascoigne was not content to follow one or the other; instead, he showed both a surprising interest in dramatic structure by combining the best elements of each version and a creative impulse in making alterations and additions, all of which result in the first really well-constructed vernacular comedy that appeared on the English stage. These same characteristics were in evidence in his translation of *Jocasta,* where this matter of dramatic structure was seen only in the alterations, since he had but one text from which to translate. However, in both the *Jocasta* and the *Supposes* are examples of Gascoigne's interest in style and expression. In the former, he was concerned with blank verse, rhetorical embroidery, and imagery, and in the latter with the structure of an ordered prose style. Exactly as his court poetry exemplified the establishment of order and form in poetic expression, so, too, his plays bear witness to a similar interest in dramatic expression.

One is tempted to speculate as to what Gascoigne would have done with an original tragedy or comedy. He seems to have had a good sense of structure and dialogue, but his other dramatic compositions are not in the great tradition of the Elizabethan stage. The masque, "shewes," and the prodigal-son play are apart from the world of Senecan tragedy and Italian comedy. Must we conclude that Gascoigne was only an imitator; that he could not have created original work? Such an assumption does not seem the real explanation, if we examine the reasons for the composition of these other dramatic productions. The masque and the "shewes" at Kenilworth and Woodstock were written for prospective patrons. In 1572/3, as we have seen from the account of his life, Gascoigne was seeking the aid of the Viscount Montague, and in 1575 he aspired for royal favor and the laurel wreath. The prodigal-son play, *The Glasse of Government,* which we shall consider below, was written as a result of the poet's own experience coupled with his residence in Holland. In other words, it would seem that opportunity, or rather the lack of it at times, and not inclination, dominated his dramatic work.

As a member of the schools, universities, or Inns of Court, a gentleman, as an amateur, could write plays for production within the particular body of which he was a member. As a member of the court circle, a gentleman could write Italianate poems; but dramatic activity in the form of masque and pageants was supplied by the Children of the Chapel and Paul's and by the Revels Office, a remunerative business. It was not until the "art for art's sake" movement of the Sidney circle some years later that gentlemen could write plays outside the restricted milieu already noted. Furthermore, court entertainment before Lyly—and it is well to remember that he was assistant master of Paul's—was largely a matter of masques and moralities.

Thus Gascoigne's dramatic activities were in large measure controlled by his social status. He was proud of his family and his title of "Esquire," and could not, therefore, accept monetary reward for his literary efforts. He could seek patronage, the reversion of an office, or royal employment consistent with his position, but not money. He was "Tam Marti Quam Mercurio," but never a professional man of letters.

THE MASQUE AND THE "SHEWES"

Tudor entertainment, though we may from the vantage of historical perspective see in it the growth of English drama, was largely concerned with pageants and masques. Reference to the surviving documents of the

Revels Office[112] confirms the preponderance of this type of semidramatic amusement in the courts of Henry VIII and his children. The origins and various classifications of this form of entertainment have been fully considered by Sir Edmund Chambers,[113] Miss Welsford,[114] and others;[115] so our present task is to examine certain problems connected with Gascoigne's productions in this genre and to relate them to the tradition of spectacular entertainment which flourished in the great halls of noble establishments or amid the natural settings afforded by the grounds of Kenilworth and Woodstock.

Gascoignes devise of a maske.—*Gascoignes devise of a maske for the right honorable Viscount Mountacute,*[116] was, as we have seen, part of the poet's attempt to secure patronage after his return from initial failure in the Dutch wars.[117] The double wedding of the son and daughter of Viscount Montague to the daughter and son of Sir William Dormer offered an excellent opportunity. The approximate but not exact date of this masque is shown by a protest to the Revels Office which has survived among the Burghley papers.[118] This document was prepared by one Thomas Giles, a haberdasher of London, who rented costumes for masques. Unfortunately for Giles's trade, the Yeoman of the Revels invaded the field and rented at low prices the royal costumes in his custody. Such misuse of and possible damage to royal property induced Giles to prepare his protest, which contained a list of all such garments rented by the Yeoman during the year 1572. Sometime between September 15 and October 6 there was lent "into the contre to the maryage of the dawter of my lorde Montague . . . the coper clothe of golde gownes" and another masque. Chambers concludes that the undescribed masque must have

[112] Feuillerat, *Documents Relating to the Revels at Court in the Time of King Edward VI and Queen Mary, Materialien zur Kunde des alteren Englischen Dramas,* Band XLIV; Feuillerat, *Documents Relating to the Office of the Revels in the Time of Queen Elizabeth, Materialien zur Kunde des alteren Englischen Dramas,* Band XXI. Cf. Steele, *Plays and Masques at Court,* which is a complete list of all Elizabethan masques.

[113] Chambers, *The Mediaeval Stage,* Vol. I, chap. xvii; Chambers, *The Elizabethan Stage,* I, chaps. v, vi.

[114] Welsford, *The Court Masque.*

[115] Cf. "Bibliographical Note" in Chambers, *The Elizabethan Stage,* I, 149.

[116] *Works,* I, 75. No. 69. The wording of the title is from *A Hundreth Sundrie Flowres,* p. 382.

[117] *Vide supra,* chap. iii.

[118] Quoted in Feuillerat, *Documents Relating to the Office of the Revels in the Time of Queen Elizabeth,* pp. 409–10. Noted by Chambers, *The Elizabethan Stage,* I, 164.

been that of the "Venetians" which Gascoigne wrote. Such a view does not seem to be supported by the introductory comments prefaced to the masque.

... there were eighte gentlemen (all of bloud or alliance to the saide L. Mountacute) which had determined to present a maske at the day appoynted for the sayd mariages, and so farre they had proceeded therin, that they had alredy bought furniture of silks, &c. and had caused their garments to be cut of the Venetian fashion ...[119]

It would thus seem that the rented costumes were for other entertainments during the festivities, since the eight gentlemen themselves bought their materials and had their own garments cut.

More important is the actual date of the marriages. Giles gives an exact date for every item on his list except this, and the limiting dates noted above are from the preceding and the following entries. It would seem that Giles was uncertain of the actual day and consequently approximated the time. That the double ceremony was performed after October 6, 1572, is suggested by our knowledge of Gascoigne's military experiences in Holland.[120] He took part in the siege of Tergoes, which was broken by Mondragon on October 21. After this failure, the English volunteers returned home. It may be that Gascoigne left before the siege ended, and we would be forced to such a conclusion were it not for Giles's seeming uncertainty of the date. In view of this, however, it seems likely that the weddings actually occurred about the beginning of November.

The scene of *Gascoignes devise* remains uncertain, in view of Giles's reference to the masques lent "into the contre." This would suggest Cowdray, the Montague seat in Sussex, but the details found in the story of the "pouer boy" do not quite agree. This youth, son of a Mounthermer (a kinsman of the Montagues) and a Montague, was rescued by Italian Montagues after the battle of Lepanto. With them he set sail for Venice, but a storm so drove the voyagers from their course that they arrived on the Kentish coast. Embarking in gondolas, they made their way up the Thames to London, where the boy heard of the double wedding. At this point in his narrative, he begs leave to introduce his Vene-

---

[119] *Works*, I, 75. The actual quotation is taken from *A Hundreth Sundrie Flowres*, p. 382. The only variation is in spelling.

[120] *Vide supra*, chap. iii.

tian rescuers, who enter, preceded by a drummer. The arrival at London on the day of the festivities and the boy's appearance on the same day at the wedding entertainment would suggest Montague House in Southwark, since a journey from London to Midhurst would require at least one day's travel. Of course, it is unwise to become too meticulous over such details, but it has seemed well to point out the possibility that the festivities may have taken place both in London and at Cowdray. Perhaps the actual weddings were performed in Montague House, after which the party set out for the country for a prolonged celebration. At any rate, Gascoigne's was not, apparently, the only masque connected with this affair, and the costumes rented by the yeoman seem to have been used at Cowdray.

Our knowledge of other contemporary masques suggests that Gascoigne's is not in the regular tradition of such entertainment. The masque for the wedding of Sir Henry Unton[121] had such figures as Mercury, Diana, nymphs, cupids, a "tronchman," and torchbearers accompanied by six minstrels. We have no record of what was said, but in contrast with Gascoigne's, this masque presumably had dancing and certainly had visual appeal. The various masques celebrating the marriage of Prince Arthur and Katherine of Arragon, in 1501, were splendid with machines, colorful costumes, mock battles, and various dances.[122] Early Elizabethan court masques were equally impressive, with mythological representations[123] and machines, while the records of the projected masque in honor of Mary, Queen of Scots[124] make Gascoigne's *devise* a puny attempt indeed.

It seems, however, that Gascoigne's purpose in writing may explain the disparity. In the introductory comments, the poet says that the eight gentlemen "entreated Master Gascoigne to devise some verses to be uttered by an Actor wherein mighte be some discourse convenient to render a good cause of the Venetians presence."[125] To this end Gascoigne composed a long narrative poem of the siege of Famagusta and the battle of Lepanto, told by a boy, a presumed connection of the Montague family.

[121] Known from a pictorial representation preserved in the National Portrait Gallery, and reproduced in Chambers, *The Elizabethan Stage,* I, frontispiece.

[122] Discussed by Miss Welsford, *op. cit.,* pp. 120–21.   [123] Steele, *op. cit.,* pp. 8, 10, 24.

[124] Discussed by Chambers, *The Elizabethan Stage,* I, 159–60.

[125] *Works,* I, 75.

His father killed by the Turks at Famagusta, he was taken prisoner and rescued at Lepanto by the Venetian Montagues, whom he desires to present to the chief of the English branch of the family. The masquers arrive, and the boy actor presents as their "tronchman"[126] Master Thomas Browne who, after consultation with the Venetians, makes a brief complimentary speech, whereupon the masquers take their leave. In other words, Gascoigne complied with the request of his friends and supplied them with a reason for wearing their costumes.

The purpose of the contemporary masque seems to have been quite different. As both Sir Edmund Chambers and Miss Welsford make clear, the Tudor masque was a combination of a variety of different elements: "mommerie," with its silent mummers who brought good luck; various dances; Italian *intermedii* and *trionfi;* and the Ferrarese use of costumes for love intrigue. The resultant mélange has no strict rules of definition; but it seems clear that dancing was an integral part of the masque, that there was visual entertainment, and that there was usually a significance attached both to the costumes and to the action. Complimentary speeches were usually made by a "tronchman." Since the literary aspects of the earlier masques do not survive, we cannot be sure of the length or the nature of the presenter's speech.

Of all these elements Gascoigne's masque has very few. There is no dancing; the complimentary speech is short and perfunctory; the costumes are explained but they have no other significance; and the masquers make no attempt to mingle with the company. The entertainment value lies solely in the long narrative poem, and it is well to recall Miss Welsford's observation that in England the chief emphasis in the masque was literary, in contrast with France and Italy, where the ballet and opera were developed from the masque.[127] The story of Famagusta and Lepanto is told for its own sake and as such amounts to a recitation—since an explanation of the costumes could have been achieved in about one-third the space. Thus it seems that we must consider *Gascoignes devise* as related to the masque tradition; but as, nevertheless, an innovation, emphasizing the idea of recitation not for compliment or explanation but for its own sake.

---

[126] There seems to be some social distinction between the "tronchman," who is a Montague and makes the complimentary speech, and the presenter, who is an actor.

[127] *Op. cit.,* p. 249.

The literary inspiration is twofold. The well-known reference to the hostility of the Capulets and Montagues attests the popularity of the Romeo-Juliet story as related by Broke and Painter, while the details of Famagusta have been recently shown to be derived from a contemporary account.[128] Thus Gascoigne put together the familiar Montagues of England and those of Italy and created a narrative based on contemporary history. Dr. R. R. Cawley has pointed out that the details of the siege and the torture of Bragadine are derived from William Malim's *The true Report of all the successe of Famagosta* (John Daye, 1572), which is a translation of an eyewitness account by Count Nestor Martinengo, printed at Verona in 1572. Gascoigne amplified and transposed his original and seemingly used some details in Malim's account for his description of Lepanto, although no source has yet been discovered for this story of Don John's victory. The poem is in poulter's measure—a form later adopted by King James for an account of the same battle—and exhibits the usual characteristics of Gascoigne's style: alliteration, embroidered imagery, and sententious or rhetorical passages noted by double commas. As a masque it is interesting; as a narrative poem it sometimes achieves vigor.

"Shewes."—Far better written and more in the tradition of Tudor revels are Gascoigne's compositions for the royal entertainment at Kenilworth in July, 1575. Two accounts of Leicester's sumptuous entertainment survive: Robert Laneham's letter[129] and Gascoigne's *The Princely Pleasures at Kenilworth*.[130] The latter is the first complete version of any Elizabethan masque or revel and as such is extremely important in understanding the precise nature of these entertainments. However, lack of knowledge should not lead to the conclusion that we are dealing with something new. One of the contributors was Ferrers, "sometime Lord of misrule in the Court," and another was Hunnis, Master of the Chapel Royal, both of whom had previously been active in court amusement, and who may, therefore, be logically expected to continue in the tradition

---

[128] Cawley, "George Gascoigne and the Siege of Famagusta," *MLN*, XLIII (1928), 296–300.

[129] Robert Laneham, keeper of the Council chamber door, wrote to his good friend, Master Humfrey Martin, Mercer. The letter is printed in Nichols, *The Progresses and Public Processions of Queen Elizabeth*, I, 426–523.

[130] Dr. Cunliffe (*Works*, II, 91–131) prints Gascoigne's account from the collected edition of 1587, since the unique copy of the first edition of 1576 was destroyed by fire in 1879.

which was familiar to them.[131] In fact, Gascoigne's first contribution to the festivities is on a familiar theme, that of the "Savage man," or, as Laneham describes him, "Hombre Salvagio."[132] Wild men had frequently appeared in masques, as Chambers has observed.[133] In the early thirteenth century, at Prato della Valle, there was performed a "magnus Ludus de quodam homine salvatico."[134] In 1502 Ercole d'Este arranged several *moriscos* and *intermedii* for his new daughter-in-law, Lucrezia Borgia, and one of the latter consisted of savages fighting for the possession of a beautiful woman;[135] while in 1515 át Greenwich "eight terrible wild men, dressed in green moss, 'came out of a place lyke a wood' and fought with the knights, who drave them out of the hall."[136]

Gascoigne's "Savage man" is content with wonder and words: he wonders what causes the magnificent assemblage of courtly folk, and, through a highly artificial dialogue with Echo, learns that Dudley is thus honoring the Queen. He then falls in submission and, continuing his flow of poulter's measure, praises Elizabeth in the usual florid vein.

More elaborate is the "shewe" of *Zabeta* which Gascoigne wrote for presentation in the forest, but which was never given, most probably, as has been observed,[137] because Elizabeth gained some knowledge of the tenor of Iris's final soliloquy urging the Queen to matrimony, presumably with Leicester. The "shewe" is comparatively short and could well be described as a masque,[138] similar to the mythological ones which, though noted in the records, do not survive in literary form. Like the court masques, it employed machines: Mercury descending in a cloud, and Iris, on a rainbow. The son of the "Savage man" appears to fill in the interval while the nymphs are searching for Zabeta, and Audax is no less complimentary than his father, Silvester. To understand his remarks on his

---

[131] An examination of Ferrers's correspondence with Sir Thomas Cawarden (Feuillerat, *Documents . . . in the Time of King Edward VI, passim*) reveals that the former was accustomed to quite as elaborate devises as those employed at Kenilworth.

[132] Nichols, *op. cit.*, I, 436. [133] *The Elizabethan Stage*, I, 123. [134] Welsford, *op. cit.*, p. 81.
[135] *Ibid.*, p. 89. [136] *Ibid.*, p. 126.

[137] Cunliffe, "The Queenes Majesties Entertainment at Woodstocke," *PMLA*, XXVI (1911), 130. .

[138] The border line between masque and pageant is very tenuous, and while this is not strictly a masque, its subject matter is close to such a true masque as that of Diana and Actaeon presented at court on Shrove Tuesday, 1559/60 (Chambers, *The Elizabethan Stage*, I, 157).

father's blindness, it is necessary to refer to the original edition of 1576, the unique copy of which was destroyed by fire in 1879. Fortunately, from a reprint of this made in 1821, we learn that during the "Savage man's," or Silvester's, speech asking the Queen to walk in the shade, Elizabeth remarked "that the Actor was blinde," seemingly because the place did not offer shelter from the sun. Such a chance remark offered Gascoigne the opportunity to develop one of his "deepe inventions." Audax, in the "shewe" of *Zabeta,* tells the Queen that his father, Silvester, has become blind as a result of royal disfavor and begs her to remove this disability.

Gascoigne's final contribution was a farewell to the Queen on her departure from Kenilworth. Since she had not heard the plea to favor Silvester, this character could not appear; so we are not surprised to discover Sylvanus as the interlocutor of this last "shewe." He is also a forest-dweller but one more accurate as to details, and proposes to accompany the Queen, telling his "certaine adventures, neither unpleasant to heare, nor unprofitable to be marked." The first of these is the contrast between Sylvanus's two visits to the Council Chamber of the Gods. At the time of the Queen's arrival all was joy, but at news of her departure, "heaven was not heaven, it was rather a verye Hell." To remedy this change, Sylvanus beseeches her to remain, promising an everlasting springtime from *Flora,* provisions from *Ceres,* and wine from *Bacchus.* At this point the narrator turns abruptly to the story of Zabeta, Diana's favorite nymph, and the subject of the never-performed "shewe." In Sylvanus's account, Zabeta appears as a sort of Circe who delights in changing her followers into plants: *Constance* has become an oak tree; *Inconstancy,* a poplar; while *Contention* has become a bramble brier, and *Ambition,* a branch of ivy. Of the two brethren, *Dewe desert* and *Deepe desire,* she has made a laurel and a holly bush. The latter, being near at hand, breaks into verse which echoes Sylvanus's requests that Elizabeth remain and so content the nymphs, gods, and goddesses. Since this is of no avail, *Deepe desire* sings a song of farewell, and Sylvanus asks the Queen's influence in releasing *Deepe desire* from the holly bush.

I have thus closely examined Gascoigne's share in the Kenilworth pleasures so that we may see the similarity between them and the court revels of the preceding years. On Shrove Tuesday, 1559/60, there was presented at court a double masque involving Diana, her nymphs, Actaeon, and hunters.[139] Part of the masque designed for Mary, Queen of Scots, portrayed Discord, False Report, Prudentia, and Temperantia.[140] In March, 1564/5, a comedy, in which Juno advocated matrimony and Diana, chastity, was followed by a masquerade of Satyrs.[141] The winter of 1573–4 saw a masque of Foresters, in green satin, and Wildmen, clad in moss and ivy.[142] The Foresters had a hollow tree which may well have concealed a speaker. The repetition of the pattern of Kenilworth in similar progresses has been noted by Sir Edmund Chambers, who observes that "classical, romantic, pastoral, and folk-lore elements blend in quite sufficient congruity."[143] The entire Elizabethan panorama of this semi-dramatic form of entertainment seems to have the same bases: allegory, either of mythological figures or personifications closely related to those of the moralities, complimentary speeches or "shewes," and above all a great interest in a pageantry that appealed to eye and ear. In such a tradition Gascoigne's Kenilworth compositions are important, not only because they provide the first record of the literary side of Elizabethan masques and pageantry, but also because they reveal another aspect of Gascoigne's versatility.

THE GLASSE OF GOVERNMENT

The Glasse of Government[144] was published by Christopher Barker sometime after April 26, 1575, the date of Gascoigne's dedication of the play to Sir Owen Hopton.[145] By this time two influences which have no connection with his other dramatic compositions were at work on Gascoigne: he had been in Holland, and he had "enjoyed" a moral reformation. The first helps to explain the form of the present work, and the second, the subject matter. Properly, a consideration of this English example of the prodigal-son play belongs to a later section of this discussion, which deals with our author as a moralist, but since a study of the dramatic qualities of this work will complete our understanding of this

---

[139] Chambers, *The Elizabethan Stage*, I, 157.   [140] *Vide supra*, n. 124.
[141] Steele, *op. cit.*, p. 25.   [142] Chambers, *The Elizabethan Stage*, I, 165.
[143] *Ibid.*, I, 124.
[144] This first edition was a separate work. It was printed as part of *The Whole Workes of George Gascoigne* in 1587. Reprinted, *Works*, II, 1–90.
[145] *Works*, II, 3.

aspect of Gascoigne's ability, it has seemed well to include the play in this section.

As Professor Herford[146] pointed out, the prodigal-son play was popular not only in the Low Countries, the land of its origin, but in England as well.[147] The Dutch Humanists produced, during the first half of the sixteenth century, a number of Latin verse plays illustrating the parable of the prodigal son. The more important of these are *Asotus* by Macropedius (*ca.* 1510), *Acolastus* by Gnapheus (1534), *Rebelles* also by Macropedius (1535), and *Studentes* by Stymmelius (1549).[148] The first two are true examples of the theme, while the last two may be best described as "school-dramas," since they elaborate the educational aspects, to the neglect of the prodigal-son idea. No single play is a direct source for Gascoigne's drama, but Professor Herford has shown in tabular form that all the elements in *The Glasse* can be paralleled in at least one of the Latin examples.[149] The contrast between the good and the bad son, or sons, is found in *Acolastus, Studentes,* and *Rebelles.* The discussion of the problem of the child's education appears in the same three. Choosing a teacher, as Phylopaes and Phylocalus select Gnomaticus, agrees with the procedure in *Studentes* and *Rebelles.* The fall from virtue to evil is an element common to all, but the parental anxiety which appears twice in *The Glasse* is found only in *Acolastus* and *Rebelles.* On the other hand, the disgrace of the prodigals is handled differently by each author. *Asotus* follows the parable; *Acolastus* necessitates repentance and then forgiveness; in *Studentes* the main problem of the seduction of an innocent girl is settled by wedded respectability; and in *Rebelles* the headsman's ax is replaced by the schoolmaster's birch. Gascoigne has his prodigals brought to ruin, for though the fathers are forgiving, their aid comes too late.

The structural basis of *Asotus* is Terentian comedy to which has been added the Christian moral, and the other Dutch plays follow this classical tradition.[150] With the exception of John Palsgrave's translation of *Acolastus* and the anonymous *Misogonus,* the English examples of this

---

[146] Herford, *Studies in the Literary Relations of England and Germany in the Sixteenth Century.* This work is the basis of any discussion of prodigal-son drama.

[147] *Ibid.,* p. 158.

[148] *Ibid.,* pp. 153–57. The dates are those of printing.

[149] *Ibid.,* pp. 162–63.

[150] *Ibid.,* pp. 152–53.

genre are really interludes. *The Nice Wanton*[151] is episodic, comparatively short, and explicit in its teachings. Thomas Ingeland's *The Disobedient Child*,[152] though better written, is equally deficient in structure.

Only Palsgrave's *Acolastus* (printed in 1540) and the anonymous *Misogonus*[153] (*ca.* 1560) present the true prodigal-son idea in English. The latter seems to have been written in emulation of *Acolastus* and preserves the classic form. The unknown author animates the type characters and has the ultimate forgiveness arise from a secondary plot. Both plays tell of a father concerned for his son's welfare, discussing the problem with a friend. The youth indulges in riotous living, loses his money, and returns to find a welcome and forgiveness. *The Nice Wanton* presents an indulgent mother chided by a friend, children fallen into ruin, the contrasting virtuous child; but its solution in Christ's forgiveness. The prodigals repent and die, but the inference is that all has ended well, since the wicked have seen and confessed the error of their ways. *The Disobedient Child,* of Thomas Ingeland, is really an attack on marriage and its only relation to the prodigal-son type lies in the child's refusal to heed his father's advice about going to school.

Although the structure of *The Glasse of Government* is based on Roman comedy, its scene is Holland, and Professor Herford[154] appears correct in his theory that Gascoigne was influenced in his choice of theme by his participation in the Dutch wars. The two fathers are prosperous citizens of Antwerp, their sons attend the University of Douai, and the two virtuous children significantly achieve their respective successes as the secretary to the Palsgrave, and as a minister in Calvin's own city. As Professor Herford has noted, Gascoigne dwelt for some time at The Hague, the native city of the author of *Acolastus,* and we know, too, that he spent some time in other cities of the Low Countries. During these years he probably became familiar with the work of the Dutch Human-

---

[151] Boas (*CHEL*, V, 110, n.) mentions this as an example of the genre in English. He also considers *Misogonus* (*ibid.,* V, 110–11) at length and notes the somewhat related play of *The Historie of Jacob and Esau* (*ibid.,* V, 111–12). *The Nice Wanton* is reprinted in Hazlitt's *Dodsley,* II, 163–83.

[152] Reprinted in Hazlitt's *Dodsley,* II, 269–320.

[153] Reprinted in J. S. Farmer, *Six Anonymous Plays.* London, 1906. The date may be *ca.* 1575. Cf. G. L. Kittredge, *Journal of Germanic Philology,* III, 335–37. Professor Kittredge suggests Lawrence Johnson as the author.

[154] *Op. cit.,* pp. 159–60.

ists, and it needed only his moral conversion to arouse his interest in the creation of an English imitation.

In this emulation he bettered his originals, at least on dramatic grounds. The action is carefully organized so that the act and scene divisions follow the rules of dramatic structure which Gascoigne had learned in his translations of Dolce and Ariosto. Act I presents the basis of the ensuing action and concludes significantly with the plans of Eccho, Lamia, and Pandarina to entrap the unsuspecting youths. Though the potential misdeeds of Phylautus and Phylosarchus are thus foreshadowed, Act II begins with Gnomaticus's second lesson, which ends with the admonition:

Lastly forget not your selves, neyther make any lesse account of your selves then to be the Temple of God, whiche you ought to keepe holy and undefiled.[155]

Only in the second scene of this act do we hear that the two elder sons are dissatisfied and have a desire for worldly experience. Yet their encounter with the harlot, Lamia, does not immediately bring about their downfall. Instead, this second act is devoted to an understanding of the way in which youth is tempted and the ease with which its ruin may be effected. Thus Gascoigne avoids the sudden and unmotivated plunge into dissipation which marks the other prodigal-son plays. Furthermore, he shows his own comprehension of the function of a second act, namely, to clarify the issues involved and to present a minor crisis. Act III continues this crisis, intensifying it by the deception which Phylautus and Phylosarchus practice on their younger brothers, as well as by the contrast between the dutiful younger sons, who have written their "themes," and their elder brothers, who plan a banquet for Lamia. A lull before the storm is Act IV. The sons are sent to Douai, while their seducers are enmeshed in the toils of the law. Gnomaticus feels that all will be well, once the boys have realized their own failure; but events move quickly in the fifth act to disprove this optimism. When the fathers receive news that the prodigals have once again fallen into evil ways, they send a faithful servant to the rescue, but he returns with the sad account of the death of Phylautus, and the disgrace of Phylosarchus—a blow somewhat tempered by the success of the two virtuous sons.

This careful division of the action is made more effective by Gascoigne's

[155] *Works,* II, 34.

dramatic instinct for events and characters. As we have noted, the prodigals do not capriciously embark on a career of evil. They learn easily, are soon bored, and long for the activity and associations of the university, characteristics of youth not necessarily vicious. Their exuberance for life and experience, accompanied by their lack of knowledge and their naïveté, aid in their seduction. In their first contact with the world they are caught, not by obvious seducers, but by evildoers whose plans are carefully laid. Eccho is no ordinary parasite, nor is Lamia a common harlot: both are clever in dealing with the youths. Eccho does not urge Phylosarchus to pursue Lamia, nor does she, on first meeting, speak with the young gallants. Later, Eccho can suggest that they call on Lamia and can devise an excuse for them to get away, but even here his cunning is of a new type. Phylosarchus offers him "twentie gildres" only to hear

What meane you sir? stay your purse untill another time, well if you will needes enforce me, I will never refuse the curtesie of a gentleman.[156]

These are not the broad strokes which portray the Vice of the interlude; they are subtle and are the results of direct observation of character.

Other events which are effective because of their realism and results are exemplified by the conduct of the Markgrave, who orders Lamia and her retinue to be seized, but whose punishment is neither swift nor arbitrary. The culprits must be treated legally. At first there is no evidence against them, and we wonder if they are to escape. The capture of Ambidexter settles their fate, but not until the last act. This attention to legal detail increases the verisimilitude of action, while the suspense is dramatic. Likewise we wonder if the prodigals are to escape: their fathers do all they can, but Fidus, who returns Ambidexter, brings word of their ruin.

The last act begins with a very real scene of contemporary life. The two parents are in the market place, anxious for news of their children, when they hear the cry, "Letters, letters, letters." A carrier from Douai fulfills the duties of the post. He can neither read nor write, but has his customers inscribe the address on a register which expectant recipients consult. We follow the two fathers in their anxiety; we hear the carrier exclaiming in his haste; and we are not too far from those realistic scenes of contemporary life in which Shakespeare excelled. Not realism, however, but dramatic choice makes the end of the play successful. Fidus has returned

[156] *Works,* II, 41.

from his errand of mercy, only to report failure. The recipient of his sad news is not his master but the idealistic schoolmaster, who has, throughout the play, believed in the ultimate success of his wayward charges. That he should hear the sorry news is, I believe, the dramatist's conscious irony.

As we have seen, Gascoigne deals successfully with characters, as well as with the choice and order of events. Eccho is a real creation, particularly if we compare him with the parasites of Roman comedy. A clever contrast is supplied by Dicke Groome, a typical low-comedy figure. He does not possess the subtlety of Eccho, but his common sense in deciding to leave Antwerp saves him from the fate which is Eccho's.[157] The latter overreaches himself in cleverness, and, in presenting this idea and contrast, Gascoigne gives very definite proof of his dramatic ability. Equally well considered as a character is Gnomaticus. Far from the birch-wielding pedagogue, he is tolerant and understanding. A Calvinist, he does not condemn completely the wanton pagans.[158] Rather he uses them as auxiliaries to the Christian ideal which is his concept of proper education. He is easily duped by Eccho, but his ideas of punishment and conduct are close to those of Ascham. The correction must suit the circumstances, since "in childhoode all punishment is terrible, but in florishing youth every punishment may not be used, but discretion must foresee what kynde of punishment wil most prevaile and best gayne reformation in the mind of the offender."[159] This understanding of youth and the confidence which Gnomaticus has in his pupils are betrayed, but that is not the fault of the dramatist. Nor is Gnomaticus guilty of false reasoning. His unworldliness is his weakness: he is deceived by Eccho, intrusts his letters to the notorious Ambidexter, and hopes for the best. In this he is far from the typical Renaissance schoolmaster and nearer to a Mr. Chips.

In depicting the fathers, Gascoigne is also original. Phylopaes and Phylocalus are citizens of Antwerp; in business together for many years, they are well off and desire for their children the benefits of education.

---

[157] Dicke is, however, finally hanged for his participation with Phylautus in a robbery.

[158] "I would not have you thinke hereby that I do holde in contempt the bookes which you have redde heretofore [i.e., "offices of *Cicero*," "Comedies of *Terence*," "Epistles of *Tully*," "some parte of *Virgill*"], but wee will (by Gods grace) take in assistance such and so many of them as may seeme consonant to the holy scriptures, and so joyning the one with the other, we shalbe the better able to bring our worke unto perfectiõ." (*Works*, II, 17.)

[159] *Works*, II, 53.

They find a tutor whom they treat as an important person, not as an inferior. The humanist ideal of the dignity of education and its responsibility for the training of youth as it is here enunciated finds a reflection in Ascham's discussion with Sir Richard Sackville, where the ideal is compared with the reality.[160]

The virtuous younger sons are necessarily dull; they lack their brothers' quick comprehension, but it is worth noting that their "themes" may not be unfavorably compared with Gascoigne's efforts in this vein. The poet's fondness for this type of composition led him to give the boys poems inconsistent with their abilities. There is little opportunity to animate these characters; but, with the prodigals, Gascoigne achieves a fluency that is not found in their Dutch or English forbears. These elder sons are not wastrels at heart. They expect something new from their master and receive a disquisition on commonplaces; very naturally they recognize the sententious, but fail to understand its significance. Quick wits are not always the best, but we can understand these two and their desire for the university. Their approach to Lamia is not brash: they behold a "peereless peece" and sympathize with her troubles like the credulous youths that they are. Phylosarchus's first desire is to write a love poem—a far cry from the riotous dissipations of other prodigals. These things we see, and it is hard to consider the youths as vicious. And so we are more ready to hear of their later ruin than we would be to witness it; the causes have been rendered understandable. Their troubles at the university do not need presentation, since the audience has already realized the fatal weakness of their unworldliness, coupled with their desire for experience. Thus the working out of their further excesses is expected. Whether this was the result of Gascoigne's attempt to preserve a unity of place or was a deliberate choice is uncertain. If it be the former, as seems likely on the basis of Roman comedy, the dramatist demonstrated not only his ability to create character but also his sense of structure, since the four sons do not depart until the middle of Act IV.

The time covered by Act V does, however, present a considerable problem. The Markgrave is still concerned with Lamia, Eccho, and their fellows, a fact which would indicate only a slight lapse of time after the

---

[160] Roger Ascham, 'The Scholemaster," in *The English Works of Roger Ascham*, ed. by W. A. Wright. Cambridge, 1904, p. 177.

departure of the students. None the less, within this period Phylautus has managed to commit robbery, and be tried and executed at the Palsgrave's court, while Phylosarchus has journeyed through France to Geneva, where he has been publicly beaten for fornication. Also, Fidus has time to journey to the Palsgrave's court, to Douai, and back to Antwerp. Indeed, with dispersed characters, the solution of the action must conflict with any unity of time. On this score Gascoigne failed. He did not employ time tags or realize that the problem could be solved by time intervals between scenes. His previous dramatic work had followed the continuous action of Greek tragedy, and his translation of Ariosto had not presented any difficulties of time relationships.

One final problem of structure, which involves consideration of the moral ideas, is the fate of the prodigals. Professor Herford noted the "stringent severity,"[161] and Dr. Boas describes it as Calvinistic.[162] The biblical story ends with the prodigal's return and with parental forgiveness, but we are unfair to Gascoigne as a dramatist if we do not point out that the fathers made a very definite effort to rescue their sons.[163] At the first temptation they sent them to the university. When things went badly there, Fidus was dispatched to bring them home. In other words, the parents are not lacking in Christian charity; they are not harsh and unforgiving. On the contrary, they take great responsibility for the welfare of their children. That death and disgrace are the fates of the sinners is due to chance, Fidus's late arrival, and to themselves, for their own deeds brought ruin upon them. In this sense the ending is harsh, but it is the harshness of the world, not that of the parents. Realism and chance destroy the happy ending.

On the purely literary side there remains to note Gascoigne's wise use of prose. The style is that which he developed in the *Supposes,* but here the sententious and moral subject matter at times creates a periodicity which is distinctly biblical. The lessons of Gnomaticus are really sermons, while the same character's soliloquy in Act IV is part of a tract on religion and education. The long speech, in a formal and heavily stylized vein, is not good drama, though it may be good prose. In the conversation of the

---

[161] *Op. cit.,* p. 161.   [162] *CHEL* V, 114.
[163] Dr. Boas (*ibid.*) says: "It pictures an unreal world of saints and sinners, ranged in symmetrical groups, with no reason for struggle and compromise, penitence and forgiveness."

morally undesirable characters there is a fluidity and phrasing that fore-
tells Pettie and Lyly. The third chorus, though heavily moral, displays
this quality, as well as the rhetorical parallelism of which Gascoigne was
fond:

> The prauncing steede, can seldome hold his flesh,
> The hottest greyhound leaves the course at length:
> The finest Silkes, do seeld continue freshe,
> The fattest men, may fayle sometymes of strength:
> Such deepe deceiptes, in faire pretence are founde,
> That vices lurke, where vertue seemes t'abound.
>
> A Spanish tricke it hath been counted oft,
> To seeme a thing, yet not desire to be:
> Like humble bees, which fly all dayes aloft,
> And tast the flowers, that fairest are to see:
> But yet at even, when all thinges go to rest,
> A foule cowe sharde, shall then content them best.[164]

This use of the chorus is, of course, derived from his contact with
Dolce and Senecan tragedy. But like the latter, it is only reflective, and its
speeches are really "themes" developing a sententious idea suggested by
the preceding action.

Though Gascoigne's moral regeneration was an integral part of his
age, and though this play is the best of its type in English, one could wish
that the technical ability suggested by his translations and here evinced
had been exercised on a subject nearer to the tradition of Elizabethan
drama. Had he not repented of his sins, Gascoigne might perhaps have
challenged Lyly's position as the first important Elizabethan dramatist.

[164] *Works*, II, 59.

VII. The Narrator

Wherefore (doubtlesse) they did him double wrong,
Which F. and J. mysconstrued have so long.

I. B.

GASCOIGNE'S INTEREST in narration, like his interest in poetry and drama, was based on tradition, but his narratives are his most original work, and, in my judgment, his claim to importance should rest more on them than previous critics have allowed. In general the historians of Elizabethan narratives have ignored Gascoigne or dismissed him in a few lines. Only recently, for example, has the originality and intrinsic worth of "The Adventures of Master F. J." been considered. On the other hand, the structure and method of composition of "Dan Bartholmew of Bathe" have seemingly escaped notice, while "The Tale of Hemetes" has been considered only in relation to the Woodstock entertainment. Equally ignored has been Gascoigne's reportorial ability as exemplified in "Dulce Bellum Inexpertis" and *The Spoyle of Antwerp*. All of these works are narratives, but since all four differ, both in their medium and *raison d'être*, and present as well a series of highly individual problems, my consideration of them will be sectional.

"THE ADVENTURES OF MASTER F.J."

Professor Saintsbury[1] noted "The Adventures of Master F. J." as "a prose tale (a version from Bandello)," while Jusserand did not consider any of the early Elizabethan tales in his *The English Novel in the Time of Shakespeare*.[2] The idea of Italian inspiration was continued by Lord Ernle[3] and Dr. Baker,[4] both of whom considered the story as either an

---

[1] Saintsbury, *A History of Elizabethan Literature*, p. 16. [2] London, 1890.
[3] Lord Ernle, *The Light Reading of Our Ancestors* (London, 1927), pp. 115-17.
[4] E. A. Baker, *The History of the English Novel* (London, 1929), II, 27-29. Dr. Baker notes the first version, but discusses the Italianate second.

imitation of or a translation from the Italian. Examining the version found in *The Posies,* we do not wonder at this when we read the title: "The pleasant Fable of *Ferdinando/ Jeron[i]mi and Lenora de Valasco,/* translated out of the Italian riding tales of *Bartello.*"[5] An omniscient author at once lays the scene somewhere in the country of Lombardy and introduces the characters: the Lord of Valasco; his daughter, Francischina; his daughter-in-law, Lenora, of the house of Bellavista; and their guest, a young man from Venice, Ferdinando Jeronimi. All the scenes are Italian, all the characters have Italian names, and there is no apparent reason to doubt that the fable is other than what it purports to be. Elyot, Painter, Beverley, and Broke had all translated Italian *novelle,* and in the past it has appeared logical to assume that Gascoigne was following the example of his contemporaries. The story as it appears in *A Hundreth Sundrie Flowres* is quite a different matter, but the traditional view has been that Gascoigne's first edition was surreptitious, even though Professor Schelling[6] and Dr. Cunliffe[7] long since observed that Gascoigne was obviously instrumental in procuring the publication.

While the weight of contemporary practice undoubtedly favors the idea of an Italian original, there is no real evidence for thinking that *A Hundreth Sundrie Flowres* was printed without authorization. Such a view is, of course, based on the anonymous introductory letters which preface "The Adventures of Master F. J." in the first edition of 1573.[8] There we learn that an anonymous *G. T.* gave to his friend *H. W.* a manuscript containing the prose tale and a number of poems. The latter, convinced of the undoubted merit of the work, made a copy which he entreated his friend *A. B.* to have imprinted.[9] The fictitiousness of this explanation is at once apparent when Gascoigne, in the prefatory letters to his revised and expanded edition of 1575, acknowledges the work as his own and, in the face of serious charges of libel and lascivious speech, does not take refuge in the obvious explanation that the work was published without his consent. Instead, he asserts that he has purified the poems and the

---

[5] *Works,* I, 383.   [6] *The Life and Writings of George Gascoigne,* p. 25.

[7] "George Gascoigne," *CHEL,* III, 204.

[8] *A Hundreth Sundrie Flowres* [1573], pp. 201–5.

[9] That Gascoigne himself wrote the letters as a protection against the charge of procuring publication (an ungentlemanly act according to contemporary practice) is the belief of Dr. Cunliffe (*CHEL,* III, 204–5). A detailed proof of this and of Gascoigne's authorship of the entire edition is part of the introduction to my edition of *A Hundreth Sundrie Flowres.*

prose narrative and, as we have seen, makes the latter appear to be a translation from a fictitious Bartello.

In thus disregarding the original version of the tale, the critics have failed to recognize Gascoigne's most important work, the first original prose narrative of the English Renaissance. Only within the last decade did Dr. Leicester Bradner[10] point out the significance of "The Adventures of Master F. J." In bringing this neglected work to the notice of the scholarly world, Dr. Bradner was necessarily limited in his discussion; hence our present task is to examine the structure of the story, its antecedents, its merits, and its influence.

In *The Posies,* as we have seen, there is a straightforward beginning: the title is given and the first paragraph lays the necessary foundation. However, the original version begins far differently, and to understand this we must briefly examine the bibliographical aspects of *A Hundreth Sundrie Flowres.* This volume begins with a letter, "The Printer to the Reader," which is followed by the text of *Supposes* and *Jocasta.* The latter ends on page 164 (sig. Xiiij^v) with the colophon: "Printed by Henrie Bynneman/ for Richarde Smith." The next page is 201 (sig. Aj^r) and there begins the letter of *"H. W. to the Reader"* which is headed: "A discourse of the adventures/ *passed by Master F. J."* Instead of beginning or even introducing the narration, *H. W.* tells how he came into possession of the manuscript of the prose tale and the poems and how he entreated his friend *A. B.* to have it imprinted. Then follows the letter by which *G. T.* entrusted the manuscript to *H. W.,* and after this we have the beginning of the manuscript itself, with *G. T.*'s editorial explanation of the arrangement and his beginning of the tale.

And to begin with this his [*F. J.*'s] history that ensueth, it was (as he declared unto me) written uppon this occasion. The said *F. J.* chaunced once in the north partes of this Realme to fall in company of a very fayre gentlewoman whose name was Mistresse *Elinor,* unto whom bearinge a hotte affection, he first adventured to write this letter following.

G. T.[11]

At this point the original and the revised versions coincide; the ensuing letter is the same in both. However, as the narrative of Master F. J. pro-

---

[10] "The First English Novel, A Study of George Gascoigne's *Adventures of master F. J.*," PMLA, XLV (1930), 543–52.

[11] *A Hundreth Sundrie Flowres,* p. 205.

ceeds, one finds that both the characters and the scene are English. In other words, the original version is an account of the love affair of F. J. and Elinor, which took place at a country house in the north of England.

The reasons for transforming the English original into a pseudo-translation from the Italian are to be found in the prefatory letters to *The Posies*. The first, addressed "To the reverende Divines," contains the following passage:

> It is verie neare two yeares past, since (I beeing in Hollande in service with the vertuous Prince of Orenge) the most parte of these Posies were imprinted, and now at my returne, I find that some of them have not onely bene offensive for sundrie wanton speeches and lascivious phrases, but further I heare that the same have beene doubtfully construed, and (therefore) scandalous.[12]

Later the tale is specifically mentioned.

> I understande that sundrie well disposed mindes have taken offence at certaine wanton wordes and sentences passed in the fable of *Ferdinando Jeronimi*, and the Ladie *Elinora de Valasco*, the which in the first edition was termed The adventures of Master F. J. And that also therwith some busie conjectures have presumed to thinke that the same was indeed written to the scandalizing of some worthie personages, whom they woulde seeme therby to know.[13]

To remedy the first fault of "wanton wordes," Gascoigne carefully excised details of the seduction scenes and omitted the poem on cuckoldry, together with its introduction. He confesses to this purification, but it will be noted that he says nothing about the metamorphosis of the English F. J. into the Italian *Ferdinando Jeronimi*. Evidently it was best not to create more problems than already faced him. By ignoring any question as to the Italianization of his story, Gascoigne seemingly hoped that it would be taken at its face value and that thus being accepted as a translation, the tale obviously could not concern contemporary figures.

This tendency on the part of his readers to find in "The Adventures of Master F. J." a veiled allusion to real people and real events was not unusual. The tradition of manifold significance was old when Dante developed it in *La Divina Commedia*. Sir John Harington appended an allegorical interpretation to each canto of his translation of *Orlando Furioso*, even though such interpretation had no foundation in his original. *Richard II* was and is thought to have a contemporary significance,

---

[12] *Works*, I, 3.   [13] *Ibid.*, I, 7.

while the repeated attempts of critics to find hidden allusions in Lyly and Spenser are a continuation of the process. That Elizabethan authors did write with a double purpose is shown by two such separated figures as Pettie and Barclay. Several editions of the latter's *Argenis* contain a table by which the reader could identify the characters as contemporary figures.[14] Pettie openly avows such a method when he says that his tales, although every one has a source, "touch nearly divers of my near friends; but the best is, they are so darkly figured forth, that only they whom they touch, can understand whom they touch."[15]

This inability to identify the persons concerned was a problem even for Gascoigne's contemporaries, since he observes that "talking with .xx. of them one after another, there have not two agreed in one conjecture."[16] This is not surprising, considering that affairs similar to F. J.'s were current, particularly in court circles. One notorious scandal was the Earl of Leicester's seduction of Douglas Sheffield, which took place in 1568 on the occasion of Queen Elizabeth's progress to Belvoir Castle. The story, as told by Sir Gervase Holles and printed by Arthur Collins in *Historical Collections of the Noble Families of Cavendish, Holles, Vere, Harley, and Ogle* (London 1752, pp. 77–78), contains similarities as striking to us as they must have been to Gascoigne's contemporaries. Mr. Fleay, in modern times, has conjectured, on the basis of the second and revised version, that here Gascoigne tells the story of Elinor Manners and John Bourchier;[17] while Mr. Ward would have us believe that it concerns the loves of Sir Christopher Hatton.[18] Dr. Bradner has demonstrated the impossibility of the former, and, in the introduction to my edition of the *Flowres*, I shall prove that Mr. Ward's entire hypothesis rests on misapprehensions. Dr. Bradner followed Professor Schelling and Dr. Cunliffe in suggesting that the story was autobiographical, and certain reasons for such a view will be made clear as we proceed. But whether the tale concerned other people or himself, Gascoigne was in a precarious position: either he was guilty of libel or he openly confessed to brazen adultery. He took the only possible course by unostentatiously describing the tale as a translation and

[14] John Barclay, *Argenis* [Latin], 1634, [English] 1628, 1629.
[15] Pettie, *A petite Pallace of Pettie his pleasure* (1576), ed. by Sir Israel Gollancz, I, 5.
[16] *Works*, I, 7.
[17] Fleay, *A Biographical Chronicle of the English Drama, 1559–1642*, I, 239.
[18] Ward, ed., *A Hundreth Sundrie Flowres* (1926), pp. xiii–xiv.

thus he hoped to avoid trouble. That he was not successful in this bold device is indicated by an entry in the "B" Book of the Stationers' Company recording the seizure, by the authorities in 1576, of "half a hundred of Gascoignes poesies."[19]

Understanding the reasons for the transformation of the prose tale does not, however, explain the original version, how it came to be written, or how it varies from the familiar type of the Italian *novelle*. Perhaps the most noticeable external feature of "The Adventures of Master F. J." is its use of poems to celebrate or to elaborate events in the narrative. Interpolated poems and letters are employed in the Italian *novelle* and in the pastoral, but in none of these is there the integration or the frequency which is here found. The explanation is suggested by the fact that the poems were written before the prose, as we may easily discover from the text itself. For example, the eighth poem beginning "Beautie shut up thy shop,"[20] uses the name "Hellen" to celebrate the Lady Elinor. In the prose narrative that follows, the latter became jealous "because hir name was *Elynor* and not *Hellen*." Then follows a discussion by the author as to whether F. J. meant Elinor or a certain Helen whom he knew some six or seven years after this affair.[21] Obviously, to discuss events later than those celebrated in the poem, the narrative must be posterior to the poem. Gascoigne's beginning of the tale, disguised as the comment of the fictitious *G. T.*, noted above, also indicates that the prose was written after the verse. Similar evidence is found in the frequent comments: "I have heard him say," or "I have heard the Aucthor saye."

One passage which indicates not only the relative time of composition but also its method and purpose is that preceding the sixth poem, *"Dame Cinthia hir selfe."* The time is the morning after F. J.'s first seduction of Elinor.

At the last *F.J.* awaked, and apparreling himselfe, walked out also to take the ayre, and being throughly recomforted aswell with the remembraunce of his joyes forepassed, as also with the pleasaunt hermony which the Byrdes made on every side, and the fragrant smel of the redolent flowers and blossomes

---

[19] Greg and Boswell, *Records of the Courts of the Stationers' Company*, pp. lvii, 87.
[20] *Works*, I, 414. "F. J." No. 8.
[21] This discussion, couched in Italian names, is found in the revised edition (*Works*, I, 415). I quote from the original version (*A Hundreth Sundrie Flowres*, pp. 244–45).

which budded on every braunche: hee did in these delightes compyle these verses following.

¶ The occasion (as I have heard him rehearse) was by encounter that he had with his Lady by light of the moone: and forasmuch, as the moone in middes of their delights did vanish away, or was overspred with a cloud, thereupon he toke the subject of his theame. And thus it ensueth, called a mooneshine Banquet.

G.T.[22]

The poem follows, but why does it require two introductions? The first is part of the narrative, while the second, even to the use of the printer's ornament, is similar to the introductory comments prefaced to the sep- arate poems which follow "F. J." and which fill the remainder of the original volume. It seems to me that this error of two introductions gives an excellent clue as to the method and, indeed, to the actual time of writ- ing the prose passages. This poem with its second introduction could well be placed among the general body of verse, and was probably intended originally for inclusion in that section. However, after, or at the earliest, during the preparation of the manuscript of the poems, Gascoigne began the prose tale and decided to make use of those verses which did in fact relate to this affair. He brought the narrative to a point where a poem was to be inserted and then included that poem. He must have first set aside certain verses for use in this tale and then, as it progressed, discovered an opportunity for employing at least one poem that he had not originally planned to use. Finding a possible place for insertion, he took the manu- script of the present poem, complete with its introduction, from among the poems signed by the various posies and physically inserted it at this point. Had he copied it, the chances are that he would have noted the double introduction, but using the already prepared manuscript, he failed to observe the redundancy. It is significant that this second introduction is omitted from *The Posies,* and, since there seem to be no moral grounds for its excision, it is apparent that in revision Gascoigne noted and cor- rected the error.

Two most important factors are, I think, to be deduced from this: first, Gascoigne had prepared his poems, or at least part of them, for publica- tion before he began the prose story of "F. J."; second, this tale bore some

[22] *A Hundreth Sundrie Flowres,* pp. 235–36.

resemblance to events in Gascoigne's own experience. The first is indicated in the preceding discussion and seems to be the only explanation for the use of two introductions. The second conclusion may be less obvious. However, let us notice how closely the details in this second introduction refer to the events related in the narrative: the encounter with and seduction of the lady and the fact that F. J. saw her in the bright moonlight. Since this introduction was composed before the prose tale and since both tell approximately the same story, the two were probably based on the same episode. If the poem were originally destined for inclusion in the verse section of the volume, it was written by Gascoigne and was probably based on his own experience. Thus it would seem that the prose tale, the second introduction, and the poem itself all dealt with one experience in Gascoigne's life.

It may be objected that the poem might have been one of those which Gascoigne wrote for other men.[23] There seems to be, however, some evidence to oppose such a view, and chief is the fact that a number of the poems in "F. J." are demonstrably linked with the narrative, as in the instance we have just noted. The verses on cuckoldry beginning, "As some men say there is a kind of seed,"[24] are intelligible only on the basis of the preceding prose account of the joint hunting expedition of F. J. and Elinor's husband. In particular the last line, "Start up a horne, thy husband could not blow it," can only be understood in relation to the whole story of the seduction. So, too, the sonnet beginning, "With hir in armes that had my hart in hold,"[25] even in the revised edition is an exact picture of the incidents related in the narrative. Likewise a phrase of the prose is used as a sort of burden in two poems, and in both instances the events are definitely connected with the prose.[26] Such a close interrelation demonstrates that both prose and verse are concerned with the same events. This being so, we find certain objections to supposing the poems were written for some friend of Gascoigne's. First, we would be forced to conclude that Gascoigne was sufficiently intimate with some one to know

[23] This custom is noted by Turbervile (*vide supra*, Chap. v, pp. 117–18) and by Gascoigne (*Works*, I, 16, ll. 32–36).

[24] The original version of this is printed in the notes to Dr. Cunliffe's edition (*Works*, I, 496). "F. J." No. 10.

[25] *Works*, I, 450. "F. J." No. 13.

[26] "I could not though I would" (*ibid.*, I, 448). "F. J." No. 12.

"And if I did what then" (*ibid.*, I, 452). "F. J." No. 14.

all the details of the love affair and to write five poems dealing with crucial events in that affair. Secondly, such a belief would indicate that the whole story concerned this friend.

Such a conclusion seems hardly possible, particularly when we can find other evidence linking Gascoigne and F. J. One of the introductory remarks to the above-noted lines on cuckold's horns is "And hereupon (before the fal of the Buck) [he] devised this Sonet following."[27] The concluding remarks to that section of the later poems entitled, "Gascoignes memorie" announce the amazing fact that the poet composed these 258 lines "riding by the way, writing none of them until he came at the end of his Journey . . . a small time for suche a taske."[28] The dedicatory letter of *The Complaynt of Phylomene* tells a similar story of the rapid production of "De Profundis," achieved while riding from Chelmsford to London.[29] Casual as these references are, they suggest for this very reason a likeness between Gascoigne and F. J.

Similar details, but indicating a physical rather than intellectual resemblance between the two men, are found in Frances's recital of her dream:

. . . for I dreamt this night that I was in a pleasaunt meadow alone, where I met with a tall Gentleman, apparelled in a night gowne of silke. . . .[30]

In the poem to Bartholomew Withypoll there are two references to Gascoigne's height.

> So shall my *Batte* prolong his youthfull yeeres,
> And see long *George* agayne, with happie dayes. . . .[31]
>
> . . . and if he bee (no, no)
> The beste compaynon that long *George* can fynde. . . .[32]

Similar mention of the poet's stature is found in his tract, *The Spoyle of Antwerpe:*

> In fine, I gotte up like a tall fellow. . . .[33]

The accumulation of evidence seems to indicate that Frances's "tall Gentleman" and George Gascoigne were one and the same person.

We can also see in the details of the story that the author, and therefore

[27] *Ibid.*, I, 496. "F.J." No. 10.   [28] *Ibid.*, I, 70. No. 61.
[29] *Ibid.*, II, 177.   [30] *Ibid.*, I, 412.   [31] *Ibid.*, I, 347. No. 67.
[32] *Ibid.*   [33] *Ibid.*, II, 595.

Gascoigne, is recounting his own adventures. For example, Elinor secretly visits F. J., who is languishing as a result of his suspicions of the Secretary. The lady assures her lover of her steadfast devotion in such fervent words that he swoons.

> It were hard now to rehearse how hee was revived, since there were none present, but he dying (who could not declare) & she living who wold not disclose so much as I meane to bewray. For my friend *F.J.* hath to me emported, that returning to life, the first thing which he felt, was that his good mistres lay pressing his brest w^t the whole weight of hir body, and biting his lips with hir friendly teeth. . . . [34]

Certainly no one would relate to another the details of this passage, and we at once see the familiar fiction of G. T. fade away to reveal Gascoigne recounting only those events which he actually remembers.

Finally, as Dr. Bradner[35] has indicated, the Gascoigne family had connections in Yorkshire and Dame Margaret was a Scargill of the same county, circumstances which would explain the locale as the North of England, particularly in view of the fact that F. J. is a kinsman of Frances.

Thus far evidence has been presented to show that the version of the tale as found in *A Hundreth Sundrie Flowres* is the original and that *The Posies'* version was made into a likeness of a translation for very definite reasons. Secondly, I have tried to prove that Gascoigne wrote the poems before the prose, that the events in the poems and prose are the same, and that George Gascoigne and F. J. are the same.[36] Unfortunately, it has been necessary to present this evidence in some detail; but it has seemed wise because, in my view, a true understanding of the merits of "The Adventures of Master F. J." rests upon the realization that it is an account of actual events, told by one of the chief participants.

And with this in mind let us consider the story. The scene is a castle or country house in the North of England, where we find the Lord of the Castle, his daughter Frances, and his married stepdaughter Elinor.[37] The

---

[34] *A Hundreth Sundrie Flowres*, p. 269.   [35] *Ibid.*, p. 546.

[36] The time when Gascoigne journeyed to the North and met Mistress Elinor is to be considered elsewhere, since it is not material to our purposes here. Suffice it to say that it was probably during his years at Cambridge or his early residence at Gray's Inn and that, in my opinion, Elinor is to be identified with the Cosmana, who was the first love of the "greene Knight." But these suppositions are tenuous and do not concern the literary values of the tale.

[37] The Lord of the Castle calls both Frances and Elinor "daughter," but Elinor's father seems to be dead, since she swears by her father's soul. In *The Posies* Elinor is the Lord's

other characters are either guests or relatives. The time covered is from early summer to the beginning of autumn,[38] and the story is that of a young man who falls in love with a married woman, enjoys success in the affair only to find disillusionment in the realization that his idol has feet of clay. On the warp of this love affair is woven a realistic picture of life and people. The events in the progress of the love story are few: F. J. meets the lady, woos, wins, and loses her. The tale is twice-told, but Gascoigne's rendition of the theme is unique in the literature of the English Renaissance and finds no equal until well over a hundred years after its publication. In other words, its importance lies less in its plot than in its method of narration. Our consideration, then, is to be based on the twofold aspect of this last: the added details which have no direct connection with the action of the love story, and the devices by which Gascoigne weaves these additions into the warp of the love story to produce the finished product.

The first of these additions or elaborations is the physical environment. The "castle," as Gascoigne calls it, resembles a late medieval structure. It has a great chamber, a base court, and several rooms, none of which is accessible to the hall. Elinor's chamber seems to be, however, since by standing in the portal of her chamber, she is able to overhear a supper conversation between Frances and F. J.[39] On the other hand, F. J. has to cross the base court to reach his room, and Frances evidently has apartments in the same section, whence she is able to observe him on his return from a meeting with Elinor.[40] Such an arrangement does not suggest the new type of Elizabethan country house of the "E" pattern, and we are evidently in a castle somewhat after the model of Kenilworth, though

---

daughter-in-law and the fact that this relationship is openly announced in the revised edition makes it, in my judgment, suspect. Therefore, I feel that Elinor's original relationship was probably that of stepdaughter. We are told that F. J. is a kinsman to Frances, but nothing is said of Elinor in this connection—a fact that seems to confirm my theory.

[38] In the opening pages Elinor gives F. J. a letter while the company is walking in the garden. The morning after his seduction of Elinor, F. J. walks in the same park and enjoys "the redolent flowres and blossomes which budded on every side." Thus the time seems to be early summer. Later we learn from Pergo, on the day after F. J.'s quarrel with Elinor, that the leaves have begun to fall and that the cuckoo is preparing to migrate. This indicates the autumn, probably September, for the cuckoo's migration begins in mid-August and ends a month later.

[39] This detail is also found in the revised version. (*Works*, I, 403).

[40] *Works*, I, 407.

we lack details of moats and drawbridges. We do, however, hear of a castle wall, for near it is a park where our characters walk to enjoy the "redolent blossomes" and to protect themselves from the heat.[41]

The characters placed in this environment are seasoned courtiers. The Lord is a generous host, concerned for the goodness of his food, the pleasure of the company, and the health of his guest. On any occasion he is ready to indulge in the game of repartee, as indeed are both Elinor and Frances, though the former usually imparts an acid rather than a dulcet tone to her remarks. Both the ladies have seen the world and have few illusions: Elinor is frankly promiscuous,[42] while Frances's gentle unrequited love for F. J. finds solace in friendship and a mildly sadistic expression in making the two lovers uncomfortable. The only other "name" character is Pergo, who, according to our author, "had stuffe in hir" and was "an old courtier, and a wylie wench."[43] Into this gathering comes a young kinsman, F. J., who in the glory of his youth rather fancies his worldliness and sophistication. In love, he begins by following the contemporary conventions of behavior, but ends as a sadder and a wiser man. In conversation he is witty, but the others usually triumph over him in verbal encounters. During these few months, however, we see him acquire a variety of experiences which contribute to his "growing-up."

The occupants of the castle lead a pleasant life. They walk in the park, ride into the surrounding country, go to chapel, have dinner in the early afternoon and supper in the evening. They find amusement in games, dancing, and singing. The round of existence proceeds, and, had one been a guest for the summer, one might very easily have missed the intrigue of Elinor and F. J., which appeared outwardly as the usual "servant and Mistress" relationship. This would have occasioned no marked attention because of its conventional nature, but beneath the outward appearance lay the reality, and in the interweaving of the inner and outward shows

[41] I have often wondered if it might be Barnard Castle, but there is no evidence to prove or disprove this.

[42] Two previous lovers, "H. D." and "H. K.," are mentioned by Frances. Full Italian names are given in *The Posies* (*Works*, I, 403).

[43] *Works*, I, 428. A further indication of the reality of the persons involved is the remark on Pergo's name, omitted in *The Posies*: ". . . whome for this discourse I will name *Pergo*, least hir name natural were to brode before, and might not drinke of all waters." (*A Hundreth Sundrie Flowres*, pp. 262–63.) This seems to mean that her real name would be too much of a clue and that its use would be displeasing to many.

of things Gascoigne achieved a literary masterpiece. To a variety of events, some casual, some amusing, some, at least to him, highly dramatic or deeply emotional, Gascoigne gave a pattern. He remembered his summer in the North; he had preserved the letters and poems, as does every young lover, but when he came to tell the story he realized the function of the artist by imposing form on the shapeless mass of remembered events. In so doing he did not destroy the complete picture of a summer's interlude; instead, he created a verisimilitude which today gives us a story with the full flavor of Elizabethan country life and which has the added distinction of being not only the first novel, but indeed the first psychological novel.

How Gascoigne achieved this is the essential problem, and we can find a clue in almost every scene. I have chosen as a first example that of the supper following the first game of questions. Although nothing which there happens or is said in any way affects the love affair of Elinor and F. J., the scene is nevertheless extremely important. In order to make it more readily understandable, I shall present it as far as possible in dramatic form:

And at supper time, the Knight of the Castel finding fault that his gestes stomacke served him no better, began to accuse the grosenes of his vyands, to whom one of the gentlewomen [Frances] which had passed the afternoon in his [F. J.'s] company [when he nearly confessed his love for Elinor], aunswered.

Frances: Nay sir, this gentleman hath a passion, the which once in a daye at the least doth kill his appetite.
Knight: Are you so well acquainted with the disposition of his body?
Frances: By his owne saying & not otherwise.
F. J.: Fayre ladie, you either mistoke me or overheard me then, for I told of a comfortable humor which so fed me with continual remembrance of joye, as y^t my stomack being ful therof doth desire in maner none other vittayles.
Knight: Why sir, do you then live by love?
F. J.: God forbid Sir, for then my cheekes wold be much thinner then they be, but there are divers other greater causes of joy, than ye doubtful lottes of love, and for myne owne part, to be playne, I cannot love, and I dare not hate.
Frances: I would I thought so.[44]

This scene may be said to have three functions. First, it displays a witty conversation which more than ever makes us wish that *Euphues* had

[44] *A Hundreth Sundrie Flowres,* pp. 219–20.

never come to England and supplanted natural wit with exotic verbal-
isms. Secondly, it tells of the social pattern: hospitality and the evening
supper. Most important, it portrays character implicitly rather than directly. The Knight is a good host, but he is ready to tease his guest.
Frances by her intervention reveals her interest in F. J.'s affair and by the
gentle ridicule of her remarks indicates her attitude toward the young
man and his "passion." She does not attack F. J. nor is she caustic here
or elsewhere; her forte is subtlety. Our hero, a bit flustered, protests that
he is not in love; in fact, he protests too much (Elinor, overhearing his
denial of love, becomes angry). The unexpected turn taken by the innocent remarks about his appetite has caught him unawares, and, though
he tries to extricate himself, he is not a master of repartee. The method
adduced from this scene is that which Gascoigne uses throughout. There
is always some bit of revelation that adds to our understanding of the
love affair or the chief actors in that affair; the conversation or event is
intrinsically witty or amusing; finally, the background of life in this
northern castle unobtrusively appears.

Gascoigne's viewpoint regarding the love affair is psychological: we
see the individuals' minds reacting to an incident or to one another. The
emphasis is not so much on what happens or what is said as upon the
meaning to the individual characters of events or remarks. The significance of the love affair to F. J., Elinor, and Frances is what Gascoigne is
interested in portraying, as we may perceive from the following scene,
where again I have employed the dramatic method of presentation. The
time is after dinner on the day following F. J.'s first seduction of Elinor.
Frances has proposed that the three of them ride out into the country
during the afternoon, and F. J., going to his room to make ready, has
become quite upset over his failure to find his sword, which Frances,
knowing at least part of its significance in connection with events of the
preceding night, has secretly removed.

(At last the Ladies going towardes horsebacke called for him in the base Court,
and demaunded if he were readie. . . .)

    F. J.: Madames I am more than readie, and yet not so ready as I would be.
(And immediatly taking him selfe in trip, he thought best to utter no more
of his conceipt, but in hast more than good speede mounted his horse, & comming toward yᵉ dames presented him self, turning, bounding, & taking up his

courser to the uttermost of his power in bravery: after suffering his horse to breath him selfe, he gan also allay his owne choller.)

F. J.: Fayre Ladies I am ready when it pleaseth you to ryde where so you commaund.

Elinor: How ready soever you be servaunt, it seemeth your horse is readier at your commaunde then at oures.

F. J.: If he bee at my commaund Mistresse, he shalbe at yours.

Elinor: Gramercy good servaunt but my meaning is, that I feare he be to stirring for our company.

F. J.: If he prove so Mistress I have here a soberer palfrey to serve you on. (The Dames being mounted they rode forthwardes by the space of a myle or very neare, & *F. J.* (whether it were of his horses corage or his own choler) came not so near them as they wished.)

Frances: Maister *J.* you said that you had a soberer horse, which if it be so, we wold be glad of your company, but I beleve by your countinance, your horse & you are agreed.

[He changes horses with his servant.]

F. J.: And why doe you thinke faire Lady that my horse and I are agreed?

Frances: Bicause by your countenance it seemeth your pacience is stirred.

F. J.: In good faith, you have gessed a right, but not with any of you.

Elinor: Then we care the lesse servaunt.

(*F. J.* looking well about him that none might heare but they two.)

F. J.: By my troth Mistres, it is with my servaunt, who hath lost my sword out of my chamber.

Elinor: (little remembring the occasion) It is no matter servaunt, you shall heare of it againe, I warrant you, and presently wee ryde in Gods peace, and I trust shall have no neede of it.

F. J.: Yet Mistresse, a weapon serveth both uses, aswell to defend, as to offend.

Frances: Now by my troth, I have now my dream, for I dreamt this night that I was in a pleasaunt meadow alone, where I met with a tall Gentleman, apparelled in a night gowne of silke all embroadered about with a gard of naked swords, and when he came towardes me I seemed to be afraide of him, but he recomforted me saying, be not afrayd fayre Lady, for I use this garment onely for myne own defence: and in this sort went that warlicke God *Mars* what time hee taught Dame *Venus* to make *Vulcan* a hamer of the newe fashion. . . .

F. J.: And what tyme of the night dreamt you this?

Frances: In the grey morning about dawning of ye day, but why aske you?

F. J.: (with a great sigh) Because that dreames are to be marked more at some hower of the night, then at some other.

Elinor: Why, are you so cunning at the interpretation of dreames servaunt.

F. J.: Not very cunning Mistresse, but gesse, like a young scholler.

(The dames continued in these and like pleasant talkes: but *F. J.* could not be mery, as one that estemed the preservation of his Mistresse honor no lesse then the obtayning of his owne delightes: and yet to avoyde further suspicion, he repressed his passions, asmuch as hee could.) [45]

How well we see and understand these three individuals, their thoughts, their motives, and the essential qualities which make them appear as real persons. F. J. is not blasé; he is really worried lest the seduction be known. Frances's seemingly innocent remarks about F. J.'s anger have hidden barbs, which the young man attempts to ignore by a great seriousness that conceals nothing. These, together with the nice circumlocution about the dream, are as nothing to Elinor. She is sure of herself, pleased with her conquest, and knows that thus she has the upper hand in any encounter with Frances. A casual horseback excursion can be made to reveal much, if the author has the eyes to see, and Gascoigne remembered only too well the agony of those moments.

A final example of Gascoigne's method of implied revelation is found near the end of the story. The break between F. J. and Elinor, though not openly known, is suspected by Frances and Pergo, who with some of the gentlewomen walk in the park, where they hear a cuckoo.

Pergo: A ha this foule byrd begines to flye the countrie, and yet before hir departure, see how spitefully she can devise to salute us.

Frances: Not us but some other whom she hath espyed.

Pergo: Why here is no body but we few women.

Frances: Thanks be to God the house is not farre from us.

Pergo: I understand you not but to leape out of this matter, shall we go visite Maister *F. J.* and see how he doth this morning?

Frances: Why, do you suppose that the Cuckoe called unto him?

Pergo: Nay marry, for (as farre as I know) he is not maried.

Frances: As who should say that the Cuckoe envieth none but maryed folkes.

Pergo: I take it so.

Frances: Yes sure I have noted as evill lucke in love (after the cuckoes call) to have happened unto divers unmaried folkes, as ever I did unto the maried. [46]

After this nothing more remains to be said about Dame Pergo, for we have seen the "wylie wench" at work and she has revealed herself. Frances's usual subtlety is apparent, as is her concern for F. J.; but we do not know the cause of the antagonism between her and Pergo. Al-

[45] *Ibid.,* pp. 239–41.   [46] *Ibid.,* p. 273.

though it has nothing to do with Frances's love for F. J., it enters our story, since Pergo is thus ready to bait Frances on any occasion. In addition to character portrayal, the scene is functional in its indication of the end of F. J.'s love affair. Frances has observed the renewed familiarity between the Secretary and Elinor, and the cuckoo's call becomes symbolic. Finally, the departure of the cuckoo points a time tag, which is nicely used later in the same scene. Frances observes that Elinor has been neglecting F. J. and adds, "I perceyve that all earthly thinges are subject unto change." Thereupon Pergo continues, "Even so they be, for you may behold the trees which but even this other daye were clad in gladsome greene, and now their leaves begin to fade and change colour."[47] F. J.'s affair has indeed flourished with the summer and faded with the autumn.

One notable exception to the revelation by implication is the account of F. J.'s suspicion of Elinor. Here we are given F. J.'s thoughts, with their swift alternation of hope and despair. Elinor visits him and is kind. At her departure he reproaches himself, rising from his bed seemingly reassured. Then he remembers that she had carried a willow branch to fan herself. Now the willow has a symbolic meaning: it indicates that a lover is rejected. At once all security vanishes; suspicion is redoubled. Though this method is different from that usually employed, it is necessary, since Gascoigne again wishes to emphasize the point of view from which he tells the entire story, namely, that of the psychological behavior of his characters and chiefly himself. He cannot yet bring himself to confide in Frances, and, since the information cannot thus be disclosed in conversation, the only available method is to present his thoughts. Elsewhere, direct description is at a minimum; only the Secretary is thus treated, mainly, we presume, because Gascoigne could not deny the desire to vilify his rival.

In this consideration of method it is interesting to note that the entire story is told on the basis of F. J.'s knowledge of events. Eventually he confides in Frances, and it is evident that she tells him of such things as the removal of the sword and seeing Elinor with the Secretary. F. J. never tells us that he gained information from Frances, but it is clear that he had. The fact that neither the Lord nor Elinor appears in scenes without F. J. again indicates that the sources of his information were limited. The

[47] *Ibid.*, p. 274.

majority of scenes are based on F. J.'s own experience, while a few come obviously from Frances. The tale is thus clearly not imaginative, and the author is not omniscient. He is the chief character and tells us only what he knows himself and what he learns from his confidante, Frances. Since Gascoigne is the author and since the author is telling of his adventures, we have another link identifying Gascoigne with F. J.

All the foregoing evidence of method leads to an evaluation of Gascoigne's achievement. He remembered his first love affair, not as a series of events which ended unhappily, but as an emotional experience that changed him from a credulous youth into a wiser man. In telling the story, therefore, he emphasized its psychological aspects: his pseudo-sophistication, his youthful confidence, Elinor's callous nonchalance, and the rather inscrutable subtlety of Frances, which he understood and appreciated only in retrospect. Since he has himself known these people, has lived with them for an entire summer in a castle in the North, he quite naturally presents them as real people in a real environment. His genius lies in his ability to create in the novel-form this verisimilitude. While it is obvious that the reality of a character or a scene cannot be achieved merely by a recital of remembered incidents, those events and conversations which Gascoigne uses are definite evidence of his conscious artistry. No single event or conversation is irrelevant; each fulfills a definite function in giving the reader an understanding of the people involved, in such a way as to heighten his comprehension of the effect of this love affair on F. J. Certainly there were many events of that summer's holiday which had no connection with the affair. F. J. must have hunted more than once; he presumably had other conversations with his host; Frances and Elinor danced in the great chamber during other evenings—yet we see none of these events. Only those happenings which are germane to the affair are reproduced, and in no two of them is the same fact revealed. The jealousy of Elinor for Frances is pointed in the dancing scene and, although this antagonism is apparent throughout, it is never again the main reason for the inclusion of any event. Growth in the relationship between F. J. and Frances is indicated progressively in their conversations, and each time we see them the young man understands more of the situation in which he is involved and more of the true friendship that Frances offers. Certainly, Gascoigne knew what he was doing in writing "The Adventures of Master F. J."

Although he was creating a unique example of the English short story, Gascoigne undoubtedly knew the Italian *novelle*. A comparison with his predecessors reveals at once that Gascoigne's point of view constitutes his real contribution. John Addington Symonds has well stated the essential nature of the *novella* as it appeared first in Boccaccio and later, in Gascoigne's time, in Bandello, Cinthio, and Masuccio.

The narrator went straight to his object, which was to arrest the attention, stimulate the curiosity, gratify the sensual instincts, excite the laughter, or stir the tender emotions of his audience by some fantastic, extraordinary, voluptuous, comic, or pathetic incident.[48] . . . The student of contemporary Italian customs will glean abundant information from these pages; the student of human nature gathers little except reflections on the morals of sixteenth-century society.[49]

The oral tradition of the *novelle* disappeared when Belleforest, Painter, Broke, and Beverley translated these tales into French and English. To these men the written, the literary form was the important consideration. They did not write down stories which they heard; they translated from the printed or manuscript page. Thus it is easy to understand their additions and elaborations. For example, Belleforest's version[50] of Bandello's "Don Timbreo,"[51] one of the sources of *Much Ado,* is quite different from its original. The events are identical, but the French translator adds the full text of love letters, conversations between the heroine and her servant on chastity and duty to one's parents, and long soliloquies by the hero, on such subjects as sacred and profane love. Peter Beverley,[52] in an English poetic version of a variant of this same story, has pages on the conventional sufferings of lovers. *The Palace of Pleasure* in a lesser degree illustrates the same practice. The early translators of the *novelle*

---

[48] Symonds, *The Renaissance in Italy,* II, 201.   [49] *Ibid.,* II, 203.

[50] François de Belle-forest, *Le Troisième Tome Des Histoires Tragiques, extraittes des oeuvres Italiennes de Bandel* (Lyon, 1574), fols. 475–515. I have used the Folger Shakespeare Library copy.

[51] John Payne, *The Novels of Matteo Bandello* (London, 1890), I, 302–38.

[52] Peter Beverley, *The Historie of Ariodanto and Ienevra, daughter to the King of Scottes, in English verse, Imprinted at London by Thomas East, for Fraunces Caldocke* [1565/6]. Unique copy in the Huntington Library. Photostat in The Folger Shakespeare Library.

found great literary value in the rhetorical. Long passages on conventional moral themes, impossible in a spoken tale, were hallmarks of fine writing in the purely literary translations and imitations.

We can thus comprehend that Gascoigne really owes little to his predecessors: he is not interested in the extraordinary, comic, or pathetic incidents of the Italian, nor does he employ the rhetoric of the French and the English translators. His narration is not objective; it is not a recital of events for their own sake. The psychological point of view is something new. The use of letters and poems finds a counterpart in the pastoral and in the contemporary *novelle,* as, for example, in the work of Belleforest, but these letters and poems were not an integral part of the story; they were ornamental. In "The Adventures of Master F. J." the author uses letters as a very real part of his method. The stylistic peculiarities of Elinor's first reply to F. J. are definitely functional, in enabling him to recognize the work of the Secretary and to realize its attendant implication. The close relation of the poems to the story has been noted above. The idea of inserting poems and letters was not new, but the integration is again Gascoigne's contribution.

What may seem to be inspired by previous literary treatment are such passages as those dealing with the *questioni d'amore* and the rules of love. Whether the Italian pattern of social behavior actually existed in England has created a considerable problem in connection with *Euphues.*[53] Miss Violet Jeffery[54] has recently examined the matter at some length, and has, I believe, offered conclusive evidence showing that English social life among the upper classes was based on the Italian model. That there was direct imitation of Italy is important, and Professor Crane's *Italian Social Customs of the Sixteenth Century* offers an infinite variety of materials for explaining the phenomenon. Professor Crane restricts himself to the appearance in literature of social customs, and therefore, in dealing with the period at hand, he considers only Tilney's *Flower of Friendship* and, later, Whetstone's *Heptameron of Civill Discourses.* From his discussion of Italy and France, however, it is apparent that the *questioni d'amore* were implicit in courtly love. Whether actual courts existed is im-

---

[53] A. Feuillerat, *John Lyly* (Cambridge, 1910), p. 60, n. 3.

R. W. Bond, *Works of John Lyly* (Oxford, 1902), Vol. II. "Note on Italian Influence."

[54] Violet Jeffery, *John Lyly and the Italian Renaissance* (Paris, 1929), chap. iv, "Italian Social Customs."

material for our purposes, since the presence of discussions of and stories illustrating the problems of love in the medieval background shows that Boccaccio, in the fourteenth century, was portraying actual customs. The famous scene of the Neapolitan youths and maidens in the *Filocolo* is the first literary presentation of the *questioni d'amore,* but that is no proof that the custom was not widespread. When, some two hundred years later, Gascoigne describes a similar gathering in the North of England, it is hardly likely that he is following a literary convention. During those two centuries the social pattern spread until, as Miss Jeffery observes, it is most reasonable to assume that English social customs similar to the Italian were in vogue before the writing of *Euphues.*

In "The Adventures of Master F. J." we find many conventional ideas, but it can be shown that frequently the convention disappears in the face of realism. Since Gascoigne was describing actual events, he was not presenting unmodified stereotypes. For example, F. J.'s jealousy presents a curious contradiction. According to the codes of love,[55] jealousy should be favorably regarded by the lady, since it emphasized her lover's devotion. On the other hand, suspicion of the lady's faith was not allowed nor was promiscuity on the lady's part. F. J.'s suspicion is unconventional because it is real, exactly as Elinor's faithlessness is real. Likewise, though the husband is a negligible object, F. J.'s frank gloating over his "deepe invention" of the hunting horn and the horns of the cuckold is very ugly realism. The open adultery of courtly love may be abstractly discussed by Monophylo,[56] but the viciousness of actual practice is only too closely revealed in this poem. This same realism vitiates the principle of secrecy. Though we are treated to a long discussion on this subject, we are allowed to see the two poems which deal with Elinor's seduction. The second of these, "That selfe same day, and of that day that hower," is not only flippant in its casualness, but brazen in its parody of the idea of Petrarch's "Benedetto sia 'e giorno e 'l mese e 'l anno." Gascoigne may not have been directly following Petrarch, for the theme was common, but whereas the Neoplatonic theme celebrated meeting the lady, Gascoigne celebrated her seduction. It is this realism in the story which enforces, in my opinion, the fact that the *questioni d'amore* were a reflection of actual events.

The interpolated stories are a structural weakness. They are too long

---

[55] *Vide supra,* chap. v, pp. 107–8.   [56] *Ibid.,* p. 106.

and have only a vague relation to the affair. The first gathering where Elinor almost traps F. J. is important, but Pergo's tale and Frances's rejoinder seem to me to be the result of the unexplained antagonism between these two characters. I cannot share Dr. Bradner's[57] feeling that Frances is telling of F. J.'s intrigue with Elinor. Frances's request that they continue the game is thus stated:

Mistresse *Fraunces,* being desirous to requite Dame *Pergoes* quippes, requested that they might continue the pastime. . . .[58]

The story obviously has some connection with Pergo, as we see in the following passage:

The Lady *Fraunces* . . . smyled in hir sleeve at Dame *Pergo,* who had no lesse patience to heare the tale recited, than the Lady *Fraunces* had pleasure in telling it, but I may not rehearse the cause why, unlesse I should tell all.[59]

I can only conclude that Pergo may have been one of the "busie brayned" sisters who tried to make the husband suspicious of his wife. There is nothing in F. J.'s relations with Elinor to indicate that the husband was suspicious; in fact, this gentleman is at home only for one short period of time. It is likely that a source may be found for Pergo's tale of a woman disdaining her lover for seven years, loving him for seven years, and being neutral for a final seven. Seven, along with three, was always a favorite number of early story-tellers,[60] while the problem of who suffered the most is likewise common among the *questioni d'amore.*[61] The nature and implications of Frances's story point, however, to a source in contemporary gossip.

The third interpolation, the translation of the story of Suspicion from Ariosto's *Cinque Canti,*[62] although a possible structural weakness, may be explained by Gascoigne's own words, as found in "Certayne notes of Instruction."

Likewise if I should disclose my pretence in love, I would eyther make a straunge discourse of some intollerable passion, or finde occasion to pleade

---

[57] *Op. cit.,* p. 549.　　[58] *A Hundreth Sundrie Flowres,* p. 278.　　[59] *Ibid.,* p. 285.

[60] Cf. *The Heptameron of Margaret, Queen of Navarre,* Novel xxiv (Third Day).

[61] Cf. Crane, *Italian Social Customs of the Sixteenth Century,* p. 10.

[62] These were appended to the first Italian editions of *Orlando Furioso,* but were omitted in subsequent editions. The story can be found in the second Canto. In the Venice edition of 1566 (Gio. Varisco) it occupies sigs. Aaa 7ᵛ–Bbb 5ʳ.

by the example of some historie, or discover my disquiet in shadowes *per Allegoriam*.[63]

The "historie" of Suspicion has the function of making clear the struggle which took place in F. J.'s mind. The power of Suspicion is too much for our hero, and through Ariosto's story we can understand the weakness of mortal man. Although the purpose is thus evident, I feel that its inclusion is superfluous, for Gascoigne had presented the conflict quite clearly.

Such weaknesses are, however, of small moment when we assess the intrinsic worth of Gascoigne's novel. Although the situation, the characters, and the events are drawn from life and are thus not imaginative creations, Gascoigne achieved in the novel what his successors were to achieve in the drama. He was able to present through the written word characters who were complete and real, not cogs in a narration of external events. He portrayed the minds of these characters in such a way as to enable us to understand them and the situation in which they were involved. And all this he achieved by inference, by letting us hear the characters speak and watch their movements. The method is essentially dramatic, as may be seen from the natural way in which the speeches may be quoted. That same ability which was evinced in his dramatic works is here present, and we can see why Gascoigne had no real imitators in the novel.[64] Whetstone imitated the form of "F. J.," but his Rinaldo and Giletta are wooden characters, hedged roundabout with the conceits and language of love.[65] The tradition of the *novelle* was too strong, and practically all Elizabethan tales, even those that follow Gascoigne's form, deal with events rather than people. The creation of character and the processes of the mind became the concern of the dramatist, since the drama was the dominant form of literary expression. The novel had to wait until the eighteenth century; by then Gascoigne was well buried in oblivion. It seems to have been Gascoigne's destiny to be trapped by circumstances. He might have written really good plays; he certainly did write a good novel, but the time was not ripe for gentlemen dramatists,

---

[63] *Works*, I, 466.

[64] There were imitations of the form but not the spirit. Cf. Percy W. Long, "From Troilus to Euphues," *Kittredge Anniversary Papers*, Cambridge, 1913.

[65] This story is found in *The Rocke of Regard*, 1576. In the Collier reprint it occupies pp. 41–90.

and the psychological novel was far away in the future, away from the heavy hand of censorship.

DAN BARTHOLMEW OF BATHE

The verse narrative "Dan Bartholmew of Bathe" is incomplete in *A Hundreth Sundrie Flowres,* and this fact indicates both the time and method of its composition. Following the poem, *His Farewell,* is a section by the Reporter which is prefaced: *"This should have bin placed in the/ dolorous discourse, before the Supplication/ to Care in Folio. 430."*[66] The page reference places this link by the Reporter between *Dan Bartholmew his Triumphes* and *Dan Bartholmews Dolorous discourses,* where it explains the seemingly abrupt transition from the joy of the former to the sorrow of the latter. This error in printing is explained by the fact that Gascoigne left England before the volume was published and that he sent the final verses back from Holland.[67] The poem which precedes "Dan Bartholmew" is "Gascoignes voyage into *Hollande"* which, as I have shown elsewhere,[68] deals with events subsequent to March 19, 1572/3, the date of Gascoigne's departure from England. That this poem, written in Holland, was placed before "Dan Bartholmew" indicates that the latter had not been printed until after Gascoigne was already in the Low Countries. Assuming that at a later date the poet sent to England the Reporter's misplaced link, we can see that it arrived too late for inclusion in its proper place. This fact indicates, however, that the printer already had in his possession the manuscript of the *Dolorous discourses, The extremitie of his Passion, His libell of request, His last will,* and *His farewell* and had seen them through the press by the time the link arrived. *The reporters conclusion unfinished,* which ends the narrative, breaks off in the middle of a line and is followed by an explanation that the author has been "more curious in deliverie of the same, than he hath bene heretofore in any other of his doings."[69] A more simple statement would be that Gascoigne was anxious for all possible speed in

[66] *A Hundreth Sundrie Flowres,* p. 441. In this section I follow the original, i.e., titles of individual poems are indicated by italics.

[67] See my article, "Gascoigne in the Low Countries and the Publication of *A Hundreth Sundrie Flowres,"* RES, XII (1936).

[68] Cf. my article (n. 67 *supra*) and chap. iii of this volume.

[69] *A Hundreth Sundrie Flowres,* p. 445.

publication,[70] but that, the work being unfinished when he left England, he continued writing in Holland and sent the manuscript to the printer. Finally, the need for haste required publication in an unfinished state.

It seems, therefore, that in the spring of 1572/3 Gascoigne was writing only parts of his verse narrative. That he was not writing each section in chronological order is evident from the foregoing discussion of the misplaced link; he was concerned only with those poems which linked the various sections. In other words, the method of "Dan Bartholmew" is the same as that of "F. J." Gascoigne had a number of poems and, wishing to unify them, he composed a narrative (this time in verse) within which he could incorporate these verses. Proof of this is found in the version which appears in *The Posies*. There we find not one but three "Triumphes."[71] The second of these is new, but the third is a poem which had appeared in the *Flowres* as a separate item signed with the posy, *Meritum petere gravé*. When he had time to revise "Dan Bartholmew," he took this poem from its original position and thus enlarged the verse narrative.

A further indication that "Dan Bartholmew" is a linking together of poems already written may be seen in the unevenness of the separate verses: some are obviously youthful compositions, others are mature; the mock-heroic spirit contrasts with the serious. Among the various comments inspired by F. J.'s poem praising Elinor under the name of Helen is the following:

And in deede, considering that it was in the first beginning of his writings, as then he was no writer of any long continuance, comparing also the time that such reportes do spread of his acquayntaunce with *Hellene* [a later love of F. J.'s], it cannot be written lesse than sixe or seven yeres before he knewe *Hellene:* mary paradventure if there were any acquayntance betwene *F. J.* and that *Hellene* afterwardes, (the which I dare not confesse) he might adapt it to hir name, and so make it serve both their turnes, as elder lovers have done before and still do and will do worlde without end.[72]

To paraphrase, Gascoigne dares not confess that he revised the poem for another beloved; but this he really did and it appears as *Dan Barthol-*

---

[70] *Vide supra,* chap. iii, for a discussion of the publication. This matter will be dealt with at greater length in my edition of *A Hundreth Sundrie Flowres.*

[71] *Works,* I, 100–104.

[72] *A Hundreth Sundrie Flowres,* p. 245.

mews Triumphes.[73] This compares his mistress with Helen and Cressida (for her beauty) and challenges Paris and Troilus to defend the beauty of their ladies, which he disparages. The figures and conceits are similar to those in F. J.'s composition, which we know from the quotation to have been one of his first. The triteness of the figures, the prosaic plodding of the verse indicate that both are creations of a young poet who is trying his muse on conventional themes. We have only to compare the *Triumphes* with the *Dolorous discourses* to realize that the latter is less trite, more fluent, and more the work of a poet who, though perhaps not great, has at least learned some lessons. The steady thump of poulter's measure is supplanted by the five-stress line, which, though rhyming as a quatrain, is not in stanzaic form. The conventional love imagery is still present, but it is secondary to the expression of a sequence of ideas—a contrast with the exploitation of imagery for its own sake, which so marks the *Triumphes*. It seems clear that a considerable time interval separated these two poems.

The bombast of the *Triumphes* and the seriousness of the *Dolorous discourses* contrast strangely with the mock-heroic spirit of *His last will and Testament*.[74] Per se, this is an amusing and well-written poem, but it belongs with its fellows: "Gascoignes Anatomie," "Gascoignes araignement," and "Gascoignes Recantation"—all of which are humourous parodies. The sad complaints of the *Dolorous discourses* have prepared us for the possible death of the stricken lover; but not for a funeral where *Pacience* is the priest, "almes of Love" are dealt out at the chancel door, and all debts are paid.

> Then for my privie Tythes, as kysses caught by stealth,
> Swete collings & such other knacks as multiplyed my wealth:
> I give the Vicar here, to please his gredie will,
> A deyntie dishe of suger soppes but saust with sorow still. . . .[75]

The lover of the *Dolorous discourses* is too unhappy and distracted a man to write such a will, which, in spite of its mock-heroic style, contains a rather touching allegory.

A similar indulgence in a "deepe invention," though not of the same

---

[73] *Ibid.*, pp. 417–19. This poem is also found in *The Posies* (*Works*, I, 100–3) as "Dan Bartholmew his first Triumphe."

[74] *Works*, I, 121–23. "Dan Bartholmew." No. 8.

[75] *Ibid.*, I, 122–23. "D. B." No. 8.

delicacy, is revealed in the short poems which precede the *last will*. *The extremitie of his Passion*[76] elaborates the sentiment of the concluding line of its first stanza,

I cannot weepe, nor wayle my fill.

The inabilities of tongue, eyes, voice, thoughts, sighs, and heart are duly catalogued, with an extravagance of metaphor that makes us realize only too well that we are near the point of exhaustion. These characteristics mark the poem as belonging among those of an earlier period, and its exact position may be ascertained. Among the poems signed *Spreta tamen vivunt* is one whose first line reads:

Now have I found the way to weepe & wayle my fill.[77]

The fact that this line directly answers that quoted above is, in my opinion, more than a coincidence. Having complained of an inability to weep and wail, what is more natural for the poet than to state the means to achieve this desirable end? The method of the answer, though not cataloguing the anatomy, is a similar exploitation of conceits, and I feel that these two poems were originally planned to be placed near one another, and that they were both inspired by the same event.

The extremitie of his Passion ends with the resolve:

Wherefore I come to seeke out care,
beseching him of curtesie,
To cut the thred which cannot weare,
by pangs of such perplexitie.[78]

Instead of the sequence proceeding to *His libell of request exhibited to Care,* an untitled link in the form and vein of the *Dolorous discourses* is inserted, not by the Reporter but by Dan Bartholmew himself. This interpolation continues the recital of his woes and Ferenda's mistreatment and only in its conclusion introduces the appeal to "Care." More than this, the inserted passage contains none of the rare figures of the preceding or following poems and is in direct contrast with them. Apparently it was written at a later time, when Gascoigne had abandoned some of his youthful excesses, and once again we have a fact which points to the assemblage of a variety of poems linked together into a narrative.

[76] *Ibid.*, I, 116–17. "D. B." No. 4.
[77] *Ibid.*, I, 45. No. 25.   [78] *Ibid.*, I, 117. "D. B." No. 4.

This and the other poem which deals with the figure of "Care" are not really integral to the story of Dan Bartholmew and Ferenda. *The extremitie of his Passion* ends with a resolve to seek out "Care"; *His libell of request exhibited to Care* exemplifies the conventional idea that rebels against Love are punished.[79] Neither of these contains specific references to the story and both require explanatory links written in the same metrical form as the *Dolorous discourses*.

A similar lack of integration is found in the details of the story. The Reporter says that Dan Bartholmew had never been in love before, while the latter, in his *Dolorous discourses,* recites the story of a previous love. The "will" fails to make any bequest to "Care," whose granting of the suppliant's request would seem to deserve some reward. Another inconsistency is found in the opening line of the *Dolorous discourses:*

I have entreated Care to cut the thred.[80]

The actual request appears some pages further on, where it is supposed to be the result of the troubles listed in the *Dolorous discourses*.

Quite clearly "Dan Bartholmew of Bathe" is not a series of well-unified poems, a fact which requires threefold explanation. First, the haste with which it was written, which we have noted, probably contributed to the lack of consistency. A second reason has been pointed out in the disparity of tone caused by the linking together of unrelated poems. Finally, we have the question of what story is being told and whom it concerns. To ascertain this last we need only consider the actual narrative, which is contained in the various sections of the Reporter, in the *Dolorous discourses,* and in Bartholmew's link between *The extremitie* and *His libell of request.* The story thus told purports to be a true "historie"[81] of the love of Dan Bartholmew for Ferenda Natura. In his middle age the hero falls in love. The lady, like Elinor, proves faithless, but Bartholmew is unable to shrug his shoulders and, like F. J., admit that the affair is ended. This time the lover is consumed by an overwhelming passion and seeks

---

[79] A familiar idea noted in *Monophylo* (*q.v., supra,* chap. v, p. 109).

[80] *Works,* I, 106. "D.B." No. 3.

[81] The distinction between the reputable true "historie," or the story founded on authority, as opposed to a feigned fable, or one without authority, which The Reporter makes, is, of course, a regular contemporary literary stereotype. Both "F.J." and "D.B." are described as "histories" and are, therefore. true stories of actual events. It is interesting to note that in the revised *Posies* the prose tale appears as a "pleasant Fable" of Ferdinando and Leonora.

to salve his sore by retiring to Bath, where he will not be tormented by Ferenda's presence. Still alternately freezing and burning, he finds solace in a recital of his woes.

The resulting *Dolorous discourses* is a heartfelt utterance. The lament is real, but we are tempted to doubt its sincerity, for it is almost too good, and we think of Sidney's comment on fashionable love poetry:

> But truely many of such writings, as come under the banner of unresistable love, if I were a Mistres, would never perswade mee they were in love: so coldely they apply fiery speeches, as men that had rather red Lovers writings; and so caught up certaine swelling phrases which hang together, like a man which once tolde mee, the winde was at North, West, and by South, because he would be sure to name windes enowe.[82]

Although the "swelling phrases" are not so much in evidence as in the majority of Gascoigne's love poems, the language of love is present. "A sparckling cole of quicke desire" kindles "flame within [the] frozen heart." Parallelism and antithesis are also used, but the poem is far superior to such verses as "I cannot wish thy griefe, although thou worke my woe."[83] The conventional nature of such earlier poems is preserved in the *Dolorous discourses,* but, as we have noted, here there is maturity: manner is subservient to matter, and Gascoigne has achieved fluency of expression.

The matter of Bartholmew's discourse is not a traditional stereotype; he tells an individual story, and it is this fact which does much to confirm our belief in the reality of the poem. The successful lover is soon rejected; Ferenda follows a "fond and newfound choice." Even then Bartholmew is faithful.

> But did I then give bridle to thy fall,
> Thou hedstrong thou, accuse me if thou can?
> Did I not hazard love yea life and all,
> To ward thy will, from that unworthy man?[84]

In his attempt to save her and her possessions from this "unworthy man," the lover is successful, but Ferenda returns again to the rival, blaming Bartholmew for all troubles. This ingratitude and faithlessness are too much for Bartholmew, who now hopes for death. The Reporter resumes

---

[82] Sir Phillip Sidney, *An Apologie for Poetrie,* ed. by Arber, p. 67.
[83] *Works,* I, 87. No. 8.   [84] *Ibid.,* I, 109. "D. B." No. 3.

the story with reflections on Ferenda's faithlessness, but the *Flowres* ends before we have any further details. In *The Posies* the story is concluded.[85] Dan Bartholmew, near unto death, is revived with a letter written by Ferenda in her own blood. She is sorry and begs forgiveness, which is at once granted. The Reporter and Bartholmew return to London for the reconciliation, but the former suggests that this is only temporary and that Ferenda will once again desert her true love.

Although the "historie" is thus ended, the matter is made even more obscure by references to Ferenda and the "greene Knight," found in poems appearing for the first time in *The Posies*. These are "The fruite of Fetters: with the complaint of the greene Knight, and his Farewell to Fansie." Gascoigne first used this pseudonym during his adventures in the Dutch wars; in "Dulce Bellum" he describes himself as "die groene Hopman" and two lines later as "the Greene knight."[86] Thus when the Reporter refers to the "greene Knights heavy plaint"[87] for further information concerning Ferenda and Bartholmew, we see that Gascoigne, the green knight, and Bartholmew are the same person. Not only is this identification confirmed by the following stanza from "The Reporters Conclusion" that first appeared in *The Posies;* but further, it is shown that Bartholmew and the hero of Bartello's riding tale (i.e., Gascoigne) are one and the same person:

> *Bartello* he which writeth ryding tales,
> Bringes in a Knight which cladde was all in greene,
> That sighed sore amidde his greevous gales,
> And was in hold as *Bartholmew* hath beene.
> But (for a placke) it maye therein be seene,
> That, that same Knight which there his griefes begonne,
> Is *Batts* owne Fathers Sisters brothers Sonne.[88]

The same riddle, as in the last two lines of the above, appears in "F. J.," when Elinor inquires who is the author of the Tyntarnell which F. J. has sung. The latter replies, "My Fathers Sisters brothers sonne," and the ensuing play on this figure shows that F. J. means that he is the author.[89] The introduction of the fictitious Bartello into "Dan Bartholmew" seems part

---

[85] *The Posies* gives the complete version, and the end as found in the *Flowres* occurs on p. 126, l. 33 of the former (*Works*, I, 126, l. 33).

[86] *Works*, I, 166.   [87] *Ibid.*, I, 136.

[88] *Ibid.*, I, 136.   [89] *Ibid.*, I, 405.

of the whole scheme to conceal the autobiographical nature of this narrative, as well as that of "F. J.";[90] in reality, once the elaborate cross-references are understood, the autobiographical nature of both poems is quite clear.

If Gascoigne is thus Dan Bartholmew, who is Ferenda? Mr. Ward thinks she is Elizabeth Bacon,[91] and certainly the story told by Bartholmew suggests parallels to this lady's career. First, the vacillations of Ferenda seem reflected in the lawsuits between Boyes and Gascoigne as to which of them was her legal husband. Secondly, Bartholmew's statement that he saved Ferenda's property parallels Gascoigne's attempts to secure from Boyes the property of William Bretton. Finally, there is the suggestion that Bartholmew and Ferenda were married, as were George Gascoigne and Elizabeth. There are, however, many "thinges [that] are misticall and not to be understoode but by Thaucthour him selfe."[92] First, the legal difficulties with Boyes were ended by 1566,[93] whereas the green knight's troubles with Ferenda seem to belong to the time of the wars in the Low Countries, for the poems dealing with them were written at this time.[94] It seems unlikely, also, that Elizabeth Bacon had continued to vacillate between Boyes and Gascoigne for some fifteen years. Furthermore, Ferenda's social position is incompatible with what we know about Elizabeth Bacon. In *The Grief of Joye* Ferenda appears as a lady of the court and a friend of Jane Townshend, Frances Pierrepont, and the Countess of Lennox.[95] Elizabeth Bacon, the daughter of an Essex yeoman and the widow of William Bretton, a minor London merchant,

---

[90] I can see no evidence for Dr. Bower's theory ("Notes on Gascoigne's '*A Hundreth Sundrie Flowres*' . . .," *Harvard Studies and Notes in Philology and Literature*, XVI, 16–19) that Bartholomew Withypoll is the hero.

[91] Ward, ed., *A Hundreth Sundrie Flowres*, pp. xxi, xxii.

[92] This marginal notation appears for the first time in *The Posies* (*Works*, I, 110). Both in "Dan Bartholmew" and elsewhere in *The Posies* similar marginal notes are used to indicate passages of obscure meaning.

[93] *Vide infra*, Appendix III.

[94] The Reporter's mention of the green knight occurs only in *The Posies*, and must, therefore, be posterior to 1573, the date of the publication of the *Flowres*. The notice of the pseudonym in "Dulce Bellum" occurs during the events of the winter of 1573, and this poem itself was written sometime after Nov., 1574, the date of Gascoigne's return to England, which is noted therein. Presumably, then, the other green knight poems are subsequent to 1573 or 1574.

[95] *Works*, II, 531. In this same poem (p. 530) Ferenda addresses Gascoigne as "Bartholmew." A few lines later (st. 26) Gascoigne tells his "ladie per a mownt" (Elizabeth Knollys) that Ferenda was his inspiration.

could hardly aspire to such a world. Finally, Elizabeth Bacon was older than Gascoigne, while Ferenda is described as being younger.

The rival adds more complications. He is also a poet and his "rimes were all in print."[96] Furthermore, he is the "Noble face."[97] Certainly nothing we know about Edward Boyes points to his possessing poetic ability, and "Noble face" suggests a series of identifications to rival those inspired by Shakespeare's rival of the *Sonnets*. The parallel with the *Sonnets* is indeed noticeable; both have a faithless lady and a noble rival. In the present instance, it seems wise to avoid tenuous identifications and to allow Gascoigne to preserve the "misteries" which he was at such pains to create.

The parallel with the literary form of the sonnet sequence is not so easy to dismiss. Elsewhere, we have noted the sixteenth-century Italian imitation of the whole of Petrarch's *Rime,* the creation of a series of poems all inspired by a single love affair.[98] I suggested in chapter v that "F. J." may have been in part inspired by Gascoigne's desire to link his verses in imitation of this idea of unity. In "Dan Bartholmew" this desire for form and unification is even more apparent, since we have a series of poems all supposedly about one love affair. Its fundamental basis is narration, and on this framework are hung a number of poems. It is debatable whether these verses were originally inspired by the poet's relations with one person, but there are poems in *A Hundreth Sundrie Flowres* which echo the story of Bartholmew. Two concern a rival,[99] one tells of a middle-aged man's falling in love with a young girl,[100] and all those signed with the posy, *Ferenda Natura,*[101] seem for this very reason, as well as for their subject matter, to concern the love of Gascoigne for this unknown lady. A possible reason why these were not used and linked together is that the Reporter covers the material which they contain. The narrative is much more easily presented by one poem than by a series of short ones, and, because of this, it seems to me that Gascoigne included short "decorative" poems, which did not directly affect or concern the events of the story, only as a means of embellishing the framework. The

[96] *Ibid.,* I, 117. Marginal notation: "Another misterie."
[97] *Ibid.,* I, 113. Marginal notation: "Another misterie."
[98] *Vide supra,* chap. v, pp. 135–36.
[99] *Works,* I, 87, 457. Nos. 8, 26.   [100] *Ibid.,* I, 93. No. 45.
[101] *Ibid.,* I, 41, 90, 92. Nos. 29, 30, 31.

addition in the revised *Posies* of two extra poems to Dan Bartholmew's *Triumphes* is once again indicative and argues for this method of selection. The fact remains that Gascoigne did, nevertheless, present a series of poems all purportedly dealing with one beloved.

Thus it seems to me that "Dan Bartholmew" has two claims to recognition: it is a continuation of Gascoigne's interest in narration, and, in a minor degree, it illustrates the impulse which produced the Elizabethan sonnet sequences. Petrarch did not confine himself to sonnets, and thus it seems reasonable to judge Gascoigne not by the form of his poems but by the idea[102] which urged him to conceive and put together "Dan Bartholmew of Bathe."

THE TALE OF HEMETES THE HEREMYTE

After her visit to Kenilworth in July, 1575, Queen Elizabeth continued her custom of a summer progress and was at Woodstock from August 29 to October 3.[103] Our knowledge of Sir Henry Lee's entertainment[104] is scanty in comparison with the rather full account which Gascoigne and Laneham give of the *Princely Pleasures at Kenilworth*. We do, however, know that Gascoigne was present at Woodstock and we have a fragmentary record of a few items devised for the royal pleasure. In 1585 Thomas Cadman printed an account of these, which, because of the lack of the first sheet, is known from the running title as *The Queenes Maiesties Entertainment at Woodstocke*.[105] This consists of a tale by Hemetes, the hermit, which is followed by a description of a woodland "house"

---

[102] Whetstone's slavish imitation of Gascoigne is revealed by three verse and prose tales found in *The Rocke of Regard* (at London for Robert Waley. Anno 1576). The first is "the discourse of Rinaldo and Giletta" which appears in the first section, entitled "The Castle of delight" (pp. 23–61). This is an imitation of "F. J." In the second section of *The Rocke*, entitled "The Garden of Unthriftinesse," is found the story of "Dom Diego" (pp. 65–71). Separate poems are "Dom Diego His Dolorous Discourse" and "Dom Diego His Triumphe." In the final section, entitled "The Ortchard of repentance," is the story of "Paulus Plasmos" (pp. 79–121), which includes a "Reporter," "P. Plasmos triumphe," "Paulus Plasmos recantation," "P. Plasmos farewell to folly," and "The reporters conclusion."

[103] Chambers, *The Elizabethan Stage*, IV, 91–92.

[104] Chambers (*Sir Henry Lee*, pp. 84–91) attributes the festivities to Lee's direction and disproves Dr. Cunliffe's view (*PMLA*, XXVI [1911], 130) that the entertainment was directed against Leicester's desire to marry the Queen.

[105] This unique item, now in the British Museum, has been twice reprinted. A. W. Pollard, ed., *The Queen's Majesty's Entertainment at Woodstocke*, Oxford, 1910. Cunliffe, "The Queenes Majesties Entertainment at Woodstocke," *PMLA*, XXVI (1911), 92–127.

prepared for a royal banquet, a pageant which took place either during or after the banquet, and a poem recited from an Oak Tree.[106] The narrator refers next to the comedy which was presented some days later, on the twentieth of September. The play, based on Hemetes's tale, carries the story to the conclusion that marriage should be subordinate to the welfare of the state. Occanon, the Duke of Cambia, learned that his daughter Candina (or Gandina, as in Gascoigne's version) was in love with a knight, Contarenus. To prevent this undesirable match, Occanon paid an enchantress to transport Contarenus to the bound of the ocean, presumably England. Candina, hearing of this device, left Cambia in search of the knight and first sought information at the cave of Sibyl, where she encountered a lovelorn knight named Loricus. A joint prophecy told Candina and Loricus that "they should never depart fellowship, till they had found out a place, where men were most strong, women most fayre, the countrey most fertile, the people most wealthy, the government most just, and the Princes most worthy: so shoulde the Lady see that would content her, so shoulde the knight heare that might comfort him."[107] Hemetes then breaks off to tell his own story of the loss of his sight, due to his failure to follow completely the Goddess of Love. From Apollo's oracle he received a prophecy that he would recover his vision when "at one time, and in one place, in a countrie of most peace, two of the most valiant knights shal fight, two of the most constant lovers shal meet, and the most vertuous Lady of the world shall be there to look on."[108] Both prophecies have now come to pass. Contarenus has met Candina; the former, jealous of Loricus, has fought with him, while the Queen, the object of the flattering prophecies, is present as a spectator. The rest of the day's entertainment is recited, and the account ends with the Queen's wish "that the whole in order as it fell, should be brought to her in writing."[109]

This indication of royal interest prompted George Gascoigne to prepare as a New Year's gift, which he presented to Elizabeth on January 1, 1575/6, an elaborate manuscript of "The Tale of Hemetes the Her-

---

[106] The Oak Tree is a frequent device. It was used by Gascoigne for the Kenilworth "shewe." Four years later, Spenser's February Eclogue contains the discourse of the Oak and the Bramble Briar.

[107] Pollard, *op. cit.*, p. xix.

[108] *Ibid.*, p. xxi.   [109] *Ibid.*, p. xxviii.

emyte" in its English original, accompanied by translations into Latin, Italian, and French.[110] These are divided by emblematic pen-and-ink drawings, and the whole is prefaced by a picture of Gascoigne kneeling before the Queen to present the manuscript.[111] Over the poet's head is suspended a laurel wreath, while through a hole in the ceiling protrudes a hand holding a ribbon which supports an elaborate frame enclosing Gascoigne's posy "Tam Marti quàm Mercurio." The motto is enforced by a sword and spear. In fact, the drawing is practically an emblem: through Mercury (his writings) Gascoigne hopes to acquire the "laurel," and through Mars (his soldiering in Holland) he hopes to gain royal employment. To prove his abilities and qualifications, he translated the tale into the three languages and in the prefatory letter recited his reformation of character.[112]

That Gascoigne was merely the translator of the tale has been clear ever since Pollard[113] first pointed out that the real author confessed to a lack of knowledge of Italian, and that Gascoigne clearly disclaimed the work in the following lines: "... nott that I thinke any of the same translacōns any waie comparable with the first invencōn/ for if yor highnes compare myne ignorance wth thaucto^{rs} skyll, or have regard to my rude phrases compared with his well polished style."[114] Pollard did, however, suggest that Gascoigne had at least a share in the comedy, which duplicated the characters and events of the Hermit's tale. Dr. Cunliffe examined this play at length and concluded that the style was much inferior to Gascoigne's and that there were external reasons which indicated that the work was by another hand.[115] Chief of these is the fact that Gascoigne never denied his other compositions and, indeed, definitely acknowledged his share in the Kenilworth "shewes." Cunliffe thought that the theme of avoiding marriage for state reasons was directed against the Earl of Leicester. Such a view has been rejected by Sir Edmund Cham-

---

[110] This manuscript survives in the British Museum, Royal MS 18 A xlviii. The dedication bears Gascoigne's autograph signature.

[111] That Gascoigne was the artist is indicated by Mr. Ward's discovery of the emblematic drawing on Gascoigne's letter to Sir Nicholas Bacon ("George Gascoigne and His Circle," *RES*, II, 32–41). Cf. *supra*, chap. iv.

[112] Dr. Cunliffe has printed the entire manuscript (*Works*, II, 473–510).

[113] Pollard, *op. cit.*, p. vii. [114] *Works*, II, 477.

[115] Cunliffe, "The Queenes Majesties Entertainment at Woodstocke," *PMLA*, xxvi (1911), 127–32.

bers, who presents a reasoned account, showing that Sir Henry Lee was entertaining the Queen and that there are no grounds for positing political implications.[116]

One potential complication is the inclusion of the English and Gascoigne's Latin version of *the pleasant tale of Hemetes the Hermite* in Abraham Fleming's translation of a tract by Synesius of Cyrene in praise of baldness.[117] As Pollard[118] remarks, "The 'recognition' by Abraham Fleming appears to amount to very little, but there is no hint that he was the author of either the original English or of the Latin." In this view both Dr. Cunliffe and Sir Edmund Chambers agree; hence a final resumé can be given.

An anonymous guest or visitor at Woodstock described, in the form of a letter, as did Robert Laneham at Kenilworth, the entertainment presented to the Queen. In this, he included the text of speeches, poems, and plays, while in his own person he recited the "business" of the action and made some comments on the subject matter. This letter was published by Cadman in 1585. Soon after the original festivities, Gascoigne, having noted the Queen's interest in the "Tale of Hemetes," secured a manuscript of this story and, desiring royal employment, thought to approach the Queen and give proof of his abilities as a linguist by preparing translations in Latin, Italian, and French. The four versions, prepared, presumably by a scribe, in a manuscript adorned with illumination and pen-and-ink sketches, were presented to the Queen on New Year's Day, 1575/6. The English version on which Gascoigne bases his translations varies in minor expressions from the version printed by Cadman, but these differences are so slight that they in no way affect either the substance or style of Hemetes's narrative.[119] We should, however, note that Gascoigne limits himself to the actual story told by the hermit. The introductory material of the account published by Cadman, and the descrip-

---

[116] Chambers, *Sir Henry Lee*, p. 90.

[117] *A Paradox, Proving by reason and example that Baldnesse is much better than bushie haire & Written by that excellent Philosopher Synesius, Bishop of Thebes, or (as some say) Cyren. A Prettie pamphlet to peruse and replenished with recreation. Englished by Abraham Fleming. Hereunto is annexed the pleasant tale of Hemetes the Heremite, pronounced before the Queenes Maiestie. Newly recognised bothe in Latine and Englishe by the said A.F. ... Printed by H. Denham. 1579.*

[118] *Op. cit.*, p. xi.

[119] Dr. Cunliffe in his notes (*Works*, II, 581–85) lists these variants.

tion of the woodland banquet are omitted, presumably for the sake of unity. Copies of "The Tale of Hemetes" were evidently circulated, since Fleming printed in 1579 the English version, together with Gascoigne's Latin translation.

Thus our interest in "The Tale of Hemetes," at least as far as Gascoigne is concerned, is limited to the translations and to the fact that, as at Kenilworth, our author came into contact with the great Elizabethan tradition of pageantry. Gascoigne's translations of "The Tale" belie the deprecatory remarks of his introductory epistle to the Queen, where he says:

... for my latyne is rustye, myne Itallyan mustye, and my french forgrowne./ I meane my lattyne over long yeared, myne Itallyan to lately lerned, and my frenche altogether owt of fashyon/.[120]

Of the three translations, the Italian seems to be Gascoigne's best, both in its use of idiom and in fluency. However, the Latin and the French reveal a certain degree of skill, indicating that Gascoigne had a good knowledge of both. We may judge more clearly of the respective merits by a direct comparison of the four renditions of the Hermit's words to the Queen:

And nowe best ladie and most beawtyfull, so termed of the Oracle, and so thoughte of in the world, what the enchauntresse told *Contarenus, Sybilla* shewed *Gandina* and *Loricus,* and what *Apollo* said to me, by your most happy comyng is veryfied/

Nunc igitur, Princeps Augustissima, mortaliū et optima ōnia et pulcherima, sic *Apollinis* oraculo dicta, sic universi terrarū orbis consensu celebrata; quicquid *Contareno* venefica, *Gandinae* et *Lorico Sybilla,* mihi autem *Apollo* praedixerant, ea ōnia tuo faelicissimo illustrantur adventu/

Hora Signora dal' oracolo chiamata la migliore e la piu bella del mondo, e cosi creduta da tutti i immortali, quel che la Incantatrice disse a *Contareno,* e tutto quel che a *Lorico* & *Gandina* predisse la *Sibilla,* e tutto quel che a mè *Apolline* promise con la vostra real a felice presenza è verificato.

Ores tresbonne et tresbelle Dame ainsi renommee de par l'oracle, et confirmée de par les opinions universelles de l'univers, Ce que l'enchanteresse a *Contarenus, Sibilla* a *Loricus* et *Gandine*; et *Apolo* a moy avoient predit, de par vostre presence tres magnifique est verifié/[121]

It is at once apparent that the Latin and Italian amplify the sentiments of the English and the French. Neither of the first two is a translation

---

[120] *Works,* II, 477. [121] *Ibid.,* II, 484, 492, 500, 508–9.

one of the other; both, on the contrary, seem separate and idiomatic versions of the English, and in both Gascoigne seems familiar with the means of expression. The comparative straightforwardness of the French emphasizes the very conscious elaboration of the preceding translations, while other passages illustrate the falsity of Gascoigne's remarks as to his lack of ability in comparison with the original author of the English.[122] This apology was conventional modesty, for Gascoigne imposed a regularity of form not found in his original. The Hermit's final words are a case in point:

Here most noble lady have I now broughte you to this most symple hermytage/ wheare as you shall see small cunnyng but of nature, and no cost but of good will/ myne hower approcheth for my orysons/ wch according to my vowe I must never breake/ I must here leave yor ma^tie, p[ro]mysing to pray (as for my soule) that whosoev^r wishe you best, may never wishe in vayne.

Iam iam (Regina modis omnibus dignissima) Ma^tem tuam in hanc Cellulam agrestem conducere prae me tuli/ ubi non artem, sed Naturae dona, neque sumptus inofficiosos, aut conditioni meae dissimiles videre dignabere/ Hora enim (orationib[us] meis assignata) appropinquanti, (vota namq[ue] maximis occasionib[us] obstantib[us] perimplenda sunt) Maiestatē tuam ibidem derelicturus veniam peto. Deum tamen ipsū obtestor, me clementiā misericordiāq[ue] suam (non secus quam pro anima mea) deprecaturū, ut qui optimè Celsitudini tuae voluerint, id nusquā nūquamve frustra deprecari valeant./

Illustrissima Regina, la mia presūtione v' hà condotta quà a questa povera stanza inculta, & manca d' ogni cosa, se non di quel che la natura produce, non vi essendo nessuna spesa se non solamente buona volontà. Ma essendo gia venuta l' hora debita delle mie divotioni (per che i voti non si deono per niente rompere) humilmente bascio le vostre reali mani, sempre fidelmente promettendo di porgere humili preghiere a Dio (come per la mia propria vita) che il desiderio di quelli che vi desiderano ogni bene e grandezza, non rieschi loro vano.

Icy (Madame tresnoble) je vous ay amenée en ma trespauvre maison/ la ou il n'y á point d'art synon le naturel, ny de fournitures sumptueuses/ tant seulement y a quelques enseignes de bon vouloir/ mais l'heure aprochant de mes oraisons (laquelle pour chose quelconque il me fault toujours observer) je vous laisseray. Icy promettant de prier Dieu (si comme pour mon ame) pour voš Majesté, Que ceux qui luy veulent plus grand bien ne le peuvent jamais soubhaiter en vain/[123]

---

[122] Cf. *supra*, n. 114.
[123] *Works*, II, 484, 493, 501, 509.

Each of the translations is an elaboration of the English. The complimentary remarks are amplified; the phrase, "small cunnyng but of nature," becomes an antithesis; and the "symple hermytage" is embroidered to become "hanc Cellulam agrestem," "questa povera stanza inculta," or "trespauvre maison." In other words, we may here see those characteristics of Gascoigne's style which have been considered in connection with his verse and his dramatic work. Had he told the truth in his preface, he would have noted the rudeness of the original in comparison with his own polished style.

Equally apparent from the quotations is the author's relative familiarity with the three languages. The Latin and the Italian are fluent and idiomatic; the French is more literal. The Latin is not, however, Ciceronian; its structure resembles that used by the legal profession. Although he had presumably read classical Latin, Gascoigne wrote in the contemporary style. Italian was probably his best language, for in it he seems most sure of himself. The addition of "humilmente bascio le vostre reali mani" indicates that he is thinking in the Italian idiom. This detail is not found elsewhere, but the custom of "bezo las manos"[124] was so identified with the social graces of Italy that in a farewell expressed in this language one would naturally follow the custom. It was literary Italian that Gascoigne knew, since he tells us that he had learned it in London.[125] To a young man aspiring for courtly grace, a knowledge of Italian literature was a necessity. On the other hand, Gascoigne's French was the result of his experiences in Holland,[126] and its origin in the wars explains the comparatively literal nature of this version of the tale. The language of soldiers and the idiom of everyday life hardly contained the vocabulary necessary for poetic compliment; so it was better to translate literally than to attempt elaboration in an unfamiliar tongue.

Gascoigne explains his translations as resulting from Elizabeth's interest in "The Tale of Hemetes," but if we depend on the spectator whose account was published by Cadman, the Queen wished for a copy of the whole proceedings, including the banquet pageants, the comedy, and other speeches. Gascoigne's choice of "The Tale" alone may perhaps be

---

[124] This phrase appears frequently in "The Adventures of Master F.J."

[125] Works, II, 477, "suche Itallyan as I have lerned in London."

[126] Ibid., "suche frenche as I borowed in Holland."

explained by its intrinsic merits. The subject matter of a Duke of Cambaya, his daughter and her lover, the locales of the river Indus, the cave of the Sibyl, and the temple of Venus at Paphos—these are not found in the *novelle*. Instead, they reflect the Greek romance, and one thinks of Theagenes and Chariclea and their wanderings.[127] Our concern is not with the development of the pastoral tale, but we may wonder how much Gascoigne, the innovator, was interested in this pale reflection of a different type of narration.

DULCE BELLUM INEXPERTIS AND
THE SPOYLE OF ANTWERPE

Environment played an important part in determining the scope and variety, even the subject matter of George Gascoigne's literary productions. At court he wrote Italianate verse, for that was the occupation of literary young men who aspired to social grace. At Gray's Inn, he followed the dramatic tradition of the Inns of Court. But in both instances, although the original impulse was imitation, the results were a development over what had been done. The tradition of martial literature was that of glorious adventure, but Gascoigne, the individual, in his two accounts of the wars in the Low Countries, described what he saw, without bowing to the tradition. The theme of his story of his own participation, "Dulce Bellum Inexpertis,"[128] indicates that point of view which caused Gabriel Harvey to note in his copy of *The Posies*,

A sorry resolution for owre Netherland Soldiours. A good pragmatique Discourse; but unseasonable, & most unfitt for a Captain or professed Martiallist.[129]

Prose accounts of wars and battles were not unusual,[130] but the use of verse for this type of narration seems to begin with Gascoigne. In 1575, the year of the first publication of "Dulce Bellum" in *The Posies, Church-*

---

[127] Thomas Underdowne's translation of Heliodorus's *Aethiopian Historie* had appeared in 1569 and was the only one of the Greek romances translated during Gascoigne's life. The connection of "The Tale of Hemetes" with this tradition has never, so far as I know, been examined.

[128] *Works*, I, 139–84. Since this poem first appears in *The Posies*, and contains a complete account of Gascoigne's martial experiences, which ended in Oct. 1574, it was probably written in the winter of 1574–75.

[129] Smith, ed., *Gabriel Harvey's Marginalia*, p. 165.

[130] Cf., *passim*, Pollard, ed., *Tudor Tracts, 1532–1588, An English Garner*, for many sixteenth-century examples.

yard's Chippes was printed and it contained an account of the recent wars in Scotland. It differs from Gascoigne's narrative in its point of view. Like the news letters[131] and pamphlets,[132] Churchyard's story is objective; the individuality of the author is not expressed. It is in this respect as well that Gascoigne established a new tradition. He was telling the story of his experiences; he was not writing an objective account.

The method by which Gascoigne achieved this individual expression is once again an interesting fusion of the traditional and the new. The poem ends with "L'envoie," but a final note is appended:

Who soever is desirous to reade this proposicion more at large and cunningly handled, let him but peruse the Proverbe or adage it self in the first Centurian of the fourth *Chyllyade* of that famous Clarke *Erasmus Roterodamus:* the whiche is there also Entituled: *Dulce bellum inexpertis.*[133]

Consulting this work by Erasmus,[134] we find that it occupies some eighteen folio columns in very small type. Indeed, the "famouse Clarke" handled the matter "more at large"! Actually, Erasmus presents a thoroughgoing study of war: its origins, its horrors, and its position in the scheme of Christian morals. The method is explanatory; Erasmus discusses and explains the ideas implicit in the homily.

This was not, however, the method in which the schoolboy wrote his "theme." As we have had reason to observe before, the ordinary procedure was to establish the validity of the proposition by quotations and examples, derived from the general fund of classical and pseudo-classical knowledge. Thus Gascoigne developed the "theme" of *Audaces fortuna iuvat* given him by his friend, Francis Kinwelmarshe.[135] The examples of Caesar, Menelaus, and Aeneas all prove the truth of the saying. A bit different is the treatment of *Satis sufficit*[136] in the same group. Croesus is the only named example; however, successive stanzas demonstrate the validity of the theme, as applied to a rich man, a conqueror, and a man married to a beautiful wife. In the same manner, Phylomusus, in *The Glasse of Government,* points the rules of a Christian life.[137]

---

[131] Cf. *The Fugger News-Letters,* 2d series, ed. by Victor von Klarwill. New York, 1926.
[132] *Vide supra,* n. 130.   [133] *Works,* I, 184.
[134] Erasmus Roterodamus, *Adagiorum Chiliades quatuor cum sesquicenturia,* Oliva Roberti Stephani [Paris] 1558, cols. 825–42. I have used the Folger Shakespeare Library copy.
[135] *Works,* I, 62. No. 57.
[136] *Ibid.,* I, 63. No. 58.   [137] *Ibid.,* II, 56.

We are not, therefore, surprised to find Gascoigne following the same method in his consideration of the theme, "Dulce Bellum Inexpertis." The opening stanzas of his narrative would, however, indicate at first glance that Gascoigne is undertaking to write on a subject of which he has no personal experience:

> TO write of Warre and wote not what it is,
> Nor ever yet could march where War was made,
> May well be thought a worke begonne amis,
> A rash attempt, in woorthlesse verse to wade,
> To tell the triall, knowing not the trade:
> Yet such a vaine even nowe doth feede my Muse,
> That in this theame I must some labor use.
>
> And herewithal I cannot but confesse,
> Howe unexpert I am in feates of warre:
> For more than wryting doth the same expresse,
> I may not boast of any cruell jarre,
> Nor vaunt to see full valiant facts from farre:
> I have nor bene in Turkie, Denmarke, Greece,
> Ne yet in Colch, to winne a Golden fleece.
>
> But nathelesse I some what read in writte,
> O[f] high exploits by Martiall men ydone,
> And thereupon I have presumed yet,
> To take in hande this Poeme now begonne:
> Wherin I meane to tell what race they ronne,
> Who followe Drummes before they knowe the dubbe,
> And bragge of *Mars* before they feele his clubbe.[188]

Nevertheless, he proceeds to discuss the nature of war, ending with his own definition:

> And for my parte my fansie for to wright,
> I say that warre is even the scourge of God,
> Tormenting such as dwell in princelie plight,
> Yet not regarde the reaching of his rodde,
> Whose deedes and dueties often times are odde,
> Who raunge at randon jesting at the just,
> As though they raignde to do even what they lust.[139]

Separate stanzas are then addressed to the "Prince," the "Nobilitie," "Prel-acie," "Lawyers," "Merchants," "Husbandmen," and the "Communal-

[188] *Ibid.*, I, 141, sts. 1–3. [189] *Ibid.*, I, 143, st. 12.

tie," urging them to avoid war.[140] Successive stanzas indicate the dangers of war to each of these classes, and then follow examples, both abstract and concrete, of the ultimate ruin of warfare to all people of all classes.

The reaction of the reader to such an academic discussion is at this point neatly anticipated by Gascoigne:

> But here (me thinks) I heare some carping tong,
> That barkes apace and killes me with his crie,
> [M]e thinkes he sayes that all this geare goeth wrong,
> When workes of warre are wrotte by such as I,
> Me thinkes I heare him still this text applie,
> That evil may those presume to teache a trade,
> Which nay themselves in Schollers roome did wade.
>
> And for bycause my selfe confessed have,
> That (more than might by writte expressed be)
> I may not seeme above my skill to brave,
> Since yet mine eyes the warres did never see:
> Therefore (say some) how fonde a foole is he,
> That takes in hande to write of worthy warre,
> Which never yet hath come in any jarre?
>
> No jarre (good sir) yes yes and many jarres,
> For though my penne of curtesie did putte,
> A difference twixt broyles and bloudie warres,
> Yet have I shot at maister *Bellums* butte,
> And thrown his ball although I toucht no tutte:
> I have percase as deeply dealt the dole,
> As he that hit the marke and gat the gole.
>
> For I have seene full many a *Flushyng* fraye....[141]

From this point on, Gascoigne deals with contemporary "broyles," which are in direct contrast to the heroic "bloudie warres" discussed in the previous section of the poem. From books we turn to the poet's own experience, but even here we do not encounter anything entirely new in Gascoigne's writings. Returning to the themes suggested by the poet's Gray's Inn friends, we find that there he employed his own experience as the illustrative material for developing the proposition. Alexander Neville delivered him the theme, *Sat cito, si sat bene,* and the resultant poem[142] is the rueful tale of the vanity and swelling pride of George

---

[140] *Ibid.,* I, 144–46. [141] *Ibid.,* I, 159–60, sts. 92–95. [142] *Ibid.,* I, 66. No. 60.

Gascoigne, the would-be courtier. Likewise, it is Gascoigne's own experience that animates "A gloze upon this text, *Dominus iis opus habet.*"[143] To the traditional procedure of theme elaboration, he thus added two things which are closely related. First, he abandoned the traditional material of elaboration; secondly, he drew from his own experience, and in so doing established the validity of the individual's reaction or emotion, as opposed to that objectivity which had hitherto been used. With these two points in mind, we can turn to his story of the Dutch wars.

The various skirmishes of the summer of 1572 are mentioned in three stanzas.[144] With dry humor, Gascoigne indicates the unheroic nature of the sieges in which he took place:

> So was I one forsooth that kepte the towne,
> Of *Aerdenburgh* (withouten any walles)
> From all the force that could be dressed downe,
> By *Alba* Duke for all his cries and calles,
> A high exployte. Wee held the Flemings thralles,
> Seven dayes and more without or bragges or blowes,
> For all that while we never herd of foes.[145]

While poor management is blamed for a series of virtual stalemates, an occasional victory is attributed less to valor than to bribery. The siege of Ramykins, a minor engagement in the attempt on Middleburgh, is treated by contemporary historians as a victory. Only Gascoigne describes the real state of affairs, and this he does with the broadest sarcasm:

> ... I was in rolling trench,
> At *Ramykins,* where little shotte was spent,
> For gold and groates their matches still did quenche,
> Which kept the Forte, and forth at last they went,
> So pinde for hunger (almost tenne dayes pent)
> That men could see no wrincles in their faces,
> Their pouder packt in caves and privie places.[146]

Thus far, the very nature of the war prohibited any opportunity for exceptional feats of bravery so necessary to attain recognition and advancement:

> And though I marcht all armde withouten rest,
> From *Aerdenburgh* and back again that night,
> Yet madde were he that would have made me knight.[147]

---

[143] *Ibid.,* I, 70. No. 62.

[144] *Ibid.,* I, 160, sts. 95–97. For an exact account of Gascoigne in the wars, *vide supra,* chap. iii.

[145] *Works,* I, 160, st. 96.   [146] *Ibid.,* I, 161, st. 102.   [147] *Ibid.,* I, 160, st. 95.

If this was a disappointment to Gascoigne, a more bitter one was yet to come. Fame was only secondary to the more tangible fortune which he hoped to find among the spoils of war. For this reason, the poet's account of the naval battle between the Dutch and Beauvois, the Spanish admiral, is a personal lament of a golden opportunity lost. Sir Roger Williams and Morgan describe the defeat of the Spaniard; Gascoigne bewails the bad management of his ship, which arrived too late to share in the plunder:

> O victorie: (whome *Haughty* hartes do hunte)
> O spoyle and praye (which greedy mindes desire)
> O golden heapes (for whom these *Misers* wonte
> To follow *Hope* which settes all hartes on fire)
> O gayne, O golde, who list to you aspyre,
> And glorie eke, by bolde attempts to winne,
> There was a day to take your prisoners in.

> The shippes retyre with riches full yfraught,
> The Souldiours marche (meane while) into the towne,
> The tide skarce good, the winde starke staring naught,
> The haste so hoate that (eare they sinke the sowne)
> They came on ground, and strike all sayles adowne:
> While we (ay me) by backward saylers ledde,
> Take up the worst when all the best are fledde.[148]

Objectively the battle was a victory; to George Gascoigne it was a tragedy that robbed him of his share of the spoils.

This individuality of treatment is present throughout the narrative. The internal dissension, of which Sir Roger Williams and Grimeston make no mention, was very real to Gascoigne, who tells of a lack of discipline and an abundance of self-will. He dwells on these points, together with other details regarding the lack of provisions and the friction between the English and the Dutch, in his attempt to justify his loss of the fort of Valkenburgh.[149]

Even more subjective is Gascoigne's account of a love affair with a lady residing at The Hague, then in Spanish possession. As we have seen above, this lady sent the poet a loving letter, which not only caused his "harmelesse hart . . . to pant apace" but also embroiled him in endless difficulty with the Dutch, who immediately suspected him of being in communication with the enemy.[150] This is, of course, irrelevant to an account of the war, but it does illustrate the diversion of an English captain

---

[148] *Ibid.*, I, 162, sts. 106, 107.
[149] *Ibid.*, I, 170–75, sts. 146–71.   [150] *Ibid.*, I, 165–66, sts. 122–29.

and the terrified suspicions of the Dutch, who were being betrayed on every side.[151]

Thus we can readily see that while Gascoigne's account of the wars in the Low Countries contains most of the facts cited by the historians of his time, the narrative is, nevertheless, something new. Gascoigne had known what war was, and in writing about it the creative artist found his medium of expression in the familiar elaboration of the theme; but he was not content with the traditional examples; he drew from his own knowledge, and in so doing he asserted the validity of the individual judgment. This was his method, but because he had a certain sensitivity to his environment and a keen awareness of details, he made his account of the Dutch wars an extraordinarily vital narrative.

Late in the summer of 1576, Gascoigne's various attempts to secure royal employment met with success. As one of Burghley's agents he went to France and later to Antwerp, where he was present during the siege and final rape of the city by the mutinous Spanish troops.[152] On the twenty-first of November Gascoigne returned to England; four days later he finished his eyewitness account of the sack of the city, which was printed in the same month by Richard Jones, under the title, *The Spoyle of Antwerp. Faithfully reported, by a true Englishman, who was present at the same.*[153]

The biographical significance and the validity of the details of this pamphlet have been considered in chapter iv; there remains an examination of the literary merits of the work. In contrast with "Dulce Bellum," this is in prose, but even so it is characteristic of Gascoigne's style and trend of ideas. The introductory paragraphs reveal both. Typical is the following:

... let these my few woords become a forewarnynge on bothe handes: and let them stande as a Lanterne of light beetween two perillous Rockes: That bothe amendyng the one, and detestynge the other, wee may gather fyre out of the Flint, and Hunny out of the Thystle.[154]

---

[151] The betrayals of the Dutch are discussed in chap. iii.

[152] Gascoigne's letters to Burghley and other references to this adventure are discussed in chap. iv.

[153] Dr. Cunliffe (*Works*, II, vi) confirmed Pollard's hypothesis (*Tudor Tracts, 1532–1588, An English Garner*, pp. 420–28) that Gascoigne was the author. The pamphlet is reprinted by Dr. Cunliffe (*Works*, II, 586–99) and by Pollard (*op. cit.*, pp. 429–49).

[154] *Works*, II, 590.

The last conceit recalls these lines from the dedication of "Dulce Bellum" to Lord Grey:

The verse is roughe. And good reason, sithence it treateth of roughe matters, but if the sence be good then have I hyt the marke which I shote at: Knowing that your Lordshippe can winne Honny out of the Thistle.[155]

The conceit, though not dominant in Gascoigne's prose style, is still a marked characteristic, but more a part of his prose are the carefully balanced clauses. Even in the heat of battle, Gascoigne seems conscious of his prose, and we find such lines as these:

So that I came down and tooke my cloake and sword, to see the certainty thereof, and as I passed toward the Bource, I met many, but I overtoke none: And those which I mette were no Townsmen, but Souldyeres: neither walked they as men which use traffique, but ran as men whiche are in feare.[156]

In addition to these stylistic characteristics, we notice Gascoigne's judgment of what he saw. We need only look back a page or so to find his definition of war in "Dulce Bellum," with which we may compare the following:

And therwithall, if the wickednesse used in the sayde towne, doo seeme unto the well disposed Reader, a sufficient cause of Gods so just a scorge and Plague: and yet the furie of the vanquishers doo also seeme more barbarous and cruell, then may become a good christian conquerour: let these my few woords become a forewarnynge on bothe handes.[157]

This idea of war as God's scourge for the wicked appears frequently in the narrative, together with reflection on the unchristian behavior of the conquerors.

But neither style nor ideas on the nature of war prevent Gascoigne from presenting a true picture—the purpose of the pamphlet, according to his own words[158]—in a style worthy of the best traditions of news reporting. He first develops the background.[159] Most important is the fact that the Spaniards had long intended to sack Antwerp, the wealthiest city of the Low Countries, and had only waited for some excuse. Antwerp was, of course, in a difficult situation. The citadel, held by the Spanish,

---

[155] *Ibid.*, I, 140.   [156] *Ibid.*, II, 594.   [157] *Ibid.*, II, 590.

[158] "But as I sayd before, mine onely entent is to set downe a plaine truthe, for the satisfiynge of sutche as have hetherto beene caried aboute with doubtfull reportes" (*Works*, II, 590).

[159] *Ibid.*, II, 590–94.

completely commanded the city, and any attempt to have given active help to Prince William would have brought destruction. Actually cannon shot had been directed on the city on the nineteenth and twentieth of October, ostensibly because Prince William's fleet had brought provisions. The Spaniards were trying to starve the city into active revolt by cutting off supplies. All these attempts to start trouble were patiently suffered by the people of Antwerp, but finally the mutinies of the Spanish armies brought matters to a crisis.

Having thus given the background, Gascoigne proceeds with an objective account of the attack on the city. The various bands of mutineers assemble; their leaders are named. William of Orange sends reinforcements and the defenses of the city are strengthened. Then the storm breaks. The Spaniards attack, the defenders flee, and the rape of the city ensues.

At this point the objective story is complete. Gascoigne then gives his own personal experiences during the battle and for the days afterwards, when the Spanish were in possession.[160] We see him hearing of the attack while he is at dinner in the house of the English Merchant Adventurers. He goes up into a high tower, whence he sees that the enemy have entered the town; he descends and ventures abroad in order to see what is taking place. Noticing the defenders in flight, he accosts a townsman, standing near-by, and inquires the reason. The latter replies, *"Helas mounsieur, il ny a poynt de ordre, & voila la ruine de ceste ville."*[161] Gascoigne's rejoinder to this is characteristic: *"Aiez courage mon amy."*[162] He proceeds and sees the rout of the defenders; but let him continue the story in his own vivid way:

... and so went onwardes yet towards the Bowrce, meeting all the way more & more which mended their pace. At last, a Wallon Trompeter on horsback (who seemed to be but a Boy of yeres) drew his sworde, and layd about him crying, *Ou est que vous e[n]fuiez canaille? faisons teste pour le honeur de la patrie.* Wherewith, fyfty or three score of them turned head, and wente backewardes towards the Bource. The which encouraged mee (*per companie*) to proceede: But alas, this comforte indured but a while: For by that time I came on the farder syde of the Bource, I might see a great trowpe comming in greater haste, with their heads as close togeather, as a skoule of yong frye, or a flocke of Sheepe: Who met me on the farder side of the Bource, toward the

[160] *Ibid.*, II, 594–99.   [161] *Ibid.*, II, 594.   [162] *Ibid.*

market place: And having their leaders formost (for I knewe them by their Javelines, Borespeares, and Staves) bare me over backwardes, and ran over my belly and my face, long time before I could recover on foote. At last when I was up, I looked on every syde, and seeing them ronne so fast, began thus to bethinke me. What in Gods name doe I heare which have no interest in this action? synce they who came to defend this town are content to leave it at large, and shift for themselves: And whilest I stoode thus musing, another flocke of flyers came so fast that they bare me on my nose, and ran as many over my backe, as erst had marched over my guttes. In fine, I gotte up like a tall fellow, and wente with them for company: but their haste was such, as I could never overtake thē, until I came at a broad crosse streate which lyeth betweene the English house & the sayd Bource: there I overtooke some of thē groveling on the ground, and groning for the last gaspe, and some other which turned backwards to avoyd the tickling of the spanishe Musquets: who had gotten the ends of the sayd broad crosse streate, and flanked it both wayes: And there I stayde a whyle till hearing the shot increase, and fearing to bee surprysed wyth suche as mighte follow in tayle of us, I gave adventure to passe through the sayde crossestreate, and (without vaunte be it spoken) passed through five hundred shotte, before I could recover the English house.[163]

The immediate story of the attack thus ends, but Gascoigne continues his picture of the rape of the city and the dangers to the house of the English Merchant Adventurers. The latter had a placard signed by King Phillip guaranteeing the safety of the house and its residents, but the mutineers disregarded this and, entering with drawn swords, forced the English Governor, "a comlie aged Man, and a personne, whose hoarie heaires might move pittie,"[164] to pay a ransom of 12,000 crowns. The English house escaped further trouble, largely through the efforts of George Gascoigne, if we may believe the letter which the Governor wrote to the Privy Council.[165] Other Englishmen were not so fortunate: some lost all their possessions, and at least four, their lives. The ruin of the city and its inhabitants was even more ghastly:

I forbeare also to recount the huge nombers, drowned in yᵉ new Toune: where a man might behold as many sundry shapes and formes of mans motiõ at time of death: as ever *Mighel Angelo* dyd portray in his tables of Doomes day. I list not to recken the infinite nombers of poore Almains, who lay burned in their armour: som thentrailes skorched out, & all the rest of the body free, some their head and shoulders burnt of: so that you might looke down into the bulk & brest and there take an Anatomy of the secrets of nature. Some

[163] *Ibid.*, II, 594–95.　　[164] *Ibid.*, II, 598.　　[165] *Vide supra*, chap. iv.

standing uppon their waste, being burnte of by the thighes: & some no more but the very toppe of the brain taken of with fyre, whiles the rest of the body dyd abide unspeakable tormentes. I set not downe the ougly & filthy polluting of every streete with the gore and carcases of men and horses: neither doo I complaine, that the one lacked buryall, and the other fleing, untyl the ayre (corrupted with theyr caryon) enfected all that yet remained alyve in the Towne: And why should I describe the particularitie of every such anoiance, as commonly happen both in campes & Castels, where martiall feates are managed? But I may not passe over with sylence, the wylfull burning and destroying of the stately Townehouse, & all the monuments and records of the Citie.[166]

Surely this devastation was the scourge of God, else how could 5,000 have defeated 15,000!

Reporting of this description has no parallel in Elizabethan days. Dramatic as was the last fight of the *Revenge,* none of the accounts of this battle have those little details, those personal observations which give flesh and blood to the bare bones of narration.[167] The creative artist devoted his talent to other fields, and it was only the chance that Gascoigne sought royal employment that has given us the artistry of visual creation revealed in *The Spoyle of Antwerpe,* "wrytten by a true English man, who was present at this pytteous massacre."

[166] *Works,* II, 596–97.

[167] I have chosen this as more or less typical of the reporting of news events, mainly because it was recounted by at least three Elizabethans.

VIII. The Moralist

The druncken soule, transformed to a beast,
My diet helps, a man, again to make:
But (that which should, be praisd aboove the rest)
My Doomes day Drum, from sin dooth you awake.
WHETSTONE

THE YEAR 1575 saw the transformation of George Gascoigne, "the ydle poett, wryting tryfles," into *"Gascoigne the Satyricall* wryter, medytating eche *Muse* that [might] expresse his reformacõn."[1] The objections raised by *A Hundreth Sundrie Flowres,* the failure of his attempts to become a soldier—in fact, the failure of all his attempts to gain fame and fortune—impressed on his mind the inexorable truth that his way of life had been wrong. He had followed the way of the world, only to find it a snare and delusion; therefore, he sought out the way of the spirit, which might justify life and bring the rewards hitherto denied. That Gascoigne was sincere I do not doubt; that his reformation was in tune with his times seems clear, and his writings after his final return from the Dutch wars seem to me to testify to the sincerity of his transformation, as well as to the fruits of the new spirit. The introductory letters to *The Posies*[2] are among the first indications of a change of heart; but, although they defend the poet against charges of lewd speech and libel and announce certain excisions, these letters are not per se evidence of reform. Gascoigne, defending himself and trying to prepare a new and acceptable version of his first book, might well be expected to use any argument. However, his first work after the publication of the revised edition confirms a new point of view.

The dedicatory letter to Sir Owen Hopton dates *The Glasse of Government* as of April 26, 1575,[3] shortly after the publication of *The Posies.* This English example of the prodigal-son play has been discussed in connection

---

[1] *Works,* II, 477.　　[2] *Ibid.,* I, 3–17.　　[3] *Ibid.,* II, 3.

with the drama[4] and Gascoigne's reformation,[5] but we may profitably recapitulate the significance of its subject matter. *"The whole Comedie* [is] *a figure of the rewardes and punishmentes of vertues and vices."*[6] The Prologue enforces this didacticism, and Christopher Barker's rules[7] for a virtuous life are constantly echoed throughout the play. The virtuous prosper while the wicked are punished, and their respective ways of life are in sharp antithesis. Quite obviously our author is here in contrast with the author of the amoral "Adventures of Master F. J." and the poems of *A Hundreth Sundrie Flowres*. The Italianate courtier has been metamorphosed into the Calvinist moralist, but the artistic ability of the former does not disappear. The skillful dramatic structure of *The Glasse*, which we have noted,[8] suggests a possible understanding of Gascoigne, the man. Although the wicked elder brothers are overwhelmed by their due punishment, we are, nevertheless, sympathetically aware of the reasons for their fall from virtue. Their wits are quick, and they find their schoolmaster's platitudes dull. Craving adventure and experience, they encounter Lamia, the harlot, but their reactions are not vicious. Her favors they presumably desire, but Phylosarchus wishes for Virgil's ability to pen her praises. Gnomaticus, their master, does not think the boys intrinsically evil; he feels that removing them from temptation will be sufficient safeguard. Thus, understanding the reasons for their downfall, may we not see a possible suggestion of Gascoigne's own ruin? The poet who laments his wasted time,[9] who finds his repentance scorned,[10] and who desires recognition of his literary productions, might well be one whose wits had been too quick, and whose desire for experience had led him into evil ways. Unlike the prodigal sons, he repented before it was too late and sought to amend his faults by virtuous and godly writings.

In fact, the dedicatory letter to *A delicate Diet, for daintiemouthde Droonkardes,* expresses just such a view to Gascoigne's friend, Lewis Dive:

But Syr, when my wanton (and worse smelling) Poesies, presumed fyrst to peark abroade, they came forth sooner then I wyshed, and muche before they

---

[4] *Vide supra*, chap. vi, pp. 180–88.   [5] *Vide supra*, chap. iv.   [6] *Works*, II, 5.

[7] The eight "sentences" which preface the play are headed: "This worke is compiled upon these sentences following, set downe by mee C.B." (*Works*, II, 7.)

[8] *Vide supra*, chap. vi, pp. 183–84.

[9] *Works*, II, 211. "I finde my self giltie of much time mispent."

[10] *Ibid.*, II, 135. "I am rygorously rejected when I proffer amendes."

deserved to be lyked. So that (as you maye sithens perceyve) I was more combred with correction of them, then comforted in the constructions, where-unto they were subject. And too make amendes for the lost time which I mis-bestowed in wryting so wantonlie: I have of latter dayes used al my travaile in matters both serious and Morall.[11]

This letter continues with a list of the works devoted to virtuous ends:

I wrote first a tragicall commedie called *The Glasse of Government:* and nowe this last spring, I translated and collected a worthy peece of worke, called *The Droomme of Doomes daie,* and dedicated the same to my Lord and Maister: And I invented a *Satyre,* and an *Ellegie,* called *The Steele glasse:* and *The complaint of Phylomene.* Both which I dedicated to your good Lord and myne, *the Lorde Greye of Wylton:* These works or Pamphlets, I esteeme both Morall and Godly.[12]

A complete list of his moral writings would include *The Grief of Joye,* which until recent times existed only in manuscript.[13] These works of George Gascoigne, moralist, would by his own definition fall into three sections: *Satire, Elegy,* and *Moral Philosophy;* and in these classifications they will be considered.

SATIRE

The Steele Glas received the commendation of "Walter Rawely," "Nich-olas Bowyer," and an anonymous "N.R."[14] That the first was Sir Walter Raleigh seems likely, even in the face of this knight's denial of a knowl-edge of law.[15] As we have seen, the Inns of Court were finishing schools as well as training schools for lawyers. Gascoigne himself was a member of Gray's Inn, yet in all his legal difficulties he never took up his own defense. The Withypolls were of the same fellowship, yet they never em-barked on legal careers. The great and near-great were members of the Inns of Court, but their interest was largely social. Thus, while we have no conclusive evidence, presumption inclines us to regard these as Ra-leigh's first published verses. Identification of Nicholas Bowyer is equally impossible of proof, but he may well have been the Bowyer who was Gentleman Usher of the Black Rod.[16] If this be so, Gascoigne had good

---

[11] *Ibid.,* II, 453.   [12] *Ibid.*

[13] British Museum, Royal MS 18 A. lxi. First printed in *The Complete Poems of George Gascoigne,* ed. by Hazlitt (1869–70).

[14] Commendatory poems by these men preface the work. (*Works,* II, 138–39.)

[15] Raleigh's recent biographer, Edward Thompson (*Sir Walter Raleigh* [New Haven, 1936], p. 10) accepts the verses as Sir Walter's.

[16] Nichols, *The Progresses ... of Queen Elizabeth,* I, 385.

sponsors for his satire, and their recognition of the poem's merit is confirmed by both its reputation and its intrinsic worth.

As Professor Schelling[17] noted, the poem has been highly regarded since the days of Warton, both as a satire and as the first original composition in blank verse. The idea of the "Glas" or mirror is not, of course, original with Gascoigne, but it had appeared before in his writings. The final act of *Jocasta* has two marginal notes which employ this familiar figure. Oedipus's lament bears the title, "A Glasse for brittel Beutie and for lusty limmes,"[18] and his concluding admonition to the citizens of Thebes is described as "A mirrour for Magistrates."[19] Frequent references are also found in the poem elaborating the theme of *Dominus iis opus habet*,[20] which follows the verses on the themes given Gascoigne by his friends at the time of his return to Gray's Inn. His mirror in this poem is "the merrie meane."

> And in that noble glasse, I take delight to vewe,
> The fashions of the wonted worlde, compared by the new.[21]

Thus comparing the contemporary scene with the past, he finds that each man is for himself and each gives the excuse, *"the Lord hath neede."*

> A noble jest by gisse, I finde it in my glasse,
> The same freehold our Savioure Christ, conveyed to his asse.[22]

After surveying the hierarchy of society, from the prince to the plowman, he finds selfishness everywhere.

> Thus learne I by my glasse, that merrie meane is best,
> And he moste wise that fynds the meane to keepe his tackling best.[23]

Not only the idea of a "glass," but also the pattern of the satire found in this poem are again employed in *The Steele Glas.*[24] In this there are two mirrors: the one, that of steel, which reflects the customs, habits, and people of the past, as well as a true picture of the contemporary world; the other, the modern, imperfect *"christal glas, which glimseth brave & bright, and shewes the thing much better than it is."*[25] There is no attempt to balance the two by contrasting the false and the true, but the crystal mirror is occasionally used.

[17] *The Life and Writings of George Gascoigne*, pp. 72, 74–75.
[18] *Works*, I, 323.   [19] *Ibid.*, I, 324.   [20] *Ibid.*, I, 70. No. 62.
[21] *Ibid.*, I, 70. No. 62.   [22] *Ibid.*, I, 71.   [23] *Ibid.*, I, 73.
[24] *Ibid.*, II, 133–74.   [25] *Ibid.*, II, 148.

Before we begin a consideration of the satire proper, we must examine the form in which it is cast. The dedicatory letter to Arthur, Lord Grey of Wilton recites the poet's unhappy circumstances and hints at those anonymous enemies who have been responsible.[26] As with Whetstone's cryptic references to Gascoigne's enemies,[27] we cannot be sure of the exact meaning. There is further talk of the poet's riotous youth, which, of course, suggests the objections caused by *A Hundreth Sundrie Flowres;* but whether the enemies were motivated by anger at hidden references in the *Flowres* or simply by jealousy, we do not know. The general theme here and elsewhere is that the wanton *Flowres* was the main cause of trouble, but more than that one cannot say. The importance of this letter lies in the reiteration of its complaints in the opening lines of *The Steele Glas*. Gascoigne invokes the nightingale to aid him in his verse and bases his appeal on the likeness of their fortunes, and in so doing he makes use of the legend of Tereus, Progne, and Phylomela. Phylomene[28] was without cause mutilated by Tereus; Gascoigne sings *"a song, in spight of their despight, which worke my woe, withouten cause or crime."*[29] In a stanza of direct address to Lord Grey, Gascoigne furthers the analogy by lamenting that Tereus's descendants still live.

> *And me they found, (O wofull tale to tell)*
> *Whose harmelesse hart, perceivde not their deceipt.*[30]

Gascoigne then proceeds to tell the story of "Satyra," the twin sister of "Poesys." The former, like Philomene, is ravished by her sister's husband, this time not Tereus but "vayne Delight." Instead of obtaining revenge, "Satyra" is accused of enticing "vayne Delight" and is clapped into the *"cage of* Myserie," where her tongue is cut out by the "Raysor *of* Restraynte." This analogy, though forced, is understandable, but Gascoigne adds to it another significance. He is "Satyra."

> *I n'am a man, as some do thinke I am,*
> *(Laugh not good Lord) I am in dede a dame,*
> *Or at least, a right* Hermaphrodite.[31]

[26] *Ibid.,* II, 135–37.

[27] Whetstone, *A Remembraunce of the wel imployed life, and godly end, of George Gaskoigne Esquire,* pp. 21–22. *Vide supra,* chap. iv.

[28] Robinson in his notes to Chaucer's "Legend of Philomela" *(The Complete Works of Geoffrey Chaucer)* says that the shift from "l" to "n" in the name is common to Chaucer, Chrétien, and the medieval MSS of Ovid. *Vide infra,* n. 56.

[29] *Works,* II, 143. [30] *Ibid.,* II, 144. [31] *Ibid.,* II, 144.

After "Satyra" is in the cage, there is another interpolated stanza with
the marginal note as follows:

note now &	*And thus (my Lord) I live a weary life,*
compare this	*Not as I seemd, a man sometimes of might,*
allegory to	*But womālike, whose teares must venge hir harms.*
the story of	*And yet, even as the mighty gods did daine*
Progne &	*For* Philomele, *that thoughe hir tong were cutte,*
Philomele.	*Yet should she sing a pleasant note sometimes:*
	So have they deignd, by their devine decrees,
	That with the stumps of my reproved tong,
	I may sometimes, Reprovers *deedes reprove,*
	And sing a verse, to make them see themselves.[32]

Then follow five short stanzas, each of which emphasizes the analogy
between Gascoigne and Philomene. He sings by night, like the nightingale, since the sun of patronage is eclipsed. He occupies a *"corner closely
cowcht, like* Philomene," since stately courts *"are no place for such poor
byrds"* as he.[33] Like Philomene with the thorn against her breast, he sings,
tormented by the worm of his conscience. The spring is the time for all
the birds to sing, and he, like the nightingale, will not be drowned out by
"jangling byrds" (other and inferior poets). His intent is true and harm-
less, even though the Cuckoo (again other poets) defiles his nest.

That Gascoigne is dealing in generalities is indicated by the fact that
the whole satire is the song of Philomene-Satyra-Gascoigne. Since the
poet has told us that his song is directed against his reprovers, and since
the satire concerns the peevish pride of the contemporary world, Gascoigne's enemies seem to be not specific individuals but the sum total of
a hypocritical social order, that masks its vices as virtues and deserts the
goodly life of the past. There is, perhaps, a specific meaning in the allegory
of Philomene's ravished tongue: the banning of *A Hundreth Sundrie
Flowres* and the seizure of *The Posies* could be considered allegorically
as cutting out the poet's tongue. Tereus's descendants are, then, a body of
people resembling those described by Turbervile, Neville, Studley, Googe,
and others as sycophants; curious, spiteful, and envious carpers; sons of
Momus; and finally as the Zoili.[34]

---

[32] *Ibid.,* II, 146.   [33] *Ibid.*

[34] Dr. Conley (*The First English Translators of the Classics,* pp. 87–91) examines the
whole question of the detractors and the use of these epithets for them. Dr. Conley discusses,
however, only the translators. Turbervile's reference is found in his "To the rayling Route of

This latter name was derived from Zoilus, a Greek grammarian of the fourth century B.C. who became proverbial as a harsh critic because of his censures of Homer, Plato, and Isocrates. As a proverbial label for all detractors, the name flourished along with that of Momus, the god of criticism, during the various literary quarrels of the sixteenth century. If we assume, however, that Gascoigne's race of Tereus and the Zoili are the same, we are led into a dilemma. The Zoili are generally those persons opposed to the demoralizing influences of profane literature. Gosson becomes a handy symbol of those who clung to the medieval critical dogma that literature was only justifiable as it induced virtuous conduct. Certainly Gascoigne's *Posies* would come under their censure, but if we are to believe the Gascoigne who lamented his ill-smelling *Posies,* he, by 1576, shared their opinion. Why then, since he belongs to the group advocating didactic literature, and since he writes in this vein, does he attack as descendants of cruel Tereus those who censured his *Posies?*

The answer seems to lie in his own words concerning the rejection of his proffered amends. The dedicatory letter of *The Steele Glas* states the problem:

> I have misgoverned my youth, I confesse it: what shall I do then? shall I yelde to mysery[35] as a just plague apointed for my portion? Magnanimitie saith no, and Industrye seemeth to be of the very same opinion.
>
> I am derided, suspected, accused, and condemned: yea more than that, I am rygorously rejected when I proffer amendes for my harme.[36]

The rest of the letter elaborates the same idea. He admits that he wasted his youth and he admits the justice of the objections raised against him. But he cries out against the seeming writ of attainder that has been levied against him. He has changed his way of life, and the sins of his youth should not be continually and everlastingly a charge against him. Like Philomene, he has once lost his tongue and can never recover it. The forces arrayed against him are not, then, individuals, but attitudes and

---

Sycophants," prefaced to his *Epitaphes, Epigrams, Songs and Sonets,* A8r–B1r. I have used the Folger Shakespeare Library copy. John Keeper, a friend of Thomas Howell, likewise referred to "Zoils snarles" in his commendatory verses to the latter's *The Arbor of Amitie* (Henry Denham [London 1568, reprinted, A. B. Grosart, 1879], p. 12).

[35] Even as Satyra was imprisoned *"in cage of* Myserie," so Gascoigne questions his yielding to "mysery." The analogy was evidently dominant in his mind as he wrote this letter.

[36] *Works,* II, 135.

concepts of a social order which has lost the virtue of magnanimity. Like Satyra *"clapt fast in cage of* Myserie," Gascoigne wonders if he must yield himself to "mysery as a just plague." "Magnanimitie saith no," but this virtue is no longer among men.

> *That age is deade, and vanisht long ago,*
> *Which thought that steele, both trusty was & true,*
> *And needed not, a foyle of contraries,*
> *But shewde al things, even as they were in deede.*[37]

The positive virtue of magnanimity[38] is mentioned only in the dedicatory letter; but its antithesis, "Surcuydry" or "peevishe pryde," is the theme of the ensuing satire, and it is to this vice that Gascoigne attributes his own lamentable condition, as well as the state of *"this weak and wretched world."*[39] Tereus's race comprehends not only the descendants of Zoilus and Momus, but also the selfish stereotypes of a society which has lost its antique virtue. Character, family, and social responsibility have disappeared. There are no longer any absolute or even relative standards by which men are judged. One fault condemns the offender for life; his repentance is viewed with suspicion, and the examples of famous men who reformed after their youthful excesses have no validity in a social order motivated only by peevish pride.

This theme was not precisely new with Gascoigne. In his verses on Alexander Neville's theme, *Sat cito, si sat bene,*[40] he told of his own desire for self-glorification. Likewise, the elaboration of Richard Courtop's *Durum aeneum & miserabile aevum,*[41] has satiric implications, in its comparison of the present with the former age. "Surcuydry" occupies a prominent position in the verses which Gascoigne wrote in Douglas Dive's commonplace book.[42] These and the poem on *Dominus iis opus habet*[43] all indicate that satire interested Gascoigne as early as 1564–65. Even then he was conscious of one aspect of his age which we are apt to ignore. Feudalism had not breathed its last on Bosworth field; instead, it died slowly during the sixteenth century. The social responsibility of the

---

[37] *Ibid.,* II, 147.
[38] It is interesting that Gascoigne, even faintly and from afar, anticipates the summation of virtue in magnanimity ("the high and triumphant vertue called Magnanimitie"), the inclusive moral attribute which Spenser calls "Magnificence."
[39] *Works,* II, 147.   [40] *Ibid.,* I, 66. No. 60.   [41] *Ibid.,* I, 69. No. 61.
[42] *Ibid.,* I, 341. No. 66.   [43] *Ibid.,* I, 70. No. 62.

feudal hierarchy, as it disappeared, left a chaotic world in which every man was for himself. The outward shows of tilting and the custom of royal champion continued, but their meanings had disappeared. The old families had to yield to the Bacons and the Burleighs, and this change in the social order is the motivating force of Gascoigne's satire, just as it is of Spenser's search for the virtuous knight. Gascoigne could only condemn, while Spenser sought a new affirmation of moral and spiritual values.

After the rather involved introduction of the Philomene analogy, Gascoigne comes to the problem at hand, the former age compared with the new, and here he explains the conceit of the mirror. His glass of steel, which reflects only the truth, was bequeathed *"to such . . . as love to see themselves, how foule or fayre, soever that they are"*[44] by that *"old satyrical Poete* Lucylius,"[45] the father of Roman satire. In this glass Gascoigne first sees himself and finds the reflection all too true. After recognizing the inevitability of his own faults, he proceeds to consider the ideal commonwealth, which is justly ruled and which lacks a lengthy enumeration of abuses. Such a state Solon and Lycurgus established, but now instead of common weal, one finds common woe. Gazing into his glass, the poet sees the four estates that should prevent such ruin.

> *The King should care for al the subjectes still,*
> *The Knight should fight, for to defende the same,*
> *The Peasant he, should labor for their ease,*
> *And Priests shuld pray, for thē & for thēselves.*[46]

This medieval basis of social organization was disappearing in Gascoigne's time, and his list of the faults of each group only too well emphasizes the transition which forced some men to look forward but him to look backward. Kings care only to maintain their pomp, but in olden times they proved their worth. Knights desire advancement to lordships and dukedoms, while in the former age they lived on their estates and were content to fulfill their duty of upholding right and banishing wrong. Soldiers (the subdivision of the defenders in the knightly group) have completely forsaken the pristine virtues of their class. They are covetous, boasting, cruel, bragging, drunken, and lecherous. Such lengthy treatment springs from Gascoigne's own martial experiences, for he frequently

[44] *Ibid.*, II, 148.   [45] *Ibid.*   [46] *Ibid.*, II, 150.

attacks the behavior of the military,[47] many of whom were, like himself, driven by changing social conditions to seek their fortunes in the wars. But this point Gascoigne ignores when he holds up as the ideals, examples from Roman history. He also fails to understand the transitional nature of his age when he castigates the "peasants" who desert their farms to seek advancement through the legal profession, trade, and minor secretarial posts.

The original four estates are expanded to include judges, lawyers, and merchants. But with these the method is the same: their vices are compared with the virtues of classic figures. Through all of these we can see Gascoigne's own experiences. Thomas Colby is evidently one of those who *"rowte (like rude unringed swine,) to roote nobilitie from heritage."*[48] The memory of his lost paternal acres still rankles in the poet's mind. Likewise, we have only to choose at random from the Close Rolls to identify the merchants who *"rule yong roysters with* Recognisance."[49] Gascoigne's many recognizances played only too great a part in his ruin for him to neglect such an opportunity for revenge.

With the discussion of the priestly estate we return to the medieval hierarchy and recognize the continuity of tradition in attacks on the clergy. Here their vices are implied, since in his glass Gascoigne sees virtuous priests of olden time who were not proud, covetous, gay, gluttonous, envious, malicious, lustful, drunken, fawning, and hypocritical. These virtuous priests Gascoigne asks to pray for those social classes whom he has castigated. Included among the beneficiaries of the prayers are the universities. Cambridge is singled out for especial consideration, but no mention is made of Oxford, which is therefore, by implication, beyond the pale. The priests begin to frown, as if inquiring when their prayers shall end, and Gascoigne uses this device to end his satire with a page and more of "when" clauses. Each of these represents some vice of society which must be amended before the prayers shall cease and a proper social order come into being. Last of all, Gascoigne asks prayers in his own behalf. An epilogue rounds out the work, with an attack on

---

[47] *Vide, passim*, "Dulce Bellum Inexpertis." Cf. also "Gascoignes wodmanship" and *The Spoyle of Antwerpe*.
[48] *Works*, II, 162. [49] *Ibid.*, II, 163.

extravagancies of dress reminiscent of similar references in the eighth poem "F. J."[50] and the warning given Bartholomew Withypoll to beware of pride in dress.[51]

As we have noted in connection with Gascoigne's earlier attempts at satire, his vein is English. The conventional classical and Italian satire of the courtly life in comparison with the rural existence was imitated by Wyatt, but Gascoigne looks to Piers Plowman and the Malvern Hills, not to Italy and its already decadent society. A direct reference to "Peerce *plowman*" is found in that concluding section of *The Steele Glas* where the author asks his priests to pray for the various members of the social order.

> *Therfore I say, stand forth* Peerce *plowman first,*
> *Thou winst the roome, by verie worthinesse.*[52]

"Peerce" is virtuous and will climb to heaven before many a shaven crown.

While the conventional satire of Italy and Wyatt's "John Poins" are limited rather closely to the social world of the upper classes, *The Steele Glas* ranges over the whole of contemporary life. Likewise, the principle of Wyatt's satire is limited. His reasons for eschewing the court are personal; it is his inability to dissemble and his personal disgust of hypocrisy of which he writes. *Piers Plowman* is objective, in that it presents the omnipresent vitiation of morality that results from the pursuit of Lady Meed. Gascoigne also deals in the larger issues: each man is driven by "Surcuydry" to seek his own advancement, and in this search he abandons all morality, all justice, truth, and social responsibility. Petrarch, Ariosto, Alain Chartier, and Wyatt ring the changes upon the familiar theme of the busy, worldly man's desire for a country retreat. It is equally valid and trite in any society and at any time. Langland and Gascoigne both were aware of the social upheaval of the times in which they lived. To both, the ideal lay in the smooth functioning of social responsibility within the medieval hierarchy.

In method as well as point of view, Gascoigne is close to Langland. His points are emphasized by significant details of ordinary life. The

---

[50] *Ibid.*, I, 414. "F. J." No. 8.   [51] *Ibid.*, I, 344. No. 67.   [52] *Ibid.*, II, 170.

entire conclusion portraying the ideal world deals not in generalities or philosophical abstractions:

> *When tinkers make, no more holes thã they founde,*
> *When thatchers thinke, their wages worth their worke,*
> *When colliers put, no dust into their sacks,*
> *When maltemen make, us drinke no firmentie,*
>
> . . .
>
> *When vintners mix, no water with their wine,*
> *When printers passe, none errours in their bookes,*
> *When hatters use, to bye none olde cast robes,*
>
> . . .
>
> *When Searchers see, al corners in a shippe,*
> *(And spie no pens by any sight they see)*
> *When shrives do serve, al processe as they ought,*
> *When baylifes strain, none other thing but strays.*
>
> . . .
>
> *When al these folke, have quite forgotten fraude.*[53]

Specific, too, are his charges against the knights, soldiers, lawyers, and merchants. He knows their tricks from bitter experience, and his satire is pungent because of this realism.

There are, of course, variations from the method of Langland. Gascoigne is not imitating directly; so we do not expect to find the biblical quotations, the dramatic scenes of real life, or the allegory which are so much a part of *Piers Plowman*. Gascoigne adds the classical examples of virtuous life, which are a part of the conventional satire of Italy. He imposes a variety of rhetorical devices, and of course he employs blank verse.

From the quotation which I have given, the nature of the poetry is apparent. Gascoigne clings to the caesura after the second foot and to the end-stopped line—two rules which make the verse rigid and which preclude the creation of the rhythmic period that the absence of rhyme otherwise allows. In fact, there are none of the characteristics of later blank verse, except the omission of a rhyme scheme. One noticeable feature, however, is the lack of alliteration. For one who had so long hunted the letter, Gascoigne here displays an admirable restraint. His experimentation is limited to stanza divisions that are of variable length and corre-

[53] *Ibid.*, II, 171–72.

spond exactly to the paragraph divisions of prose. Equally effective is his
general use of parallelism. Several passages have lines beginning with
the same word and it is a nice observation which prevents the parallelism
from continuing to the grammatical structure of these lines.

> *No crueltie, nor tyrannie can raigne,*
> *No right revenge, doth rayse rebellion,*
> *No spoyles are tane, although the sword prevaile,*
> *No ryot spends, the coyne of common welth.*[54]

He also employs antithesis to good purpose:

> *These be the Knights, which shold defend the lãd,*
> *And these be they, which leave the land at large.*[55]

It is not, however, in the mechanics of poetry that we may find the true
merit of *The Steele Glas*. However interesting may be Gascoigne's hesi-
tant use of the new medium, the matter is far more unusual than the
manner. Satire did not flourish in the great days of Elizabethan literature,
and one reason may lie in the social status of the creators of that literature. George Gascoigne came of an old family, well established in the
medieval tradition. To him the changing social pattern was an upsetting
force that prevented his following the accustomed pattern of life. He
therefore felt the force of change strongly enough to cry out upon it. On
the other hand, this same transition which stifled the feudal families was
favorable to the emergence of men from the lower classes. To these men
the age was one of opportunity, and what cause had a Marlowe, son of
a Canterbury shoemaker, to cry out for a return to the virtues of a rigidly
stratified society? George Gascoigne was proud of his family tradition
and his right, as the eldest son of a knight, to the title of "armiger." But
in the new world of the Tudors the significance of family was not what
it had been; hence Gascoigne looked back to the days when the world
was well ordered, when the eldest son of a knight would have fared better.

ELEGIES

Gascoigne describes both *The Complaynt of Phylomene* and *The Grief
of Joye* as elegies, but any real similarity between the two is not easily
discerned. *The Complaynt of Phylomene* is a retelling of the old legend

---

[54] *Ibid.*, II, 149.   [55] *Ibid.*, II, 155.

of Tereus, Progne, and Philomela, or Philomene, as the name is spelled in the medieval MSS of Ovid[56] and in the commentaries of the Renaissance.[57] This poem, begun in April, 1562, was continued in April, 1575, and finally concluded a year later.[58] We may therefore expect to find a change in Gascoigne's purpose of composition, which is ultimately didactic. The results of lust, the suffering of the innocent, and finally the inexorable punishment of sin are the themes of the poem's conclusion. A similar didactic aim is to be found in *The Grief of Joye,* where the successive vanities of Youth, Beauty, Strength, and Ambition are revealed in all their evanescence, as compared with the stern reality of death. All joy is implicitly sad by reason of its mortality; therefore the wise man will scorn the transitory and prepare himself for the eternal. But whereas *The Complaynt* achieves its purpose in the manner of the exemplum, *The Grief* is an exhortation, with only incidental narrative references. Thus Gascoigne's definition seems curious in its grouping of two disparate poems. The inclusive nature of the elegiac classification is not revealed by Puttenham, who notes only the lamentation of a lover[59] and the lengthy obituary notice as of this type.[60] A more revealing definition is found in Thomas Cooper's *Thesaurus,*[61] where the Latin "Elegia" has as its English equivalent, "Lamentableness: a lamentable songe." Both *The Complaynt* and *The Grief* may be designated "lamentable songes," and it was presumably this meaning of the word "elegy" which Gascoigne employed.

The lamentableness of the harsh fate of Philomela was, as we have seen in connection with *The Steele Glas,* very real to George Gascoigne. He found the cruelty of Tereus to the innocent Philomela analogous to his own persecution by a world that attacked his verses, banned his books, and refused to forgive the repentant sinner. That this analogy was the original impulse which urged him to a paraphrase of the Ovidian story is

---

[56] Cf. *Chrétien de Troyes, "Philomena,"* édition critique avec introduction par C. De Boer [Paris, 1909], Appendices I–III. *Vide supra,* p. 243, n. 28.

[57] *Vide infra,* n. 76, for a list of the Renaissance editions in The Folger Shakespeare Library which I have used.

[58] *Works,* II, 207.

[59] Puttenham, *The Arte of English Poesie,* ed. by Arber, p. 41.

[60] *Ibid.,* pp. 70–71.

[61] Thomas Cooper, *Thesaurus Linguae Romanae & Brittanicae,* H. Wykes, London 1565. Copy in The Folger Shakespeare Library.

doubtful. The conditions which made his lot similar to Philomela's existed only after the publication of *A Hundreth Sundrie Flowres,* and we know that the composition of the narrative began in April, 1562.[62] At this time Gascoigne was still an apprentice, whose early poems dealt with traditional ideas expressed in traditional form and language. It is, of course, a truism that every great age of literature begins largely with translation, and that the career of the individual poet resembles in outline the pattern of the age. The *Metamorphoses* was known to every schoolboy, and the story of the nightingale had been frequently told throughout the Middle Ages.[63] The fact that Gascoigne began his version in April may suggest a cause. Evidently he had been in the country near Chelmsford, since it was on his journey from this city to London that he began his verses.[64] Probably during his country visit he heard the first songs of the newly returned nightingales, and on his homeward journey he passed the time, as he frequently did, in the composition of a poem. The journey was, however, interrupted by "a sodaine dash of Raine" which turned his rather volatile mind to a new theme, that appeared in print as the *De profundis.*[65] Philomela's tale remained unfinished until April, 1575, when presumably Gascoigne either found it accidentally among his papers or else had occasion once again to be in a receptive state of mind when he heard the first song of the nightingale. But the poet of 1575 was a wiser and sadder man than the young courtier of 1562, and the original exercise in paraphrasis became a didactic narrative, emphasizing by analogy the cruel fate which time had brought to the erstwhile gallant. In 1575 the metamorphosis of Tereus, Progne, and Philomela had a very real meaning for Gascoigne. By telling the story and by using the analogy in *The Steele Glas,* he hoped to explain himself to Lord Grey, just as he hoped by the dedication of the two poems to gain favor from this nobleman.

Even more interesting in its relation to Gascoigne's life than the history of the poem is the method of its composition. The story of Philomela was probably first told in literary form in Sophocles's lost tragedy of Tereus, but after this it appears frequently in literature. Apollodorus retold it in *The Library,* Conon in his *Narrationes,* Hyginus in his *Fabulae,*

---

[62] *Works,* II, 207.
[63] By Chaucer, Gower, Chrétien de Troyes, and the anonymous author of the *Ovide Moralisé.*
[64] *Works,* II, 177.   [65] *Ibid.*

Ovid in the *Metamorphoses,* and among many others, Pausanias in the *Periegesis.*[66] In the Middle Ages, Chrétien de Troyes made the story into a lengthy narrative, which was taken over and enlarged by the anonymous author of the *Ovide Moralisé,*[67] while both Chaucer[68] and Gower[69] told it in English. The Renaissance saw it as an incidental reference or allusion, a problem for the commentators of Ovid, a moral narrative in Gascoigne, Pettie, and *The Passionate Pilgrim,* and a potential source for *Titus Andronicus.*

In this lengthy descent, the story lost some of its original details and acquired new ones. In fact the story told by Apollodorus differs materially from that told by Gascoigne. According to the former, Pandion gave his daughter Procne to Tereus as a reward for the latter's help in war. Soon after a son, Itys, was born, Tereus seduced his sister-in-law, Philomela, telling her that Procne was dead. Philomela learned the falsity of this and, though deprived of her tongue by her seducer, she wove the story in a web and thus informed Procne, who promptly killed Itys and fed his body to Tereus. The father, learning of this foul deed, took an ax and pursued the sisters, whom he overtook at Daulia, in Phocis. Procne and Philomela thereupon prayed to be turned into birds, with the result that Procne became a nightingale, Philomela, a swallow, and Tereus, an hoopoe. The cry of each bird was that which was on his or her lips when transformed. Thus Procne laments Itys, Philomela chatters with her stump of tongue, and Tereus cries Pou, Pou (where, where).[70]

Gascoigne's poem[71] differs considerably from this Greek tale. The first important addition occurs when Progne, desirous of seeing her sister, Philomene, urges Tereus to journey to Athens and bring the maiden to Thrace. Tereus undertakes the journey and, arrived in Athens, is soon inflamed with lustful desire for the beauteous Philomene. Pandion is at first unwilling to allow his daughter to leave, but Tereus becomes eloquent in advancing his passions under the guise of urging his wife's desires. Philomene herself begs her father to permit the journey, and finally Pan-

---

[66] These details are derived from Sir James Frazer's extensive discussion of the story in the notes (II, 98–100) of his edition of *The Library* of Apollodorus in the "Loeb Classical Library."

[67] The text of both is found in C. De Boer, *op. cit.*

[68] *The Legend of Good Women,* "The Legend of Philomela."

[69] *Confessio Amantis,* v. 5551 ff.

[70] Apollodorus, *The Library,* III, xiv, 8 ff. (Frazer's ed., II, 98–101.)

[71] *Works,* II, 182–206.

dion yields. In a farewell speech the aged king confides his daughter to Tereus and urges her to remember her father's age and loneliness. No sooner are Tereus and Philomene embarked than the former exults in his triumphs and gazes lustfully upon his prey. Arrived on land, Tereus conveys the maiden to a sheepcote, where he rapes her. Philomene then laments her fate and swears revenge upon Tereus, who proceeds to cut out her tongue. Leaving her in the sheepcote, Tereus returns to Progne, telling her that Philomene is dead. The Queen at once dons mourning garments and builds an empty sepulchre to the memory of her sister. Twelve years pass before Philomene can devise her revenge, but finally she makes a garment on which, in needlework, she tells her story. A trusty servant conveys this to Progne who, though desiring vengeance, bides her time until the triennial rites of Bacchus give her an opportunity to assume a disguise and rescue Philomene. Progne swears revenge in a long speech, which is interrupted by the entrance of Itys calling for his mother. In a scene reminiscent of *The Sacrifice of Isaac* in its pathos and struggle, but lacking the fortunate ending of that play, Progne kills her child whose flesh she serves to his father. Philomene, unable to restrain her joy of revenge, emerges clad in the disguise of a worshiper of Bacchus and hurls the head of Itys at Tereus. The father, realizing the horrid truth, starts up in pursuit, but the gods, to stop the strife, change Progne into a swallow, Tereus into a lapwing, Itys into a pheasant, and Philomene into a nightingale. The story ends with an explanation of the nightingale's song, which Gascoigne divides into three words: Tereu, fye, and jug-jug.

The variation between the accounts of Apollodorus and Gascoigne can be largely explained by a reference to Ovid's version,[72] which is the framework of Gascoigne's narrative. Practically all the events and their sequence are derived from Ovid, but Gascoigne paraphrases rather than translates. The tragic irony of Progne's desire to see her sister, as well as that of Philomene to journey to Thrace, are from Ovid, as is the scene of Progne's conflicting emotions before killing her son. The time intervals are Ovidian, but other details appear which are not in the text of the *Metamorphoses*. Recently Professor D. T. Starnes[73] has commented on

[72] *Metamorphoses*, VI, ll. 412–676.
[73] "Literary Features of Renaissance Dictionaries," *S. in Ph.*, XXXVII (Jan., 1940) 38, 43–44.

Gascoigne's version and concluded that the poet had two sources: Gold-ing's translation of Ovid and the synopsis of the story given by Thomas Cooper in his *Thesaurus*.[74] That Gascoigne, who translated *Hemetes* into Latin and who says that he had studied Latin at Cambridge,[75] should use a translation of such a well-known text as the *Metamorphoses* seems unusual. Actually, there are good reasons for concluding that Gas-coigne not only based his paraphrase on the original Latin, but also used a text whose notes contained the details not found in Ovid.

There are in the Folger Shakespeare Library four copies of sixteenth-century Latin editions of the *Metamorphoses*.[76] All were printed abroad, and all contain an elaborate commentary by Raphael Regius, as well as an introductory synopsis for each story by Lactantius Placitus. Two vol-umes contain contemporary English marginalia and interlinear transla-tion which reveal that they were used in the universities before 1560.[77] A third volume was similarly employed by an Italian student.[78] The im-portance of these books is that they furnish evidence of the text which students used and which, therefore, we may logically conclude Gascoigne employed. This evidence seems to me only contributory, both because a well-educated Elizabethan would hardly have thought of consulting a translation of a familiar classic and because Gascoigne's paraphrase

[74] The concluding section of the *Thesaurus* is a dictionary of proper names in classical lit-erature and mythology.

[75] *Works*, II, 477.

[76] *Publii Ovidij Nasonis . . . Metamorphosis*, Denis Roce, Paris 1510; *Metamorphoseos* [title page missing] Nicolaus Wolf, Lyon 1511 [from colophon]; *P. Ovidij Metamorphosin*, Leo-nardo Lauredão, Venice 1509; *P. Ovidij Nasonis Metamorphoseon*, Ioan. Gryphius, Venice 1565.

[77] The Lyons edition of 1511 has on the end paper this inscription, "ffor as muche as yt hath pleasyd all myghty god To call To hys merce Our Soveren Ladie Quene Mary," which must have been written soon after 1558. The Paris edition of 1510 has on the title-page the name "Edwarde Watmoughe," followed by the date "1555." I have been unable to identify this one-time owner of the volume, but the unusual surname may place him among the for-bears of John Watmoughe, who matriculated at Christ's College in 1627. It would seem that Edward was a student at Corpus Christi College, Oxford, since the following is in his hand. Folio ten is printed in its upper corner "Fo x." This, of course, spells "Fox" as well as "folio ten"; so Watmoughe has written before it "Richarde" and after it "Fundator Collegii C.C." Since Richard Fox was the founder of Corpus Christi, presumably an undergraduate of that College was responsible for the emendation. Both of these volumes are well covered with names, and the interlinear translations are in a number of different hands, showing the suc-cessive uses of the volume.

[78] The Venice edition of 1509.

reveals several direct contacts with the original. Examples showing Gascoigne's use of the Latin rather than Golding's translation are most easily understood by direct comparison, so I shall present the Latin, Golding's translation, and Gascoigne's rendition in sequence.

> Facundum faciebat amor[79]
>
> Love gave him power to frame his talke at will[80]
>
> Love made him eloquent[81]

That Gascoigne here consulted the original seems self-evident.

> Et quoties amplectitur illa parentem
> Esse parens vellet; neque enim minus impius esset.[82]

> As oft as she hir father did betweene hir armes embrace,
> So often wished he himselfe hir Father in that case.
> For nought at all should that in him have wrought the greater grace.[83]

> And wisht himselfe hir sire,
> When she hir sire embrast,
> For neither kith nor kin could then
> Have made his meaning chast.[84]

Again Gascoigne seems to be using the Latin directly.

> Vicimus, exclamat: mecum mea vota feruntur.
> Exsultatque, & vix animo sua gaudia differt
> Barbarus:[85]

> The fielde is ours he cride aloude, I have the thing I sought
> And up he skipt, so barbrous and so beastly was his thought,
> That scarce even there he could forbeare his pleasure to have wrought.[86]

> Ne could the *Barbrous* bloud,
> Conceale his filthy fyre,
> *Hey: Victorie* (quoth he) my shippe
> Is fraught with my desire.[87]

---

[79] *Metamorphoses*, VI, l. 469. I am quoting from the contemporary text, but I give line numbers for use in any modern edition.

[80] Arthur Golding, *The XV Bookes of P. Ovidius Naso, Entytuled Metamorphosis* (William Seres, 1567) fol. 75ᵛ.

[81] *Works*, II, 184.   [82] *Metamorphoses*, VI, ll. 482–83.

[83] Golding, *op. cit.*, fol. 75ᵛ.   [84] *Works*, II, 185.

[85] *Metamorphoses*, VI, ll. 513–15.   [86] Golding, *op. cit.*, fol. 76ʳ.   [87] *Works*, II, 186.

These examples of Gascoigne's use of Ovid rather than Golding may be concluded with one which indicates not only a Latin source but also the use of the commentary of Raphael Regius which we have noted above.

> Non secus exarsit conspecta virgine Tereus;
> Quam si quis canis ignem supponat aristis:
> Aut frondem, positasque cremet foenilibus herbas.[88]

> King Tereus at the sight of hir did burne in his desire,
> As if a man should chaunce to set a gulfe of corne on fire,
> Or burne a stacke of hay.[89]

> And as the blazing bronde,
> Might kindle rotten reeds:
> Even so hir looke a secret flame,
> Within his bosome breedes.[90]

Why Gascoigne used the phrase "rotten reeds" is not explained either by the Latin or by Golding, but the commentary of the contemporary editions does suggest the source. There the adjective "canis" is thus emended: "flavis, & iam aridis"[91]—yellowed and dried—and so the commentary, plus text, gives "as if someone placed a fire under yellowed and dried straw,"[92] which Gascoigne renders colloquially as "rotten reeds."

Another example of the use of details found only in the commentary is revealed in the following comparison:

> Hoc quoque post facinus (vix ausim credere) fertur
> Saepe sua lacerum repetisse libidine corpus.[93]

> And after this most cruell act, for certaine men report
> That he (I scarcely dare beleve) did oftentimes resort
> To maymed Philomela and abused hir at his will.[94]

> I blush to tell this tale,
> But sure best books say this:
> That yet the butcher did not blush
> Hir bloudy mouth to kisse.[95]

---

[88] *Metamorphoses*, VI, ll. 455–57.   [89] Golding, *op. cit.*, fol. 75ʳ.   [90] *Works*, II, 184.

[91] *P. Ovidij Nasonis Metamorphoseon*, Ioan. Gryphius, (Venice, 1565), p. 134. The commentary is the same in all editions, and I quote from that of 1565 because it has regular pagination and is in Roman type.

[92] The modern meaning of "arista" is "the beard of the ear of corn," but this is corn in the generic sense of a cereal, not maize. Cooper simply gives the one word "corne," but Ovid's meaning seems to be that part of the wheat or rye which is stacked and is withered and yellow. This may be rendered by "straw."

[93] *Metamorphoses*, VI, ll. 561–62.   [94] Golding, *op. cit.*, fol. 77ʳ.   [95] *Works*, II, 191.

The connection between the Latin and Gascoigne's version is understandable only when we realize that the commentary[96] explains "lacerum" as "Lingua mutilatum." Thus I think that we may reasonably conclude that Gascoigne not only used a Latin text, but that he availed himself of the commentary of Raphael Regius, as found in the four contemporary editions noted above. Incidentally, by availing himself of this rendition, the poet achieved one of those realistic details, horrid to the point of perfection.

This use of the commentary also invalidates Professor Starnes's theory that Gascoigne used Cooper's *Thesaurus* for those details not found in Golding's translation, since all three of the examples of supposed borrowing from Cooper can be traced to the notes of Regius, the synopsis of Lactantius Placitus, or the additional notes of Henricus Glareanus. The first detail is Gascoigne's account of the transformations of all the characters: Tereus into a lapwing; Itys, a pheasant; Progne, a swallow; and Philomena, a nightingale. These facts are to be found in Cooper, but they also exist in the synopsis of Lactantius Placitus, as well as in the commentary. I quote from Lactantius Placitus:

Philomela cubiculo exiliens caput filii ac pedes in Tereum coniecit, qui stricto ense cum ambas persequeretur, ipse quidem in upupam[97] Itys in phasianum, Progne in hirundinem, Philomela in lusciniã conversi fuisse narrantur.[98]

Since Gascoigne had these facts thus available in the text from which he was working, it seems that we must abandon Cooper and conclude, instead, that the source of the information in the *Thesaurus* was the same commentary used by Gascoigne.

[96] *P. Ovidij Nasonis Metamorphoseon* (Venice, 1565), p. 136. The commentator's note on "Mutilatae colubrae" as "incisa serpentis in duas partes" explains the detail found only in Gascoigne, "so stirres the serpent's taile when it is cut in twaine."

[97] Strictly this means "hoopoe," as does Ovid's "Epops." However, Tereus appears as a lapwing in Gower, Cooper, Golding, Gascoigne, and Sandys. I can only conclude that Ovid's description of the bird applies equally well to both the hoopoe and the lapwing, and that the existence of the proverb about the latter led the translators so to identify him. In 1760 John Clarke, in his translation of Ovid, still used "lapwing" as a translation. The proverb, as given by Gascoigne, is

"*Then (Lapwinglike) the father flies about,*
"*And howles and cries to see his children stray,*
"*Where he him selfe (and no man better) mought*
"*Have taught his bratts to take a better way.*"
[*Works*, II, 206.]

[98] *P. Ovidij Nasonis Metamorphoseon* (Venice, 1565), p. 132.

The other two points adduced by Professor Starnes[99] are the means by which Philomela inscribed her message to Procne and the person by whom the message was conveyed. Since both points derive from the same passage, which is rather obscure, it has seemed well to consider them together.

> . . . grande doloris
> Ingenium est, miserisque venit solertia rebus.
> Stamina barbarica suspendit candida tela:
> Purpureasque notas filis intexuit albis,
> Indicium sceleris: perfectaque tradidit uni:
> Utque ferat dominae, gestu rogat, Illa rogata
> Pertulit ad Prognen: nec scit quid tradat in illis.
> Evolvit vestes saevi matrona tyranni.[100]

> With curious needle worke,
> A garment gan she make,
> Wherin she wrote what bale she bode,
> And al for bewties sake.

> This garment gan she give
> To trustie Servants hande,
> Who streight cōveid it to the queen
> Of *Thracian Tirants* lande.[101]

The first point is Gascoigne's use of "trustie servant," which is not suggested by the one word "uni." Cooper's version reads she "sent the same by a servaunt."[102] Actually, Gascoigne is closer to the Latin in his use of the indirect object, and the "trustie servant" is explained by the commentary, which reads "Uni: ex ancillis."[103]

The second point is more complicated and concerns Gascoigne's use of "curious needle worke" and "garment." That Philomela sent a garment is, I think, shown by Ovid's use of "vestes," but whether this was woven or embroidered is the question. Cooper says, "She beinge very cunnynge in workyng and imbrodering, did in such sorte set out the whole matter in a garment." Gascoigne's "curious" and Cooper's "cunnynge"

---

[99] *Op. cit.* [100] *Metamorphoses,* VI, ll. 574–81. [101] *Works,* II, 192.

[102] As I have noted, Cooper tells the story under the name "Philomela" in the concluding section of his Thesaurus. Pagination varies according to edition, but it is easily found under the name.

[103] *P. Ovidij Nasonis Metamorphoseon* (Venice, 1565), p. 137.

can be traced to "miserisque venit solertia rebus." The work was something familiar to Philomela and she was presumably clever at it. Thus both Cooper and Gascoigne are translating and getting approximately the same result. What the work was is baffling. Modern editions of Ovid read "callida" for "candida" and thus have an adverb; however, Renaissance texts had the adjective, and that was what Gascoigne read. The obscurity of the passage is attested by Henricus Glareanus, whose comment is appended to the various books of the 1565 Venetian edition:

Si tela est opus ipsum, quod ex stamine & trama paulatim conficitur, hic certe abusus videtur nomine, & vel pro iugo vel transversa pertica in altum suspensa, accipiendum, quomodo texunt, qui pretiosa conficiunt texta.[104]

Further evidence of the variety of meanings to be derived is Dr. C. De Boer's rendition of the passage in his comment on Chrétien de Troyes' *Philomena.*

Ovide nous raconte que Philomena brode avec du fil rouge dans un voile blanc l'histoire de son malheur.[105]

My purpose is not to establish an authoritative reading, but to show that the meaning is sufficiently loose to allow of the idea of needlework. If Philomela embroidered, say in the style of petit point, she would use a needle and "intexuit" could be used as a proper verb. It thus seems probable that Gascoigne was simply giving his version of these obscure lines, and there is no apparent evidence that he was following Cooper.

Our consideration of Gascoigne's paraphrase is not complete with this establishment of his source as a contemporary annotated edition of Ovid. There remain at least two matters which have no explanation in the early editions, or any of the versions of the story that I have examined. Gascoigne describes the scene of Philomene's rape as

> A sheepecote closely builte
> Amid the woodds, where many a lāb
> Their guiltlesse bloud had spilte.
>
> There (like a lambe,) she stoode,
> And askte with trimbling voice,
> Where *Progne* was.[106]

---

[104] *Ibid.*, p. 142.   [105] *Op. cit.*, p. xcvii.   [106] *Works*, II, 187.

Ovid's scene is a barn or stable, but he does use the figures of the lamb and a dove to describe Philomela after her rape.

> Illa tremit, velut agna pavens, quae saucia cani
> Ore excussa lupi, nondum sibi tuta videtur.
> Utque columba, suo madefactis sanguine plumis,
> Horret adhuc, avidosque temit, quibus haeserat, ungues.[107]

Gascoigne uses the second of these figures at the same point in the narrative, but not the first. Thus we seem to have once more an example of Gascoigne's own initiative in translation. The idea of the lamb was developed into that of a sheepcote, and from that figure he achieved a poignancy for the scene which does not exist in Ovid or the other versions. The change is of a familiar type: it is Gascoigne's "deepe invention." If Philomene were like a lamb torn by a ravening wolf, then it was much better that she be violated in a place where countless innocent lambs had been slaughtered to satisfy the hunger of men. The analogy was too good not to be used.

Similar in origin, as it seems to me, is Gascoigne's conclusion, wherein he explains the song of the nightingale. Neither Ovid nor any of his Renaissance commentators whom I have read discuss the song. Apollodorus mentions the hoopoe (Tereus) as crying "Pou, Pou" (the words on his lips at the time of his transformation),[108] and Pausanias says that Philomela cried "Tereus," while Procne lamented her son, calling "Ityn."[109] Beyond these I have been unable to discover an exact source for Gascoigne's lengthy explanation of the song of the nightingale, with its three notes: Tereu, fye, and Jug, Jug, Jug. It seems that Gascoigne may have himself noted or have heard of the Tereu-Tereus significance and, being pleased with the "deepe invention," developed it fully.

The moral lesson implicit in the legend had been pointed out by Golding, but it remained for Gascoigne to add not only the analogy to his own life, but also the themes of the inevitability of God's punishment and the desirability of strict sexual morality. The story interested him from an artistic point of view, as we have seen, but I think there can be no doubt

---

[107] *Metamorphoses*, VI, ll. 527–30.
[108] *The Library*, ed. Frazer, *op. cit.*, II, 100.
[109] Pausanias, *Periegesis*, 1, 41, 8 ff.; x, 4, 8 ff.

that his purpose had become didactic, particularly when we read his final lines to Lord Grey:

> *Beare with me (Lord) my lusting dayes are done,*
> *Fayre* Phylomene *forbad me fayre and flat*
> *To like such love, as is with lust begonne,*
> *The lawful love is best, and I like that.*
> *Then if you see, that (Lapwinglike) I chaunce,*
> *To leape againe, beyond my lawful reache,*
> *(I take hard taske) or but to give a glaunce,*
> *At bewties blase, for such a wilful breache,*
> *Of promise made, my Lord shal do no wrong,*
> *To say* (George) *thinke on* Phylomelâes song.[110]

Although the spring of 1576 thus saw Gascoigne considering the possibility of future lapses from virtue, in a comparatively short time sickness had come upon him, and his thoughts were turned toward the inevitability of death. *The Droomme of Doomes day* ends with a letter "teaching remedies against the bytterness of Death,"[111] and the dedicatory letter to the Earl of Bedford concludes: "From my lodging where I finished this travayle in weake plight for health as your good L: well knoweth this second day of *Maye.* 1576."[112] The late summer found both Gascoigne's health and fortunes improved: he received royal employment and was evidently well enough to undertake a mission to France and Antwerp. The attitude with which he accepted this favor is, I think, revealed by the fact that his leisure moments were occupied with the writing of *The Grief of Joye,* as he told the Queen in the dedicatory letter of this work.[113] His theme was the omnipresence of death, in comparison with which all the delights of the body were but snow upon the desert's dusty face. It is curious, however, that this lamentable song is different in mood and inspiration from those gloomy translations of Innocent and Augustine which occupied the poet just before he left England.

For his last song Gascoigne turned to one of the masters of his youth, Petrarch. That he did so may be attributed to an ironic melancholy or simply to the fact that he wished to write a suitable New Year's present

---

[110] *Works,* II, 206.   [111] *Ibid.,* II, 437.   [112] *Ibid.,* II, 214.

[113] *Ibid.,* II, 514. The poem was presented as a New Year's gift on Jan. 1, 1576/7. The presentation MS survives in the British Museum (Royal MS 18 A lxi). It was first printed by Hazlitt (*The Complete Poems of George Gascoigne*).

for the Queen. The heavy-handed asceticism of *The Droomme of Doomes day* or *A delicate Diet* would not meet with royal favor as would the glib superficiality of a Petrarchan imitation, particularly one that would enable him to eulogize the Queen and her court. In spite of his general disillusionment and despair, Gascoigne may still have thought it well to be politic and to convince the Queen of his serious purpose in a poem which had a recognized literary sanction in Petrarch.

Such a view is confirmed by a comparison of *The Grief of Joye* with Petrarch's *De Remediis Utriusque Fortunae,* which Gascoigne says was his model.[114] Petrarch's pseudo-philosophical dialogue is divided into two books: the first dealing with Good Fortune and the second with Bad Fortune. Joy recounts some fact or experience which gives pleasure, whereupon Reason points out the frailty or danger of the enjoyment. Included in the first book are such topics as: "Flourishing Yeeres," "The Goodly Beautie of the Body," "Freedome," "Daunsing," "Playing at Dice and Lottes," and "Sundry Spectacles and Shewes." The second half is devoted to the laments of Sorrow, to which Reason replies so glibly that the character seems to us a Devil's Disciple, finding sorrow in joy and joy in such Bad Fortune as "Deformitie of the Bodye," "An Unchaste Wyfe," "Blyndnesse," and "Payne of the Guttes."[115]

Actually Gascoigne's only indebtedness to Petrarch is the idea of a literary treatment of the vanity of all things mortal and the subject of each of his songs. The English poet does not adopt the dialogue form, but in his own person plays the parts of Joy and Reason. He notes both the seeming Joy and its attendant Grief, and thence derives his title: the grief that is implicit in any joy. His first song deals with "The greeves or discommodities of lustie yowth"; the second, "The vanities of Bewtie"; the third, "The faults of force and strength"; while the last, which was "left unperfect for feare of Horsmen,"[116] points out "The vanities of Activityes." Each of these has a counterpart in Petrarch, but Gascoigne, having borrowed the idea, proceeds to its development in his own fashion.

[114] "Towching the *Methode* and *Invention,* even as *Petrark* in his workes *De remediis utriusque fortunae,* dothe recoũpt the uncerteine Joyes of men in severall dialogues, so have I in thes *Elegies* distributed the same into sundrie songes." (*Works,* II, 514.)

[115] I have consulted the Folger Shakespeare Library copy of Thomas Twyne's translation, which appeared in 1579 with the title *Phisicke Against Fortune.* For a notice of the philosophical background, *vide supra* chap. iv.

[116] *Works,* II, 557.

It is this individuality of development which differentiates the mood of these songs from that of Gascoigne's excursions into "morall philosophie." The most obvious in its treatment is the second song, "The vanities of Bewtie." Instead of a harangue on tombs and corpses, we have a lengthy account of the Queen and the ladies of the court, whom the poet, in his imagination, sees assailing his muse that dares to "attempt to find a newfound griefe."[117] Gascoigne's admonition to his muse sets the tone for the ensuing stanzas, which are in reality the memoirs of a courtier recalling the women he has known.

> MUSE: plaie thy parte/ & fend thy head frō blowes/
> I see a swarme, wch coome thee to assayle,
> Ne canst thow well, defend so many foes,
> Yf harte wax feynt, or courage seme to quayle/
> Behold, beholde, they come, as thyck as hayle,
> And threat to pluck the tongue owt of thy jawes,
> Which darest presume, to clapp on such a clawse/[118]

The "swarme" is led by the Queen, and she receives a full measure of praise from her loyal subject, who carefully disassociates his thoughts from those of his muse. Those who follow the Queen are mentioned sometimes by name, at other times by puns, but all have their initials carefully noted in the margin. Practically all of these beauties can be identified, and their names are to be found in Appendix VI.

Suddenly, however, there appears another "troupe of Dames" whom Gascoigne does not at once recognize, because "Thes Starres of Cowrte had bleared [his] better eye."[119] Chief among this new group, come to attack the spiteful muse, is the elusive Ferenda Natura. Two stanzas describe her manifold attributes, but they yield no tangible clue to her identity:

> My *Sweetest sowre*, my Joy of all my griefe,
> My *Frendly foe*, myne ofte *Reviving death*,
> My first *Regreate*, my right and last *Reliefe*,
> My *frewtful cropp*, and yet my *Barreyne heath*,
> My *store* and *stocke*, wch spares & spends my breathe/
> My *Hope forlorne*, my *Heyght* of all my *Happe*,
> My *Love* first *lulled*, in golden fancies lappe.

---

[117] *Ibid.*, II, 526.   [118] *Ibid.*   [119] *Ibid.*, II, 530.

My *Hollow tree*/ my banishment to *Bathe,*
Ferenda Shee, who eke, *Natura* hight,
My *Ground* of *Greene,* w^{ch} (myxt wth black) is rathe,
My *Porte* of *Peace,* whose warres yet dubd me knight,
My *Livia,* my love, and my delight,
Myne *A per se,* my *All,* myne onely *Sum,*
Before this heape, in hasty heate dothe cõme/[120]

She addresses Gascoigne as Bartholmew, and so we realize that she and Gascoigne are the lovers of "Dan Bartholmew of Bathe," yet we know not who she is. "Her playfellowes" are Jane Townshend, Frances Pierrepont, and the Countess of Lennox,[121] but I have been unable to find any indication through these friends that would serve to name her. That she occupied a position of some importance is attested by her friends, and this inclines me to exclude Elizabeth Bacon. Mr. Fleay attempted to make her Helen Suavemberg, because Gascoigne's appellation of "hollow tree" suggests the heraldic use of a boat, and Helen Suavemberg's arms were a lighter boat in fosse.[122] This same method could be employed with equal success for such other of her attributes as *"frewtful cropp," "Barreyne heath,"* and *"Ground* of *Greene."* It would seem that the identity of Ferenda, like that of the Dark Lady, must remain for yet a little time a thing "mistical and not to bee understoode but by Thaucthour him selfe."[123]

After concluding his memoirs with some of those Beauties of the Low Countries who helped him while away his leisure hours not only during the years 1572–74, but also during the siege of Antwerp when he was writing this philosophical treatise, Gascoigne returns to his theme of vanity. "Lust," "false suspect," and "wormes of wonton wyll" infect *"Bewties* bones." Young men desert their prayers to pursue a Beauty thus infected, but Gascoigne is still too much of a gallant to condemn all his ladies.

If Dames demaund, howe they the same might deeme?
I answere thus: the fayre which is content,
Withe natures gyftes/ and neither dothe esteeme,

---

[120] *Ibid.*   [121] *Ibid.,* II, 531. Cf. Appendix VI.
[122] Quoted by Schelling (*op. cit., p.* 20) from *Transactions of the Royal Historical Society,* n. s., I (Pt. II), 130.
[123] A marginal note to "Dan Bartholmew of Bathe" (*Works,* I, 110).

Yt selfe to muche: nor is to lightnes bent,
Nor woulde be loved, but with a true entent:
And strives in goodnes, likewise to excell,
I say thatt *Bewtie,* beares awaie the bell./[124]

True Beauty is not a vanity, and Gascoigne, the poet, can never wholly scorn the world which once he had enjoyed.

Likewise, it is the poet echoing the old cry for the snows of yesteryear who dominates the first song, where the sins of youth are occasionally condemned, but where the loss of youth and the haste of Time are Gascoigne's real sorrows.

„The heavens on highe perpetually doe move/
„By mynutes meale, the howre dothe steale awaie/
„By howres, the daie, by daies, the monethes remove/
„And then by monethes, the yeares as fast decaie/
„Yea, *Virgills* verse, and *Tully,* truth do saie,
„*That tyme flieth on, and never claps her wings,*
„*But rides on clowdes,* & *forward still she flinges.*[125]

He could have spent his youth more wisely, but such repentance brings him no sorrow like that of the realization that "the best is over."

The third and fourth songs, dealing with strength and activities, are a curious mixture of ideas. Strength is vain because the biggest and strongest are the first on whom Fortune wreaks her will. Activities, however, are only a grief when they go to extremes. In his advocacy of the humble life of a weakling, a life that does not tempt Fortune, Gascoigne is definitely medieval, but in admitting that only extremes are bad he is a true Humanist. In his attack on Strength we find the man who sees no justice, no reason, and no purpose, only a capricious Fortune; while the man who deems many things virtuous and desirable in moderation affirms a purposeful growth.[126]

These contradictions seem to find at least a partial resolution in the songs themselves. All four are written from Gascoigne's own point of view: he laments his youth now lost, beauty that once he knew, strength that brought disaster, and activities that caused minor difficulties.

I have bene stronge (I thanke my God therefore)
And did therein, rejoyce as most men dyd/

---

[124] *Works,* II, 538.   [125] *Ibid.,* II, 522.
[126] For an extended examination of these two concepts, see Farnham's *The Medieval Heritage of Elizabethan Tragedy,* chaps. i, ii.

> I lept, I răne, I toylde and travailde soore,
> My might and mayne, didd covett to be kidd/
> But lo: beholde; my mery daies amydd,
> One heady deede, my haughty harte did breake,
> And since (full oft) I wisht I had bene weake./[127]

>   Amongst the vaynes, of variable Joyes,
> I must confesse, that *Musicke* pleasd me ones
> But whiles I searcht, the semyquaver toyes,
> The glăncing sharpes, the halfe notes for the nones;
> And all that serves, to grace owre gladsome grones;
> I founde a flatt, of follye owt of frame,
> Whiche made me graunt my *Musicke* was but lame.[128]

Strength is to be wholly condemned because it brought ruin; music can exist in moderation because it caused him less hurt. What great disaster strength brought upon him we do not know. Presumably it was the publication of *A Hundreth Sundrie Flowres,* which could be considered an instance of the strength of dangerous ambition. Similarly we know not what song displeased what person.

In retrospect we see that Gascoigne, the moralist, lamented in his elegies the misfortunes which had been his. He, like Philomene, had been the victim of wanton aggression. He knew the grief implicit in joy, and he knew through bitter personal experience. His are no general or fashionable laments, but the disillusioned reflections of a man who understood too well "the troubles of [his] proud and angry dust." Virtue thus was no set code, governing all of life's activities; instead, it was a negation of those deeds and desires which had brought trouble to George Gascoigne, who, now that youth was done, saw himself

>   Muche lyke to them, who (sitting in a shipp)
> Are borne forthright, and feele no footing sturr./
> In silent sleepes, the tyme awaie dothe slipp./
> Yt neither bawlethe (like a contrie curre)
> Nor standeth styll, to byde a hasty spurre/
> But slily slydes, and never maketh noyse,
> And much bewrayes; with verie little voyce./[129]

---

[127] *Works,* II, 542.   [128] *Ibid.,* II, 551.   [129] *Ibid.,* II, 523.

MORAL PHILOSOPHY

I was (now almost twelve moneths past) pricked and much moved, by the grave and discreete wordes of one right worshipfull and mine approved friend, who (in my presence) hearing my thryftlesse booke of *Poesyes* undeservedly commended, dyd say: That he lyked the smell of those *Poesies* pretely well, but he would lyke the Gardyner much better if he would employe his spade in no worse ground, then eyther Devinitie or morall Philosophie.[130]

Thus urged to serious labor, Gascoigne found two apt subjects among the manuscripts in his library.

I chaunced to light upon a small volumne skarce comely covered, and wel worse handled. For to tell a truth unto your honor, it was written in an old kynd of Caracters, and so torne as it neyther had the beginning perspycuous, nor the end perfect. So that I can not certaynly say who shuld be the Author of the same.[131]

This manuscript, or "Paumphlette" as Gascoigne terms it, contained Pope Innocent's *De Contemptu Mundi* and St. Augustine's sermon on drunkenness. In addition to these there were two other treatises, one on sin and the other on the rules of the Christian life.[132] These last, whose authorship I have been unable to determine, Gascoigne combined with the *De Contemptu,* to which he added a letter on the bitterness of death, and thus compiled a volume under the title of *The Droomme of Doomes day,* which was published by Gabriell Cawood in 1576.[133] The dedicatory letter[134] to the Earl of Bedford sets the more exact date of 2 May, 1576, as the backward limit of publication.

Evidently Gascoigne was engaged in his translation of those parts of the manuscript included in *The Droomme* at about the time he was finishing *The Complaynt of Phylomene* and *The Steele Glas,* whose dedicatory letters are dated April 16 and April 15, 1576. Some months elapsed, however, before the publication of *A delicate Diet, for daintiemouthde Droonkardes,* based in part on the sermons of Augustine. This work

---

[130] *Ibid.,* II, 211–12.   [131] *Ibid.,* II, 212.

[132] There were probably several MSS gathered together, since Gascoigne says in connection with *A delicate Diet:* "Whyles I travayled in Translation, and collection of my *Droomme of Doomes daye:* and was busyed in sorting of the same (for I gathered the whole out of sundry Pamphlets:)." [*Works,* II, 455.]

[133] *Works,* II, 209.   [134] *Ibid.,* II, 214.

bears the title-page[135] date "Aug. 22, 1576," while the dedication[136] to Lewis Dive was written on 10 August, 1576.

The spring and summer of 1576 thus appear to have been times not only of great labor but also of sincere moral purpose. As we have noted, Gascoigne told the Earl of Bedford of his sickness during the first week in May, and this fact must be considered when we attempt a judgment of these works of "morall Philosophie."

Both these excursions into the writings of the Church Fathers were translations[137] and are not, therefore, direct expressions of Gascoigne's own beliefs. In the preceding pages devoted to the Elegies, I suggested that Gascoigne's concept of virtue was based on a negation of those ideas or pursuits which had caused him harm. In the present discussion, it will be well to think of these two translations as contributory to this whole process of negation, rather than as affirmations of an attitude toward life. In other words, Gascoigne did not change his philosophy and then adopt a specific philosophical or religious viewpoint; rather, his changing attitude toward the world, brought on by his realization of failure, induced in him a philosophical outlook that took pleasure in lamenting and castigating all things that had brought disaster. Thus, in 1576, his ideas were congenial to the virulent asceticism of Pope Innocent, as well as to St. Augustine's strictures on drink. These two works, although grouped by Gascoigne as "morall Philosophie," are hardly comparable in tone and scope, so that they require individual consideration.

The Droomme of Doomes day.—The source of the first section of *The Droomme of Doomes day,* entitled "The vewe of worldly Vanities," was first recognized by Professor Schelling[138] as the *De Contemptu Mundi* of Pope Innocent III. Professor Schelling[139] also noted another version of this work, printed in the same year. The translator, H[enry] K[irton], entitled his work *The Mirror of Mans Lyfe.*[140] That Gascoigne and Kirton worked independently is indicated by the lack of any definite

---

[135] *Ibid.,* II, 451.   [136] *Ibid.,* II, 454.

[137] For the significance of the original sections of *A delicate Diet, vide infra,* pp. 274–75.
[138] *Op. cit.,* pp. 96–97.   [139] *Ibid.*

[140] Printed by Henry Bynneman, who had printed *A Hundreth Sundrie Flowres, The Posies, The Steele Glas,* and *The Complaynt of Philomene.* Stephen Gosson's first published work, *Speculum Humanum,* was printed at the end of *The Mirror of Mans Lyfe.* I have consulted the Folger Shakespeare Library copies of the two editions of 1576.

verbal similarities. In general both works are good translations in the latinistic biblical style.

It is difficult to estimate how closely Gascoigne followed his manuscript original, since we have no means of knowing how accurate a version that was. By comparison with a modern definitive text of Innocent, Gascoigne seems to have been more literal in his rendition of this tract than he had been in his more secular translations. He does, nevertheless, emphasize those stylistic devices of which he was fond. The various forms of parallelism, antithesis, series, and repetitions are all present as the devices of that style which is familiar to us in Cranmer's *Prayer Book,* as well as in the King James version of the Bible. Certainly the Latin original was constructed in a style very close to this, so we cannot be certain as to the extent of Gascoigne's contribution. Therefore, although we can find in his other translations definite evidence of his own stylistic desiderata, here we are limited by the traditional nature of the translation. This may be confirmed by reference to Kirton's translation, which, in general matters of style, is close to that of Gascoigne.

Likewise, our interest in the subject matter is necessarily limited by the fact of translation. The student of an emergent Puritanism could undoubtedly find much of interest; but it is best to limit our application of the ideas to the more general aspects of Gascoigne's life. The theme of "The vewe of worldly Vanities"[141] is, of course, the utter vileness of life in all its physical manifestations, from birth to death. Whereas Job's cry as to the purpose of birth and existence is an attempt to solve the problem of evil; Innocent's "O mother (may I well saye) wherefore hast thou begotten or conceyved me the sonne of bitter sorrow and payne?"[142] has already admitted the essential evil of life and asks a rhetorical question. The remainder of the tract is an amplification of this theme, consisting largely of an enumeration of the sorrows, troubles, torments, and punishments which man encounters during his terrestial pilgrimage to the grave. That Gascoigne could share this complete negation of physical life is understandable. Life had treated him badly and, though he could sigh for his lost youth,[143] it was easy, particularly in his present sickness, to deny

---

[141] *Works,* II, 217–74. [142] *Ibid.,* II, 217.
[143] Cf. *The Grief of Joye,* "The First Songe."

that which he could no longer enjoy and which he now perhaps actively disliked. The man who had seen the error of his ways could cast the world aside, at least until he had a promising opportunity to enter it once more.

The final sections of *The Droomme* are separate tracts similar to the *De Contemptu.* The second part is entitled "The Shame of Sinne," the third, "The Needles Eye," and the last, "The Bytternes of Death." Gascoigne tells us that the second and third were a part of the same manuscript from which he took "The vewe of worldly Vanities," but I have been unable to discover their authors. Evidently the manuscript or manuscripts were devoted to worthy tracts by eminent divines, and thus identification probably lies somewhere among the manifold volumes of the *Patrologiae Latinae* or the *Patrologiae Graecae.*

"The Shame of Sinne,"[144] the second section of *The Droomme,* may be classified as Puritan or Calvinistic, but it does not have those Manichean characteristics which mark "The vewe of worldly Vanities." Its manner is the familiar one of assembling relevant material from all biblical sources, with a sectional unity based on various sentences which preface each "article." Some of these are the following:

That only sinne causeth a reasonable creature to be displeasaunt, dispisable and odious unto God.[145]

That the greatnesse and enormitie of sinne is comprehended (by generall speech) in sixe poyntes.[146]

What sinne is.[147]

That we are not able in this life fully to comprehend the enormitie of sinne.[148]

How a man ought to behave himselfe heere in earth, which desireth to attayne unto perfection of life.[149]

The third section, "The Needles Eye,"[150] is described by Gascoigne as the rules of Christian life, but it is a far more lengthy and rambling disquisition than such a subtitle implies. It ranges over the whole of life, physical and spiritual, with admonitions on all manner of topics such as these:

A reprehention of our sloth, necligence, & dastardlinesse.[151]

What it is to contempne and despise the wor[l]dly.[152]

---

[144] *Works,* II, 275–331.　　[145] *Ibid.,* II, 277.　　[146] *Ibid.,* II, 281.　　[147] *Ibid.,* II, 283.
[148] *Ibid.,* II, 312.　　[149] *Ibid.,* II, 328.　　[150] *Ibid.,* II, 332–437.　　[151] *Ibid.,* II, 348.
[152] *Ibid.,* II, 358.

The consideration of our owne perilles enduceth us to cõtempne the worlde.[153]

The world is to be cõtempned because it is hard (therein) to attayne salvation.[154]

It is good to pray and sing Psalmes.[155]

The Droomme concludes with a letter written by I.B. to "his famyliar frende G.P. teaching remedies against the bytternesse of Death."[156] The argument is the usual one that death is the beginning, not the end. The joy with which the Christian can approach the grave is contrasted with the heathen views of Aristotle, Cicero, and Marcus Aurelius, each of whom feared the end of life. A short quotation will show not only the philosophical basis, but also the more familiar style in which the letter is couched, in contrast with that of the three main sections:

But as to the heathen the ende of lyfe & being, is and (for causes aforesayd) must be dreadfull, so unto a christian man it neither is nor should seeme so, unto whom death is yᵉ beginning of lyfe, the gate of blysse, the ende of sorow and mortal greefe. Whereof he is not onely informed by conjecture lyke to be true, but assured by promise of him yᵗ can be all thinges saving false, so that a scholer of Christe should rather doubt whether the Sunne shyne by daye, or whether he feele being awaked, then whether the promises made thereof be assured or no.[157]

If Gascoigne's illness were serious, as it seems to have been by reason of his delay from May to August in completing *A delicate Diet, for daintiemouthde Droonkardes,* his mind must many times have turned to thoughts of death, and we can only wonder how much consolation he found in the evanescence of physical life and the reality of death which he had affirmed in *The Droomme of Doomes day.*

A delicate Diet, for daintiemouthde Droonkardes.—That *A delicate Diet, for daintiemouthde Droonkardes*[158] was derived, at least in part, from the manuscripts in his possession and from which he translated the various sections of *The Droome* is clearly indicated by Gascoigne's own words:

Whyles I travayled in Translation, and collection of my *Droomme of Doomes daye:* and was busyed in sorting of the same (for I gathered the whole out of

---

[153] *Ibid.,* II, 380.   [154] *Ibid.,* II, 383.   [155] *Ibid.,* II, 426

[156] *Ibid.,* II, 437–49. A similar letter on death is the concluding item in Edward Hake's *Newes out of Powles Churchyard,* 1579. This volume of verse satires was entered in 1567/8 and therefore antedates *The Steele Glas* as satire, but it is topical and is in fourteeners.

[157] *Works,* II, 439.   [158] *Works,* II, 455–71.

sundry Pamphlets:) I chaunced at passage, to espye one shorte Epistle, written against Dronkennesse. And though the rest of such Treatises, as I founde in the same Coppie, dyd carrye none expresse name of theyr severall Aucthours: yet this Epystle was therein entytuled:

An Admonition of Saint Augustine the Bishoppe, for the eschewing of Droon-kennesse.[159]

Having perused the tract and mediated upon the dangerous increase of drunkenness within the realm, Gascoigne decided to translate the words of St. Augustine. The translation, which occupies some four pages, is preceded and followed by Gascoigne's own reflections and admonitions.

The original from which Gascoigne derived his version of Augustine's remarks would seem at first to be easily identified. The translator describes it as an "Epystle," while Professor Schelling[160] says that the whole tract "is a translation of the epistle of Saint Augustine, *De Ebritate*." As a matter of fact, there is no epistle among the extant writings of Augustine which bears this title, nor is there any epistle which could serve as the source of Gascoigne's four pages of translation. There are, however, among the doubtful sermons of St. Augustine, two which are concerned with the problem, and it is on the first[161] of these that Gascoigne's manuscript was based. The sermon itself runs to three and one-half large quarto columns of small print and is thus double or triple the length of Gascoigne's version, so it would appear that the transcriber of Gascoigne's manuscript was guilty of an all-too-frequent sin. He began with the idea of making a complete transcript, but as he proceeded, he decided to condense. Such would appear to be the case, since the translation compares closely with the first paragraph and then lapses into summaries of the ensuing sections. I shall quote the first and last sections of both the Latin and the English so that the method of Gascoigne's translation may be apparent.

Licet propitio Christo, fratres charissimi, credam vos ebrietatis malum velut inferni foveam expavescere, et non solum ipsi non velitis amplius bibere, sed nec alios adjurare vel cogere plus quam oportet accipere: tamen quia non potest fieri ut non sint aliqui negligentes, qui sobrii esse non velint, vos qui

[159] *Ibid.*, II, 455.   [160] *Op. cit.*, p. 97.

[161] Migne, ed., *Patrologiae Latinae*, Vol. XXXIX. "Sancti Augustini Hipponensis Episcopi, Opera Omnia" V, Sermo CCXCIV, "Admonitio ut ebrietatis malum totis viribus caveatur," cols. 2303–6. This is one of the supposititious sermons of Augustine and was probably composed by Caesar of Arles. (col. 2303 n.)

semper convivia sobria exhibetis, nolite ad vestram injuriam revocare, quia nobis necesse est alios ebriosos arguere.[162]

Although, my deerly beloved, I hope y^t you through the grace of Christ, wyll feare Droonkennesse, as you feare the pit of Hell: and that not only you wyl drinke no more then is convenient, but also that you wyll not compell or allure any other to drinke more than wyll suffise: yet shall you take in good part this councell of mine, because it can not be chosen, but that some will be necligent, and are not able to keepe them selves sober. But you which doo alwayes banquette soberlie, and temperately, take not this as spoken to your reproche: for it is necessarie that we do sometimes rebuke dronkardes.[163]

Sed credo de Dei misericordia, quod ita vobis inspirare dignabitur, ut tam lugendum et etiam erubescendum malum ita vobis in horrorem veniat, ut illud nunquam fieri permittatis; sed quod in illa ebrietate periturum erat, in pauperum refectionem proficiat: praestante Domino Jesu Christo, qui cum Patre et Spiritu sancto vivit et regnat Deus in saecula saeculorum. Amen.[164]

Wherefore, I beseech God of his mercie, that he vouchsafe to enspire you with such grace, that this so shamefull and lamentable an evyl and wickednesse, maye become such an horrour unto you, as that you suffer it never to be committed, but that you convert that to helpe & refresh the poore, which shoulde have bene cast away in superfluous droonkennesse. And this by the helpe & grace of our Lorde Jesus Christ, who with the Father and the holy ghost, lyveth and raigneth God, world without ende. *Amen*.[165]

Thus I think it is clear that Gascoigne translated from a manuscript which began and ended as a literal transcript, but which abbreviated and summarized the central portions of the sermon. It is also important that while Gascoigne's whole tract occupies some twenty pages, the actual translation of Augustine requires but four of these. In other words, the bulk of the tract is of Gascoigne's own composition.

His method is easily recognized as the familiar one of the "theme." His introductory remarks explain the discovery of the manuscript of Augustine, which led him to reflect not only upon the increase of drunkenness but also upon the proposition *"That all Droonkardes are Beastes."*[166] The words of the good bishop completed, Gascoigne advances to the proof of his proposition. He adduces the examples of Holofernes, Alexander of Macedon, and Lucullus to prove the metamorphoses wrought by the Circe of drink. This achieved, there remains the contemporary world,

---

[162] Migne, *op. cit.*, col. 2303.   [163] *Works*, II, 457.   [164] Migne, *op. cit.*, col. 2306.
[165] *Works*, II, 460.   [166] *Ibid.*, II, 456.

where he summons forth not only "the *Germaines* (who of auncient tyme have beene the continuall Wardens of the Droonkards fraternitye and corporation,) but . . . our new-fangled Englyshe men, which thinke skorne to leave any newe fashion (so that it be evyll) untryed or unfollowed."[167] These unfortunates are guilty of the enormous sin of the "drinking of harty draughtes." This custom of drinking toasts is, of course, derived from abroad. Even as extravagancies of dress had been imported from Italy, Spain, and Turkey, so this habit of drinking came from "the *Almaines* and other of the low Countreyes."[168] Finally, Gascoigne avails himself of scriptural authorities who condemn drunkenness, and the tract ends with this exhortation:

Nowe if these aucthorities, examples, counsels, and commandements, seeme not sufficient to terrifye us from falling into this swynish and filthye abhomination, I can doo no more, but praye unto God, that some better learned, and more eloquent then I, maye (by assistance of his holy spyrite) be made able to set downe such wholsome lessons for the avoyding thereof, that the excesse and custome of the same, maye generallye throughout all Christendome, and especially heere in England, be reformed: And the plagues and punishmentes by him threatened and pronounced (by his clemency and mercy) may be withdrawne and remytted: So that in all cleanesse and purenesse of hart, we maye praise his name: To whome with the Sonne and the holy Ghost, bee all dominion, power and glory, nowe and for ever. So bee it. FINIS.[169]

A delicate Diet is interesting from several points of view. It is among the earliest temperance tracts in the language, it reveals to us the Puritan spirit in its attacks on clothes as well as drink, and, lastly, it presents us with a final picture of Gascoigne, the moralist. He has changed considerably from the man who wrote *The Steele Glas*. In that work, he was a critic observing social change, and we can sympathize with the justice of his satire, which dealt in a specific manner with the whole question of a

---

[167] *Ibid.,* II, 465.

[168] *Ibid.,* II, 466. A seventeenth-century tract, Matthew Scrivener's *A Treatise Against Drunkenesse* (Cambridge, 1685) contains a complete translation of both of Augustine's sermons (the second, not used by Gascoigne, is No. CCXCV in Migne). He does not borrow from Gascoigne, but he does attack the drinking of toasts. In one passage, there are references which are amusing when we think of Gascoigne, the soldier, and Gascoigne, the moralist: "When Queen *Elizabeth* gave assistance to the distressed *Netherlands,* these succours soon learn'd the art, and catched the Disease of Drinking, rife in those countries, and transported the same soon after into England." (Page 114.) Cf. "Gascoignes voyage into *Hollande.*" (*Works,* I, 354. No. 74.)

[169] *Works,* II, 471.

society in a state of flux. This larger attitude toward the world is in strange contrast with that of the ascetic whose idea of moral philosophy finds expression in a negation of physical life and a bitter attack on the evils of drink. There is always, however, the possibility that he wrote for reasons of expediency, and this finds confirmation in his royal employment a short time after he finished *A delicate Diet*. On the other hand, the change from *The Glasse of Government* to *A delicate Diet* is a progression to a logical conclusion. If literature were didactic and if Gascoigne turned with bitterness upon those aspects of life of which he had reason to repent, then it is understandable that he should become a Puritan Cato, crying out upon the wickedness of the world. Always the superficial vices have been the more interesting, because they are more picturesque and allow of greater fluency in their castigation. We need only compare Gascoigne's attack on the disappearance of social responsibility with *A delicate Diet* to realize how much more lurid the latter appears. The specific, the common, and the picturesque—these are the subjects which men can understand. Social responsibility was vague and intangible, even though its disappearance caused more harm than all the drink and the outlandish clothes in London. Gascoigne was great as a satirist; as a moralist he was a bitter and disillusioned Puritan.

Epilogue

Tam Marti, Quam Mercurio.
GASCOIGNE

AND so from the young man hunting and hawking and taking his pleasure in Queen Mary's Honour of Ampthill we have seen George Gascoigne become successively the amorous poet, the young lawyer writing for the stage, the teller of tales, the unlucky soldier, and finally the disillusioned moralist, sighing in his last song for the youth that had vanished. But what final picture may we draw of this mortal fusion of Mars and Mercury? The elephantine Harvey made many observations on the life and doings of George Gascoigne and, singularly enough, some of these are most revealing. Among the marginalia in his copy of *The Posies* are the following lines:

Want of resolution & constancy, marred his witt & undid himself.[1]

Sum vanity: & more levity: his special faulte, & the continual causes of his misfortunes. Many other have maintained themselves gallantly upon sum one of his qualities: nothing fadgeth with him, for want of Resolution, & Constancy in any one kind. He shall never thrive with any thing, that can brooke no crosses, or hath not learned to make the best of the worst, in his Profession. It is no marvell, thowgh he had cold successe in his actions, that in his studdies, & Looves, [he] thowght upon yᵉ Warres; in the warres, mused upon his studdies, & Looves.[2]

These same criticisms are repeated by Harvey in *The Letter-Book*, where in addition Gascoigne is baited as to his "posy" and his seriousness in upbraiding the contemporary scene. The first passage concerns Gascoigne's vanity exemplified in his "posy."

> In effigie Gascoigni
> Gascoignus Mercurium atque
> Martem suum inuocat
> Illi verbo respondent.

---

[1] Smith, ed., *Gabriel Harvey's Marginalia*, p. 166.   [2] *Ibid.*, pp. 166–67.

G. Mercuri ades: M. Venio. G. Mars adsis: M. Protinus adsum. G. Quid datis?
M.M. Ah, miser est, qui petit G. Ecce miser.

> Gascoignus solus, seipsum cum Hercule
> Strozza comparat, homine Italo
> Eodemque viro generoso ac poeta nobili.

In eo discrimen notatur quod cum Mars et Venus utrique dominaretur, haec tamen illum, hunc potius ille perdiderit.

> Mercurius linguam: Mars dextram: Cypria mentem:
> Et parvam mentem parve Cupido dabas.
> Scilicet ista isti dederant eadem omnia iidem.
> Strozza tibi: nec aquam sic aqua pura refert.
> Ambo infaelices: sed erat discrimen in illo
> Incidit tibi Mars: Cypria falsa mihi.
>
> G.H. invita Minerva F[ecit].[3]

In this brief dramatic sketch Harvey, by imagining Gascoigne in conversation with Mars and Mercury, punctures the vanity of the posy and chastises the poet for hoping to gain rewards merely by asking. This latter point is also noted in Harvey's copy of *The Posies,* where in connection with the posy, *Meritum petere, gravè,* he remarks:

Meritum petere, vile: capere, generosum. In hoc mundo, non loquendum de meritis, sed reverâ merendum. Jactare industriam, vanum reipsa extendere, virile.[4]

In other words, if Gascoigne had done more to deserve reward and had thought less of what was due him as the elder son of a good family, he would have achieved far more than he did.

This serious tone of criticism disappears in Harvey's two English poems on Gascoigne. The first imagines the poet's arrival in the nether world, and the second is presumably Harvey's description of his vision of Gascoigne in that region. Both lack introductions and are separated by several leaves from their seeming introduction and from Harvey's statement that he was writing an obituary notice of the poet. What appears to be the introduction again plays on Gascoigne's vanity.

A suttle and trechrous advantage (poetically imagined) taken at unawares by the 3 fatall sisters to berive M. Gascoigne of his life, notwithstandinge a former

---

[3] *The Letter-Book of Gabriel Harvey, A.D. 1573–1580,* ed., by E. J. L. Scott. Camden Society Publications, LXXXIV (1800), 54.

[4] Smith, *Marginalia,* p. 167.

composition solemely and autentically agreid uppon betwene Mars Mercury and them to the contrarye. His lively and vitall spiritts grauntid and (by allegoricall interpretation) restorid unto him of . . . .

After four excised leaves we encounter the poem describing Gascoigne's entry into the Elysian Fields:

> And if with pleasure thou delightes
>   To feede thine eie, injoye thy fill;
> Here mayst thou gratis vewe the gostes
>   That Socrates surveyith still.
>
> He longed to dye, thou wottst it well
>   To looke ould Homer in the face
> And to dispute with Hesiode
>   Queinte mysteries towchinge Poets grace.
>
> To marke withall Ulisses sleites,
>   And heare Sir Nestors eloquence,
> And Hercules countenaunce beholde,
>   And note sage Dias sapience.
>
> Methinkes thow gleekiste[5] many a lorde
>   And spees out maddames for the nonce
> And sporte thyselffe with this and that
>   And specially with ther deinty bones.[6]
>
> And all that glorious cumpany
>   Of parsonages heroicall,
> To greete with salutations
>   Divine and metaphysicall.
>
> Of purpose framed longe before,
>   And kennd by heart as many yeares,
> As Horace would have poems kepte
>   Before in printe on worde appeares.[7]
>
> This pleasure reape: and shake thou hands
>   With auncient cuntrymen of thine:
> Acquayntaunce take of Chaucer first
>   And then with Gower and Lydgate dine.

---

[5] Jest, scoff at.

[6] Cf. "His last will and Testament" (*Works,* I, 121. "D. B." No. 8), in which he leaves his body to be embalmed and preserved against the time of her (Ferenda's) death. Then "hir bones" are to be placed over his body, which will thus become the first object of the "greedy wormes."

[7] Presumably a jibe at Gascoigne's pride in his ability to improvise verses which he later set down. Cf. *Works,* I, 70, 479 (n. to p. 59).

And cause thou art a merry mate
　Lo Schoggin where he lawghes aloane
And Skelton that same madbrayne knave
　Looke how he knawes a deade horse boane.

Perdy thou art much to reioice
　That good Syr Thomas More will deyne
His cuntryman at first insight
　So curteously to interteyne.

And loa my lorde of Surrey tooe
　What countenaunce he shows to the
O happye and thrise happye man
　That fyndes sutch heavenlye curtesye.

But preythe see where Withipolls cum
　Daniel and Batt[8] both atonse
In soothe their odd copesmate thou werte
　Else would not they voutsafe the onse. . . .[9]

Finally, there is another poem without introduction, but which obviously refers to Gascoigne, and is Harvey's last judgment on our poet.

A.B.[10] Me thinkes I see the bite ye lipp,
　At queinte newfanglid vanities,
At strange outlandishe forreyne wares,
　At monstrous disguised guises.

Me thinkes I see the hange ye browe,
　At periuryes and blasphemies,
At payntid vizardes and wizards,
　At highe and deepe hypocrisees.

Me thinkes I see the shake ye hedd,
　At such and such collusions,
As these and these have putt in me,
　To his and her confusions.

Me thinkes I see the make a mowthe
　At certayne Tuscane brave conceites,
And so thou doist, and so thou maiste,
　At many Florentyne receytes.

---

[8] Gascoigne's friendship with Bartholomew Withypoll is discussed in chaps. ii, iii, and iv.
[9] *Letter-Book, op. cit.,* pp. 56–57.
[10] This reference to "A.B." and the final "A.C." presumably refers to Gascoigne's use of initials for the letters prefacing the *Flowres. Vide supra,* chap. vii, pp. 190, 191.

(Whuist, not a worde nor halfe a worde
    Of perfumes or the pike sauce,
Or Fico foistid in thy dishe,
    Or thy first P. or Batts first pawse.) [11]

And sithe I am nowe in the veyne
    Me thinkes ten millions of deceiptes
Must nedes amounte to greate huge summes
    Of iestes and laughtures and sutch baytes.

Me thinkes I heere a comicall scoff
    Against sum persons tragicall,
Upbraiding the of tyrannyes,
    And outrages and divell, and all.

Me thinkes thou sckornist seigniores,[12]
    And gibist at thrise mightye peeres,
And maakst a ieste of monumentes,[13]
    And caarest not for a thousand yeeres.

Me thinkes I see a newe Steele Glasse,
    A second girdinge satyre,
Not sutch a saincte againe in heaven
    Do moove us silly sowles to ire.

What George? I pray the spare the world
    And give men leave to temporize;
Our tyme is shorte, weele lawghe with the,
    If once to heaven we take our rise.

Inioye thine owne pleasures aboove,
    Lett us aloane with ours beneathe,
And yet ifaythe sum fooleryes
    Will Sumner moughte to Patche[14] bequeathe.

Those frumpe a gods name to thy fill,
    Good leave thou haste such toyes to skoffe;
But thinke in worlde a worlde must be,
    And swine you wott will to ye troffe.

And where is huffcapp there is huff,
    And where is revell there is rowte.
What marvell, thoughe a London stage
    With fooles be compasd rounde abowte?

---

[11] Cf. *Works*, I, 344–47 (No. 67), where Gascoigne warns Bartholomew Withypoll against Italian poison, and pride.

[12] A reference to the libelous nature of some of Gascoigne's poems.

[13] Cf. *Works*, I, 73–74 (No. 68), an epitaph spoken by a tombstone.

[14] Patch, jester to Cardinal Wolsey.

I did longe since drawe to an ende,
   But to what pleasure pleasures have,
Your ioyes no sooner cam to minde,
   But they a fresh discourse did crave.

My only purpose was to quote
   A epitaph to fitt your tum;
If for the iest a name you will:
   Call it A.C.'s[15] memorandum.[16]

The worthy Hobbinol has, it seems to me, shrewdly observed the character of George Gascoigne. Of the faults of levity and vanity the poet must plead guilty. Harvey noted the vanity of his posy, and we need only look at his writings to see it over and over again. In the guise of *G.T.*, Gascoigne took great pleasure in commending the verses of his *alter ego*, F.J.[17] His inordinate pride in his "deepe inventions" is found in the comments on the Phoebus-Cynthia conceit of the sixth poem of "F.J." The opening lines of the account of his voyage to Holland swell with pride at his wondrous new conceit,[18] while "the greene Knights farewell to Fansie" boldly states his desire "To heare it sayde there goeth, the *Man that writes so well.*"[19] We can note how quickly and seriously his personal vanity is touched when Elinor and Ferenda prefer the hated rival. Of levity there are many instances. Harvey noted the rather macabre humor of the epitaph on Captain Bourcher, spoken by one "Marmaduke Marblestone,"[20] while we have observed that defamation of the ideals of Petrarchan love found in the "Anatomie."[21] Certainly "Phillip Sparrow"[22] is a form of jesting, hardly in the best of taste.

In his life, as well as in his verse, these qualities evidently played a part. We can only too well imagine the truth of his own account of his prodigal expenditure as an aspiring courtier. He would keep up the appearance of a young gallant, regardless of cost. So too the poem comparing G[ascoigne] and B[oyes] reveals the poet's hatred of his rival.[23] The fight in Redcross Street, the legal battles, all show his injured vanity. How great a blow were his father's suspicion and his mother's preference for the younger son, we do not know; but certainly the Cardington sheep-stealing had

---

[15] *Vide supra*, n. 10.   [16] *Letter-Book, op. cit.,* pp. 68–70.
[17] These comments follow practically every poem in "F.J." They are, however, omitted in *The Posies.*
[18] *Works,* I, 354. No. 74.   [19] *Ibid.,* I, 381.   [20] *Ibid.,* I, 73–74. No. 68.
[21] *Ibid.,* I, 37. No. 48.   [22] *Ibid.,* I, 455. No. 21.   [23] *Ibid.* I, 502, No. 38.

more behind it than the title to a few lambs. Unfortunately, the law is a serious business, and we have no records of Gascoigne as the potential comrade of Scoggin and Skelton; but it is not too much to imagine the household that included George and Elizabeth Gascoigne and John and Elizabeth Gostwick.

If vanity, levity, and a want of resolution were the causes of his misfortunes, Gascoigne was the last to deny his own responsibility. He admits to lavish spending, to failure as a student, lawyer, and courtier; but he had the courage to struggle on. *A Hundreth Sundrie Flowres* met with official disapproval, yet he tried to salvage the wreckage in *The Posies*. Financially ruined, he sought a patron and finally interested the Queen. Of his virtues we may praise his courage, that did not let him fall into the ranks of the decayed gentlemen who lived by their wits.

Above all, Gascoigne is to be commended for his versatility. He tried many things: philosophy, the law, farming, court life, the wars, and finally a literary career. This wide field of interest is in evidence in his works. He was the first to write an English treatise on poetry, the first to translate a prose comedy from the Italian, the first to put Greek tragedy, even at secondhand, on the English stage. The *Steele Glas* is the first original nondramatic blank verse in English, while it is unique in Elizabethan satire in its essentially English character. "The Adventures of F.J." is the first purely English story of the Renaissance, and its equal is not found until the eighteenth century. "Dan Bartholmew" is the first English attempt to tell a love story in a series of poems and in this respect is the predecessor of the flood tide of Elizabethan sonnet sequences. His masques are among the earliest English representations of this type of dramatic art. Finally, *The Spoyle of Antwerpe* is an early example of news-reporting. To such a variety of literary interests was joined an ability to compose music and to sketch remarkably well.

Truly Gascoigne was a man of the Renaissance, with an interest in all forms of human activity. His friends included other poets: Whetstone, Barnaby Rich, Gabriel Harvey, Turbervile, Spenser, and probably Sidney and Churchyard. He knew the great courtiers of his day: Leicester, Bedford, Warwick, Essex, Oxford, Northumberland, Ormont, Lincoln, Kildare, Worcester, and Grey of Wilton—as well as the ladies of the court: Lettice, Countess of Essex; Anne, Lady De la Warr; Maria Hopton;

Lady Bridges; Katherine, Frances, and Mary Howard; Mary Burrowe; Lady Mary Vere; Mary Sidney; Lady Susan Bowcher; the Countesses of Huntington, Warwick, Oxford, Rutland, and Bedford; and many more. The prelates of the church—Archbishop Parker, Bishops Sandys and Cooper, and Dean Nowell of St. Paul's—were among his friends, as were many lawyers and London merchants.

In both his life and his writings Gascoigne was a man of his times. The elder son of an established family, he tried to succeed in a changing world. How many others of his class failed we do not know. We think of the successful men, because they left their names in history, but we do know Sidney's unhappiness in the courtly world and we know of Spenser's experiences in Ireland. Turbervile sought reputation in wildest Russia and hated travel and the sea ever after. Sir Humphrey Gilbert was deluded by fool's gold. Men failed and old families disappeared. Change was everywhere. The drama was not of age, and the novel was still in the future. Satire had little place in a youthful society. And finally poetry had to become sated before it could be purged of its triteness. Being of his time, Gascoigne was before his time. In the next generation his abilities could probably have achieved more, but in his own day he had to explore the means of success in both the economic and literary worlds. The fates were against him, as he says in his own best couplet:

> The fatal Sisters three, which spun my slender twine,
> Knew well how rotten was the yarne, frõ whence they drew their line.

> My penne is stubbed, my paper spente, my Inke wasted,
> my wittes gravelled, and (to be shorte) tyme
> calleth me away: wherefore standing
> to your curtesies, and hoping of
> your good acceptance hereof,
> wishyng to you as to my
> selfe, in haste I
> bid you Farewell.

GRANGE

Appendix I

THE DATE OF GASCOIGNE'S BIRTH

Mr. B. M. Ward first discovered the Inquisition Post Mortem on Sir John Gascoigne, which he used to place the date of birth of George Gascoigne as shortly before April, 1542.[1] Miss Genevieve Ambrose discussed the same document and showed that according to it, the date of the poet's birth lay between the limiting dates of April 5, 1541, and April 4, 1542.[2] The evidence for both assertions is the following sentence from the document:

Quidam Georgius Gascoygne tempore mortis predicti Johannis patris sui fuit etatis vigenti sex annorum et amplius.[3]

Since the death of Sir John occurred on April 4, 1568,[4] and since Miss Ambrose assumes that "amplius" means part of a year, the manner of establishing her limiting dates is apparent.

There is, however, some reason to doubt Miss Ambrose's assumption that the term "amplius" means part of a year. The Inquisition Post Mortem taken on William Bretton is most precise in its statement of the age of Richard Bretton, the heir:

Et quod Ricardus Breton . . . est etatis die capcionis hujus Inquisitionis XVI annorum XI mensum et duorum dierum.[5]

This exact information is typical of many inquisitions, even as the vague "amplius" is typical of others. It will therefore be apparent that we need to know something more about Inquisitions Post Mortem before any certain conclusions can be drawn.

Mr. C. G. Crump,[6] late an Assistant Keeper at the Public Record Office, wrote a most valuable "Note of Criticism of Records," which is indeed helpful in assessing the truth and the value of their evidence. Mr. Crump's thesis is that the testimony of records depends on the circumstances in which the records were written. Such a warning is very necessary in judging the value of

---

[1] Ward, "George Gascoigne and His Circle," *RES*, II (1926), 34–35.

[2] Ambrose, "George Gascoigne," *RES*, II (1926), 163–64.

[3] Quoted by Ward, *op. cit.*, p. 35.

[4] This date is found in the Inquisition.

[5] Quoted by Ward, *op. cit.*, p. 37.

[6] C. G. Crump, "A Note on the Criticism of Records," *Bulletin of the John Rylands Library*, VIII (1924), 140–49.

Inquisitions Post Mortem.[7] The escheator called together a group of citizens to bear witness to the assessment of a deceased person's estate. In general, the escheator or one of his clerks presented the evidence, which was then sworn to by the inquisitors. As Mr. Crump points out, such a system did not produce absolute truth. For example, none of the inquisitors might be familiar with the family of the deceased. If this were true and if the heir was not present at the Inquisition, there would be no immediate way of knowing the exact age of the heir. In such circumstances a reasonable guess at the age would be sufficient, since the only reason for stating the age was to ascertain whether the heir was to be made a ward or to be allowed the possession of the property. If he were a minor, the former course would have been followed. With this in mind, we can see that the inquisitors would probably be as accurate as possible by saying: "He's at least twenty-six." *or* "He's more than twenty-six."

That these gentlemen were uncertain concerning the age of George Gascoigne is indicated by the document's use of "amplius" and by other facts known about the poet. George Gascoigne married Elizabeth Bacon Bretton Boyes on November 23, 1561.[8] If he had been under twenty-one at that time, he would have needed his father's consent. It is most strange that in all the subsequent litigation no mention is made of this permission, and we can be almost sure, by reason of what we know of Edward Boyes, that it would have been mentioned, had he been under twenty-one.

In his reply[9] to a suit filed against him by the Bretton children, Boyes claimed that the children were not of legal age and could not bring action, and this plea quashed the proceedings. Surely, if George Gascoigne had been under age when he married Elizabeth, Edward Boyes would have made some technical objection. Similarly, we may consider the suit that Gascoigne brought against Boyes. A decree in this action is dated October 1, 1562.[10] The Michaelmas term had not then begun, so we may conclude that the action had been initiated at the very latest in the Easter term which lasted from April 15, 1562, until May 11, 1562.[11] If one may judge by other chancery proceedings, the initiation of proceedings and the rendering of a decree in one term would have been most unusual. Such a case[12] began with a petition for a writ; then it took some time for the Chancellor to decide to issue the writ. Following the issuance, it was necessary for the defendant to make an answer. With this answer the real business began. Interrogations were made out on both sides; commissioners were appointed to hear witnesses; and finally there were warnings and

---

[7] *Ibid.*, pp. 141–42.   [8] *Vide infra*, Appendix III.

[9] *Vide infra*, Appendix III. PRO Chanc. Proc. (Ser. II) C3, 27/51.

[10] *Vide infra*, Appendix III. PRO Chanc. D & O C33/28, fols. 122ᵛ–123ʳ.

[11] For the dates of court terms, *vide* Fry, *Almanacks for Students of English History*.

[12] This account of procedure is based on my own observations in examining chancery records. Confirmation of this account can easily be checked in the various cases which I have used in connection with Gascoigne's life.

permissions of publication. Since the decree was dated as October 1, 1562, all this preamble would have had to have been finished by the end of the Easter term, for legal action was almost completely stagnant during the Long Vacation. That the original petition was entered in the Easter term becomes highly doubtful, and if the proceedings began before the Easter term, say in the Hilary term, which ran from January 23, 1561/2, to February 12, 1561/2, George Gascoigne would, according to the calculations of Miss Ambrose, have been under twenty-one years of age. The fact that Boyes did not raise this technical question seems to me to indicate that the poet was born before April 5, 1541.

Further evidence for such an assertion is to be found in the Close Rolls. If George Gascoigne had not been born before April 5, 1541, he could not legally have signed a bond jointly with his father to William Wytte on October 13, 1561, nor could he have signed his own bond to Brian Ledes on November 6, 1561.[13]

The same question of minority must also be considered in connection with the poet's parliamentary career. Although minors did sit in Parliament,[14] Professor J. E. Neale assures me that it is highly unlikely that a boy of sixteen would have been elected to the Commons. If George Gascoigne was born after April 5, 1541, he would have been only sixteen and a half when the elections took place, since the Parliament of 4 & 5 Philip & Mary, of which he was a member, met in January, 1557/8.[15] The elections must have been held at least two months before.

To this we can add the fact that in the masque written for the Montague marriage Gascoigne describes "a boy of twelve or .xiiii. yeeres."[16] If the poet was born after April 5, 1541, he would have been a boy of ".xiiii. yeeres" when he went to Gray's Inn, and he most certainly does not consider himself a boy in the poems written about this period, nor do the records so reveal him.

This cumulation of discrepancies seems to point to an error on the part of the inquisitors or to the necessity for a more liberal interpretation of the word "amplius." At the time of his father's death, George Gascoigne was probably between twenty-six and twenty-eight years of age. On the basis of the election to Parliament, the fact that the first Close Roll entry is 1561, and the date of Elizabeth Bacon's marriage to him, I am inclined to assign 1539 as the probable year of birth.

[13] *Vide infra,* Appendix IV, where all Close Roll entries are listed.
[14] For references to the poet's parliamentary career, *vide supra,* chap. i.
[15] The writ of his return is dated Jan. 2, 1557/8, and is noted in *Parliamentary Papers,* XVII, 396. This same page gives the date of the opening of the Parliament.
[16] *Works,* I, 75. No. 69.

Appendix II

THE VARIOUS GEORGE GASCOIGNES

DURING the middle years of the sixteenth century, there were, according to the records, probably three men who bore the name "George Gascoigne." Therefore, one must be careful in ascribing documents and references to any particular one of them. However, there is evidence to show that, with very few exceptions, all the references in this work do belong to the poet. I shall note such evidence before discussing either the questioned documents or the other bearers of the name.

Whetstone, in his *Remembraunce . . . of George Gaskoigne,* notes that the poet was "Sir John G. sonne and Heire Disinherited."[1] According to all the known pedigrees of the family,[2] there was only one Sir John Gascoigne who had a son George, and this was Sir John Gascoigne of Cardington, Bedfordshire. Such evidence is not, of course, absolute, but other facts that we do possess concerning this son of Sir John show that he was the poet. Sir John's son married Elizabeth Bacon, daughter of John Bacon of Hesset, as is proved by the pedigree and by a Chancery suit that tells of a dowry for this lady provided by her uncle and her father-in-law.[3] Certain legal disputes which arose out of this marriage describe George Gascoigne as of Walthamstow,[4] and the first prefatory letters of *The Posies of George Gascoigne* are signed "From my poore house at Waltamstow."[5] I submit that it is highly unlikely that there were two George Gascoignes living in Walthamstow, and it will be seen below that none of the other George Gascoignes is mentioned as living there. Finally, we know from the introductory remarks to "Gascoignes memorie"[6] that the poet was a member of Gray's Inn. A Close Roll entry describes "George Gascoigne of Graies Inne son & heir apparent of Sir John Gascoigne of Cardington Beds."[7] This seems to me final proof that George Gascoigne the poet was son and heir of Sir John Gascoigne of Cardington, Bedfordshire.

This fact being established, it becomes possible to prove that various descrip-

---

[1] Whetstone, *A Remembraunce of the wel imployed life, and godly end of George Gaskoigne, Esquire,* ed. by Arber, p. 17.
[2] *The Visitations of Bedford 1566, 1582, 1634,* Harl. Soc. Pub., XIX, 116, 173.
[3] PRO Chanc. Proc. (Ser. II) C3, 41/22.
[4] PRO Close Roll 693 (7 Eliz. pt. 21) no. 43.
[5] *Works,* I, 8, 14.   [6] *Ibid.,* I, 62. No. 57.
[7] PRO Close Roll 769 (10 Eliz. pt. 13) m. 46d.

tions of residence indicate the poet. We have seen the validity of Cardington, Walthamstow, and Gray's Inn, in this respect. Another document related to the marriage difficulties describes George Gascoigne of Willington,[8] and thus this place of residence can be added to the list.

There now remain several documents in which the evidence is not absolute, but presumptive. First of these is that listing George Gascoigne as Member of Parliament from Bedford Borough in 1557/8.[9] The same document notes the election of Sir John Gascoigne as Member for Bedford County. I can see no reason to doubt the logical inference that this George Gascoigne was the son of Sir John Gascoigne of Cardington. In Elizabethan times, a large percentage of members of Parliament resided in the counties of their election, and certainly the son of a local squire would be a more logical candidate than any other. If this conclusion seems reasonable, then equally so is the fact that the George Gascoigne elected to the first Parliament of Queen Elizabeth, from the same division, was the poet.[10]

Secondly, there are certain Close Roll entries[11] which refer to George Gascoigne of London. Such an ascription makes identification difficult. None of these are important for any purpose of the present work, but at least one refers definitely to the poet. Close Roll 638 (5 Eliz. pt. 9) no. 20 is a bond of George Gascoigne of London, to William Wytte. Reference to Appendix IV will at once show that this is the poet, since there are several other bonds to Wytte which are by the poet. There are no means of proving that bonds of George Gascoigne to William Pelham and Robert Drury were made by the poet, but they are not important enough to examine further.

That the anonymous letter to the Privy Council[12] can describe anyone but the poet has never been questioned, since among the allegations is the charge of being "a Common Rymer and a deviser of slaunderous Pasquelles."

Thus I feel that I have given proof or at least strong evidence that all the documents which I have used relate to the poet. There now remains to note briefly the other George Gascoignes. The old story of "Mr. Gastone, the lawyare,"[13] who, in 1548, was in custody for felonious acts can no longer be ascribed to the poet. The earliest possible date of birth makes the poet too young to have "hadde an old wiffe." Finally, there is no evidence to show that this wretched individual was named George.

---

[8] PRO Chanc. Proc. (Ser. II) C3, 78/55.

[9] "Return of the Name of Every Member of the Lower House," *Parliamentary Papers*, XVII, 396. Miss Ambrose (*MLR* [April, 1927] p. 219) is in error when she says that this source shows that "the poet George was returned to parliament 2 Jan. 1557/8." The document mentions nothing more than the mere name, and date, and gives no identification.

[10] *Ibid.*, p. 400. [11] *Vide infra*, Appendix IV.

[12] PRO *State Papers Domestic*, lxxxvi, no. 59.

[13] Edward Underhill, *Autobiographical Anecdotes, Narratives of the Reformation*, Camden Society Publication, p. 175. Noted by Professor F. E. Schelling, *The Life and Writings of George Gascoigne*, p. 6.

In various records there appear two other George Gascoignes. George Gascoigne, a younger son of the family of Lasingcroft, Yorkshire, was admitted to the Middle Temple in 1560.[14] A Close Roll entry of August 31, 1566, notes a bond given by George Gascoigne of the Middle Temple to Thomas Parker as a guarantee that the former will marry Mary Stokesly, daughter-in-law of the latter.[15] There are other Close Roll entries of this George, and most interesting is an indenture between Thomas Parker of Shenfield, Essex, and George Gascoigne of Shenfield, Essex.[16] The connection with Parker proves, I think, that the same George Gascoigne is concerned and that in 1576 he was living at Shenfield. This explains a presentment, in the local records of Chelmsford, against Mary Gascoigne, wife of George Gascoigne, for failure to attend divine service.[17] This Gascoigne owned lands in various counties[18] and was successful as a lawyer. He was a master of the bench of the Middle Temple, and this allowed his son, Nicholas, to enter the Inn without payment of a fee.[19]

Of the third George, less is known. He appears in two Chancery cases[20] in which he and his wife, Jane, are suing Ed. Wood, Thos. Bote, and Wm. Richardson for lands in Pinxton, which Edmond, Lord Sheffield had sold to Anthony Richardson, the late husband of Jane. The proceedings are undated, and it may well be that this is the same as the Lasingcroft man; perhaps he had taken a second wife. I have not thought it worth while to examine this matter further, since it has no connection with any records or facts which concern George Gascoigne, the son of Sir John Gascoigne of Cardington, Bedfordshire.[21]

---

[14] A. R. Ingpen, *The Middle Temple Bench Book* (London, 1912), p. 162.

[15] PRO Close Roll 721 (8 Eliz. pt. 24) no. 33.

[16] PRO Close Roll 996 (18 Eliz. pt. 15).

[17] *Hist. MSS Comm. Rep.*, MSS of Marquess of Salisbury, IX, pt. 1, 468.

[18] PRO Close Roll 993 (18 Eliz. pt. 12), Close Roll 954 (16 Eliz. pt. 29).

[19] Ingpen, *op. cit.* Miss Ambrose (*RES*, II [1926], 167–68) notes the Inquisitions on this George Gascoigne.

[20] PRO Chanc. Proc. (Ser. I) C2, Gg 8–60, and Rr 4–45.

[21] This summary should establish the fact that Mr. Kittle's five different George Gascoignes, none of whom is supposed to be a poet, are the result of a misunderstanding of the facts. Such a variety of men is very helpful to Mr. Kittle's thesis that "George Gascoigne" was an imaginative creation of the Earl of Oxford. (William Kittle, *George Gascoigne* [signature]*April 1562 to January 1, 1578 OR EDWARD DE VERE . . . 1550–1604,* Washington, 1930.)

Appendix III

GEORGE GASCOIGNE AND ELIZABETH BACON BRETTON BOYES GASCOIGNE

A SERIES OF PROBLEMS AND THEIR ANSWERS[1]

By C. T. Prouty

The marriage of George Gascoigne and Elizabeth Bacon Bretton Boyes and the various problems arising from this marriage have been the source of considerable discussion and some theorizing.[2] As a result of my researches, I am able to present certain new facts which will, I trust, clarify the general situation and resolve several moot points. The first of these debatable topics is that of the genealogy of Elizabeth Bacon and the exact degree of her relationship to Sir Nicholas Bacon. Second is the date of Elizabeth's marriage to William Bretton. The third is the problem of her marriage to Edward Boyes, concerning whose identity certain facts are here for the first time revealed. Fourth we have the question of the exact date for the marriage between Elizabeth and George Gascoigne. Finally there is the vexatious riddle of the sequence and meaning of various legal documents involving Gascoigne, Elizabeth, and Boyes.

Mr. B. M. Ward has put forward a genealogical chart showing what he considers to be the relationship of Elizabeth Bacon to Sir Nicholas.[3] Furthermore, Mr. Ward has demonstrated by means of evidence contained in the will of John Bacon of Hesset (P.C.C. 16 Chaynay)[4] and in the will of William Bretton (P.C.C. 51 Welles)[5] that this John was the father of Elizabeth. However, there is, as far as I know, no proof for Mr. Ward's hypothesis that this John was the son of John, brother to Robert Bacon, the father of Sir Nicholas.

---

[1] [Reprinted from *The Review of English Studies*, July, 1938.]

[2] B. M. Ward, "George Gascoigne and His Circle", *Review of English Studies*, January 1926, pp. 32–41. "The Death of George Gascoigne", *R.E.S.*, April 1926, pp. 170–2. *A Hundreth Sundrie Flowres*, ed B. M. Ward, London, 1926, Introduction, p. xvi.

Genevieve Ambrose, "George Gascoigne", *R.E.S.*, April 1926, pp. 166–7,

Genevieve Ambrose Oldfield, "New Light on the Life of George Gascoigne" *R.E.S.*, April 1937, pp. 135–8.

[3] B. M. Ward, "George Gascoigne and His Circle", *op. cit.*, p. 38.

[4] *A Hundreth Sundrie Flowres*, *op. cit.*

[5] B. M. Ward, "George Gascoigne and His Circle", *op. cit.*, p. 37.

Mr. Ward indicates in the pedigree above mentioned that John, the brother of Robert, died in 1538. The will of a John Bacon of Hesset, who names his brother Robert as one of his executors, was proved on September 27, 1538,[6] and I presume that this is the gentleman Mr. Ward had in mind. An examination of this will, made in 1536, reveals that the son John, whom Mr. Ward would have to be the father of Elizabeth, was under twenty years of age at

BACON PEDIGREE

CHART I

Thomas Bacon[7]=Anne

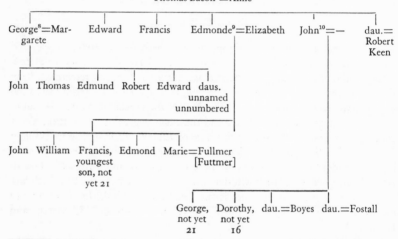

George[8]=Mar-   Edward   Francis   Edmonde[9]=Elizabeth   John[10]=—   dau.=
garete   Robert
                                                                            Keen

John Thomas Edmund Robert Edward daus.
                                      unnamed
                                      unnumbered

John William Francis, Edmond Marie=Fullmer
               youngest   [Futtmer]
               son, not
               yet 21

George, Dorothy, dau.=Boyes dau.=Fostall
not yet not yet
21   16

---

[6] P.C.C. 10 Crumwell.

[7] Thomas Bacon of Heggesset "gentilman." P.C.C. 41 Alen. Will proved "30 June, 1547." Executors: "Edmonde Bacon, John Bacon, & George Bacon my sons." Supervisor: "Nicholas Bacon attorney." Witnesses: Nicholas Bacon, Robert Bacon, Edmonde Bacon, John Bacon, George Bacon.

[8] George Bacon of Hedgeset, gent. P.C.C. 24 Sheffeld. Will proved "28 Nov. 1569." Executors: "Thos. Badbie, esq., Thos. Andrewes of Bury gent." Supervisor: "Mr. Robt. Asshefelde of Stow." Witnesses: "Anthony Gosnold, John Bacon, Frauncis Bacon, Robt. Cottenn, Wm. Burton clerk, vicar of Thurston, Phillip Page of Thurston, Henry Hunte." Mentions "my nevye George Bacon."

[9] Edmonde Bacon of Hedgesset, "gentilman." P.C.C. 20 Tashe. Will proved "13 Nov. 1553." Executors: "Robert Kene, my bro.-in-law, & Iohn Bacon, my eldest son." Supervisor: "Brother, George Bacon." Witnesses: "Edmund Iermyn, Master Ambrose Iermyn, Robt. Kene." Mentions "my brother in law Robt. Kene."

[10] John Bacon of Bury St. Edmunds, "gentilman." P.C.C. 16 Chaynay. Will proved "10 May, 1559." Executors: "son Geo. Bacon, brother Geo. Bacon of Heggesset, Suff. 'gentilman,' Thos. Androwes of Bury 'gentilman.' " Supervisor: "Rt. Hon. Sir. Nicholas Bacon knt. Lord Keeper of the Great Seal of England." Mentions "my brother George's sons," "my brethren Geo. & Francis."

that time. Now when it is known that Elizabeth married William Bretton in 1545—as I shall later demonstrate—one is tempted to speculate concerning the early marriage ages of both father and daughter. Wonder increases as one realizes that there is no evidence in the wills of the supposed father and son to indicate their relationship.

However, an examination of the wills of Thomas, Edmund, and George Bacon—all of Hesset—together with the will of John, the known father of Elizabeth, shows a definite genealogical relationship which can be placed in its proper position in the main Bacon pedigree.[11] Chart 1 shows the genealogy of the Bacons of Hesset according to their wills, and contains the reference for each will, the date of proving, and the names of executors, witnesses, supervisors, children, and other relatives. Proof that Edmund, George, and John are sons of Thomas is shown by references in the wills of each of the brothers to land messuages and rents which Thomas in his will bequeathed to his sons Edmund, George, and John. Specifically identification of this latter John, the son of Thomas, with John, the father of Elizabeth, is proved by references in the wills of both father and son to lands at West Wreatham. Thomas bequeathed these lands jointly to John and his brother Francis; John, the father of Elizabeth refers to these lands as being held jointly with his brother Francis. Therefore it seems reasonable to conclude that Thomas Bacon of Hesset is the paternal grandfather of Elizabeth. Further detailed accounts of land and bequests to prove the general relationships of Chart 1 seem both tedious and beyond the scope of this article. However, certain contributing evidence is shown in the chart itself where are recorded the names of executors, supervisors, and witnesses. For example, Thos. Andrewes of Bury, gent., acts as executor for both John and George Bacon; Robert Keene, called "son-in-law" by Thomas Bacon, is executor for Edmund, who describes him as "brother-in-law"; and Nicholas Bacon is supervisor for Thomas and John.

To locate this segment of the family in the main Bacon pedigree, it is necessary to refer to Davy's Suffolk Pedigrees,[12] wherein are found the two main lines of descent recorded in Chart 2. In the descent from John Bacon by his wife Julian [a], the eldest son of the third generation is Thomas, who has a second wife, Anne, sons Edmund, Thomas, John, and a daughter Anne married to a Robert Keene. Now the Thomas Bacon of Chart 1 also has a wife Anne, sons Edmund and John, and especially a daughter married to a Robert Keene, whose name is mentioned by both Thomas, the father, and Edmund, the brother. From this evidence it seems reasonable to identify the Thomas Bacon of Chart 1 with the Thomas Bacon of Chart 2. Thus it seems that not only the pedigree of Elizabeth Bacon but also the exact degree of her relation-

---

[11] Since I list the reference for each will on Chart 1, I shall refrain from further annotation in the text.

[12] British Museum, Add. MS, 19,116, folio 23.

ship to Sir Nicholas Bacon can at last be ascertained and proved. Elizabeth is no longer a second cousin to Sir Nicholas; she is now a cousin many times removed.

Even though Sir Nicholas and his father Robert are thus but distantly connected to the Hesset branch of the family, we can see evidence in Chart 1 to indicate a friendship much closer than the distant ties of kinship. Thomas had as supervisor of his estate "Nicholas Bacon, attorney," and as one of his witnesses "Robert Bacon." Later "Sir Nicholas Bacon knt. Lord Keeper of the Great Seal of England" is supervisor of the estate of John Bacon. This close contact with the Lord Keeper proved valuable to Elizabeth when, after the death of her husband William Bretton, she became involved in the legal difficulties of her subsequent marriages.

Mr. Ward conjectured from the Inquisition Post Mortem on William Bretton that Elizabeth married him *circa* 1550.[13] Actually this marriage took place

BACON OF HESSET

CHART 2

(Davy: Suffolk Pedigrees, B.M., Add. MS 19,116.)

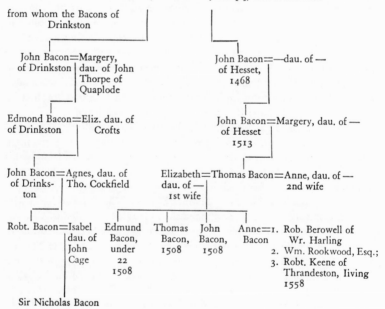

Helena Tillott=John Bacon=Julian[a], dau. of Berdwell

from whom the Bacons of
Drinkston

John Bacon=Margery,
of Drinkston | dau. of John
Thorpe of
Quaplode

John Bacon=—dau. of —
of Hesset,
1468

Edmond Bacon=Eliz. dau. of
of Drinkston | Crofts

John Bacon=Margery, dau. of —
of Hesset
1513

John Bacon=Agnes, dau. of
of Drinks- | Tho. Cockfield
ton

Elizabeth=Thomas Bacon=Anne, dau. of —
dau. of — | 2nd wife
1st wife

Robt. Bacon=Isabel   Edmund   Thomas   John   Anne=1. Rob. Berowell of
dau. of   Bacon,   Bacon,   Bacon,   Bacon   Wr. Harling
John   under   1508   1508   2. Wm. Rookwood, Esq.;
Cage   22   3. Robt. Keene of
1508   Thrandeston, living
1558

Sir Nicholas Bacon

---

[13] B. M. Ward, "George Gascoigne and His Circle," *op. cit.,* p. 37.

five years earlier, for Boyd's Marriage Register shows that the wedding occurred at Hesset in 1545.[14] This new fact is not only valuable because it gives us exact knowledge but also because it aids us in following the pedigree as I have noted above.

William Bretton died January 12, 1558/9,[15] and left Elizabeth quite wealthy. Soon either her money or her beauty found her another husband, for, as Mr. Ward has pointed out, the will of John Bacon[16] and the Inquisition Post Mortem on William Bretton[17] indicate that Elizabeth had married Edward Boyes by April 7, 1559. John Bacon in his will speaks of his "daughter Boyes" and bequeaths "to Mr. Boyes my son-in-law 2 angels to make them rings." It may be pure speculation, but perhaps John had some doubts as to the circumstances of this marriage and therefore thought that "rings" would make the union more binding. Be that as it may, the marriage is later described by Elizabeth's own children in this fashion:

That one Edward Boyes of Nonnington in the county of Kent by and under colour of a pretended marriage solemnised between the said Edward and the said Elizabeth ... hath had received and gathered into his hands ... divers great sums of money.[18]

This hitherto unknown discussion of the marriage is from a Chancery Bill brought by the Bretton children against Edward Boyes. Not only does this Bill make clear the general marriage problem, but also it tells us that Edward Boyes came from Nonnington in Kent. Hitherto nothing has been known about Elizabeth's second husband.

The clue of Kent and particularly that of Nonnington lead to the various genealogical studies of Kent,[19] where there are recorded numerous Boyes families, but only one family of the town of Nonnington. In these various families there are several Edwards who lived during the sixteenth century; however, there is only one Edward Boyes of the Nonnington family who lived during the sixteenth century and who was of an age to have contracted a marriage in 1558/9, and herewith I give his pedigree.[20]

---

[14] *Boyd's Marriage Register,* ed. Percival Boyd, Society of Genealogists, folio 106.

[15] B. M. Ward, "George Gascoigne and His Circle," *op. cit.,* p. 37.

[16] *A Hundreth Sundrie Flowres, op. cit.,* Intro., p. xvi.

[17] B. M. Ward, "George Gascoigne and His Circle," *op. cit.,* p. 37.

[18] P.R.O. Chanc. Proc. Eliz. Series II., 27/51.

[19] *The Visitations of Kent* 1530–1, 1574. The Publications of the Harleian Society, vol. 74, London, 1923. *The Visitations of Kent* 1574, 1592. Pub. Harleian Soc., vol. 75, London, 1924. *The Visitations of Kent* 1619. Pub. Harleian Soc., vol. 42, London, 1898. Berry, *County Genealogies Kent.*

[20] Compiled from *Visitations of Kent* 1619, *op. cit.,* pp. 39–40; *Visitations of Kent* 1574, 1592, *op. cit.,* pp. 123–24; Berry, *op. cit.,* pp. 478–9. The various sons of each generation are given in the above sources and among them is no Edward of Nonnington except those noted. The son, Edward Boyes, Miles, was born in 1558, as is known from the Inquisition Post Mortem on Edward Boyes noted below.

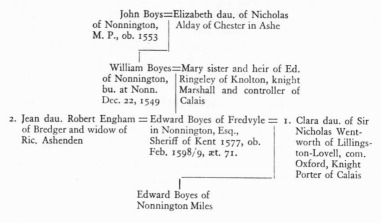

John Boys=Elizabeth dau. of Nicholas
of Nonnington, | Alday of Chester in Ashe
M. P., ob. 1553

William Boyes=Mary sister and heir of Ed.
of Nonnington, | Ringeley of Knolton, knight
bu. at Nonn. | Marshall and controller of
Dec. 22, 1549 | Calais

2. Jean dau. Robert Engham = Edward Boyes of Fredvyle = 1. Clara dau. of Sir
of Bredger and widow of   in Nonnington, Esq.,   Nicholas Went-
Ric. Ashenden   Sheriff of Kent 1577, ob.   worth of Lillings-
                   Feb. 1598/9, æt. 71.   ton-Lovell, com.
                                        Oxford, Knight
                                        Porter of Calais

Edward Boyes of
Nonnington Miles

That this onetime Sheriff of Kent had certain good connections and that he achieved a position of some eminence are evinced, I think, by the pedigree. Furthermore, the Inquisition Post Mortem on his estate,[21] which I have examined, shows that Boyes had managed on more than one occasion to gather into his hands "divers great sums of money," for the property therein noted is considerable. Whether or no these later transactions were honourable, the Bretton children depict him on one occasion as the deep-dyed villain striving to cheat little children out of their lawful inheritances.

But before we consider the Chancery Bill it is necessary to solve one more problem: the exact date of the marriage between Gascoigne and Elizabeth. The Christ Church Newgate register lists under the year 1562, the following:

23 Nov. George Gascoyne and Elizabeth Brytayne.

Although Miss Ambrose has discussed quite fully the problem presented by this register,[22] a brief recapitulation is necessary fully to understand the question. The original year dates of Births and Marriages in the register have been crossed out and in certain year groups post-dated by three years and in other groups by four years. Thus the original entry for the Gascoigne-Bretton marriage is 1558 and has been altered to 1562. As this latter date is untenable for many reasons, some of which Miss Ambrose has noted and others of which will be made clear as I proceed, the actual date of the ceremony has been hitherto unknown. This question was, however, answered some years ago by Mr. J. Challenor Smith, whose article[23] on the Harleian Society's reprint of the Christ Church Register has seemingly escaped the notice of those

---

[21] P.R.O. Chancery I. P.M. Series II.; 250/85.

[22] Genevieve Ambrose, "George Gascoigne," *op. cit.*, p. 167.

[23] J. Challenor Smith, "The Harleian Society's Reprint of the Christ Church Newgate Register," *The Genealogist*, vol. XII, pp. 223–225.

interested in Gascoigne research. Mr. Smith, examining the problem of the date change, says:

In the marriages the year 1538 in the original has been altered by a later hand to 1542. . . . But a comparison of the register with the Harleian Society's volumes of marriage licences amply proves that although most of the dates of marriages were incorrect as they originally stood in MS., they are all wrong as altered.

Mr. Smith continues with an examination of each year group, and compares the marriage entries with the licence entries. By this method he determines the date error for each particular year group. For the years from 1557 to 1584 as recorded in the register, he concludes that the entries should be antedated one year, i.e. 1562 in the register should be 1561. Therefore on the basis of this highly conclusive evidence, George Gascoigne married Elizabeth Bretton on November 23, 1561.

Even though this date be now ascertained, there remains the question of how Elizabeth was legally able to marry Gascoigne since, as has been noted, she was already married to Boyes. Miss Ambrose has solved the dilemma by maintaining that the marriage to Boyes never took place.[24] Other investigators do not seem to have attempted an answer. However, the new evidence of the Chancery Bill, noted above, seems to settle the question by revealing what actually did happen; so I shall quote the pertinent sections of the Bill.

Mulrowe (24 Nov. ?) 1566
[Date of filing in another hand]

To the right honourable Sir Nicholas Bacon knight, Keeper of the great seal of England.

Right humbly complaining sheweth unto your honourable Lordship your humble and daily orators Richard Britten, Nicholas Britten and Thamar Britten the children of William Britten late of London gent. deceased [Here follows a recital of the will of William Bretton and his various legacies] . . . So it is if it please your good Lordship that one Edward Boyes of Nonnington in the county of K[e]nt gent. by and under colour of a pretended marriage solemnised between the said Edward and the said Elizabeth mother to your Lordships said orators and executrix of the said last will and Testament of their said late father hath had received and gathered into [hi]s hands of and from the said creditors divers great sums of money amounting to three hundred pounds and more and all or the greatest part of the said parcels of plate jewels apparel and household stuff and other legacies before bequeathed remaining in the custody of the said Elizabeth And notwithstanding that the said Edward Boyes hath been sithence by due order and sentence in form of law divorced from the said Elizabeth mother to your Lordship's said orators . . . And hath appealed from the said s[ente]nce and in his said appeal hath been eftsoones by due order and sentence in form of law divorced from the said Elizabeth and adjudged as guilty in his said complaint of appeal and license given by the said sentence to the said Elizabeth to marry again at her election and disposition. And notwithstanding that he

---

[24] Genevieve Ambrose, "George Gascoigne," *op. cit.*, p. 167.

hath been by divers and sundry means required to redeliver the said sums of money and the said parcels of plate jewels apparel and household stuff and legacies aforesaid into the safe custody of the said Elizabeth as executrix of the will or into the safe custody of the right worshipful Thomas Seckford one of the Masters of Requests and nominated and app[oin]ted to be supervisor of the said last will and testament . . . In tender consideration whereof and forasmuch as now there is none appeal strife demand or other question hanging or depending between the said Edward and Elizabeth whereby he might have or pretend any colour to detain the same sums of money or parcels of plate jewels apparel and household stuff . . .

Bound with this Bill are several other documents: first, the inventory of those items in the estate of William Bretton which the children are trying to recover from Boyes; second, the answer of Boyes; finally, the rejoinder of the original complainants. In his answer, Boyes maintains that the children are not yet of the age designated in their father's will as the time for them to receive their legacies, and that on this account they have no basis of legal action; furthermore Boyes alleges that the children are not of legal age and in consequence have no right to bring suit. He adds that the suit has been urged on by George Gascoigne merely to cause him "great vexation." The rejoinder of the children practically calls Boyes a liar, and then recapitulates the whole story as in the original Bill.[25]

It is, I think, obvious from the evidence in the selection which I have quoted that Elizabeth actually did marry Boyes, for unless there had been such a marriage and unless this marriage had been valid, no decree of divorce could have been issued. Had there been no real marriage between them, the courts would have decided on this question of fact, and the decree in such a case would have recognized that no valid ceremony had been performed. It seems, therefore, that the phrasing "by and under colour of a pretended marriage" reflects the opinion that there was something of a deceitful or questionable nature concerning the means by which "one Edward Boyes" lured Elizabeth into the holy estate of matrimony. Elizabeth must have been of such an opinion, and probably she thought the ceremony itself invalid, for otherwise she would not have married Gascoigne, unless, like Fielding's Huncamunca, she joyfully contemplated bigamy with, "First I married him; now I'll marry you."

No sooner had she married, however, than a dispute arose. The entry in Machyn's diary has been noted before, but I think it worth repeating.

The xxx day of September [1562] . . . the same day at night between viii and ix was a great fray in Redcrosse Street between two gentlemen and their men for they

---

[25] The various documents which I have found and which relate to this problem are P.R.O. Chanc. Decree, vol. xxxv., fo. 172, and P.R.O. Chanc. Proc., Series II., 202/7. The decree permits Gascoigne and Elizabeth to join with the children and thus jointly to prosecute their cases to recover from Boyes the estate of William Bretton. The Chanc. Proc. is a Bill brought by these new complainants.

did marry one woman and divers were hurt; these were their names Master Boysse [Boyes] and Master Gaskyn [Gascoigne] gentlemen.[26]

Although recorded physical encounters between the two "husbands" did not occur until September, legal encounters had begun some time before. On October 1, 1562, there was recorded in the Chancery Decree Book a Memorandum[27] which, although it is mentioned in a later proceeding quoted by Mr. Ward,[28] has not hitherto been considered. I shall quote this neglected Memorandum because it has a most important bearing on the problem.

primo die Octobris 1562

G. George Gascoyne pl.⎱ Memorandum upon the hearing and examination of
Edward Boys   def.⎰ the causes and matters in controversy between the said
parties before the Master of the Rolls Mr. Recorder of London and D. Yale, to whom the same was committed and upon their report made unto the L. Keeper of the great seal of England, It is this day ordered by the said L. Keeper and by thassent of both the said parties in manner and form following / First that the said George Gascoyne and Elizabeth Brytaine alias Gascoyne alias Boys shall immediately renounce and relinquish his or her appeal depending before the Queen's Majesty's Delegates assigned by commission out of the Court of Chancery. And that the matter in law shall proceed without any delay to be sought by the said Gascoyne and Elizabeth and shall be tried between this and the feast of all Saints next by Mr. D. Weston with the assistance of Mr. D. Lewis and Mr. D. Yale, and that both the said parties and the said Elizabeth shall stand to their sentence and judgment without any further appeal./ In the mean season the possession of the house in London with certain Goods as hereafter in this order is expressed shall remain with the said Elizabeth / And if by the means or delay of the said Gascoyne or of the said Elizabeth or for want of bringing in the proofs the said matter in law shall not be decided between this and the feast of all Saints as is aforesaid, then the possession of the said house with the said goods shall be restored to the said Bois / And it is further ordered with like assent that so much household stuff and goods as were of the said Elizabeth before marriage with the said Boys or gascoyne remaining in the said house or in any other place as shall be by the said Mr. of the Rolls Mr. Recorder and Mr. Yale thought meet and necessary to be assigned unto the said Elizabeth, shall be delivered unto her upon sufficient surety that the same shall be truly answered and redelivered unto him whose wife she shall be adjudged (to be) [struck through] by order of law upon this appeal now pending / And that the rest of the said stuff and goods shall remain in the hands and custody of indifferent men such as the said Mr. of the Rolls Mr. Recorder and Mr. Yale shall assign, until such time as the matter and controversy between the said parties and the said Elizabeth shall be decided and determined upon the said appeal. / And thereupon the same goods together with the possession of the said house to be delivered unto him,

[26] F. E. Schelling, *The Life and Writings of George Gascoigne.* Univ. of Pennsylvania Publications, Series in Philology, Literature and Archæology, vol. II, no. 4, p. 9. Prof. Schelling also shows why this is to be identified with the poet.

[27] P.R.O. Chancery Decrees and Orders, vol. XXVII, fos. 122ᵛ–123ʳ.

[28] B. M. Ward, "The Death of George Gascoigne," p. 171.

unto whom the said Elizabeth shall be adjudged wife / In the mean season It is ordered that neither the said George Gascoyne nor Edward Boys shall have access or shall at any time repair unto the said Elizabeth, nor she to any of them. / And as touching the rents and profits of the lands of the said Elizabeth now due or to be due It is further ordered that the same shall be brought and delivered into the Rolls / and that thereof so much shall be assigned & delivered unto the said Elizabeth for the maintenance and sustentation of herself and her children, as shall be thought meet by the said Mr. of the Rolls Mr. Recorder and Mr. Yale, The rest of the said rents & profits there to remain to be delivered unto him whose wife the said Elizabeth shall be adjudged to be upon the said appeal determined / And it is further ordered that all such goods and chattels which were the proper goods of the said George Gascoyne, as have come to the hands or possession of the said Edward Boys, he the same Edward shall forthwith redeliver unto the said George / And likewise that all such goods & chattels which were the proper goods of the said Edward Boys, as have come to the hands or possession of the said George Gascoyne or Elizabeth he the same George shall forthwith redeliver unto the said Edward / And it is further ordered by like assent that as touching the jointure which the said Elizabeth might claim out of the lands of the said Edward Boys / if she should not be adjudged his wife, and touching such [*Altered from* "the"] lands as the said Edward standeth bounden for the payment of certain legacies and other things towards the performance of Mr. Brytaines will and touching all matters of variance which might or shall rise or grow between the said parties not comprised in this order, the said George and Edward shall stand to and abide the order and determination of the said Mr. of the Rolls Mr. Recorder and Mr. D. Yale.

/ powle / .

Since this Memorandum and Order is dated October 1, 1562, and since the Michaelmas Term of Court for 1562 did not begin until October 9,[29] it is therefore obvious that proceedings must have been instituted either in the Easter or the Trinity Term of the same year. But before examining the evidence of this Memorandum it will be well to conclude the story as it appears in legal documents. Mr. Ward has noted and partially printed a Chancery Petition[30] which Gascoigne brought before the Lord Keeper between February 13 and March 25, 1562/3.[31] The importance of this document seems to have been overlooked, for in it Gascoigne not only complains of the delay

---

[29] E. A. Fry, *Almanack for Students of English History,* Phillimore and Co., London, 1915, p. 137.

[30] B. M. Ward, "The Death of George Gascoigne," *op. cit.,* p. 171.

[31] P.R.O. Chanc. Proc., Series II., 78/55. Ward quotes only in part, and so I give the original reference of the document which I examined. The date must be 1562/3, for although the date of swearing on the document is 1562, the Petition refers to a suit brought by Boyes against Gascoigne, and the date of the documents in this latter action is Easter Term 1563. Now the Easter Term began on April 28, 1563, so we must conclude that (1) the date of swearing is incorrect, or (2) Boyes filed suit between the end of the Hilary Term (February 12, 1563) and the beginning of the Easter Term. The latter seems more logical. Therefore we can date the petition as between February 13 and March 24, 1562/3.

in settling the matter according to the terms of the Chancery Decree, but also reveals that he has been sued by Boyes on an action of Debt. This strange turn of events is the result of the delay and of a bond which Boyes and Gascoigne signed to each other. An agreement and bond for £500 was made between the two to secure their faithful observance of that part of the Decree which forbade either of them to repair to Elizabeth. When the matter was not settled by the Feast of All Saints, Gascoigne, feeling that "the said Edward Boyes ... by the strictness of the said words in the said order and thinking all his lifetime to keep your said Orator separated from his wife by the delays and means of his Counsel," nevertheless made his repair to the said Elizabeth. Thereupon Boyes brought action[32] to recover the £500 of the bond because Gascoigne had broken the letter of the agreement. In this Boyes is consistent with his policy in the suit of the Bretton children; in both instances he bases his argument on technicalities. To remedy this obviously unjust prosecution Gascoigne beseeches Sir Nicholas to grant him a writ of injunction against his persecutor so that the £500 may not be forfeit. This request was granted, as is shown by a Chancery Decree which I have found,[33] dated May 24, 1563.

Now that this story has been told, we may examine the significance of the above documents in the light of the evidence found in the Chancery Bill of the Bretton children. This latter Bill says that Elizabeth had been divorced from Boyes, that Boyes had appealed, and that not only had the sentence been upheld but Boyes had been adjudged as guilty in his appeal. Further, by this last sentence licence was given to Elizabeth to marry again at her election and disposition. The Memorandum of October 1, 1562 refers to matters in dispute before the Mr. of the Rolls (William Cordell),[34] Mr. Recorder of London, and D. Yale. It orders that an appeal which Elizabeth and Gascoigne had made to the Queen's Majesty's Court of Delegates, assigned by Commission out of the Chancery, be dropped and commits the whole question of the marriage problem to three new commissioners: D. Weston, D. Lewis, and D. Yale. Finally, Gascoigne, in the Chancery Petition mentioned in the previous paragraph, refers to D. Weston, D. Lewis, and D. Yale as the Court of the Arches.

These various pieces of evidence may be reconstructed in the following manner. Since the Memorandum committed the marriage problem to D. Weston, D. Lewis, and D. Yale, whom Gascoigne describes as the Court of the Arches, it seems that commissioners appointed out of Chancery to hear a mar-

---

[32] Coram Rege Roll (K.B. 27) 1206 (East. 5. Eliz.) 1563. Mrs. Genevieve Ambrose Oldfield mentions this action in a recent article (*R.E.S.*, xiii, 137), but she gives the reference in a footnote to a series of Chancery Proceedings. More important is the fact that Mrs. Oldfield attributes this suit to the dispute over the Bretton children's inheritance. There is no evidence in the documents to substantiate this assertion.

[33] P.R.O. Chanc. Decrees and Orders, vol. xxvii, fo. 490.

[34] Wm. Dugdale, *Origines Juridiciales*, London, 1680, p. 91.

riage question, always a matter of ecclesiastical jurisdiction, constituted a Court of the Arches. Therefore, the Master of the Rolls, Mr. Recorder of London, and D. Yale to whom the marriage problem had been committed, according to the Memorandum, were a first Court of the Arches. They must have decided in favour of Boyes, since George and Elizabeth are the appellants to the Queen's Majesty's Court of Delegates, an ecclesiastical court of appeal.[35] This appeal was ordered to be dropped and the new group, consisting of D. Weston, D. Lewis, and D. Yale were appointed a second Court of the Arches to decide the matter. Their decision was unfavorable to Boyes and he appealed, but to no avail. Elizabeth was divorced from Boyes and given licence to marry again. The necessity of marrying again is, I think, evinced by the preceding facts, for on November 23, 1561, Elizabeth was the lawful wife of Edward Boyes and her marriage to George Gascoigne was therefore illegal. In view of this conclusion Elizabeth and George must have had the ceremony performed anew. Where and when such a marriage was performed is at present unknown, but it can be dated between May 1563, the date of the Chancery Decree preventing Boyes from prosecuting his action of Debt, at which time matters in law were still in process, and November 1566, the date of the Bretton Bill which states that there was no other strife or appeal pending between Elizabeth, Gascoigne, and Boyes. Thus the story of the marital difficulties of Elizabeth Bacon Bretton Boyes Gascoigne seems at last to be somewhat clarified.

---

[35] M. S. Giuseppi, *A Guide to the Manuscripts Preserved in the Public Record Office.* H.M. Stationery Office, London, 1923, vol. 1, p. 292. The problem of procedure in the Ecclesiastical Courts is one concerning which no other evidence seems available. These courts were of recent origin, and their powers were undefined. The problem is further complicated by the seeming absence of all records of the Courts for this period.

Appendix IV

A LIST OF CLOSE ROLL ENTRIES

---

13 Oct. 3 Eliz. 1561
Close Roll 601 (3 Eliz. pt. 19) no. 36.
    Bond
    Sir John Gascoigne of Card., Beds., & George Gascoigne his son.
to
    William Wytte, citizen & saddler of London.
    £1,000, payable at feast of St. Andrew Apostle following.

Condition: Unless John & George keep the articles of an agreement between them & George Bacon esq. dated as above.

Memo: Cancelled on 17 May 4 Eliz., Wm. Wytte acknowledged that he was satisfied.

6 Nov. 3 Eliz. 1561
Close Roll 599 (3 Eliz. pt. 17) no. 50
    Bond
    George Gascoigne of Card., Beds., esq.
to
    Brian Ledes of North Middleforthe, York., esq.
    £40, payable at feast of St. Andrew Apostle following.

16 May 4 Eliz. 1562
Close Roll 627 (4 Eliz. pt. 24) no. 25.
    Bond
    Sir John Gascoigne of Card., Beds., & George Gascoigne of London, esq., his son & heir apparent.
to
    Henry Everard of Beiston, Beds., gent.
    £100.

20 May 4 Eliz. 1562
Close Roll 617 (4 Eliz. pt. 14) no. 33.
    Indenture of lease
made between: John Gostwicke of Willington, Beds., & Elizabeth his wife
and   George Gascoigne, esq.
    In consideration of £100 paid by Gascoigne, Gostwick lets to farm the manor

of Willington, together with all other his lands in Copley, Beds., with all rights, household utensils, etc., to hold to Gascoigne, his executors, etc., for twenty-one years from the feast of Annunciation last, paying to Gostwicke & his wife the yearly rent of £105.

Memo: On 4 June 4 Eliz. John Gostwyke came into Chancery & acknowledged the above deed.

7 Nov. 4 Eliz. 1562
Close Roll 625 (4 Eliz. pt. 22) no. 29.
        Bond
        George Gascoigne of Willington, Beds., esq.
to
        Arthur Hall of Grantham, Lincs., esq.
        £200, payable at Easter following.

Condition: Unless £140 is paid on 25 Oct. 1565, at the tenement "wherin the said George Gascoigne nowe inhabiteth and wherin one William Britton lately inhabited and dwelled . . . in Redcrostrete in . . . Sainte Giles withoute Crepulgate of London," if Hall appears bringing testimonials proving that he has been to the city of Toledo in Spain after the date above written.

9 Dec. 5 Eliz. 1562
Close Roll 635 (5 Eliz. pt. 6) no. 40.
        Bond
        George Gascoigne of Willington, Beds., esq.
to
        Sir William Vavasour of Hasylwood, York.
        £1,000, payable at Christmas following.

Condition: Unless the said George and Elizabeth his wife perform the articles of indentures, dated the same day, between them and Sir William.

9 Dec. 5 Eliz. 1562
Close Roll 650 (5 Eliz. pt. 21) no. 64.
        Bond
        William Redman of Twiselton, York., esq.; Anthony Cavallery of Furnival's Inn, gent.; & Christofer Vavasor of Gray's Inn, gent.
to
        George Gascoigne of Willington, Beds., esq.
        £1,200

Condition: Payable unless William Vavasor of Hasilwood, York., pay Gascoigne £1,000 as follows:—21 June next, £600; on feast of St. Martin the bishop in Winter, £400; "in the hall of Graies Inne";

and unless William Vavasor keep articles in an indenture of this
same date made between Gascoigne and Elizabeth his wife and
William Vavasor.

11 Dec. 5 Eliz. 1562

Close Roll 630 (5 Eliz. pt. 1) no. 46.
    Bond
    Sir John Gascoigne of Card., & George Gascoigne his son & heir apparent.

to

    Thomas Wood of London, gent.
    £400, payable at Christmas following.

Memo: On 6 July 5 Eliz. Thos. Wood came into Chancery & acknowledged
        he had been paid.

12 Dec. 5 Eliz. 1562

Close Roll 630 (5 Eliz. pt. 1) no. 10.
    Bond
    John and George Gascoigne (as *ibid.,* no. 46), the latter of Gray's Inn.

to

    Thomas Wood of London, gent.
    £100, payable at Christmas.

Memo: On 10 Feb. 5 Eliz. 1563 cancelled (as *ibid.,* no 46) by Wood.

18 Dec. 5 Eliz. 1562

Close Roll 630 (5 Eliz. pt. 1) no. 13.
    Bond
    George Gascoigne of Gray's Inn, esq., son & heir of Sir John Gascoigne of
    Card.

to

    Thomas Wood of London, gent.
    £100, payable at Christmas following.

Memo: On 24 Feb. 5 Eliz., Wood acknowledged payment in Chancery.

28 Jan. 5 Eliz. 1562/3

Close Roll 633 (5 Eliz. pt. 4) no. 55.
    Bond
    George Gascoigne of Willington, Beds., esq.

to

    Thomas Cornwallis of London, esq.
    £200, payable at Easter following.

Condition: Unless Arthur Hall of Grantham, Lincs., esq.; John Farneham of
        London, esq.; and George Gascoigne, or any of them pay Corne-

wallys £100 on 6 Jan. following, at house of Humfrey Shelton of London, gent., in Coleman St., London; according to a former recognizance, dated 13 Jan. 5 Eliz. in which Hall and Farneham are bound to Cornewallys in £200 for the sure payment of the said £100.

29 Jan. 5 Eliz. 1562/3

Close Roll 650 (5 Eliz. pt. 21) no. 65.
    Bond
    Arthur Hall of Grantham, Lincs., esq.

to

    George Gascoigne of Willington, Beds., esq.
    £240, payable at Easter next.

Condition: Unless Hall discharge Gascoigne from obligations of a recognizance for which he is bound to Thomas Cornwallys for a debt owed by Hall. (Cf. C.R. 633 [5 Eliz. pt. 4] no. 55)

Memo: On 2 Dec. 17 Eliz., George Gascoigne appeared in Chancery & acknowledged satisfaction. Signature of George Gascoigne in the margin.

3 April 5 Eliz. 1563

Close Roll 636 (5 Eliz. pt. 7) no. 75.
    Bond
    George Gascoigne of Graies Inne, son & heir apparent of Sir John Gascoigne of Card., Beds.

to

    John Peers, citizen & fishmonger of London.
    200 marks, payable at Michaelmas following.

14 May 5 Eliz. 1563

Close Roll 638 (5 Eliz. pt. 9) no. 20.
    Bond
    George Gascoigne, esq., & William Wytte, citizen & saddler of London.

to

    John Marshall, citizen & fishmonger of London.
    £200, payable at Whitsun following, to perform articles of an indenture dated 12 May 5 Eliz. between Gascoigne & Marshall.

Memo: On 12 July 5 Eliz., cancelled by Marshall.
    Cf. C.R. 717 (8 Eliz. pt. 20) no. 20.
    Cf. C.R. 672 (6 Eliz. pt. 21) no. 36.

12 July 5 Eliz. 1563
Close Roll 650 (5 Eliz. pt. 21) no. 98.
  Bond
  Sir John Gascoigne
to
  George Gascoigne his son of Willington, Beds.
  £1,000, payable at feast of St. James Apostle following.

Condition: Unless John does not alienate the lands assured to George, but allows them to descend to George & his heirs, according to an indenture between the parties, dated 10 July 5 Eliz.

14 March 6 Eliz. 1564
Close Roll 672 (6 Eliz. pt. 21) no. 36.
  Bond
  George Gascoigne of Gray's Inn, & George Wytt, citizen & saddler of London.
to
  John Rawlyns of the Tower of London, yeoman.
  £200, payable at Easter following.

24 Nov. 7 Eliz. 1564
Close Roll 693 (7 Eliz. pt. 21) no. 43.
  Bond
  George Gascoigne of Walthamstowe, Essex, esq.
to
  George Bacon of Hegessett, Suff., gent.; Thomas Andrewes and George Bacon Jr. of London, gent.
  £1,000, payable at Easter following.

Condition: That Gascoigne & Elizabeth his wife, late the wife of Wm. Breton of London gent. deceased, have in their possession messuages, lands, money & household goods, which by the will of Wm. Breton, dated 12 Feb. "1557" were bequeathed to his children, if George or Elizabeth pay to Richard, Nicholas and Thamar Breton their bequests according to the will, & meanwhile maintain & bring them up so far as the goods & revenues will allow, and discharge George, Thomas & George of all charges & demands connected with the bequests, then this recognizance is to be void.

29 March 8 Eliz. 1566
Close Roll 717 (8 Eliz. pt. 20) no. 20.
  Bond
  George Gascoigne of Grayes Inn, & William Wytt, citizen & saddler of London.
to
  John Rawlyns of the Tower of London, yeoman.
  £200, payable at the Nativity of St. John the Baptist following.

26 Dec. 9 Eliz. 1566

Close Roll 729 (9 Eliz. pt. 3) no. 10.
    Bond
    George Gascoigne of Gray's Inn, esq.

to

    John Wynche of Northyell, Beds., esq.
    £500, payable at Annuciation of the Virgin following.

Condition: Unless Gascoigne before 12 May next discharges Wynche of re-
    cognizance dated same day made between Wynche, Gascoigne, &
    Danyell Snowe of Gray's Inne esq. in £400 to John Clarke gent., or
    unless Gascoigne before 12 May next makes an assurance to Wynche
    of a messauge & 120 acres of land in East Cotes alias Cotten Ende
    in Cardyngton, Beds., late parcel of the inheritance of Sir John
    Gascoigne, father of the said George.
    [Noted by Miss Genevieve Ambrose, *RES*, II, (1926), 165. She
    prints the name "Windre," but actually it seems to be "Wynche."]

27 Feb. 9 Eliz. 1566/7

Close Roll 731 (9 Eliz. pt. 5) no. 8.
    Bond
    George Gascoigne of Grayes Inne, esq., son and heir apparent of Sir John
    Gascoigne of Cardington, Beds.

to

    John Rawlyns of the Tower of London, yeoman.
    £200, payable at Easter following.

Condition: Unless Gascoigne keep article of indenture made between the two
    on 3 Feb. 9 Eliz.
    [Noted by Miss Ambrose, *RES,* II (1926), 165.]

5 Oct. 9 Eliz. 1567

Close Roll 757 (10 Eliz. pt. 1) m. 27d.
    Bond
    George Gascoigne of London esq., & William Pelham of Brokelsbye, Linc.

to

    Tristran Decharte of London, merchant-stranger.
    £200, payable at Christmas following.

Condition: Unless they pay him £100 on 5 April following [sic] at home of
    Vincent Guychardyne, merchant-stranger, in Mark Lane, London.
    [Noted by Miss Ambrose, *RES,* II (1926), 165. She gives the name
    as "Tristram Deacher."]

5 Oct. 9 Eliz. 1567
Close Roll 756 (9 Eliz. pt. 30) m. 16d.
    Bond
    George Gascoigne of London, esq.

to

    William Pelham of Brokelsby, Linc., esq.
    £300, payable at Christmas following.

Condition: Unless Gascoigne pay £100 on 5 April following to Tristran
    Decharte, and discharge Pelham from recognizance made between
    them & Decharte.
    [Noted by Miss Ambrose, *RES*, II (1926), 165.]

12 Nov. 9 Eliz. 1567
Close Roll 769 (10 Eliz. pt. 13) m. 46d.
    Indenture
made between: Sir John Gascoigne of Card., Beds., & George Gascoigne of Gray's
    Inn, his son & heir apparent.
and   Thomas Colby of London, esq. & Elizabeth his wife.
    In consideration of £940 paid by Colby, Sir John & George have sold him
    the manor of Escottes alias Cotton in Card. Beds.

Memo: On 15 Dec. 10 Eliz. John & George appeared in Chancery & ac-
    knowledged indenture.

15 Nov. 9 Eliz. 1567
Close Roll 744 (9 Eliz. pt. 18) no. 38.
    Bond
    George Gascoigne of London, esq.

to

    Robert Drurye of Rougham, Suff., esq.
    200 marks, payable at Christmas following.

Condition: Unless Gascoigne perform articles of an indenture of the same
    date made between the same parties.
    [Noted by Miss Ambrose, *RES*, II (1926), 165.]

15 Dec. 10 Eliz. 1567
Close Roll 769 (10 Eliz. pt. 13) m. 48d.
    Bond
    Sir John "Gascon"

to

    Thomas Colbye of Gray's Inn, esq.
    2000 marks
    To perform indenture of C.R. 769 (10 Eliz. pt. 13) m. 46d.
    [Mrs. Genevieve Ambrose Oldfield notes this bond (*RES*, XIII [1937], 133).

The indenture, which is dated 10 Eliz., is noted by Miss Ambrose (*RES*, II [1926], 164) as 9 Eliz. This latter must be the correct dating, since Sir John died 4 April 9 Eliz. The original document is in error.]

10 March 10 Eliz. 1567/8

Close Roll 769 (10 Eliz. pt. 13) m. 48d.
    Bond
    Sir John Gascoigne of Card., Beds.
to
    Thomas Colby & Robert Rynge of Wroteham, Kent.
    £200
    To perform indenture dated 20 Feb. 10 Eliz. made between Sir John & George Gascoigne and Thos. Colby.

12 March 10 Eliz. 1567/8

Close Roll 759 (10 Eliz. pt. 3) No other ref.
    Bond
    George Gascoigne of Gray's Inn, esq.
to
    Edward Russell of London, esq.
    £200, payable at the Nativity of St. John the Baptist following.
Condition: Unless within one month after Russell returns from Jerusalem bearing proof of having been there Gascoigne pays £100. [Noted by Miss Ambrose, *RES*, II (1926), 165.]

25 April 10 Eliz. 1568

Close Roll 769 (10 Eliz. pt. 13) m. 44d.
    Bond
    George Gascoigne of Gray's Inn, esq.
to
    John Rawlins of the Tower of London.
    £1000, payable on 30 April 10 Eliz.

10 May 10 Eliz. 1568

Close Roll 772 (10 Eliz. pt. 16) m. 36d.
    Indenture
made between: George Gascoigne of Gray's Inn.
and   Sir George Speke of Whytelakynton, Somerset.
    In consideration of £540 paid by Speke, Gascoigne sells him the manor of Cardyngton, late property of Sir John Gascoigne, deceased, father of said George. This also includes Fenlake Barnes, the advowson of the vicarage of Cardyngton, & his term of years in Hawnes Park, Hardnes, Beds. Bases his right on indenture of assignment of said parsonage & manor made from

Sir John to George, dated 15 June 5 Eliz., of all which George is seised in remainder expectant upon an estate for life held by Dame Margaret, late the wife of Sir John deceased.

Condition: That should George pay £540 at one payment on 2 Nov. following, in the Hall of Gray's Inn, then the indenture is void.

Memo: On 31 May 10 Eliz. George Gascoigne appeared in Chancery & acknowledged above indenture.

10 May 10 Eliz. 1568

Close Roll 772 (10 Eliz. pt. 16) m. 36d.
    Bond
    George Gascoigne of Gray's Inn.

to

    Sir George Speke of Whytelakynton, Somerset.
    1000 marks, payable at Michaelmas following.

Condition: Unless Gascoigne keep covenants of above indenture.
    [Noted by Miss Ambrose, *RES,* II (1926), 165.]

12 June 10 Eliz. 1568

Close Roll 789 (11 Eliz. pt. 3) m. 15d.
    Bond
    George Gascoigne of Walthamstowe, Essex, esq.

to

    Thomas Browne, citizen & writer of London.
    100 marks, payable at Michaelmas following.

3 July 10 Eliz. 1568

Close Roll 772 (10 Eliz. pt. 16) m. 24d.
    Bond
    George Gascoigne of Walthamstow, Essex, esq.

to

    Thomas Colby of London, esq.
    £500, payable at feast of St. Bartholmew following.

6 Nov. 10 Eliz. 1568

Close Roll 767 (10 Eliz. pt. 11) m. 33d.
    Bond
    George Gascoigne of Walthamstow, Essex, esq.

to

    Richard Ratcliff of London, gent.
    200 marks, payable 1 Dec. following.

Condition: Unless Gascoigne pay £100 on 6 Dec. following at house of Barnard Garter of London, notary, in Chrystchurche [ward] in Newgate.
[Noted by Miss Ambrose, *RES,* II (1926), 165.]

28 May 11 Eliz. 1569
Close Roll 806 (11 Eliz. pt. 20) m. 34d.
    Bond
    George Gascoigne of Walthamstow Tony, Essex.
to
    Richard Ratcliff, citizen & clothworker.
    £100, payable 1 June following.

Condition: Unless Gascoigne pay Ratcliff £70 in house of Edmond Bysshopp of London in St. Paul's yard i.e., £40 on 24 June and £30 on 29 Sept. following.

Appendix V

THE "DISINHERITANCE" OF GEORGE GASCOIGNE

GEORGE WHETSTONE was the originator of the statement that George Gascoigne was disinherited by his father, Sir John Gascoigne of Cardington, Bedfordshire. A marginal note in Whetstone's rhymed obituary notice reads: "He was Sir John G sonne and Heire Disinherited."[1]

From this beginning and from an examination of the will of Sir John Gascoigne[2] has arisen a controversy:[3] was the poet really disinherited? Recently, Mrs. Genevieve Ambrose Oldfield[4] reviewed the question and arrived at certain conclusions about the terms of Sir John's will. Since some of these seem to be based on a misapprehension, it will be well to review the evidence.

It is known from the Inquisition Post Mortem taken on Sir John Gascoigne[5] that this knight died on April 4, 1568, and a document[6] which I have found reveals that the will was made on his deathbed. From the nature of this latter document, it is unlikely that the poet was present on this occasion. That he knew or thought he knew, however, something of the terms of his father's will is confirmed by an indenture of May 10, 1568,[7] in which George sells to Sir George Speke of Whytelakynton, Somerset, the manor of Cardington, the parsonage of Cardington called Fenlake Barnes, the advowson of the vicarage of Cardington, and an interest for a term of years in Hawnes Park. All this Gascoigne claims he is to inherit from his late father, except Hawnes Park, which Sir John had given him by an indenture of June 15, 1563. A marginal note on the Close Roll shows that on May 31, 1568, the poet appeared in Chancery and acknowledged this indenture. Clearly, then, one day before his father's will was proved, Gascoigne appeared certain of his inheritance.

---

[1] Whetstone, *A Remembraunce of the wel imployed life, and godly end, of George Gaskoigne Esquire*, ed. by Arber, p. 17.

[2] PCC 12 Babington. Noted and partially printed by Ward, "George Gascoigne and His Circle," *RES*, II (1926), 32–35.

[3] Ward, *op. cit.* Ambrose, "George Gascoigne," *RES*, II (1926), 163–66.

[4] "New Light on George Gascoigne," *RES*, XIII (1937), 129–35.

[5] Noted by Ward, *op. cit.*, pp. 34–35.

[6] PRO St. Ch. 5, G36/14.

[7] PRO Close Roll 772 (10 Eliz. pt. 16) m. 36d. Noted by Ambrose, "George Gascoigne," *RES*, II (1926), 165.

What then were the terms of the will which have caused such argument? Briefly stated these are the provisions of Sir John's will:

1. Household stuff to Dame Margaret to the value of 300 marks;
2. 200 marks owed to Robert Carpender;
3. The lease of the parsonage of Fenlake Barnes to son, John Gascoigne;
4. £10 to Richard Lambe, servant;
5. A quarter's wages to all servants in the house;
6. £6 13s. 4d. to Church of Cardington, where he desires to be buried, for the part purchase of a bell;
7. 2 shillings to every poor cottager of Cardington;
8. . . . and as touching all my manor lands tenements and hereditaments whatsoever they be heretofore not granted or bequeathed I give unto my son George Gascoigne and to his heirs upon this condition faith confidence and trust and not otherwise. That my said son George shall permit and suffer my executors . . . to take and receive the rents issues and profit of my said manors lands tenements and hereditaments until my said executors have levied . . . so much money as shall be sufficient to pay . . . my debts legacies and bequests mentioned . . . in this my said last will and testament or otherwise by me lawfully due and payable or else pay them him self within one year next after my decease.
9. An annuity of £20 to "Anne Drewry sometime my servant" is to be compounded and paid off by son George within a year's time;[8]
10. . . . and if it happen that my said son George do not procure or discharge whereof [the annuity] And also pay and discharge my debts and legacies within one year after my decease And likewise pay and discharge my funeral charges in convenient time if sufficient of my goods and chattels do not remain in the hands of my executors to satisfy and discharge the same after my wife be satisfied of such portion of such utensils and household stuff as before mentioned Then I will and give to my said executors all my lands tenements and hereditaments not given or appointed to the Jointure of my said wife And so much of the reversion of my other lands [etc.] . . . to her appointed in Jointure as shall amount to the yearly value of Sixteen pounds by the year To the intent that my said Executors shall within a convenient time after sell the said lands [etc.] . . . and with the money thereof coming to satisfy and pay the said annuity and other my debts legacies and charges hereafter following;
11. Here follows a list of persons to whom Sir John owes money: (1) To Mr. Wynche as shown by a covenant between them, (2) £5 to Elizabeth, the kinswoman of Gregory Rodwell's wife, (3) Seven quarters of barley to Mr. Gostwick of Bedford, (4) £7 to one Bridges of Jewelry, (5) £50 to Isabell, wife to his servant Robert Bray;
12. £40 to William Curson of Norfolk, nephew, if he serve as executor and faithfully carry out the terms of the will;

---

[8] Mrs. Oldfield (*op. cit.*, p. 132) has noted Patent Roll, 7 Eliz., pt. 8, m. 1, which shows that Anne Drewry had sued Sir John in Common Pleas. Sir John had not appeared in court and was outlawed. However, on paying £200 awarded to Anne Drewry and 68 shillings damage, Sir John's outlawry was pardoned by the Queen. I have been unable to find the original action in Common Pleas.

13. . . . and where there is a recognizance acknowledged unto me by my said son George Gascoigne my mind and intent is and also I desire my said Executor that if it happen the same to be forfeit by my said son and that Thomas Colby of Gray's Inn . . . be any ways troubled or molested by my said son for or concerning any the lands tenements or hereditaments which he the said Thomas Colby hath bought and purchased of me and of the said George Then if the said Thomas Colby do desire my said Executor to sue execution thereof [presumably upon the recognizance noted above] That then my said Executor upon the said desire shall from time to time do and suffer to be done without revocation disabling or denial of the said suits at the cost and charges in the law of the said Thomas Colby his executors or assigns all reasonable acts and things that shall be devised by the said Thomas Colby his executors [etc.] . . . as well for the presenting and suing of execution of the said bond [recognizance] against my said son his heirs or assigns as also for the permitting & suffering of the said Thomas Colby his executors [etc.] . . . peaceably and quietly to have and enjoy all such sums of money to the only use of the said Thomas Colby . . . as by the said suit or execution shall be recovered [etc.];

14. Robert Bray, servant, to have all goods now in his possession whether his own or Sir John's;

15. Any residue to the payment of debts, charges, etc.

Here we have the evidence from which Mrs. Oldfield deduces that "Sir John practically disinherited his son and heir."[9] She further concludes:

This [Item no. 13] left matters so that George, if he had wished to recover the premises involved, not only would have had to repay the original sum of £940 received from Colby for the manor and appurtenances, but also the additional 2,000 marks and £200 advanced to his father by Colby.[10]

In the first place, there is no evidence to show that Colby advanced to Sir John 2,000 marks and £200. These were the sums which Sir John gave in the two bonds guaranteeing performance of the original indenture of sale; Sir John was to pay these sums if Colby did not secure possession of the manor of Eastcottes. Secondly, there is nothing in the original indenture or in either of the bonds to indicate that the property could be recovered. Colby had legal title and bonds for the performance of the indenture. Finally, Mrs. Oldfield does not note a bond of £500 which Gascoigne gave to Colby on July 3, 1568.[11] There are no terms for this bond, but its appearance within a month of the proving of Sir John's will seems to relate to this matter of the quiet possession of Eastcottes.

But in what way does Sir John's will practically disinherit his son and heir? According to the Inquisition Post Mortem taken on Sir John's estate in April, 1569, George received the manor and a quarter part of the barony of Bedford, which were worth, by the year, £20 14 s. 11 d. and 12 s. respectively, a not

---

[9] Oldfield, *op. cit.*, p. 134.   [10] *Ibid.*, p. 133.
[11] PRO Close Roll 772 (10 Eliz. pt. 16) m. 24[d].

inconsiderable sum.[12] In addition the poet may have received other lands, as well as goods, chattels, and money which are not mentioned in the Inquisition. It is well to remember that an Inquisition covered lands held of the Crown, but not a man's entire estate. Furthermore, the conditions laid down by Sir John are not excessive. Sir John seems to have been preoccupied with two matters: first, the payment of his debts and bequests; secondly, the guaranteeing of Colby's possession of the manor of Eastcottes. For the performance of the first he gave his son two alternatives: the executor could take the revenue of the property until there was sufficient to cover the debts and bequests, or the son could take possession and pay off the debts and bequests within a year. Certainly Sir John was wise to take some precaution, in an age of sharp practice, by setting a time limit. As regards the manor of Eastcottes, Sir John's mind was far from easy. He had sold the manor to Colby and had received payment; but as we have noted above, Sir John had sold, in 1562, the same manor to Francis Bacon as a jointure for Elizabeth, and George knew this.

Finally, Sir John had been involved in another suspicious transaction with his son George. The latter claimed that Sir John had given him by indenture the manor of Fenlake Barnes. The dispute that subsequently arose over this property presents to us for the first time the true story of Sir John's will and also explains why Dame Margaret did not mention her son George in her will.

Tithe lambs were the first cause of trouble and, since the tithe lambs were taken by force, George Gascoigne brought action against his brother, John, in the Star Chamber,[13] where, as we have seen before, matters involving "weapons, invasive and defensive" were tried. The account, as found in the records, reveals the true story in a most dramatic fashion, so it will be best to let the documents speak for themselves:

To Our Sovereign Lady
The Queen's Most Excellent Majesty

In most humble wise showeth and complaineth unto your most excellent majesty your highness true faithful and obedient subject George Gascoigne esquire that whereas your majestys said subject was lawfully possessed of and in one flock of sheep depasturing and feeding within his landship of Cardington in your highness County of Bedford being in the whole about the number of XX and your said subject thus being possessed thereof So it is most gracious sovereign Lady that one John Gascoigne gent. younger Brother to your majestys said subject being Accompanied with John Ayleford Richard Lambe Lawrens Osborne John Walters John Byrd and other lewd and evilly disposed persons to the number of VIII being Riotously arrayed with force and arms that is to wit with swords Bucklers daggers staves and divers other kinds of weapons both invasive and defensive the twenty

---

[12] PRO Court of Wards, v. XI, No. 139. Ward (*op. cit.,* p. 34) prints a summary; Mrs. Oldfield (*op. cit.,* p. 134) notes the value.

[13] PRO St. Ch. 5, C36/14. In the ensuing quotations I have omitted tiresome legal verbiage, but in no way have I omitted anything which alters any material fact.

day of September last past in the tenth year of your majestys most prosperous Reign assembled themselves together in very Riotous and disordered manner at Cardington aforesaid then and there the said John Gascoigne and the other Riotous persons by his abetment commandment and procurement did Riotously chase course and disturb the said flock of sheep and chattel of your said subject and them would take violently driven and carried away with great force saving that one John Rogers being your majestys said subjects shepherd and servant seeing the said flock . . . disturbed as aforesaid and in driving away by the said Rioters and meaning both to stay the said sheep and to know the cause why the same should be driven away as Reason it was he should so do did therefore in quiet and peaceable manner repair unto them of a narrow lane at Cardington aforesaid through the which the said John Gascoigne and the other Rioters were then prepared to drive the said sheep but also demanded of the said Rioters what they meant to do with the said sheep but . . . John Gascoigne being maliciously minded rather with violence and force to carry away the . . . sheep than peaceably and quietly to show what cause he had so to do did therefore not only crowd by enforce and drive the said sheep with violence meaning to carry away the same in despite of your said subjects said servant but also animated abetted & commanded the other said Rioters to strike and overthrow your said subjects servant and . . . John Gascoigne seeing that his other Rioters were not as willing to satisfy his present fury as he was to command them to commit that outrage therefore he himself in very furious manner having in his hand a long staff did hastily set upon your . . . subjects . . . servant and him did then and there sore hurt wound and evil intreat and him overthrew and there he and the said Riotous company did take drive and chase away the score and four of the said sheep of the proper goods and chattels of your majestys subject and the same did presently drive unto a market Town called Leighton . . . and sold the same to them that listed to buy for the half that the same were worth not only to the great loss and hindrance of your majestys said subject but also to the lewd and evil encouragement of others to do and practice the like attempts if the Rioters should escape unpunished In tender consideration whereof may it therefore please your majesty to grant your several writ of sub poena to be directed to the same John Gascoigne John Ayleford Richard Lambe Lawrens Osborne John Walters and John Bird commanding them personally to appear before your majestys honorable council in your highness Court of Star Chamber then and there to answer to the premises and your majestys said subject shall daily pray unto almighty god for the preservation of your majestys most Royal person long over us to Reign.

To these charges John Gascoigne replied that the lambs belonged to his mother, Dame Margaret, from whom the complainant, being an "unnatural" son, had stolen them. Dame Margaret, hearing of this theft, sent her dutiful son, John, along with several servants, to regain possession. They espied the tithe lambs among George Gascoigne's flock of sheep and drove the whole lot to an "apt place" to separate the lambs from the sheep. This being done, they returned George's sheep to John Bird, "being then the said complainants own shepherd." John and the other defendants denied the charges of riotous behavior and the possession of weapons, saying the only weapons carried by

John, Lambe, and Osborne were "a little walking stick either of them in the hand." Walters and Bird had only "their shepherd hooks."

The poet was not the man to submit easily to a charge of sheep-stealing, particularly one made by his mother, so he prepared a replication to establish his ownership of the lambs as well as the truth of his original complaint.

Replication of George Gascoigne Esquier complt.
to the Answer of John Gascoigne & others defts.

Complainant sayeth that his Bill is true and sufficient in the law to be answered unto and the Answer is untrue uncertain and insufficient in the law to be replied unto but saving to himself the advantage of exception to its uncertainty and insufficiency complainant saith as he did before in his Bill and will prove every matter therein to be good just and true Further for a full declaration of the truth Complainant saith that John late Prior of the Dissolved Monastery of St Paul of Newnham in the county of Bedford and the Convent of the same place were seized in their demesne as of fee of and in the parsonage of Cardington called Fenlake Barnes with all . . . the tithes obligations glebe lands emoluments and advantages to the said parsonage belonging . . . and the said John late Prior . . . and the said late Convent . . . being so seized . . . did by their deed indented under their Convent seal bearing date the xvjth day of May in the xxviijth year of the Reign of the late King of famous memory Henry the eight demise grant and let to farm to Sir William Gascoigne knight grandfather to this Complainant Dame Elizabeth his wife and Sir John Gascoigne knight father to this Complainant by the name then of John Gascoigne son and heir apparent of the said Sir William the said parsonage of Cardington called Fenlake Barnes with all manner of glebe lands meadows and pastures to the said parsonage belonging and almoner of Tithes as well of Corn hay and wood as of wool and Lamb within the whole parish of Cardington . . . To have and to hold . . . to the said Sir William and Dame Elizabeth and John their executors administrators and assigns from the feast of the annunciation of our Lady then last past before the date of the said Indenture unto the end and term of lxxxxix years then next ensuing yielding and paying therefore yearly . . . to the said prior and Convent and to their successors xxiiij [pounds] x s[hillings] of lawfull English money as by the said indenture of lease among other thing therein contained it may appear by force whereof the said Sir William Gascoigne entered into the said parsonage with the premises and was thereof possessed and he being thereof possessed died and after the said Dame Elizabeth died By force whereof the said Sir John Gascoigne father to this Complainant as survivor to the said Sir William and Dame Elizabeth entered in the said parsonage with the premises and was thereof by virtue of the said indenture of lease lawfully possessed and he being thereof so possessed did by his deed indented bearing date the xvth day of June in the fourth year of the reign of our Sovereign Lady the Queens Majesty that now Reigneth aswell for and in Consideration of the natural love that the said Sir John did bear to this Complainant being his son as also for and in consideration that this Complainant payed for the mere and only debt of the said Sir John the sum of two hundred pounds of lawfull English money grant assign and set over unto this Complainant all his Right Estate title interest and term of years then to come in the said parsonage with the premises and all and singular the appurtenances providing by special Covenant in the said Indenture that the said Sir John Gascoigne should

enjoy the said parsonage and other the premises during the natural life of the said
Sir John Gascoigne and no longer and after died after whose death this Complainant
by force of the said deed indented bearing date the said xvth day of June . . . entered
into the said parsonage with the premises and was thereof lawfully possessed and he
being thereof so possessed did on saint Marks day in the Tenth year of the Reign of
our said sovereign Lady or very near about that time at Cardington aforesaid quietly
and peaceably gather the tithe lambs of the inhabitants of Cardington aforesaid being then due to this Complainant as in his right to the said parsonage and after that
this Complainant had in quiet and peaceable manner without any contradiction of
any of the inhabitants of Cardington aforesaid and without contradiction of any
other person gathered the said tithe lambs in manner above rehearsed this Complainant did in like manner set his brand on the one side of the said lambs as lawfull
it was for him to do by means whereof this Complainant was lawfully possessed of
the said tithe lambs to the number of lxiiij or thereabouts and . . . did entreat the
inhabitants of Cardington . . . that the said tithe lambs might still remain with
the Ewes amongst their several flocks until the said tithe lambs were stronger and
better able to be drawn from the said Ewes the which the said inhabitants did very
willingly grant unto this Complainant for one month and more during which time
the said defendants did in very disordered manner come to the several flocks of the
said inhabitants of Cardington . . . and then and there did take away from their
shepherds the said tithe lambs or the greater number of them after that this Complainant had in quiet and peaceable manner branded the same as is before rehearsed
and the same did in very disordered manner convey and carry away into one pasture
of Dame Margaret Gascoignes named in the said answer commonly called the park
and notwithstanding that this complainant did at sundry times and by sundry means
in most obedient humble and submissive manner beseech the said Dame Margaret
being his mother to redeliver the said lambs unto this Complainant and also to become good and natural loving mother to this Complainant in such sort as all vari-
ances or demands depending between the said Dame Margaret and this Complainant
or between this Complainant and the said Defendants might be fully agreed compounded and determined so that there might be an unfeigned love between this
Complainant and the said defendant being brothers and a natural love as well on
the behalf of the said Dame Margaret towards this Complainant as a due obedience
on the behalf of this Complainant towards . . . Dame Margaret yet nevertheless the
said Dame Margaret of some unnatural disposition utterly to overthrow and undo
this Complainant being her own natural child and such one as hath always behaved
himself most obediently and lovingly towards his said mother and hath not spared
to adventure the losses both of life and living at all times in her behalf and of an
unmeasurable love and affection that she hath conceived towards the said defendant
being her younger son did not only refuse the humble and reasonable petitions of
this Complainant But did also dissuade the younger son to refuse any such agreement or composition to be made for the establishment of a brotherly love and concord between the . . . defendant and this Complainant And further did contrary to
all right and order of laws detain from . . . Complainant the . . . tithe lambs or the
greater number of them in the . . . pasture called the park by the space of one month
or more as . . . Complainant hath been credibly informed during which time it
fortuned that . . . Complainant having a pasture at Cardington then in his occupation

called somerfeild adjoyning to the . . . pasture of . . . Dame Margaret called the park
the said tithe lambs together with other sheep of . . . Dame Margarets and others for
as much as the grass in the said pasture then of this Complainant called Somerfeild
was much better than the grass in . . . the Park break through the hedge of the . . .
Park into . . . Somerfeild And this Complainant having understanding that a great
number of sheep had broken into his . . . pasture repaired thither to see whose sheep
the same were and perceiving that the same were the sheep of . . . Dame Margarets
his mother and that a great number of . . . Complainants tithe lambs were amongst
the same did in very quiet and peaceable manner and without any Contradiction of
any person draw as many of the . . . tithe lambs as were branded with the brand of
. . . Complainant from the rest of the . . . Sheep and although . . . Complainant might
by just occasion lawfully have impounded the sheep . . . of Dame Margaret for trespass in eating the grass of . . . Complainant in the . . . pasture yet . . . Complainant
of a dutiful love towards . . . Dame Margaret his mother did forbear to take advantage in that behalf and did of Courtesy drive the . . . sheep through the hedge
of the . . . park in the same place where they before had broken through and did
stop up the said gap or hole in the said hedge so that the . . . sheep might not easily
break through again and after did in quiet manner and without contradiction of any
man carry and drive the . . . tithe lambs unto the house of John Rogers servant to
. . . Complainant & named in the said answer at Cardington . . . and immediately
this Complainant did set his brand on both sides of the . . . lambs and likewise on
both sides of all his other lambs as lawfull it was for him to do and after delivered
them unto John Birde being then the shepherd of . . . Complainant and now one of
the said defendants who kept the same with divers other sheep of this Complainants
in quiet and peaceable manner in the common fields of Cardington by the space of
two months or thereabouts until the said defendants the xxth day of september last
past with force and arms as . . . in the said Bill . . . the Complainant hath before
alleged did take and drive the greater number of the said tithe lambs together with
certain other sheep of . . . Complainant from the . . . servant of . . . Complainant and
out of the flock of . . . Complainant and did in very disordered manner contrary to
all right . . . drive the same to market and did there sell them as this Complainant
hath been credibly informed for very small prices in effect for less than the one half
that the same were worth to the great hindrance and damage of . . . Complainant
and to the evil example of such like riotous and disordered persons and only of purpose to undo this Complainant knowing very well that this Complainant would
rather bear a great Injury than seem to contend in law with . . . Dame Margaret
his mother the said defendants have therefore falsely and colourably surmised in
their said answer that the . . . tithe lambs should be the proper goods and Chattels
of . . . Dame Margaret without that the said John Waters did in quiet manner drive
the rest of . . . Complainants sheep unto the Common flock and there deliver them
to the shepherd of this Complainant And without that it was . . . lawfull for any
man . . . to drive or carry the goods and chattels of any person to an open market and
. . . to sell them before the said parties can have knowledge thereof And without that
any other thing . . . in the said Answer . . . not herein sufficiently confessed and
avoided . . . or denied is true All which matters Complainant is ready to prove And
prayeth the Court to determine the right of the parsonage and to take possession

thereof to avoid disorders and that a brotherly concord may ensue between Complainant and defendants which hitherto this Complainant cannot by any mediation of friends or any other means obtain

Bell

Now that the real point of dispute between George and his brother—the ownership of Fenlake Barnes—was stated, John again entered the lists. This time he denied that George had paid any debt of £200 owed by Sir John or that Sir John had given the lease of Fenlake Barnes to his elder son by an indenture of June 15, 1562. John proceeds to the story of his father's deathbed will in these words:

... and afterwards lying on his death bed [Sir John] for some preferment in living to this defendant and for the natural zeal he bare to this defendant his son and for the accomplishing of his former promise covenant or agreement before made to the right honorable Earl of Bedford and Sir George Conyers knight did by his last will and testament amongst other things devise and bequeath the said lease whole unto the said John his son declaring then also on his death bed that the said complainant had nothing at all to do with the said lease or parsonage And yet nevertheless for that the said Sir John had some suspicion of the said complainants evil doings he the said Sir John then also gave warning both unto the said Dame Margaret and also unto the said John ... to take good heed and to beware of the said complainant saying if they did not so the said complainant would them beguile which thing by experience they have now found true. ...

All of George's charges arising from his ownership of the parsonage of Fenlake Barnes are denied, as well as the allegations against Dame Margaret, of whose love and affection for her elder son proofs are given.

... Howbeit for a declaration of the said Dame Margarets dealing herein they the said defendants say that the said Dame Margaret doth bear good love favour and affection unto the said John her son for that she hath found of him an obedient son and willing to please his said mother the contrary whereof she hath by experience tried and found in the complainant And yet the said Dame Margaret hath before this time assured unto the complainant and his heirs of her lands tenements and hereditaments being her inheritance to the clear yearly value of one hundred marks and above And also when the said Sir John lying on his death bed was fully minded and did purpose to disinherit the said complainant and to give his lands from him for his misbehaviour towards his father yet the said Sir John at the earnest entreaty of the said Dame Margaret did leave to the complainant in lands of good inheritance to the value of two hundred marks and above Whereby it may evidently appear unto this Honourable Court what a good and natural mother the said Dame Margaret hath been to the said complainant. ...

George, in his reply to this wholesale indictment, prepared a list of questions to be administered to the defendants.[14] From this interrogatory we learn sev-

---

[14] PRO St. Ch. 5, G13/30.

eral additional facts about the sheep stealing and about the characters of the principals involved.

The first to answer the questions was John Gascoigne, who at that time, May 4, 1569, described himself as of Staple Inn. He had evidently set out upon a legal career in imitation of his brother; indeed, he imitated his brother only too well, since later we find him being sued for debt, selling his patrimony, and being charged with forgery,[15] but in 1569 he was still his mother's "natural son." His answers show that nearly every question is a true statement of fact. All violence is denied, but John admits that the defendants did show a paper to Bird telling him that they had, thereby, the right to take him to gaol if he refused to let the sheep go. He denies striking Rogers and says his mother made no such remark to him as "Goe to leave you ffolysshe boye stryke him not," but admits that she did say, "I will have the sheep thow Knave." The only weapons were daggers, which Osborne and Lamb had at their backs. The only staves are disparagingly referred to as "little hawking staves of the bigness of a mans thumb." There is a deal of equivocation over the ownership of the sheep, but John claims that he had sold them to his mother and affirms that he had earmarked them before George branded them. The charge that Rogers and his master broke in to steal the sheep is admitted as hearsay and, strangely enough, John does not know for how much the sheep were sold. The general run of the other depositions is about the same, the only additional information being Ayleford's statement that the lambs were sold for 17 nobles 4^d which, he adds, was all they were worth.

The subsequent course of the litigation need not delay us further; the documents at hand are sufficient to show quite clearly that George Gascoigne was not disinherited. It must be observed, however, that Sir John was not on friendly terms with his elder son and therefore, although leaving him a considerable patrimony, did not bequeath as large an amount as his heir might have expected. We are thus made aware that the point of view must be considered in discussing the meaning of such a word as "disinheritance." To Dame Margaret and John Gascoigne, it seemed that the poet had fared better than he deserved; to George Gascoigne, such bequests as he received seemed the equivalent of disinheritance. As in the case of his marriage to Elizabeth Bacon, knowledge of the exact facts revealed the various complications; so here the story of the interrelations of the Gascoigne family reveals the source of George Whetstone's prejudiced accusation.

---

[15] PRO St. Ch. 5, M56/10; Chanc. Proc. (Ser. I) C2, Mm14–54; Chanc. Proc. (Ser. I) C2, Gg4–10; Chanc. Proc. (Ser. I) C2, Gg4–14.

Appendix VI

LADIES OF THE COURT
Mentioned in "The Second Song" of *The Grief of Joye*

THE FIRST THREE ladies listed by Gascoigne were all daughters of Sir Francis Knollys and Catherine Carey, cousin of Queen Elizabeth.

E.K.   Elizabeth Knollys.

C. of Ess.   Countess of Essex—Lettice Knollys, then married to Walter Devereux, Earl of Essex. After his death she married Robert Dudley, Earl of Leicester.

A.W.   Anne West—Anne Knollys, the wife of Thomas West, Lord Delaware.

Gascoigne's kinswoman.

M.H.   Mary Hopton, daughter of Sir Owen Hopton, Lieutenant of the Tower of London, and Anne Itchingham. She married William Brydges [Bruges], Lord Chandos. Gascoigne claimed that he was a kinsman "by alliance" of Sir Owen.

The next three ladies were daughters of William, Lord Howard of Effingham by his second wife, Margaret Gamage: K., F., & M.H.

K.   Katherine.

F.   Frances, who became the second wife of Edward Seymour, Earl of Hertford.

M.   Mary[?], Martha[?]. Mary, the second daughter, married first Edward, Lord Dudley, and secondly, Richard Mompesson [Montpesson]. Martha, the fourth daughter, married Sir George Bourchier. As Gascoigne is here listing the youngest daughters and those presumably unmarried at the time, it is most likely he meant Martha.

M.B.   Mary Borough [Burrowe]—daughter of William, Lord Borough and Katherine, daughter of Edward Clinton, Earl of Lincoln. She later married Sir Richard Bulkeley.

L.M.V.   Lady Mary Vere—daughter of John Vere, Earl of Oxford and Margaret Golding. She subsequently married Peregrine Bertie, Lord Willoughby.

M.S.   Mary Sidney—daughter of Sir Henry Sidney by Lady Margaret, daughter of John, Duke of Northumberland, and sister of Sir Philip Sidney. She married Henry Herbert, Earl of Pembroke.

L.S.B.   Lady Susan Bourchier—daughter of John Bourchier, Earl of Bath by his third wife, Margaret Donington.

Cs. of Hŭt., War., Ox., & Rut.

Hŭt.   Countess of Huntingdon—Catherine, daughter of John Dudley, Duke of Northumberland, and wife of Henry Hastings, Earl of Huntingdon.

War.   Countess of Warwick—Anne, daughter of Francis Russell, Earl of Bedford and Margaret St. John, and third wife of Ambrose Dudley, Earl of Warwick.

Ox.   Countess of Oxford—Anne, daughter of William Cecil, Lord Burleigh and Mildred Cooke, and wife of Edward Vere, Earl of Oxford.

Rut.   Countess of Rutland—Isabel, daughter of Sir Thomas Holcroft and wife of Edward Manners, Earl of Rutland.

With the Countess of Bedford a rather complicated sequence of ladies is introduced, comprising the Countess herself, her own two daughters by a former marriage, and her stepdaughters by her present marriage.

C. of Bed.   Countess of Bedford—Bridget, daughter of John, Lord Hussey and Anne, daughter of George, Earl of Kent. She married successively Sir Richard Morysin, Henry Manners, Earl of Rutland, and Francis Russell, Earl of Bedford.

L. Grey   Lady Grey—Jane Sibilla Morysin, daughter of the Countess of Bedford by her first husband. Jane married first Edward, Lord Russell, son of Francis, Earl of Bedford, and secondly, Arthur, Lord Grey of Wilton. The death of Lord Grey's first wife, Dorothy Zouche, is mourned by Gascoigne in his poem, "In prayse of *Zouche* late the Lady Greye of Wilton." (*Works*, I, 53. No. 51.)

L.E.R.   Lady Elizabeth Russell—daughter of Francis, Earl of Bedford by his first wife, Margaret St. John. She later married William Bourchier, Earl of Bath.

L.M.R.   Lady Margaret Russell—youngest daughter of Francis, Earl of Bedford by his first wife. On June 24, 1577, she married George Clifford, Earl of Cumberland.

E.M.   Elizabeth Morysin—daughter of Bridget, Countess of Bedford by her first husband. Elizabeth was subsequently married to William Norris and to Henry Clinton, Earl of Lincoln.

L. R., A., Sh., Ch., & S.

L.R.   Lady Russell—Elizabeth, daughter of Sir Anthony Cooke and Anne Fitzwilliam, and wife of John, Lord Russell. Before becoming Lady Russell, she was the widow of Sir Thomas Hoby.

L.A.   Lady Audley—Elizabeth, daughter of Sir William Snede, and wife of Henry Touchet, Lord Audley.

L. Sh.   Lady Sheffield—Douglas, daughter of William, Lord Howard of Effingham and Margaret Gamage, and wife of John, Lord Sheffield. [This seems to be the lady meant, although Douglas was secretly married to Robert Dudley, Earl of Leicester about this time.]

L. Ch.   Lady Chandos—Frances, daughter of Edward, Lord Clinton by his second wife, Ursula Stourton, and wife of Giles Brydges [Bruges], Lord Chandos.

L.S.   Lady Sands—Catherine, daughter of Edmund Brydges [Bruges], Lord Chandos and Dorothy Bray, and sister of Giles who married Frances Clinton [the Lady Chandos noted above]. Soon after Catherine married William, Lord Sands, Gascoigne wrote a poem, "In prayse of *Bridges,* nowe Lady *Sandes.* (*Works,* I, 52. No. 50.)

Other ladies

E.D.   Elizabeth Drury—Elizabeth, daughter of Sir William Stafford of Grafton by his second wife Dorothy, daughter of Henry, Lord Stafford, only son of Edward, Duke of Buckingham. Elizabeth's mother was one of the principal ladies of the bedchamber to Queen Elizabeth. Elizabeth married Sir William Drury of Hawsted.

L.Th.   Lady Thynne—Joan, daughter of Sir Rowland Hayward and wife of Sir John Thynne.

J.T.   Jane Townshend—daughter of Sir Michael Stanhope and Anne Rawson, and wife of Sir Roger Townshend. After the death of her husband [1590] she married Henry, Lord Berkley.

F.P.   Frances Pierrepont [Perpont]—daughter of William Cavendish and Elizabeth Hardwick, and wife of Sir Henry Pierrepont.

328 LADIES OF THE COURT

C. of L.   Countess of Lennox—Elizabeth, daughter of William Cavendish and Elizabeth Hardwick, and sister of Frances Pierrepont
[q.v.]. She was the wife of Charles Stuart, Earl of Lennox.

Pagetts   [?] William, Lord Paget, and Anne Preston had six daughters:
Elianore, Grisild, Joane, Dorothy, Anne, and Etheldred [the
latter noted only in Collins's *Peerage* (1779), VII, 11]. Of these,
Eleanor was married to one Palmer in 1560, as is noted in her
father's will. Which two of the remaining girls comprised the
"payre of *Pagetts*" is difficult to say.

Bibliography

SELECTED LIST OF THE PRINCIPAL
WORKS QUOTED

Ambrose, Genevieve. "George Gascoigne," *Review of English Studies,* Vol. II (1926).

——— "Review of B. M. Ward's edition of A Hundreth Sundrie Flowres," *Modern Language Review,* Vol. XXII (1927).

Arber, Edward. Transcript of the Registers of the Company of Stationers of London, 1554–1640. 5 vols., Birmingham, 1875–94.

Ariosto, Lodovico. Le Commedie, edited by Michele Catalano. 2 vols., Bologna, 1933.

Berdan, John M. Early Tudor Poetry. New York, 1931.

Boas, F. S. "Early English Comedy," in Cambridge History of English Literature, Vol. V.

——— University Drama in the Tudor Age. Oxford, 1914.

Bowers, F. T. "Notes on Gascoigne's 'A Hundreth Sundrie Flowres' and 'The Posies,'" *Harvard Studies and Notes in Philology and Literature,* Vol. XVI (1934).

Bradner, Leicester. "The First English Novel, a Study of George Gascoigne's Adventures of Master F.J.," *Publications of the Modern Language Association,* Vol. XLV (1930).

Calendar of State Papers, Domestic, 1547–1580.

Calendar of State Papers, Domestic, Addenda, 1566–1579.

Calendar of State Papers, Foreign, 1572–1574.

Cambridge History of English Literature, The. 15 vols., Cambridge, 1932.

Camden, William. The History of The most Renowned and Victorious Princess Elizabeth. London, 1675.

Camden Society Publications. Camden Miscellany, Vols. VI, IX, London, 1871, 1895.

——— Letter-Book of Gabriel Harvey, A.D. 1573–80, edited by E. J. L. Scott. London, 1884.

Campbell, Lily B. Scenes and Machines on the English Stage. Cambridge, 1923.

Cawley, R. R. "George Gascoigne and the Siege of Famagusta," *Modern Language Notes,* Vol. XLIII (1928).

Chambers, E. K. The Elizabethan Stage. 4 vols., Oxford, 1923.

—— The Mediaeval Stage. 2 vols., Oxford, 1903.

—— Sir Henry Lee. Oxford, 1936.

C[hurchyard], T., and Ric. R[obinson]. A True Discourse Historicall of the Succeeding Governors in the Netherlands and the Civill Warres there begun in the yere 1565. London, 1602.

Conley, C. H. The First English Translators of the Classics. New Haven, 1927.

Cooper, C. H., and T. Cooper. Athenae Cantabrigienses. 2 vols., Cambridge, 1858.

Courthope, W. J. A History of English Poetry. 6 vols., London, 1920.

Crane, T. F. Italian Social Customs of the Sixteenth Century. New Haven, 1920.

Cunliffe, J. W. Early English Classical Tragedy. Oxford, 1912.

—— The Influence of Seneca on Elizabethan Tragedy. London, 1893.

—— "The Queenes Majesties Entertainment at Woodstocke," *Publications of the Modern Language Association,* Vol. XXVI (1911).

—— "George Gascoigne," in Cambridge History of English Literature, Vol. V.

Cunliffe, J. W., ed. The Complete Works of George Gascoigne. 2 vols., Cambridge, 1907–10.

—— Supposes and Jocasta, by George Gascoigne. Boston, 1906. "The Belles-Lettres Series."

Cunningham, Peter. Extracts from the Accounts of the Revels at Court, in the Reigns of Queen Elizabeth and King James I. Shakespeare Society, London, 1842.

Dictionary of National Biography.

Dodd, W. G. Courtly Love in Chaucer and Gower. Boston, 1913.

Dugdale, William. The Baronage of England. 2 vols., London, 1675.

—— Origines Juridiciales. London, 1680.

Eccles, Mark. Christopher Marlowe in London. Cambridge [U.S.A.], 1934.

Farnham, Willard. The Medieval Heritage of Elizabethan Tragedy. University of California Press, Berkeley, 1936.

Fenton, Geoffrey. Monophylo, a philosophicall discourse of love. London, 1572.

Feuillerat, A., editor. Documents Relating to the Revels at Court in the Time of King Edward VI and Queen Mary, *Materialien zur Kunde des alteren Englischen Dramas,* Band XLIV, Louvain, 1914.

—— Documents Relating to the Office of the Revels in the Time of Queen Elizabeth, *Materialien zur Kunde des alteren Englischen Dramas,* Band XXI, Louvain, 1908.

Fleay, F. G. A Biographical Chronicle of the English Drama, 1559–1642. 2 vols., London, 1891.

Fletcher, J. B. The Literature of the Italian Renaissance. New York, 1934.

Fletcher, R. J. The Pension Book of Gray's Inn, 1569–99. London, 1901.

Foster, Joseph. Register of Admissions to Gray's Inn. London, 1889.

Foxwell, A. K. A Study of Sir Thomas Wyatt's Poems. London, 1911.

Fry, E. A. Almanacks for Students of English History. London, 1915.

Fuller, Thomas. The History of the Worthies of England, edited by John Nichols. London, 1811.

Gascoigne, George. A Hundreth sundrie Flowres bounde up in one small Poesie. Gathered partely (by translation) in the fyne outlandish Gardins of Euripides, Ovid, Petrarke, Ariosto, and others: and partly by invention, out of our owne fruitefull Orchardes in Englande: Yelding sundrie sweete savours of Tragical, Comical, and Morall Discourses, bothe pleasaunt and profitable to the well smellyng noses of learned Readers. Meritum petere, grave. At London, Imprinted for Richarde Smith. [1573.]

——— The Complete Works of George Gascoigne, edited by J. W. Cunliffe. 2 vols., Cambridge, 1907–10.

——— Supposes and Jocasta, edited by J. W. Cunliffe. Boston, 1906. "The Belles-Lettres Series."

——— The Complete Poems of George Gascoigne, edited by W. C. Hazlitt. "Roxburghe Library," 2 vols., 1869–70.

——— A Hundreth Sundrie Flowres, edited by B. M. Ward. London, 1926.

Googe, Barnabe. Eglogs, Epytaphes, and Sonettes, (1563), edited by Edward Arber. London, 1871.

Gosson, Stephen. The Schoole of Abuse and A Short Apologie of the Schoole of Abuse, (1579), edited by Edward Arber. London, 1868.

Greene, Robert. Menaphon, edited by G. B. Harrison. Oxford, 1927.

Greg, W. W., and E. Boswell. Records of the Court of the Stationers' Company. Bibliographical Society, London, 1930.

Grimeston, Edward. A General Historie of the Netherlands. London, 1627.

Harleian Society Publications:

Visitation of Yorkshire, 1563–4, Vol. XVI.

Visitation of Kent, Vol. XLII.

Visitation of Bedfordshire, Vol. XIX.

Visitation of Somersetshire, Vol. XI.

Hasted, Edward. A History of the County of Kent. 4 vols., Canterbury, 1778–99.

Herford, C. H. Studies in the Literary Relations of England and Germany in the Sixteenth Century. Cambridge, 1886.

Holinshed, Raphael. The Whole Volume of Chronicles. 2d edition, 3 vols., London, 1587.

Hunter, Rev. J. South Yorkshire, The History and Topography of the Deanery of Doncaster. 2 vols., London, 1828–31.

Journals of the House of Commons, Vol. I (1547–1628), London, 1803.

Kervyn de Lettenhove, J. M. B. C. Baron, and L. Gilliodts van Severen. Réla-

tions Politiques Des Pays-Bas et de l'Angleterre sous le règne de Phillippe II. 11 vols., Brussels, 1882–1900.

Lee, Vernon [Violet Paget]. Euphorion. 2 vols., London, 1884.

Lewis, C. S. The Allegory of Love. Oxford, 1938.

Lucas, F. L. Seneca and Elizabethan Tragedy. Cambridge, 1922.

Migne, J.-P., editor. Patrologiae Latinae. Vol. XXXIX, Paris, 1861.

Motley, J. L. The Rise of the Dutch Republic. 3 vols., New York, 1859.

Nichols, John. The Progresses and Public Processions of Queen Elizabeth.
3 vols., London, 1823.

Oldfield, Genevieve Ambrose. "New Light on the Life of George Gascoigne,"
Review of English Studies, Vol. XIII (1937).

Ovid, Metamorphoses. For editions used, see chap. viii, notes 76, 80.

Painter, William. The Palace of Pleasure, edited by Joseph Haslewood. 2 vols.,
London, 1813.

Pasquier, Etienne. Oeuvres Choisies d'Etienne Pasquier, edited by Léon
Feugère. 2 vols., Paris, 1849.

Pettie, George. A petite Pallace of Pettie his pleasure (1576). "The King's
Classics," edited by Sir Israel Gollancz, 2 vols., London, 1908.

Pollard, A. F. editor. Tudor Tracts, 1532–1588, An English Garner. New
Yord, n.d.

Prouty, C. T. "Gascoigne in the Low Countries and the Publication of A
Hundred Sundrie Flowres, "*Review of English Studies,* Vol. XII (1936).
―――― "George Gascoigne and Elizabeth Bacon Bretton Boyes Gascoigne,"
Review of English Studies, Vol. XIV (1938).

Public Record Office. M. S. Giuseppi. A Guide to the Manuscripts preserved
in the Public Record Office. 2 vols., London, 1923–24.

Puttenham, George. The Arte of English Poesie (1589), edited by Edward
Arber. London, 1869.
―――― Edited by Gladys D. Willcock and Alice Walker. Cambridge, 1936.

"Return of the Name of Every Member of the lower house of the parliaments
of England Scotland and Ireland. 1213–1874." *Parliamentary Papers.* 3 vols.,
1878.

Robb, Nesca. Neoplatonism of the Italian Renaissance. London, 1935.

Robinson, F. N., editor. The Complete Works of Geoffrey Chaucer. Cambridge [U.S.A.], 1933.

Rollins, Hyder E., editor. The Paradise of Dainty Devices (1576–1606). Harvard University Press, Cambridge, 1927.

Saintsbury, George. A History of Elizabethan Literature. London, 1891.
―――― A History of English Prosody. 3 vols., London, 1923.

Schelling, F. E. The Life and Writings of George Gascoigne. "Publications
of the University of Pennsylvania, Series in Philology, Literature and
Archaeology," Vol. II, No. 4.

Seneca His Tenne Tragedies, Translated Into English, edited by Thomas

Newton. "Tudor Translations," Second Series, 2 Vols., London, 1927. (Introduction by T. S. Eliot.)

Smith, G. C. Moore. The Family of Withypoll. "Walthamstow Antiquarian Society Official Publication No. 34," (1936).

───── editor. Gabriel Harvey's Marginalia. Stratford, 1913.

Smith, G. Gregory. Elizabethan Critical Essays. 2 vols., Oxford, 1904.

Songes and Sonettes (1557) ("Tottel's Miscellany"), edited by Edward Arber. London, 1870.

Spenser, Edmund. The Poetical Works of Edmund Spenser, edited by J. C. Smith and E. de Selincourt. Oxford, 1926.

Spingarn, J. E. Literary Criticism in the Renaissance. New York, 1899.

Steele, Mary Susan. Plays and Masques at Court. New Haven, 1926.

Strype, John. The Life and Acts of Matthew Parker. 3 vols., Oxford, 1822.

───── Ecclesiastical Memorials. 6 vols., Oxford, 1822.

Surrey. The Poems of Henry Howard, Earl of Surrey, edited by F. M. Padelford. "University of Washington Publications," Seattle, 1928.

Symonds, John A. The Renaissance in Italy. "Modern Library," New York, n.d.

Tillyard, E. M. W. The Poetry of Sir Thomas Wyatt. London, 1929.

Turbervile, George. Egyptaphes, Epigrams, Songs and Sonets. London, 1570.

───── Tragical Tales and Other Poems. Reprinted from the Edition of M. D. LXXXVII. Edinburgh, 1837.

Usher, Roland G. The Rise and Fall of the High Commission. Oxford, 1913.

Victoria County History: Bedfordshire, Vol. III.

───── Sussex, Vol. I.

Ward, B. M. "George Gascoigne and His Circle," *Review of English Studies,* Vol. II (1926).

───── "The Death of George Gascoigne," *Review of English Studies,* Vol. II (1926).

Webbe, William. A Discourse of English Poetrie (1586), edited by Edward Arber. London, 1870.

Welsford, Enid. The Court Masque. Cambridge, 1927.

Whetstone, George. A Remembraunce of the wel imployed life, and godly end, of George Gaskoigne Esquire, (1577), edited by Edward Arber. London, 1868.

Williams, Sir Roger. Actions of the Lowe Countries. London, 1618.

Willis, Browne. Notitia Parliamentaria. 3 vols., London, 1716–50.

Wright, H. G. The Life and Works of Arthur Hall of Grantham. Manchester University Press, 1919.

Wright, Louis B. Middle Class Culture in Elizabethan England. University of North Carolina Press, 1935.

Wyatt. The Poems of Sir Thomas Wiatt, edited by A. K. Foxwell. London, 1914.

Index